Environmental Physiology
of Plants

EXPERIMENTAL BOTANY

An International Series of Monographs

CONSULTING EDITORS

J. F. Sutcliffe and J. Cronshaw

Environmental Physiology of Plants

A. H. FITTER

Department of Biology, University of York, England

and

R. K. M. HAY

Department of Environmental Sciences, University of Lancaster, England

1981

ACADEMIC PRESS

A Subsidiary of Harcourt Brace Jovanovich, Publishers

London   New York   Toronto   Sydney   San Francisco

ACADEMIC PRESS INC. (LONDON) LTD.
24/28 Oval Road,
London NW1

United States Edition published by
ACADEMIC PRESS INC.
111 Fifth Avenue
New York, New York 10003

British Library Cataloguing in Publication Data

Fitter, A. H.
    Environmental physiology of plants.—(Experimental
botany
    1. Plant physiology.   2. Botany—Ecology
    I. Title   II. Hay, R. K. M.   III. Series
    581.1   QK711.2   80–42083
    ISBN 0–12–257760–4
    ISBN 0–12–257762–0 Pbk

Filmset in Great Britain by Latimer Trend & Company Ltd, Plymouth
and printed by St Edmundsbury Press, Bury St Edmunds, Suffolk

Preface

This book arose from the perception of a need for a text which examines the physiology of plants from an ecological and evolutionary standpoint. It is a curious observation that zoologists refer to the "grey area" between physiology and ecology as "environmental physiology", whereas botanists generally use the term "physiological ecology". The reason for this difference lies, perhaps, in the differing developments that physiology and ecology have undergone at the hands of plant and animal biologists. For zoologists ecology has always involved the study of populations, but botanists have only recently become aware of their importance. Plant ecology has been based, from its beginnings, on a distinction between synecology (the study of communities rather than populations) and autecology (the study of individual plants or plant species); the animal equivalent of autecology, in contrast, has tended to verge on behavioural studies, especially in the study of vertebrates. As a result the relationship of the individual organism to its environment was an early fascination of plant ecologists, and this, in turn, has led to the stress laid on "physiological ecology". The zoologist, however, came to the same problems from a primary interest in the physiology of organisms. It therefore comes as a surprise to find that the word ecology, at least in its modern sense, was coined by Haeckel, a zoologist, in 1886 as the "relation of the animal to its organic and inorganic environment".

This book is an attempt to bridge the gap between the physiology and biochemistry of plants on the one hand, and their ecological behaviour on the other, starting from this "zoological" standpoint. It asks the question: "how do the intricate physiological mechanisms which have been elucidated over the last 100 years by plant physiologists really operate under natural conditions?" The structure of the book is dictated by the underlying concept that plants sense the environment in two distinct ways: first, as a source of energy and materials, and second as a compendium of potentially damaging stresses. Thus Chapters 2 to 4 treat the environment as a fund of resources (light, minerals, water), whereas Chapters 5 to 8 examine the various environmental stress factors (temperature, toxins, and other organisms). The introductory Chapter serves to set the ecological and evolutionary framework within which plants operate. An important paradox in plant ecology is that, although there is an overall similarity amongst plant species in their biochemistry and physiology, evolution has acted on this uniformity to give ecological diversity. Consequently, within the factorial structure of this book, we have emphasized the importance of a comparative approach, recognizing the significance of inter-specific differences.

We have written this book for the use of second and third year undergraduates, as well as postgraduates, and have therefore been generous with literature references to encourage familiarity with original material. To those to whom "plants" means the whole plant kingdom we must apologize for the emphasis on Angiosperms: space and personal acquaintance are our excuses.

Finally we should thank all those colleagues who have read parts of the manuscript: their comments were invaluable. They were as follows: Chapter 1 (A.H.F.)—A. D. Bradshaw, T. J. Crawford; Chapter 2 (A.H.F.)—J. P. Grime; Chapter 3 (A.H.F.)—P. B. Tinker; Chapter 4 (R.K.M.H.)—W. J. Davies, T. A. Mansfield, E. I. Newman; Chapter 5 (R.K.M.H.)—J. A. Bryant; Chapter 6 (A.H.F.)—M. J. Chadwick; Chapter 7 (R.K.M.H.)—J. A. Bryant, T. A. Mansfield; Chapter 8 (A.H.F.)—J. H. Lawton, M. H. Williamson. In addition Professor J. F. Sutcliffe read the entire manuscript and made valuable comments.

Our most heartfelt thanks, however, go to our families, who had to put up with distracted husbands and parents for too long.

January, 1981   A. H. FITTER
                                                                   R. K. M. HAY

Acknowledgements

We are grateful for permission, from the following authorities, to use materials for the figures and tables listed. Academic Press Inc. (London) Limited and the appropriate authors—Figs 4.7, 5.8 and 7.2; Agriculture Canada and the Minister of Supply and Services Canada— Fig. 5.2; Agriculture Research Council—Fig. 7.6; The American Chemical Society, Washington—Fig. 7.7; Ann Arbor Science Publications Ltd and Professor R. M. M. Crawford—Figs 7.3 and 7.4; Blackwell Scientific Publications Ltd, Oxford—Figs 1.6, 4.8, 4.9 and 8.4, Table 4.4; Cambridge University Press and Professor W. D. Billings—Table 5.3; Dr M. C. Drew—Fig. 3.13; Macmillan Journals Ltd and the appropriate authors—Tables 7.2 and 7.3; Macmillan Publishing Co. Inc., New York—Fig. 4.4; Professor T. A. Mansfield —Fig. 4.5, Table 4.1; Professor H. Meidner—Fig. 4.6; The Royal Society and Professor T. C. Hsiao—Fig. 4.2; Springer Verlag, Heidelberg and the appropriate authors—Figs 5.1, 5.3, 5.5, 5.6, 5.7, Tables 4.3, 5.1 and 5.4; Springer Verlag, New York, Inc.—Table 4.6.

To
Rosalind and Dorothea

Contents

PART I. INTRODUCTION

1. The Physiological Basis of Ecology

PART II. THE ACQUISITION OF RESOURCES

2. Light

3. Mineral Nutrients

4. Water

PART III. RESPONSES TO ENVIRONMENTAL STRESS

5. Temperature

6. Ionic Toxicity

7. Gaseous Toxicity

8. Interactions between Organisms

Part I

Introduction

1. The Physiological Basis of Ecology

The canals of Mars and a wealth of twopenny science fiction testify to the pedigree of Man's belief that life could exist on other planets. But when Jules Verne took his improbable train to the moon his expectation of encountering living creatures was not based on knowledge of the versatility of living systems, but on ignorance of the real conditions on other planets. We know enough of those environments to persuade any rational Victorian that they must be as barren as the summit of Everest; yet in 1975 a vehicle was launched to Mars to look for evidence of life, with curiously ambiguous, but probably negative results.

This strange paradox illustrates our new awareness of the ability of living systems on our own planet to withstand stress. Bacteria are now known which can persist at temperatures as high as 90°C (Brock and Darland, 1970), and other simple organisms will tolerate equally bizarre stresses. The adaptive power of higher plants, with which this book is concerned, is less dramatic, but it is sobering to consider how few terrestrial environments admit no plant growth, and how plants have colonized man-made terrain well beyond their normally experienced environmental range, such as metal-mine spoil heaps.

The concept of "normal" and "extreme" ranges of an environmental factor highlights the great variability of all such factors, in both space and time. The few exceptions to this are consequently of little physiological or ecological significance. Nevertheless, most physiological experiments are performed in constant or optimal environments, for the excellent reason that only there can the basic physiological processes be studied. Outside the laboratory these same processes cope with great variation, for plants have colonized all but the most extreme environments. Volcanoes achieve temperatures too high and ice-caps too low for plants; a few deserts are too dry, and deep caverns are too dark. Only the oceans represent an apparently favourable environment uncolonized by higher plants, but the problems are not physiological, for they can tolerate salt water in salt marshes. It seems probable that the shore is too rough and the algal holdfast better than the roots of higher plants at maintaining a hold there, while unicellularity is the optimum form for the open sea.

Only a few species are capable of colonizing extreme environments, whereas more moderate environments can support many more. The diversity of species in a habitat is thus controlled by the environment, whether by soil fertility (Thurston, 1968), altitude (Del Moral, 1972a), or any other factor. This diversity reflects the number of species adapted to grow in the habitat, and the nature of this adaptation must be examined in the light of the physiological effect of the environmental factors making up the habitat, and of their variation in time and in space.

A. Favourability and Toxicity

It is valuable when considering the physiological impact of an environmental factor to distinguish between unfavourability and toxicity. In ecological terms, favourability is a concept of limited value, as its definition tends to circularity (Terborgh, 1973), but the ecological tautology hides a physiological point of substance: favourable conditions are those which permit maximum growth for most species. Certainly some plants will continue to respond in culture to high nitrogen levels, which are no longer useful or even deleterious to others (Bradshaw et al., 1964; Fig. 1.1), but many of the species apparently adapted to the least "favourable" habitats, such as Deschampsia flexuosa (Hackett, 1965), will in fact grow far better in a monoculture in "favour-

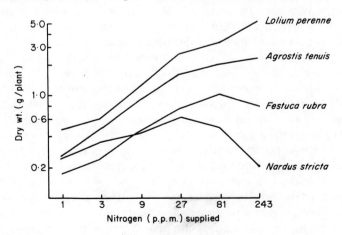

Fig 1.1. Effect of nitrogen supply on the dry weight of four grass species grown in sand culture for eight weeks. (From Bradshaw et al., 1964).

have a greater effect on species diversity than unfavourability. Good data to test such hypotheses are hard to come by, but Fig. 1.3 shows some from Grime and Lloyd (1973) on the frequency of grassland species on soils of different pH. Soil pH is a complex factor, but on the

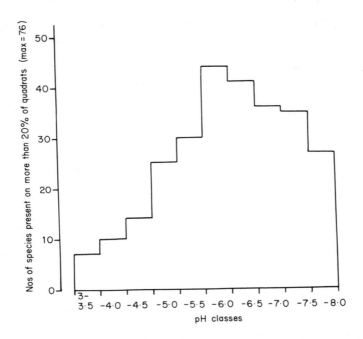

Fig. 1.3.   Distribution of species' optima with respect to pH. The histogram shows the number of species present in more than 20% of the quadrats in each pH class (data from Grime and Lloyd, 1973).

whole high pH represents unfavourability (deficiency of Fe, P, etc.) and low pH toxicity (mainly of Al and Fe). It is apparent that the decline in the number of species reaching their optimum is greatest on the toxicity side (low pH) than on that of increasing unfavourability: from the maximum of 44 species at around pH 6, there is a decline to 28 at pH 8 and to 10 at pH 4.

B. The Significance of Growth Rate

For a plant to achieve dominance in favourable environments it requires the ability fully to exploit the environment. In favourable environments free from catastrophic disturbance this means the species which can grow largest and, by means of over-shadowing leaf canopies and widely ramifying root systems, obtain the largest share of the environmental cake—in simpler terms, trees. Over large areas of the earth trees are dominant, but their life-cycle is long and they are at a disadvantage in areas of intense human activity. In such circumstances herbaceous vegetation appears, characterized by fast rather than large growth.

Grime and Hunt (1975) have analysed a large number of herbaceous plants in terms of the maximum rate of growth they are capable of achieving, and have found a good correlation between this and habitat. The fastest growing plants are found in productive habitats, whereas unfavourable and toxic sites support slower growing species (Table 1.1).

TABLE 1.1. Mean frequency (%) of species of different maximum relative growth rates (R_{max}) in different habitats (from Grime and Hunt, 1975).

Habitat	R_{max} (week $^{-1}$)			
	< 1	1–1·24	1·25–1·44	> 1·44
Acidic pastures	23	17	10	3
Limestone pastures	22	23	19	17
Rocks	6	12	8	7
Cliff	5	8	6	4
Soil heaps	6	10	21	17
Arable	2	11	19	20
Manure heaps	0	13	18	23

The measure of growth used was the *relative growth rate*, a concept introduced to describe the exponential phase of growth of annual crop plants (Blackman, 1919), which assumes that new growth is simply related to the existing biomass. The relationship between plant weight and time (i.e. growth rate) can be described as:

$$\frac{d \ln W}{dt} = \frac{1}{W} \cdot \frac{dW}{dt} = R \qquad (1.1)$$

so that R represents, at an instant in time, the rate of increase in plant weight (or other variable) per unit of existing weight per unit time. If growth were truly exponential R would be constant and a plant characteristic, but in reality this is only the case for short periods. What is normally calculated is the mean value of **R** over a period of time, which can be calculated as (Radford, 1967):

$$\overline{\mathbf{R}} = (\ln W_2 - \ln W_1)/(t_2 - t_1) \qquad (1.2)$$

The value of this equation is considerable as it permits the comparison of the growth of dissimilar plants, but because of deviations from exponentiality the value of **R** is continually changing, usually declining. Many workers have therefore sought to define the course of growth by means of a single equation. Williams (1964) has compared the fitting of a logistic curve, a series of sequential exponential functions, and a polynomial equation to the same data set, to show that none of them precisely describes the growth curve (Fig. 1.4). Logistic curves and

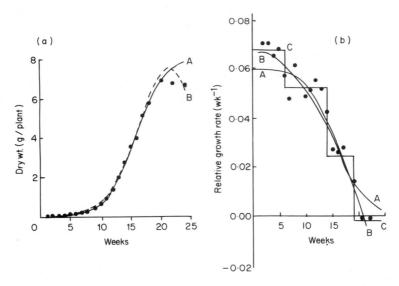

FIG. 1.4.　(a) Rates of dry matter increment of field-grown wheat with fitted curves of logistic equation (A) and polynomial (B). (b) Relative growth rate as calculated from logistic equation (A), polynomial (B), and by fitting a sequence of exponential equations (C). (From Williams, 1964).

similar equations such as the Gompertz function (Richards, 1969; Lioret, 1974) may not take account of end-of-season behaviour and are anyway cumbersome. Sequential exponentials often give a close fit to data and Williams was able to demonstrate that the points at which one equation gave way to the next could be related to major changes in the plant's ontogeny, such as the switch from root to shoot growth (postulated), flowering, fruiting, and the like. Such an approach has great biological appeal, but suffers from the drawback of implying that growth rate declines in a series of steps, which is manifestly untrue. A selection of frequently used equations is shown in Table 1.2.

The growth of a plant is the sum of the growth of its component cells and so it is improbable that any single equation will realistically describe it. More recently workers have adopted a purely empirical approach in which polynomials are fitted to the data to describe the changes without attempting to provide biological insight. From such polynomials, however, values of **R** can be calculated for any desired time interval or instant (Hunt and Parsons, 1974; Nicholls and Calder, 1973). The values for maximum growth rate (**R**$_{max}$) obtained by Grime and Hunt (1975) and mentioned above, were obtained in this way.

This approach assumes that the growth rate of a plant is in some way related to its mass, as is generally true of annuals, and is dramatically illustrated by the duckweed *Lemna minor* growing in uncrowded culture (Fig. 1.5). If perennials, particularly long-lived woody perennials, are considered, however, it is at once apparent that the trunk of an oak tree contributes to the tree's welfare by supporting the leaf canopy in a dominant position and does not directly augment the growth rate. If

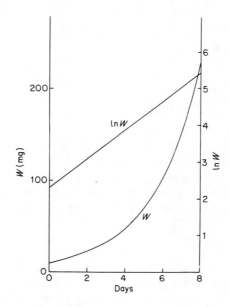

Fig. 1.5.   Growth in dry weight (W) of duckweed *Lemna minor* in uncrowded culture. Hypothetical data based on maximum growth rate of 0·39 mg mg^{-1} d^{-1}.

TABLE 1.2. Equations used to describe growth.

Name	Type	Form	Logarithmic transformation	Growth rate (**R**)
Exponential	Exponential	$W = be^{kt}$	$\ln W = \ln b + kt$	k
Time Power	Exponential	$W = be^{k}$	$\ln W = \ln b + k\, \ln/t$	$k\left(\dfrac{b}{w}\right)^{1/k}$
Monomolecular or Mitscherlitsch	Sigmoid	$W = A(1 - be^{-kt})$	$\ln \dfrac{A-W}{A} = \ln b - kt$	$k\left(\dfrac{A-W}{W}\right)$
Logistic	Sigmoid	$W = A/(1 + be^{-kt})$	$\ln \dfrac{A-W}{W} = \ln b - kt$	$k\left(\dfrac{A-W}{W}\right)$
Gompertz	Sigmoid	$W = Ae^{-be^{-kt}}$	$\ln \log_c \dfrac{A}{W} = \ln b - kt$	$k\ln\left(\dfrac{A}{W}\right)$
Polynomial	Sigmoid		$\ln W = a + bt + ct^2 \ldots nt^{n-1}$	differential $d\ln W/dt$

relative growth rate were calculated for a tree in the way outlined above, ludicrously small values would result. Alternative models have been proposed to take account of such points (e.g. Dudney, 1973), but it is still important to bear in mind the ecological limitations of the concept of relative growth rate. Plants use the carbohydrate produced by photosynthesis for a range of functions, such as support, resistance to predators, reproduction, and so on, which reduce growth rate from its potential maximum—indeed that would be attained by a plant consisting solely of leaves. It is no accident that the fastest growth rate measured by Grime and Hunt (1975) was for *Lemna minor*, a plant comprising one leaf and a single root a few millimetres long, and which rarely flowers in Great Britain. Logically, then, one would expect (and indeed finds) that unicellular algae, the closest approximations to free-living chloroplasts, are the fastest-growing of all green plants. R_{max} is therefore a useful indicator of the extent to which a species is using its photosynthate for growth and further photosynthesis—the production and functioning of more chloroplasts—as opposed to secondary functions, such as defence, support, reproduction, and nutrient and water gathering. In many habitats, usually unfavourable or toxic ones, growth is disadvantageous and acquisition of water and nutrients or protection from grazing or disease is the first priority.

Growth analysis can also be used to investigate the way in which environmental factors influence plants. One of the most useful parameters is the net assimilation rate (*NAR* or **E**) which is the increase in plant weight per unit area of assimilatory tissue (usually leaf area; A_L) per unit time, or:

$$\mathbf{E} = \frac{1}{A_L} \cdot \frac{dW}{dt} \qquad (1.3)$$

which can be related to **R** *via* the leaf area ratio (*LAR* or **F**) which is the ratio of assimilatory tissue to plant weight. The relationship is:

$$\frac{1}{W} \cdot \frac{dW}{dt} = \frac{1}{A_L} \cdot \frac{dW}{dt} \times \frac{A_L}{W} \qquad (1.4)$$

$$\mathbf{R} = \mathbf{E} \times \mathbf{F}$$

E and **F** can therefore be thought of as representing the photosynthetic efficiency and capacity of the plant respectively, and it follows that a plant can maintain a constant growth rate, if for some reason the rate of photosynthesis is reduced, only by increasing the leaf area. Plants growing in shade generally have larger, thinner leaves than those in the open, illustrating this point (cf. Chapter 2).

An example of the use of growth analysis to investigate adaptation to environment comes from the work of Callaghan and Lewis (1971) on the grass *Phleum alpinum* in Antarctica. They obtained populations from exposed and sheltered sites and cultivated them under standard conditions. They maintained similar relative growth rates, but this was achieved by high **F** and low **E** in the plants from the sheltered habitat, and by high **E** and low **F** in the exposed-site plants. The latter had adapted by producing few leaves, clearly valuable in an exposed situation, whereas the plants from the sheltered sites were in competition with other plants for light and benefited from more vigorous growth; the correlated changes in **E** resulted in similar values of **R**.

Changes in **E** and **F** do not necessarily balance one another to produce constant **R**. Goodman (1968) showed that the crop growth rate of sugar beet (*CGR* or **C**, defined as the increase in crop weight per unit area of ground surface per unit time), the product of **E** and leaf area index (*LAI* or **L**, leaf area per unit ground surface), was directly proportional to **L**. This occurred because, as **L** increased, so leaves started to shade one another and **E** decreased. As a result, yield was inversely proportional to **E**, but increases in **L** more than compensated, and the amount of leaf area became the major determinant of growth rate.

Increases in **L** tend to increase growth rate, but eventually a value is reached at which sufficient self-shading occurs to reduce **E** so far as to cause a decrease in growth. There is then an optimum value of **L** ($\mathbf{L_{opt}}$) that varies with species and with the nature and intensity of incident radiation. Plants with large, thick, entire, horizontal leaves will intercept more light per unit leaf area than those with opposite characteristics, and will cause more self-shading at a given **L**; $\mathbf{L_{opt}}$ for these will therefore be lower. Black (1964) has determined the relationship between **C** and **L** for *Trifolium subterraneum* growing near Adelaide, Australia, and has shown that $\mathbf{L_{opt}}$ increases with increasing radiation input up to a ceiling value (Fig. 1.6).

In favourable environments the attainment and maintenance of $\mathbf{L_{opt}}$ is likely to have been selected for, since during a growing season **L** will successively be sub-optimal, optimal, and supra-optimal. Both the first and last phases represent lost potential production, but one would expect the latter to be more serious as the plant has to invest energy into achieving a supra-optimal **L**. Black has again shown that near Adelaide losses of production in *T. subterraneum* due to sub-optimal **L** are about one-fifth of those due to supra-optimal values. Morphogenetic mechanisms such as leaf shedding and development of leaf mosaics in trees have developed to prohibit the surpassing of $\mathbf{L_{opt}}$, but in most natural communities biotic processes act to ensure that these are unnecessary, prime amongst which is grazing.

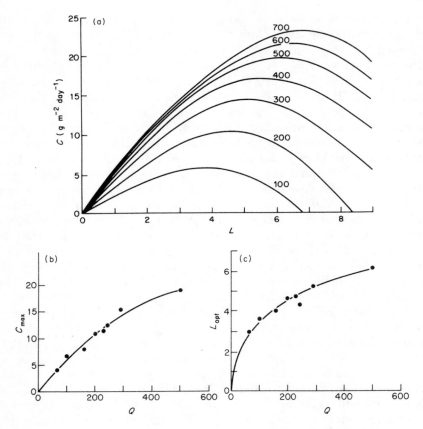

FIG. 1.6.   (a) Inter-relationships of C, the crop growth rate, L, the leaf area index, and Q, incoming radiation. Figures on curve represent values of Q in cal cm^{-2} d^{-1}, where 100 cal cm^{-2} d^{-1} equals approximately $4 \cdot 2$ MJ m^{-2} d^{-1}. The plant used was subterranean clover, *Trifolium subterraneum*. (b) and (c) Relationship of C_{max}, the maximum value of crop growth rate, and L_{opt}, the leaf area index at which C_{max} is attained, with Q. (Reproduced, with permission, from Black (1964). *J. appl. Ecol.* **1**, 3–18. Blackwell, Oxford).

C. The Influence of Environment

Since growth depends on the activity of the photosynthetic system, this has inevitably been subject to intense selection pressure—either on the ability to produce photosynthetic machinery or to photosynthesize more efficiently. Although most natural soils are nutrient-deficient (in the sense that fertilization causes either enhanced growth or changes in species composition or both), only toxic and arid soils inhibit growth to such an extent that there is no overlap between adjacent plants and therefore no competition for light. Ultimately selection acts upon the ability of a plant genotype to produce enough dry matter to transmit sufficient propagules to the next generation.

The photosynthetic machine has, however, adapted not only to the supply of its raw materials—photons, carbon-dioxide, and water—but also to the supply of soil nutrients and the additional water required to transport them, without which the carbohydrate produced would be unusable; to effects of temperature, which may impose additional constraints on leaf design and may again require water for cooling; and to many other environmental features, such as the activity of animals, other plants, fungi, microbes, and so on.

It is pertinent to ask, therefore, what features of a plant life-cycle are peculiarly susceptible to environmental influence. In marked contrast to most animals, which receive their food ready packaged in concentrated form, plants depend on concentrating very dilute resources— CO_2 at 300 p.p.m. in the air and soil nutrients whose concentrations are often in the micromolar range. Only light is usually abundant, and then only for the top leaves in a community, but it is unique in its transience—a photon missed is a photon lost. It follows then that a plant must expose itself to the environment, must maximize its surface area, and must feed externally. In most cases, then, there can be no fixed plant size or endpoint of growth, for the plant must be capable of continuous growth with many growing points, to give the potential for continual exploration and exploitation of the environment. Since nearly all plants are stationary and so cannot escape environmental stress, except by changes in the life-cycle, they must be capable of adaptation. Indeed every individual must be able to adopt a range of different phenotypes depending on environment; in other words it must possess phenotypic plasticity (Bradshaw, 1965, 1973).

The effects of environment on plant growth may be divided into enforced damage effects, controlled by environment, and adaptive responses, controlled by the plant. Damage, which may be manifested as actual injury (death of all or part of the plant) or merely as reduced growth rate due to physiological malfunction, is a common phenomenon and the agents are various: wind, ions, temperature, grazing and many others. Clearly, however, the occurrence of damage implies a lack of resistance on the part of the plant, and plants differ greatly in their resistance to damage. Resistance may be conferred by molecular, anatomical or morphological structure, or by phenology, and is a fundamental component of a plant's physiology and ecology, being responsible for all major differences in plant distribution. The critical feature is that such resistance is constitutive: a particular enzyme will be capable of operating over a certain temperature range and beyond that range damage will occur.

Adaptive responses, however, are the fine control on this constitutive damage resistance. They involve a shift of the range over which resistance occurs, which may be reversible (and usually, therefore, physiological) or irreversible (usually morphological). Levitt (1972) has used the terminology of physics to distinguish elastic strains, which are reversible, from irreversible plastic strains, in response to environmental stress. Thus the same stress, for example shade, may induce a reversible physiological response in photosynthetic activity in a woodland herb, but an irreversible morphological response in a weed or crop plant (cf. Chapter 2). Both responses are adaptive within the context of the plant's normal environment, and both require phenotypic flexibility.

Phenotypic plasticity of morphology is a universal feature of plants and conspicuous examples, such as the heterophylly of water buttercups (*Ranunculus aquatilis*), are well known. The ubiquity of reversible, adaptive, phenotypic changes is less clearly appreciated, but good examples are changes in amounts of enzymes, particularly inducible enzymes such as nitrate reductase (cf. Chapter 3), and behavioural responses, such as the opening and closing of flowers (*Bellis perennis, Mesembryanthemum*) and compound leaves (*Trifolium repens*), and sun-tracking by flowers (*Cotula coronopifolia, Helianthus annuus*). These may be more or less direct responses to environment, or may in some cases have developed an endogenous rhythmicity that permits them to continue without the environmental cue.

Each individual plant is thus capable of a range of response to environmental fluctuation. Clearly all must have some molecular basis but it is possible to classify them according to whether the molecules directly provide the adaptation, or act by creating structures or behaviour patterns that are adaptive. Resistance to injury can be classified simply on this basis: either the molecules themselves are resistant to stress, as with the enzymes of thermophilic bacteria, or the molecules are protected from damage by other molecules, special structures, or behaviour patterns. Plastic responses are, however, more complex and a simple classification is suggested in Table 1.3. Which of these responses types are utilized by plants depends upon the way in which the environmental stimulus presents itself.

TABLE 1.3. Classification of response types.

***

I Adaptations explicable in molecular terms
(a) Changes in molecular structure—Qualitative
    (i) to resist denaturation if molecule would not survive stress—e.g. reduction in number of SH groups in proteins of cold-hardened plants (Chapter 5).
   (ii) to improve operation—i.e. molecule would operate sub-optimally in changed conditions—e.g. changes in affinity of uptake systems of nutrient-stressed plants (Chapter 3).
(b) Changes in amounts of molecules—Quantitative
    (i) to adjust capacity if insufficient or excess molecules would otherwise be present—e.g. differences in ribulose bis-phosphate carboxylase activity in shaded and unshaded leaves (Chapter 2) or synthesis of phytoalexins in response to fungal attack (Chapter 8).
   (ii) to protect metabolic system from injury—e.g. osmotic balance by amino acid synthesis in halophytes or toxic ion chelation (Chapter 6).
(c) Changes in functional types of molecules
    (i) to operate alternative pathway—i.e. one set of molecules not appropriate for changed conditions, but no synthesis required—e.g. switch of anaerobic respiratory pathways in flood-tolerant plants (Chapter 7).

II Adaptations requiring explanation in morphological or behavioural terms
(a) Adjustments to temporal changes in the environment
    (i) immediate reactions—i.e. behavioural responses such as leaf and stomatal movements (Chapter 4).
   (ii) long-term reactions: seasonal differences in growth form, including dormancy, juvenile and mature leaves, etc. (Chapters 2, 4, 5).
(b) Adjustments to spatial changes in the environment
    (i) qualitative responses: different structures produced, such as sun and shade leaves, aquatic heterophylly (Chapter 2); aerenchyma in flooded plants (Chapter 7).
   (ii) quantitative responses: changes in resource allocation, such as morphological reactions to density and shading (Chapter 2) or to nutrient stress (Chapter 3).

***

D. Strategies of Response

Viewed as an individual, the plant must be capable of one or more of the responses described above to survive environmental vicissitudes. One strategy then available to a plant population is that all individuals should possess damage resistance or be capable of a plastic response. In this situation the response may be expressed as phenotypic differences between individuals or within one individual at different times.

For an outbreeding species with more or less free gene exchange, however, an alternative strategy is for the members of a population to be capable of different responses. Then only some of the individuals will be adapted to any given environment. This initially implies genetic polymorphism, with distinct genotypes maintained in the population by, for example, selection favouring heterozygotes, or disruptive selection, favouring two distinct genotypes contemporaneously. The latter can lead, through geographical, ecological, or chromosomal isolation, to the delimitation of differentiated populations with reduced gene exchange, which would be recognizable as ecotypes, possessing contrasting ecological and physiological responses. Ultimately divergence of such populations could lead to the production of two distinct species.

At first sight it would seem that a population comprising individuals capable of phenotypic adaptation to environmental stress would always be favoured over another containing members with distinct, but more fixed developmental patterns, since in the former all members can adapt to changes in the environment. This will depend partly on the ability of the plastic individual to achieve the same degree of adaptedness as the ecotypically differentiated populations. More importantly, perhaps, it will depend on the probability that the individual will in fact experience more than one state of the environment; in other words that the environmental fluctuations will actually affect the fitness of the various genotypes. This fitness, the number of offspring that survive to reproduce, can be altered in three ways:

(i) Fluctuations in *time* can mean that a stationary individual will experience distinct states of the environment. Daily and seasonal changes are clear examples.

(ii) Fluctuations in *space* can occur where an individual occupies a heterogeneous environment, such as an air–water interface. The soil–air interface is also important for plants with diageotropic stems, such as rhizomes and stolons, and the spread of an individual by such means may also involve encountering environmental changes.

(iii) Fluctuations in *space* are also experienced by the offspring of a plant after seed or propagule dispersal. The chance of an offspring landing in a similar environment to the parent will influence the selective advantage of plasticity.

1. Fluctuations in Time

The strategy adopted in temporally fluctuating environment depends on two factors: the time-scale of the fluctuations in relation to the life-cycle of the plant and the predictability of the change.

All environments change slowly over long periods of time and much of the entire evolutionary progress of life over the last 3.2×10^9 years has been a response to this. On time-scales far longer than the life-cycle of any individual, responses are determined solely by the changes of gene frequencies arising primarily from selection of adapted genotypes.

Where the time-scale is comparable with life-cycles, however, population gene frequencies may not adjust rapidly enough and plasticity is necessary.

Within the life-time of an individual there will certainly be significant environmental fluctuation. Much of this, however, is catered for by predetermined ontogenetic changes, such as the progressive increase in leaf dissection that occurs in many seedlings with successive leaves. This can be interpreted as a change from a shade-adapted entire leaf at the base of the canopy, to the more dissected leaf form adopted by most sun plants (cf. Chapter 2). The timing of such ontogenetic changes and the duration of the life-cycle may be highly plastic and an important part of adaptation to temporal fluctuation. Thus, the autumn-shedding of leaves by deciduous trees is wholly under environmental control, and continuous leafiness can be maintained under long days. Similarly, populations of *Poa annua* vary from ephemeral to short-lived perennial, depending upon the stability of the habitat, and hence the scale of temporal fluctuation (Law *et al.*, 1977); indeed the distinction between annuals and perennials can be seen as an extension of this.

Plants also experience fluctuations on a very short time-scale, and here the degree of predictability is critical. Some short-term fluctuations, such as that between day and night, are highly predictable, and precise signals are available to the plant by which it can recognize the onset of the change. In such cases morphological plasticity is inappropriate, but behavioural responses, such as leaf-movements, and physiological responses are possible. These may become tied to the march of the environmental stimuli, and an endogenous rhythm be set up, as with the daily fluctuation in the nitrate reductase level in cow parsley *Anthriscus sylvestris* (Janiesch, 1973) or the flower movements of daisy *Bellis perennis*.

Where the stress is unpredictable, however, the appropriate response will depend upon the severity of the stress and the amplitude of constitutive resistance. If the stress is mild in relation to resistance, the plant may recover by a plastic response: *Ranunculus flammula* from shores of lakes with fluctuating water levels shows greater plasticity of leaf shape than populations from lakes with more constant levels (Cook and Johnson, 1968). Presumably the experienced submergence is not sufficiently damaging to reduce plant survival before the adaptive morphological changes can occur.

Under conditions of greater stress, however, the plant must be "pre-adapted" by a greater amplitude of constitutive resistance, and selection may favour a phenotype that is sub-optimal for the normally prevailing conditions, but capable of withstanding occasional, unpredictable stresses. This is illustrated by the success of many alien, often sub-tropical plants when introduced into temperate regions; these frequently grow well for a few seasons before succumbing to a particularly severe season. Similarly, agricultural grasses planted in upland areas often grow much better than the native species for a few seasons, before being killed by a hard winter. Indeed, it must be common for the occasional environmental extreme to have profound effects on the differential survival of genotypes, particularly for plants at the edge of their range. In the long term, exceptional seasons such as the winter of 1962–3 or the summer of 1976 must have effects on gene frequencies quite unrelated to normal climatic adaptation.

As significant may be the effects of factors, such as wind speed (Grace, 1977), which may force plants to produce supporting tissue. Clearly where photosynthate is being diverted into structural (or defensive) tissues rather than assimilatory organs, growth rate will be reduced. For much of the time the plant will be operating sub-optimally, but such "pre-adaptation" is essential.

2. Fluctuations in Space
Where spatial variation occurs in an environmental factor, adaptation by change in gene frequency is possible, but as with temporal fluctuations, the effect is related to the scale. Clearly where the change occurs over a distance less than the size of the individual (or its relevant organ system) a plastic response is required. Such distances may be remarkably large: many dipterocarp trees and conifers such as *Sequoia* typically approach 100 m in height at maturity, while root systems may reach to depths as great as 40 m (alfalfa; Meinzer, 1927, quoted by Daubenmire, 1947). *Prosopis velutina* forms a small tree on flood plains with a tap-root descending to 12 m or more, and a shrub on desert soils, with a small tap-root but a lateral spread of more than 15 m (Cannon, 1911). Over such distances one must expect variation. Indeed all plants which produce leaf area indices greater than 1 are likely to experience some

self-shading, and for many trees the contrasts in light levels are sufficient
to elicit the production of morphologically and physiologically distinct
"sun" and "shade" leaves on each individual (cf. Chapter 2). Other
classic examples of such variation are the heterophylly of *Ranunculus*,
already mentioned (cf. Fig. 2.6), and of the aerial and appressed
branches of *Hedera helix* (Fig. 1.7).

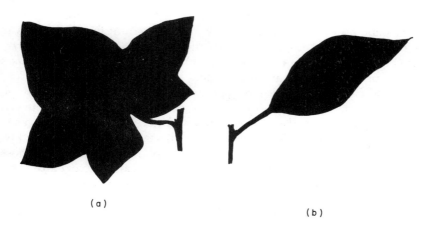

(a)

(b)

Fig. 1.7.   Silhouettes of ivy leaves, showing the difference between the palmate leaves
from appressed, vegetative stems (a) and the oval leaves of flowering stems (b).

The definition of an individual is notoriously difficult in higher
plants, many of which reproduce vegetatively, and nowhere more so
than in the tillering grasses. Harberd (1961) has shown that single
clones of *Festuca rubra* can be spread over a distance as great as 240 m;
in this instance 51% of the tillers from a 100 square yard quadrat were
of a single genotype, and 82% were accounted for by the six commonest
genotypes. Any spatial variation within this quadrat must therefore be
coped with by each genotype by plasticity, and the same must be true
for those water plants that rarely or never reproduce sexually and which
are therefore huge clones, for example *Elodea canadensis* in Britain and
particularly the duckweeds (*Lemna* spp.) which are free floating and for
which the spatial scale of the environment may thus be vast.

For sexually reproducing species and where the spatial scale of variation is greater than that of the individual or clone, the situation is more
complex. Certainly, here differentiation into ecotypes by adaptive
changes in gene frequency is possible, and its occurrence is determined
by the balance between the force of selection acting to create ecotypic

adaptation to local conditions, and the extent of gene flow between such contrastingly selected individuals. Such gene flow will usually result from pollen flow, but can also occur as a result of seed dispersal, if selection pressure is insufficient to eliminate the "foreign" genotype prior to reproduction. There is good evidence that if selection co-efficients are sufficiently high, local pockets of distinct genotypes can be maintained as little as 10 cm apart, even in outbreeding species (Snaydon, 1970; Davies and Snaydon, 1974). In an inbreeding species, where gene flow is negligible, this alone can account for adaptation to the environmental mosaic, as can readily be observed in *Erophila verna*, where genetically distinct inbred lines may co-exist. By contrast *Festuca rubra* is predominantly an outbreeder, but in the study by Harberd (1961) at least 17 distinct genotypes were recorded from a 10×10 yd ($\simeq 9\cdot 1 \times 9\cdot 1$ m) quadrat and two of the most abundant of these showed contrasting responses that correlated with their distribution over a soil pH range of $5\cdot 0$ to $6\cdot 6$. In this case local adaptation was maintained by vegetative reproduction. In other words all plant species, except those relatively rare obligate outbreeders lacking means of vegetative re-production (e.g. *Anthemis arvensis* and *A. cotula*, Kay (1971)), can by these means maintain sharp genotypic discontinuities where corresponding environmental boundaries occur. The exceptions are generally weeds of transient habitats, where such spatial adaptation is not re-quired. The importance of the breeding system is underlined by the demonstration that discontinuities such as these may be sharp to the windward, but blurred to the leeward of an environmental boundary in anemophilous grasses (MacNeilly and Bradshaw, 1968). In fact so strongly leptokurtic is pollen dispersal in most plants (Fig. 1.8), and so powerful are the selection pressures acting on such stationary organisms, that even in many outbreeding plants the population size in terms of gene flow can be measured in metres or even centimetres (Bradshaw, 1972). Of course many species have breeding systems which permit or encourage inbreeding, and the extent of this may be related to en-vironment.

There is, of course, an important interaction between temporal and spatial variation, since any environmental factor must show variation on some scale in both respects simultaneously. Nevertheless, these arguments perhaps lead us to imagine that environmental variation on a vertical axis, and for clonal species horizontally as well, will be re-sponded to by plasticity, but that other horizontal variations may be more conductive to genetic differentiation, so that both will be essential components of the armoury of all plant species. Again, as with variation in time, predictability must be considered as determined by seed

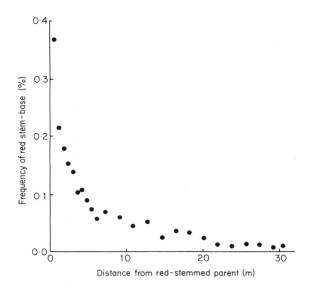

FIG. 1.8. Frequency (%) of a genetic marker (red stem-base) in an experimental population of *Lolium perenne*, as a function of distance of the white-stemmed parent from a block of red-stemmed plants. The distribution implies a strongly leptokurtic pollen distribution. (Data of Griffiths (1950), as plotted by Gleaves, T. J. (1973). *Heredity* **31**, 355–366.)

dispersal. Many species, such as groundsel *Senecio vulgaris*, are fugitive (*r*-selected in the terminology of population dynamics), relying on wide dispersal and fast growth rate to exploit ephemeral habitats. For these species the predictability of spatial variation is minimal and they may need to maximize plastic responses to permit offspring to colonize a wide range of habitats, implying that species of unstable habitats would display more plasticity than those of mature communities.

E. Physiological Tactics

There are, then, two conceptually well-contrasted strategies in response to environmental variation, depending on the nature, scale and predictability of the fluctuations. On the one hand stand mechanisms by which individuals can respond, such as phenotypic plasticity and what may be termed ontogenetic polymorphism, typically the existence of juvenile phases, as with the young leaves of *Eucalyptus*. On the other hand are population responses of which the most frequently quoted is ecotypic differentiation, but genetic polymorphism and other mechanisms maintaining genetic variation within the population (e.g. polyploidy) are included here.

For any character a particular balance and blend of the two strategies will be selected for in each situation—neither operates in isolation. Indeed, the basis of plasticity is genetic, or it could not be acted on by selection, and adaptive differences in the degree of plasticity can be discovered, as in *Ranunculus flammula* (see above, p. 20) or *Camelina sativa*. In the latter case the var. *sativa*, a general arable weed, is highly plastic, but var. *linicola*, a specific weed of flaxfields is scarcely so at all, having a morphology well adapted to growing with its room-mate, flax, the result of selection that has ensured its perpetuation both during the growing season and at harvest time. Even so major differences in life-style are linked with this distinction, demonstrated with respect to the time factor by annuals and perennials, and on a spatial dimension by trees and herbs.

This evolutionary dichotomy has a profound influence on the type of environment experienced by the plant, and this necessitates physiological adjustments. In deserts there is marked temporal fluctuation in water supply, and plants have evolved different mechanisms to cope with this. Thus one response is to avoid the dry season altogether by assuming dormancy either as seed or as rootstock or entire, but leafless plant. Such species require less physiological adaptation to drought stress but their life-cycle, particularly for the ephemerals, must be cued precisely by environmental stimuli such as rainfall (Went, 1974). By contrast, cacti have adopted a life-style which involves less morphological and phenological plasticity but vastly more physiological adaptation, as growth continues, albeit slowly, in dry conditions. Similar contrasts in tactics could be demonstrated by other stresses. Overall three distinct sets of tactics can be recognized:

(i) *Avoidance*—growth ceases for the duration of the stress, which is not therefore experienced. This is an option only appropriate for surviving time-varying stresses, except in animals where behavioural responses can be used to avoid spatial variations. It is the commonest method of surviving adverse seasons, such as winters. Typically it involves phenological adjustments.

(ii) *Amelioration* involves adaptive modifications of the internal environment, such that growth can occur under stress. Organisms adopting this tactic give the appearance of true physiological tolerance, but in fact survive by protecting internal metabolic processes. Thus cacti can store water and other desert shrubs, such as *Prosopis*, have enormous root systems which help maintain water supply. This tactic is analogous to homeostasis in animals.

(iii) *Tolerance* strictly refers to situations where the physiology and often the biochemistry of the organism are adapted to operate under stress. It is most clearly shown by bacteria and other unicells which lack structures capable of amelioration.

These three approaches are not mutually exclusive. The tolerance mechanism is by its nature quantitative and tolerance of a small intensity of stress may be used in conjunction with both avoidance and amelioration. The main disadvantage of avoidance mechanisms is that they reduce the available growth period and partial tolerance may then allow an extension. Thus, temperate trees, though avoiding winter by leaf-fall, are still more frost-resistant and more capable of photo-synthesis at low temperatures than tropical species. Similarly, amelioration responses, such as the exclusion of toxic ions or salt by roots, may be only partly effective, but the degree of tolerance required by a plant possessing such a mechanism is far less than it would be in an un-protected species.

In summary, there are two basic modes of response to environmental stress, namely that each individual should be capable of the response— plasticity—or that different individuals within the population should exhibit different reponses—genetic differentiation. The actual responses that occur may involve escaping altogether from the stress, ameliorating it so that metabolic processes at least are protected, or true physiological tolerance to the stress.

Part II

The Acquisition of Resources

2. Light

Owing to the fundamental role of photosynthesis in plant metabolism, light is one of the most important environmental factors. Visible light represents a small part (*c*. 400–700 nm) of the full solar radiation spectrum and plants are also sensitive to other wavelengths—the crucial importance of far-red radiation (far-red "light" is a convenient misnomer) of wavelength *c*. 700–800 nm in morphogenesis is well documented elsewhere. Radiation affects organisms by virtue of its energy content and is only active if absorbed. Thus, ultra-violet "light" is strongly absorbed by proteins and can cause damage; blue light is absorbed by carotenoid pigments and chlorophyll, red light by chlorophyll, and both red and far-red by phytochrome. The existence of pigments, therefore, is basic to any response and most plants appear green simply because most plant pigments absorb green light weakly.

At longer wavelengths one can no longer think in terms of pigments (which of course strictly refer to only the visible range), since long-wave radiation is absorbed by all plant surfaces with consequent heating. The biophysics of the energy budgets of plant organs are discussed in Chapter 5 and are fully considered elsewhere (Gates, 1962; Monteith, 1973); they are of great importance in regulating the temperature of plants, particularly in extreme climates. Because of this dual effect of solar radiation—in supplying the energy for metabolism and in controlling the temperature of plants—responses to sunlight may have no photosynthetic or morphogenetic basis. For example, flowers in Arctic regions, such as *Dryas integrifolia* and *Papaver radicatum* are saucer-shaped and follow the sun, acting rather in the manner of a radio telescope, concentrating heat on the reproductive organs in the centre of the flower and so attracting pollinating insects to these hot spots. A temperature differential of 7°C or more is frequently attained between flower and air, with a maximum temperature of 25°C being recorded (Kevan, 1975).

Physiologically, light has both direct and indirect effects. It affects metabolism directly through photosynthesis, and growth and develop-

ment indirectly, both as a consequence of the immediate metabolic responses, and more subtly by its control of morphogenesis. Light-
controlled developmental processes are found at all stages of growth
from seed germination and plumule growth to tropic and nastic
responses of stem and leaf orientation, and finally in the induction of
flowering (Table 2.1). There may even be remote effects acting on the

TABLE 2.1 Some light-controlled developmental processes.

Process	Control
Germination	Light-requiring seeds are inhibited by short exposure to far-red (FR) light. Seeds capable of dark germination may be inhibited by FR irradiation.
Stem extension	Most plants show etiolation in dark. Red (R) light stops this but brief FR irradiation counteracts R. Prolonged FR irradiation can have similar effects to R.
Hypocotyl hook unfolding	Occurs with R or long-term exposure to FR.
Leaf expansion	Require prolonged illumination for full expansion. Short-term FR inhibitory, long-term may or may not be inhibitory.
Chlorophyll synthesis	
Stem movements	Blue light most effective.
Leaf movements	Blue and red light active. R/FR reversible.
Flower induction	In short-day plants, R can break dark period. FR reverses effect.
Bud dormancy	Usually imposed by short-days. Behaves as for flowering.

next generation by maternal carry-over; Shropshire (1971) has shown
that dark germination of seed is affected by light quality incident on the
flower-head in *Arabidopsis thaliana*, a small ephemeral crucifer. Dark
germination of seed was much greater when the parents had been
grown in fluorescent light than in incandescent light, which contains
much more far-red.

These responses are mediated by three main receptor systems:
chlorophyll absorbing at around 660 nm for photosynthesis, phytochrome absorbing in two interchangeable forms at 660 and 730 nm
for many photomorphogenetic responses, and (probably) carotenoids
absorbing at around 450 nm for tropisms and high-energy photomorphogenesis. All plants contain a wider variety of compounds

capable of absorbing light, and no function is known for many; it is likely that in some the absorption is chemically fortuitous. In algae, however, the accessory pigments are known to play an important auxiliary role in photosynthesis.

I. THE LIGHT ENVIRONMENT

A. Radiant Flux Density (Intensity)

Light, considered as energy, reaches maximum input on cloudless days with minimum particulate matter or water vapour in the atmosphere, and when the sun is at its zenith. The differences in flux density between this situation and that on a cloudy winter day, and between that and bright moonlight, encompass several orders of magnitude. Strikingly, plant response covers a parallel range (Table 2.2).

The main effects of changes in flux density occur on the process that uses light as an energy source—photosynthesis—rather than on those which use light as an environmental indicator. For most plants photosynthesis becomes light saturated at flux densities well below the maximum they occasionally experience, largely due to the problems of CO_2 supply, but in temperate and arctic regions the converse often holds, with photosynthesis limited by low light intensity. Variation in radiant flux density is a universal feature of habitats colonizable by plants, and the complex nature of this variation is well shown in woodlands where any point on the forest floor will experience first, seasonal variation; secondly, a diurnal cycle; thirdly, random "weather" effects due to cloud cover; and fourthly, canopy shade effects such as sunflecks. In addition to this temporal variation, immediately adjacent points may differ radically in the last two factors, as shown by Anderson (1964). Leaf canopy effects on light are discussed later.

Solar radiation reaching vegetation has two components:

(i) direct sunlight or irradiance (I), and
(ii) diffuse skylight from both clouds and clear sky (D).

Diffuse light increases in importance as the solar beam is attenuated, either by actual obstruction (clouds, leaves, etc.) or by scattering due to particles and molecules in the atmosphere. Scattering is affected by the density of these particles, and also by the path-length of the direct solar beam through the atmosphere, both of which increase the chances of scattering occurring. Particles such as dust and smoke, and molecules

TABLE 2.2. Variation of radiant flux density in the natural environment and of plant response to it (adapted from Salisbury, F. B. (1963), "The Flowering Process").

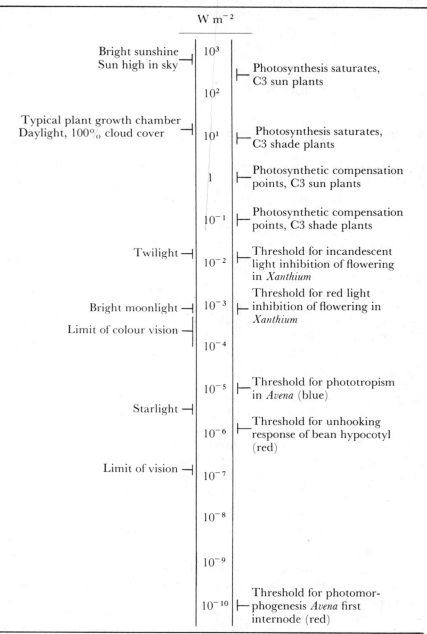

$W\ m^{-2}$

Bright sunshine Sun high in sky	10^3	
		Photosynthesis saturates, C3 sun plants
	10^2	
Typical plant growth chamber Daylight, 100% cloud cover	10^1	Photosynthesis saturates, C3 shade plants
	1	Photosynthetic compensation points, C3 sun plants
	10^{-1}	Photosynthetic compensation points, C3 shade plants
Twilight	10^{-2}	Threshold for incandescent light inhibition of flowering in *Xanthium*
Bright moonlight	10^{-3}	Threshold for red light inhibition of flowering in *Xanthium*
Limit of colour vision		
	10^{-4}	
	10^{-5}	Threshold for phototropism in *Avena* (blue)
Starlight		
	10^{-6}	Threshold for unhooking response of bean hypocotyl (red)
Limit of vision	10^{-7}	
	10^{-8}	
	10^{-9}	
	10^{-10}	Threshold for photomorphogenesis *Avena* first internode (red)

such as water vapour, cause scattering in inverse proportion to the wavelength; the power function of the relationship depends upon particle size, but the net effect is to reduce the blue content of direct radiation and increase that of diffuse light. Thus, although the sunset is red, the consequence of the long path-length of the beam at such a low solar angle, the overall radiation load is blue-shifted at that time, since diffuse light predominates.

In effect the reductions in light intensity caused by occlusion of the direct solar beam are partially offset by the enhanced blue component of diffuse radiation and by the fact that water vapour in particular absorbs in the infra-red region, radiation which is not photosynthetically active. About one-third of direct solar radiation is photosynthetically active (PAR, i.e. 400–700 nm) as compared with over two-thirds of diffuse radiation. Under most meteorological conditions, therefore, PAR as a fraction of total solar radiation remains conveniently constant at 0.5 ± 0.02 (Szeicz, 1974).

In considering flux density it is possible for these reasons to disregard wavelength differences between direct and diffuse irradiance. Direct sunlight will of course be more intense than diffuse light, but at least in temperate climates, diffuse radiation is a major part of the incident light. Theoretical calculations by Avaste show that even under cloudless skies diffuse radiation (D) may account for between one-third and three-quarters of the total (T), and in a series of measurements in Cambridge the ratio D/T was always greater than 0.5 (Szeicz, 1974).

The maximum intensity of bright sunlight (for most purposes) depends on the solar constant, the radiant flux density at the outer margin of the earth's atmosphere, confirmed by satellite measurements to be about 1400 W m^{-2}. Typical instantaneous values for PAR at vegetation surfaces are 500–1000 W m^{-2} for sunlight and 50–200 W m^{-2} for overcast skies. Other units of measurement are frequently encountered since some workers have averaged flux densities over time periods.

Irradiation is reduced not only by cloud, dust, water vapour, and other atmospheric obstructions that increase the D/T ratio, but also through shading by terrestrial objects. Shadows may be divided into those caused by selective filters, letting a part of the spectrum through, such as leaves (considered below), water (cutting out long wavelengths), soil, and so on; and those that are opaque or act as neutral filters, such as tree trunks and rocks. The two are clearly not exclusive; in sites to the north of vegetation a mixed shade occurs, having both the enhanced far-red component of leaf-transmitted shade and the enhanced short-wave content (mainly blue) of diffuse light. It has been termed "open shade" (Stoutjesdijk, 1974).

B. Quality and Period

Diurnal and seasonal variations not only affect energy inputs but also introduce an important periodic factor. Daylength at different times of the year is, for non-tropical organisms, the most reliable indicator for predicting, and hence avoiding, unfavourable conditions, and most plants are photoperiodic. Spring bud-break, flowering, and leaf-fall are only the most obvious processes to be controlled by daylength, which is measured by means of the third parameter in which light varies— quality. Direct irradiance at dawn and dusk contains more long-wave radiation, owing to the longer atmospheric path-length and consequent scattering of short-wave radiation; it is therefore often visibly red, but always contains an even more enhanced far-red content (Kasperbauer, 1971; Shropshire, 1971). In this situation the plant can use phyto-chrome, reversibly absorbing in both red and far-red; the rate of decay of the FR-absorbing form may be involved in the operation of a daily clock, although the evidence here is conflicting (Vince-Prue and Cockshull, 1980).

Photoperiod varies both seasonally and with latitude, but not significantly in other ways, whereas light quality is almost as variable as intensity. Many substances absorb light preferentially at some wave-

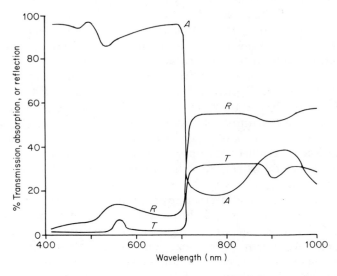

Fig. 2.1.   Generalized spectral characteristics of plant leaves between 400 and 1000 nm (from various sources). Abbreviations: *A*, absorption; *R*, reflection; *T*, transmission.

lengths (for example water and soil components both of which reduce long wavelengths), increasing the red/far-red (R/FR) ratio. Leaves, on the other hand, absorbing in blue and red (Fig. 2.1), greatly reduce the ratio. Leaf canopies, therefore, produce a light climate varying in both intensity and quality factors in a most complex manner.

C. Leaf Canopies

Light can penetrate a leaf canopy in four ways:

(i) Unintercepted direct irradiation is represented by sunflecks. These have the characteristics of direct irradiation except where penumbral effects occur (Anderson and Miller, 1974). Direct sunlight is likely to be of less value to most sub-canopy species than might be expected in densely shaded environments, since their photosynthetic response curves tend to saturate at lower light intensities. Where spreading occurs, however, the sunfleck will occupy a larger area at lower flux density and is more likely to be used photosynthetically. Sunflecks are by nature transitory, but since flashing light can be as effective for photosynthesis as a continuous source (Emerson and Arnold, 1932), it is striking that Anderson (1970) has found that a photocell of 1 mm diameter placed below a crop canopy can give readings fluctuating by as much as 80% several times a second, whereas a larger cell gives an averaged, more or less uniform reading. Evidence from the field is scarce and conflicting; Kriedemann et al. (1973) found that grape leaves utilized flashing light effectively, but Huxley (1969) was unable to find differences in plant growth under shades that covered and uncovered the light source at different rates. Perhaps the most important findings were those of Woods and Turner (1971), who found that shade-resistant trees tended to exhibit more rapid stomatal responses to changes in light intensity than shade-sensitive ones, suggesting that they showed some adaptation to utilizing sunflecks.

(ii) Unintercepted diffuse radiation is the diffuse skylight counterpart of the sunfleck.

(iii) Reflection—leaves do not simply transmit light but in common with all other biological surfaces reflect a certain proportion. The amount reflected will depend upon several parameters, such as leaf shape and cuticle thickness. Reflected light is also altered spectrally in much the same way as transmitted light.

(iv) Transmission—the degree of shade clearly depends upon the amount of light absorbed and reflected by the leaves. Light passing through a leaf is not simply reduced in intensity, but is also radically altered in terms of spectral quality, due to the action of the various leaf pigments. Typically leaves transmit a small portion of incident light (*c.* 1–20%) in the green band at around 550 nm, but are otherwise effectively opaque in the visible range. There is almost invariably a dramatic change from opacity to near transparency above 700 nm, so that transmitted light has a very high FR/R ratio. This is shown for various canopies in Fig. 2.2. Detailed analyses of spectral energy distribution under leaf canopies are given by Holmes and Smith (1977).

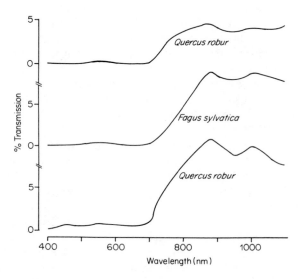

FIG. 2.2.   Transmission spectra of three woodland canopies. Note the transition at about 700 nm from opacity to near transparency (redrawn from Stoutjesdijk, 1972).

The relative contribution of these four components, and hence the depth and nature of the shade, depends upon the number, thickness, and type of leaves in the canopy. The number is usually expressed as the leaf area index (*LAI* or **L**), a dimensionless parameter representing the area of leaf surface over unit area of ground. It is possible to relate the rate of attenuation of solar radiation through a canopy to **L**; differences between species in such a relationship reflect differences in leaf geo-

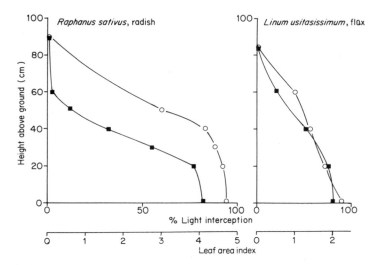

FIG. 2.3.   Correlation between interception of light with depth in stand (o) and cumulative leaf area index (■) for two contrasting crops (from Newton and Blackman, 1970).

metry, arrangement, and thickness (Fig. 2.3). This relationship is approximately exponential and can be simply described by the formula:

$$I_L = I_0 \cdot e^{-kL} \tag{2.1}$$

where I_0 and I_L are the radiation flux respectively above the canopy and at a point above which there are L layers of leaf, and k is the extinction coefficient, varying between species as just described. A plot of ln I_L/I_0 against L therefore should reveal a straight line of slope k.

A wide variety of more sophisticated models have been advanced to describe this relationship, taking into account such important additional factors as the angle of the leaves (which may itself alter with the angle of the sun in heliotropic species), the solar angle, anisotropy of the radiation field, and the distribution of leaves (Ross, 1970). The complexity of the light climate is illustrated by Acock et al. (1970), who show that the frequency distribution of flux density inside, but very near the top of a Chrysanthemum canopy is actually bimodal, as a result of the simultaneous penetration of large amounts of unintercepted light and significant quantities of both reflected and transmitted light.

Most work concerned with characterizing the light climate within plant canopies has been on agricultural, mono-specific stands, with the aim of maximizing photosynthetic production. In a natural situation, however, we must also consider the environment of subordinate layers in a complex community. For instance, a temperate oak wood (*Quercus robur* on mull soil) may have a closed canopy of oak leaves with a leaf area index (**L**) of between 2 and 4, a lower, usually more broken canopy of shrubs such as *Corylus avellana* (hazel), a herb layer whose density will be dependent partly on the upper layers, but which, in the case of *Mercurialis perennis* forming mono-specific stands, may itself have **L** = 3·5, and beneath all these a layer of mosses such as *Atrichum* and *Mnium* species and possibly soil algae as well, which must still achieve net photosynthetic production.

Radiant flux density beneath the tree and shrub canopies can be as low as 1·0% of levels in the open; beneath the herb canopy it will be even less. In deciduous woods, however, and in most herbaceous plant communities (reedbeds, tall grassland, etc.) this massive reduction is a seasonal phenomenon. Salisbury (1916) pointed out the importance to the ground flora in *Quercus–Carpinus* woods in Hertfordshire of the switch from light to shade conditions that occurred at the time of leaf expansion, and Blackman and Rutter (1946) showed that the distribution of the bluebell (*Endymion non-scriptus*) was profoundly influenced by it. Coombe (1966) gives seasonal irradiance data for a shaded site in Madingly Wood, Cambridge, showing a clear peak of irradiance from March to May. The effects of this peak on the distribution and phenology of woodland herbs is immense; no analogous situation occurs in evergreen or tropical forests, except where a dry season causes leaf fall.

Under leaf canopies, therefore, all three aspects of the light environment, intensity, quality, and periodicity, are modified to produce a distinct environment to which photosynthetic and morphogenetic adaptation has been necessary.

II. EFFECTS OF LIGHT QUALITY OF PLANTS

A. Responses to Ultra-violet Radiation

Light of altered quality is found in two main terrestrial situations: under leaf canopies and at high altitudes where radiation of enhanced ultra-violet (UV) content occurs. At lower altitudes UV is progressively filtered out by the atmosphere, particularly by oxygen and ozone. The differences in UV between high and low altitude sites are, however, relatively small, and though UV is biologically an extremely potent form of radiation, there is little evidence of the effects of UV on high

altitude vegetation. Caldwell (1968) found a 26% increase in direct
solar radiation in the 280–315 nm band at 4350 m as compared with a
station at 1670 m, but this was largely counteracted by a decrease in
diffuse UV radiation, so that overall UV input was little changed.
Caldwell also covered alpine vegetation at altitudes up to 4000 m in
Colorado with UV-excluding filters and could find no changes beyond
an increase in the number of flowering heads of *Trifolium dasyphyllum*.
He was able to show significantly greater UV transmission by epidermal
cells of arctic as compared with alpine populations of *Oxyria digyna*, but
the differences were small. Overall it is unlikely that enhanced UV
levels are a major factor for alpine plants, although generally UV
stimulates phenolic acid production (see e.g. del Moral, 1972b). Since
phenolics absorb UV this may possibly be a widespread protective
response.

B. Germination

The seeds of many species will not germinate in the dark—they require
a light stimulus. There appear to be two sets of ecological pressures that
favour this: first, the seeds of many weeds, such as those of various
Chenopodium species (Cumming, 1963), which are characteristic of disturbed ground and may be buried to considerable depth by cultivation,
are obviously most likely to encounter favourable conditions if they do
not germinate until they are returned to the surface. It is a common-
place that ploughed land quickly comes to support a crop of such plants
as *Stellaria media* and *Veronica persica*. The second situation in which
light-stimulated germination is favoured is where the species develops
a reservoir of buried seeds, for example in *Calluna vulgaris*, *Deschampsia
caespitosa* and many others. In both cases the seeds are usually very
small (Grime, 1979). Light stimulation of germination is, however, a
red/far-red reversible phenomenon, implying the involvement of
phytochrome. Typically light-sensitive seed will germinate when exposed to red light, but this stimulation can be erased by subsequent
treatment with far-red; in this case it is the final exposure which is the
determinant of germination.

Several workers have shown that light-sensitive seed will not germinate under leaf canopies (Black, 1969; Stoutjesdijk, 1972; King, 1975),
presumably because of the enhanced FR levels. Gorski (1975) found
germination inhibition in all of seven species with light stimulated seeds
and in 14 out of 19 insensitive species. Of the four light-inhibited seeds
he used, however, only tomato (*Lycopersicon esculentum*) was inhibited by

a leaf canopy. There is, however, a problem in interpreting such experiments because of the demonstration mentioned above (Shropshire, 1971) of parental habitat effects on light control of germination. Thus, of three dock species, *Rumex crispus*, *R. obtusifolius*, and *R. sanguineus*, only the latter, a woodland species, shows appreciable germination under FR, but seed from *R. obtusifolius* growing in shade had greater germination in FR than that from the same species grown in the open (Table 2.3); such differences could clearly be due either to ecotypic differentiation or to direct environmental effects on the seed during maturation of the parent plant.

TABLE 2.3   Germination of seed of three dock species, *Rumex crispus*, *R. obtusifolius*, and *R. sanguineus* from open and shaded habitats, under different light conditions. Only *R. sanguineus* is normally a woodland plant. Fitter (unpublished).

Species	R. crispus		R. obtusifolius		R. sanguineus	
Habitat	Open	Shade	Open	Shade	Open	Shade
Treatment						
Dark	89	95	74	94	96	99
Far-red light	12	14	7	26	55	49

Figures are percentages of germination in full light, which was between 90 and 97% in all cases.

It seems, therefore, that light controlled germination is an adaptation of plants which are intolerant of shade. If the seed of such plants is exposed to high FR levels, in nature implying that it is under a leaf canopy, or is in the dark, which would normally mean burial, it does not germinate. Clearly such a mechanism could be used to adjust the timing of germination to take advantage of seasonal "windows" in the canopy. Seed of shade-resistant plants such as *Rumex sanguineus* on the other hand, will not be at a disadvantage if it germinates under a closed canopy, as this is the normal habitat for the adult plant. In addition there is the as yet unexplored possibility that plants may be able to confer upon their seeds germination characteristics which will suit them to the environment in which the parent plant is growing. For species of limited dispersal power this would provide the implied advantage of local ecotypic adaptation, without the necessity for genetic differentiation by selection.

C. Morphogenesis

Far-red light acts on most plants that have been studied in the laboratory *via* the phytochrome system; Mohr *et al.* (1974) have summarized
the known morphogenetic responses that are phytochrome mediated.
Virtually all such physiological work has been carried out using briefly
raised levels of FR, presumably to simulate sunrise and sunset effects.
For example, tomatoes given 5 min FR at the end of each day produce
no side shoots (Tucker, 1975). Kasperbauer (1971) has suggested that
such short-term changes are responsible for the fact that tobacco plants
in the centre of a stand have longer internodes and paler, thinner
leaves than those at the edge. As the sun passes through very low angles
at dawn and dusk, light received by central plants would be filtered
through the leaves of the marginal ones and so have enhanced FR
levels. He was able to mimic all the responses of mid-row plants by
growing them in controlled conditions with a short pulse of FR at the
end of each light period. Kasperbauer and Peaslee (1973) subsequently
demonstrated that FR-treated plants (i.e. analogous to mid-row
plants) had longer, narrower, lighter leaves with fewer stomata and less
chlorophyll per unit area. Carbon-dioxide assimilation was the same
on an area basis, but greater on a leaf weight basis, showing that FR-
treated plants had maintained photosynthetic assimilation at a lower
flux density by increasing leaf area.

The mechanism and ecological significance of the elongation response are presumably similar to that of etiolation, allowing plants
shaded by other leaves to grow into better illuminated regions. The
situation under a plant canopy, however, has two important characteristics:

(i) the alteration in R/FR ratio is permanent (at least in the "leafy"
season) and not a 10 min dawn or dusk effect;
(ii) the distance from the ground to the unfiltered light may be as
much as 100 m, though in temperate woods 15–25 m is more likely;
no etiolation responses will be of value to a herbaceous plant in these
conditions, although sustained extension growth might be important
for tree seedlings.

The effects of variations in light quality on plants have been examined only recently. Erez and Kadman-Zahavi (1972) grew peach trees
(*Prunus persica*) under neutral shades and filters giving respectively blue
light (no transmission above 550 nm), blue with FR (transparent above
660 nm), and red with FR (transparent above 500 nm). They found
that leaf area, as well as most other growth parameters was greatest

under R + FR and least under blue + FR. The latter correspond to the conditions termed open shade by Stoutjesdijk (1974).

The role of phytochrome under natural conditions is now becoming clear: plants appear to use it to detect shading. Holmes and Smith (1975) measured the photostationary state of phytochrome under leaf canopies, finding it to be similar to that under an FR filter. They showed that incandescent lights (producing more FR) stimulated greater stem extension growth in two arable weeds than fluorescent tubes, and were able to relate this to measurements showing a shift of phytochrome to the P_r (red-absorbing) form in etiolated seedlings. In plants characteristic of shaded conditions, however, the situation may be different. Fitter and Ashmore (1974) used two species of speedwell, *Veronica montana* and *V. persica*, the latter an arable weed, the former growing typically in deep shade. Under neutral shade both species showed reductions in various growth parameters, but under continuous FR at the same flux density, *V. persica* exhibited a further decline in leaf area, whereas *V. montana* was not affected differently by the FR and neutral shade treatments (Table 2.4). In very deep shade cast by a

TABLE 2.4   Differences in total dry weight, dry weight distribution, and leaf area of two *Veronica* species in full light (O), neutral shade (NS) and far-red treatment (FR) of equal intensity to NS. Plants were grown for 3 weeks.

	V. montana			V. persica		
	FR	NS	O	FR	NS	O
Total dry weight (mg)	70·3	67·8	101·2	32·5^a	41·7^a	66·5^b
Proportion of dry wt in :						
Leaf (*LWR*)	0·48	0·50	0·49	0·55	0·61	0·64
Stem	0·29	0·27	0·26	0·25^a	0·23^a	0·07^{b*}
Petiole	0·12	0·12	0·09	0·09	0·07	0·10
Root (*RWR*)	0·12	0·12	0·15	0·10	0·11	0·13
Leaf area (cm²)	15·7	16·3	22·8	9·7^a	16·3^b	27·3^{c*}

Within any set of three figures, those superscripted differently are significantly different by Duncan's test with $P=0.05$, except those asterisked where $P=0.01$. Where no subscripts are given, no significant differences exist.

tobacco leaf canopy both species grew very poorly, but whereas *V. persica* became etiolated, *V. montana* showed no alteration to its development pattern. It is now apparent that stem extension rates, leaf weight ratio and petiole length are all characteristically more labile in plants adapted to open conditions than in those found growing in shade (Morgan and Smith, 1979).

D. Photoperiodism

Although strictly a different aspect of the light factor from quality, periodic effects are mediated *via* the red/far-red reversible pigment phytochrome. Most temperate region plants are photoperiodic; in equatorial regions daylength shows little seasonal march and so photoperiodism would be of less value. Since the beginning and end of the day are marked and measured by changes in the R/FR ratio, it may well be that effects such as those shown by Kasperbauer (1971; and see p. 41) for tobacco, could have an important influence on processes that are under photoperiodic control; apparently the question has not been raised experimentally.

Keeping a photoperiodic plant under a constant daylength will usually maintain it in one developmental stage. Thus *Epilobium hirsutum* and *Lythrum salicaria* flower if given 16 h days, but will remain vegetative indefinitely under a 9 h photoperiod (Whitehead, 1971), although if the photoperiod promotes flowering, it will normally be stopped eventually by other processes. Not all temperate zone plants however are photoperiodic: many weedy species, such as groundsel (*Senecio vulgaris*) will flower in all months of the year if the weather is favourable, and *Impatiens parviflora* is an example of a large group of plants which flower at a particular stage of development, irrespective of photoperiod.

The photoperiodic response enables the plant to time vegetative and floral growth to fit seasonal changes in environment. If a plant is moved to a different latitude it will then be out of phase and may die from, for example, attempting vegetative growth in the winter or too late in spring. This was what led to the first recognition of the phenomenon (Garner and Allard, 1920) and its importance was quickly seen by silviculturalists, who discovered that a wide-ranging tree species may have well-marked photoperiodic races or ecotypes as for example in birches (*Betula*) (Vaartaja, 1954). The same is true of grasses (Olmsted, 1944) and of other herbaceous plants such as *Oxyria digyna*, the mountain sorrel, a circumpolar arctic–alpine species that descends as far south as California in the North American Rockies (Fig. 5.4). Mooney and Billings (1961), in a comprehensive study of the different arctic and alpine races of this species, found that the arctic populations required a much longer day to induce flowering; arctic plants could be kept vegetative in growth room photoperiods that stimulated flowering in alpine populations.

III. EFFECTS OF RADIANT FLUX DENSITY ON PLANTS

A. Patterns of Response

Flux density, or intensity, exerts its primary effect on photosynthesis, acting secondarily on morphogenesis; most morphogenetic responses are to low intensities, but some require greater energy (Mancinelli and Rabino, 1978). The ecology of a plant with regard to light intensity is governed by two considerations:

(i) placing the leaves in the positions that will maximize light inter-ception. This is above the canopy and in a complex community most of the leaves cannot achieve this. Most leaves will therefore exist at reduced light intensities, where they must

(ii) maximizing photosynthesis for the energy received, assuming this to be below the light-saturation point for normal photosynthesis, so as to remain in net positive carbon balance (photosynthetic CO_2 fixation greater than the sum of respiration and carbohydrate ex-port). A leaf in negative C-balance will need to import sugars from the rest of the plant and will reduce overall fitness.

Patterns of leaf placement are more complex than a first glance sug-gests. Horn (1971) has suggested two basic architectures for forest trees —monolayer and multilayer. The monolayer is defined as a complete, uniform layer of leaves and lets through little photosynthetically active radiation (PAR), but it will have low productivity since it has a maxi-mum **L** of 1. The multilayer species has a broken canopy but relies on the facts that:

(i) an individual leaf only casts a shadow for a certain distance (Horn uses 70 diameters), and

(ii) light-saturation for most species occurs at intensities well below full sunlight,

so permitting several layers of leaves (high **L**) all operating at high photosynthetic rates. The multilayer can therefore grow faster, but since it lets through more PAR, it is more open to invasion. Even though Horn's theory does not take account of variation in photo-synthetic response to light intensity (see p. 55) it has important im-plications.

Within this basic dichotomy the plant needs to be able to control both leaf production and placement. The morphogenetic responses involved are closely tied to the phytochrome system. Typical responses include stem elongation and leaf orientation.

1. Etiolation

Bringing the plant's leaves up into more brightly illuminated regions, is only of value to plants of low-growing communities or those that typically form the canopy, except in the case of hypocotyl elongation in hypogeal seeds. Significantly etiolation is normally demonstrated with crop plants (beans, mustard, etc.) and is absent from species adapted to and resistant to shade, such as *Veronica montana* (Fitter and Ashmore, 19 . .) Grime (1966) has suggested that resistance to etiolation is found in two ecologically contrasted groups of plants—those adapted to dense shade, and those that normally grow in open habitats. In his experiments *Arenaria serpyllifolia* and *Hieracium pilosella*, species of open communities, showed no elongation growth in shade, apparently owing to exhaustion of carbohydrate reserves, whereas *Betonica officinalis*, a grassland species, became very etiolated. In a low but closed canopy this would enable *Betonica* to reach the light, where, since it is a relatively large plant, with leaves capable of overshadowing competitors, it is likely to be successful; once it has penetrated the canopy the consequent increase in intensity would inhibit further extension growth. Trenbath and Harper (1973) showed that the elongation response of oats (*Avena sativa*), a species selected for growth in herbaceous stands ecologically similar to tall grassland, resulted in about 20% extra weight in each seed when grown in mixed culture with *A. ludoviciana*, as compared to the estimate for a shaded plant.

2. Phototropism and Orientation

Tropic responses remain a physiological enigma. Much of the ground work was laid by Darwin and an apparently adequate explanation was propounded by Went and his co-workers in the 1920s, based on a theory of auxin movement. Recently doubt has been cast on this explanation, at least for geotropism (Firn and Digby, 1980). What is certain is that the action spectrum is complex, with as many as four peaks between 370 and 470 nm, suggesting the involvement of flavins and carotenes, and that the response is dramatically affected by IAA. Whatever the physiology, the adaptive significance is clear, and is enhanced by the partial reversibility of the process, since although it involves differential growth, this can be reversed by complementary growth opposite the original site. Generally, however, phototropism will be a response to a more or less fixed spatial pattern in the light environment.

Phototropic responses are adaptive; differences between plants adapted to contrasting habitats should therefore occur. Genotypic differences in the patterns of leaf arrangement occur in forage grasses, and the same phenomenon was recognized early for uncultivated plants (Turesson, 1922).

Plants with prostrate leaf arrangements have very much higher extinction coefficients for light (k) within the canopy than those with erect leaves (Cooper and Breeze, 1971), a situation analogous (for a very different growth form) to Horn's (1971) distinction between mono- and multilayer tree strategies. As a result, under agricultural conditions, long-leaved, erect plants of low k can grow faster, a discovery that may be exploited for higher productivity (Table 2.5). Indeed in terms of plant breeding it seems that much more can be obtained by alterations in canopy architecture than in photosynthetic rates, which Sheehy and Peacock (1975) found to be unrelated to growth rate.

TABLE 2.5.   Crop growth ratios of six common forage grasses in relation to the extinction coefficient of light in the canopy and the leaf area index (Sheehy and Cooper, 1973).

Species and cultivar		Crop growth rate $(\mathrm{g\ m^{-2}\ d^{-1}})$	Extinction coefficient (k)	Leaf area index
Festuca arundinacea	S170	43·6	0·34	11·2
Dactylis glomerata	S 37	40·5	0·23	13·7
	S345	25·0	0·91	14·9
Phleum pratense	S 50	36·4	0·30	15·5
	S 48	28·9	0·39	10·4
	S352	21·9	0·55	14·5

In natural conditions, however, the prostrate form will often be favoured, since the advantage of the erect types increases with longer intervals between cutting, and under very frequent cutting regimes (intervals of less than 10–14 days), the short-leaved genotypes are favoured (Rhodes, 1969). Under these conditions, which would be produced in the wild by grazing animals, the erect types never produced an adequate canopy. Very severe environments will also enforce the same result, as shown by Callaghan and Lewis (1971) for *Phleum alpinum* in Antarctica (see p. 13).

Where changes in the spatial pattern of light are more short-lived, however, more rapid, nastic responses will be necessary. Leaf and petiole movements, operated by turgor changes, occur more or less continuously in controlled conditions, as can be shown by time-lapse photography. The function of these rather slight movements in the field is unclear, as they will often be swamped by air turbulence. Nevertheless, nastic movements as dramatic as those of the leaves of the sensitive plant, *Mimosa pudica*, or the compass plant, *Lactuca serriola*, whose leaves tend to orient themselves north–south, can readily be observed in the field. For plants growing in low light intensities these movements typically follow the sun to ensure maximum illuminations; for plants in strong light they are normally avoidance reactions to reduce the heat load on the leaf and to allow subordinate leaves in the canopy to receive the light. When the sun is far from the zenith such movements can also markedly influence the effective leaf area index.

B. Responses to Low Light Intensity

1. Temporary Stress

As shown above, there is a distinct peak of irradiance in temperate deciduous woods in early spring, and a well-marked group of plants takes advantage of this. Deciduousness in trees in response to seasonal temperature changes (as opposed to variation in water supply) is, however, an adaptive response to avoid frost damage to leaves capable of high productivity, so that the herbs which photosynthesize during this brief seasonal window need to be frost resistant (see Chapter 5). To take full advantage of the radiation peak they must also have fully expanded leaves by April at the latest, so that leaf growth must take place at very low temperatures in February and March, when photosynthetic activity will be low. This growth therefore requires stored reserves and almost all these species are perennials with underground storage organs, whether bulbs (*Hyacinthoides non-scripta*, *Allium ursinum*), corms (*Cyclamen*), tubers (*Ranunculus ficaria*), or rhizomes (*Anemone nemorosa*). These storage organs are re-charged during the radiation peak.

Occupation of this particular niche, therefore, requires modification to all other parts of the life-cycle. Whereas some species, such as *Hyacinthoides*, complete their life-cycle during the light phase and remain dormant for the rest of the year, others, such as *Oxalis acetosella*, remain active for a large part of the shade phase. This activity occurs in very dim light and so requires a change in physiology, which is brought about plastically in two distinct ways. *Oxalis* has a photosynthetic system capable of adjustment without morphological change (Daxer, 1934), whereas *Aegopodium podagraria*, a garden weed in northern Europe, but a woodland herb in central Europe, has two leaf types produced by a single plant: thin broad summer leaves, and thicker spring

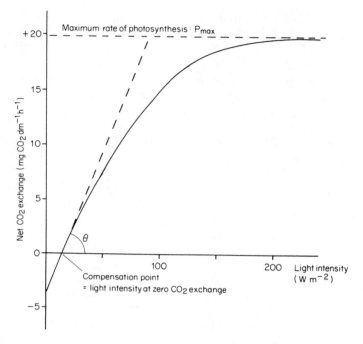

Fig. 2.4. Representative photosynthetic response curve showing the compensation point, the light intensity at which net CO_2 exchange is zero, as the point at which gross photosynthesis equals respiration.

leaves, adapted to higher light levels. These two mechanisms are of general significance in the adaptation of plants to low light intensity and the physiological background to the ecological switch will be examined below.

Of course, any change in physiology to maintain carbon balance involves changes in respiration rate too. This typically means a lowering of the compensation point, where respiration exactly balances photosynthesis (Fig. 2.4) which is not in any way fixed, as shown by McCree and Troughton (1966) for white clover.

2. Long-term Stress

If a plant is shade resistant and makes no attempt either to place its leaves in unshaded positions, or to restrict their activity to periods of high illumination, selection will act more on the photosynthetic process itself. This is inescapable for the lower leaves of a plant forming a multi-layer canopy, and it follows that both plastic (within a genotype) and genetic (between genotypes) differences must exist in the photosynthetic system.

The problem faced by a shaded leaf is to maintain a positive carbon balance, and the flux density at which this is reached is the compensation point (Fig. 2.4). Under low light stress three options are open:

(i) reduced respiratory rate, to lower the compensation point;
(ii) increased leaf area, to provide a greater surface for light absorption; and
(iii) increased photosynthetic rate per unit light energy and leaf area.

All these three courses are adopted by shaded plants, but they impose particular restraints.

(a) *Reduced respiratory rate.* At the compensation point photosynthetic carbon fixation equals respiratory loss. A reduction in respiration will therefore lower the compensation point, but respiration has a purpose and a reduction is likely to slow growth down, which could lower the competitive ability of the plant in relation to faster growing species. As a response to low light stress it is therefore only likely to be advantageous in severe shade where growth rates are sufficiently reduced to minimize competitive interactions. It is certainly true that plants capable of growth in deep shade have low relative growth rates (Grime and Hunt, 1975), and Mahmoud and Grime (1974) found that at extremely low illumination (down to 0.07 W m^{-2}) *Deschampsia flexuosa* showed zero growth rate, whereas *Festuca ovina* and *Agrostis tenuis* had large negative **R** below their compensation points at about 0.7 W m^{-2} (Fig. 2.5). *Deschampsia flexuosa* survived four weeks in deep shade; the two latter species senesced. Although respiratory rates were not measured, the clear implication is that *D. flexuosa* owed its resistance to a virtual cessation of respiratory activity. Certainly McCree and Troughton (1966) found that white clover, a species unable to survive in deep shade, when grown at 65 W m^{-2} and transferred to a range of intensities from 88 to 3.7 W m^{-2}, had respiration rates varying from 7.0 down to 0.7 mg CO_2 dm^{-2} h^{-1}.

A small reduction in respiratory rate is then a fairly general response to reduced light intensity, but as a major adaptive response it is only of value to severely shaded plants, and particularly as a survival mechanism for long-lived plants to persist during periods of temporary stress (cf. above). This is clearly the value of the near-dormant behaviour of *D. flexuosa* and has previously been recognized, for example by Chippindale (1932), who observed that seedlings of *Festuca pratensis* were

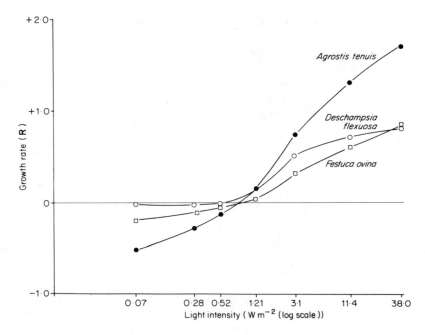

Fig. 2.5.   Effect of very low light intensity on growth rate in three grass species. Note the very small negative **R** of *Deschampsia flexuosa* (from Mahmoud and Grime, 1974).

able to survive long periods without growing when under severe competitive stress from older plants of *F. pratensis* and *Lolium italicum*, but could resume normal growth when the stress was removed. He termed the phenomenon inanition.

A similar case has been reported by Cross (1975) for *Rhododendron ponticum* seedlings, and Hutchinson (1967) showed that woodland plants, such as *Digitalis purpurea* and *Bromus ramosus* could survive for 5–6 months in complete darkness, and very strikingly that *Deschampsia flexuosa* could persist for as long as 227 days. He was able to demonstrate that generally small-seeded, pioneer plants, such as *Betula pubescens* and *Erophila verna* were least resistant to this stress, and that plants grown on nutrient-deficient soils which reduced growth and probably also respiration rates, actually could survive for longer in complete darkness than those grown on fertile soils.

(*b*) *Increased leaf area*. Plant growth can be described by the classic growth equation (see p. 12):

$$\mathbf{R} = \mathbf{E} \times \mathbf{F} \qquad\qquad (2.2)$$

The immediate, enforced response on a plant removed to a lower light intensity will be a reduction in $\mathbf{R}$ caused by a lowering in $\mathbf{E}$ (net assimilation rate), reflecting the effect of light on photosynthesis. To maintain $\mathbf{R}$ therefore, assuming no change in the light-dependence of photosynthesis, the plant must raise the leaf area ratio $(\mathbf{F})$. $\mathbf{F}$, as the ratio of leaf area to plant weight, is a complex function without any obvious biological interpretation. It can, however, be thought of as:

$$\mathbf{F} = LWR \times SLA$$
$$A_L/W = W_L/W \times A_L/W_L \qquad (2.3)$$

Leaf area ratio = leaf weight ratio × specific leaf area
$$cm^2 \, g^{-1} = g \, g^{-1} \times cm^2 \, g^{-1}$$

LWR is the ratio of leaf weight to plant weight, SLA that of leaf area to leaf weight. Leaf area described by LAR or $\mathbf{F}$ can therefore be discussed in terms of two components:

(i) the proportion of plant weight devoted to leaf material; i.e. how much leaf is there?
(ii) the area: weight ratio of the leaf itself; i.e. how thick is it?

Changes in leaf dry weight. It is well established (cf. Chapter 3) that the ratio of root weight to shoot weight is very plastic—plants grown in infertile soils tend to have very high root : shoot ratios. Since for most herbaceous plants the leaves are a large proportion of the shoot weight, and since the main function of the stem is to place leaves in an appropriate light climate, one would expect the leaf weight ratio (LWR) to be equally variable. Evidence on this point is surprisingly unclear. Evans (1972) suggests that LWR is susceptible only to changes in temperature, daylength, and soil factors, and not to light intensity, the daily total of irradiance, or the spectral composition of radiation. This is largely based on experiments on one plant—*Impatiens parviflora*. Fitter and Ashmore (1974) found LWR to be unaltered by severe shade stress in *Veronica montana*, a shade-resistant species, but to be reduced by shade in *V. persica*, an arable weed. Most probably LWR is a reflection of the plant's ability to maintain its normal developmental pattern, and it will be found to be constant over the range of light intensities to which a plant is adapted. Under shade stress, however, particularly if etiolation occurs, LWR will be reduced.

Specific leaf area. SLA is a much more variable parameter than LWR; in other words leaf area is more plastic than leaf weight. A striking illustration is that, immediately subsequent to germination, there is a marked rise in *SLA*, caused by expansion of the first leaves, whose dry weight, of course, changes only slightly during expansion. *SLA* also responds to environmental changes. Newton (1963) showed that the leaf area of cucumber plants (*Cucumis sativa*), a light-demanding species, was proportional to the total radiation, with an optimum at about 100 cal cm^{-2} d^{-1} (equivalent to 4·19 MJ m^{-2} d^{-1} or about 73 W m^{-2} for a 16 h day) and that changes in both daylength and intensity (as components of irradiation) had no effect if the daily total was the same. The reduction in leaf area at the highest irradiances was due to a reduction in cell size, whereas cell number increased to a plateau (Milthorpe and Newton, 1963).

Apparent effects of light intensity may therefore be responses to total irradiance; this is probably the case for *Impatiens parviflora* which shows an almost three-fold increase in *SLA* when grown in 7% of full daylight (Evans and Hughes, 1961). When plants are grown under field conditions, responses are even more dramatic—*SLA* changing from 4·9 to 12·7 dm^2 g^{-1} for plants growing under 48 as opposed to 13 cal cm^{-2} d^{-1} (Hughes, 1959; see conversions above). The plasticity of the character is emphasized by the rapidity with which *SLA* adjusts when plants are transferred from one light regime to another.

These differences are for whole plants. Similar effects can be found between leaves of a single plant exposed to heterogeneous light, as in a forest canopy. Such differences are the basis of the sun and shade leaves, first recognized by Haberlandt. In beech (*Fagus sylvatica*) the phenomenon is very clear-cut (see Table 2.6), but as with *LWR* the degree of plasticity appears to be related to the ecological niche of the species. Shade-resistant species, such as *Veronica montana* (Fitter and Ashmore,

TABLE 2.6   Characteristics of sun and shade leaves of mature and young beech trees *Fagus sylvatica*, from Nordhausen, quoted by MacGregor Skene (1924) in "The Biology of Flowering Plants".

| | Mature | | Young | |
	Sun leaves	*Shade leaves*	*Sun leaves*	*Shade leaves*
Leaf thickness (μm)	210	108	117	90
Number of palisade layers	2	1–2	1–2	1
Thickness of upper palisade layer (μm)	60	28	39	24

1974) and *Rhododendron ponticum* (Cross, 1975) show much less striking changes in *SLA* under low light stress than species from open habitats.

Leaf morphology. The relative constancy of *LWR* and plasticity of *SLA* imply that the plant has an optimum developmental pattern in terms of dry weight distribution, achieving adaptation to light intensity by changes in leaf morphology. The increased ratio of leaf area to weight (*SLA*) must imply important anatomical changes in the mesophyll and palisade layers, and this is clearly shown in *Mimulus* (Hiesey *et al.*, 1971) and in a wide range of deciduous trees (Jackson, 1967). In all cases the palisade layer is reduced from 2–3 cells to 1 cell in the shaded or shade-resistant leaves. Such thin leaves produce high values of *SLA*.

These changes have been shown to affect CO_2 diffusion. In plants of *Solidago virgaurea* from exposed sites, high light intensity causes a thickening of the leaf that lowers resistance to CO_2 diffusion by increasing the pore space in the mesophyll layers (Holmgren, 1968). Since CO_2 is limiting for photosynthesis at high intensities this enables the plant to raise its effective light saturation point; plants from shaded habitats show no such response.

Similar effects can be demonstrated in the field. Fekete *et al.* (1973) examined photosynthetic rates in trees of *Quercus pubescens* in sites varying in illumination and soil moisture and found a high correlation between the rate and the palisade/mesophyll thickness ratio ($r = 0.753$), the mesophyll chamber size ($r = -0.949$), and the ratio of intercellular spaces to assimilating cells ($r = 0.892$); there was no relationship, however, with stomatal number. All these parameters influence the rate of CO_2 diffusion to the chloroplasts, important at high light intensities, and all are plastic in response to changes in irradiance.

Leaf morphology, then, affects photosynthesis *via* factors such as CO_2 diffusion, but is controlled to a great extent by light intensity. A good analysis of photosynthetic limitation by CO_2 diffusion based on the generally accepted resistance analogy can be found in Zelitch (1971), and Lommen *et al.* (1975) and more recently Tenhunen *et al.* (1976) have presented photosynthetic models of this type. Nevertheless, changes in morphology will certainly influence light interception. Horn (1971), in developing his concept of mono- and multilayer canopy strategies claims that monolayers will tend to have large, unlobed leaves to maximize ground coverage with minimum overlap, whereas multilayer species will favour smaller, more dissected leaves. He cites the ontogenetic changes in *Quercus velutina*, which has large, toothed leaves in the seedling stages, when the monolayer will be favoured, and smaller, deeply lobed leaves in the adult. Adult leaves of

Q. velutina show a similar plastic gradation in response to illumination, brightly lit leaves being most dissected. The latter exemplifies a general distinction between sun and shade leaves (Vogel, 1968), and is to a great extent explicable in terms of heat budgets (cf. Chapter 5), since large leaves with greater boundary layer resistance are less susceptible to convective cooling and may overheat in full sun.

Leaf cooling is largely brought about by evaporation of water as vapour through the stomata, and is controlled by factors such as size and frequency of stomatal apertures, but also by the boundary layer conditions of the leaf surface atmosphere (Gates, 1968). If this layer is turbulent (in wind, or on flat or smooth leaves) evaporation will be faster; a stable boundary layer will provide a large resistance to the movement of water vapour. Boundary layer resistance can be reduced by leaf dissection, as long as each individual leaf segment maintains a discrete boundary layer. Where the distance between segments is too small, a common boundary layer will form over the whole complex and boundary layer resistance will be considerably increased. A fuller discussion of leaf cooling is given in Chapter 5.

Apart from water vapour, the other important gas moving through the stomata is CO_2, and the same constraints will apply. It becomes of particular importance in water, however, where CO_2 diffusion is much slower and where its concentration is very sensitive to pH as a result of bicarbonate ion formation; and the characteristic feathery leaf of water plants (*Myriophyllum, Ranunculus* subgenus *Batrachium, Hottonia palustris*, see Fig. 2.6) is largely a mechanism for increasing surface area to allow greater CO_2 uptake. Significantly, the response is frequently light-triggered, by perception of photoperiod (Cook, 1972).

Leaf morphology, therefore, affects photosynthesis in four main ways:

(i)   light interception;
(ii) temperature regulation;
(iii) water balance;
(iv) CO_2 diffusion.

(ii) and (iii) are probably the most important. In all cases the environmental stimulus to which the plant responds is light, whether as flux density, duration, or their product, irradiance.

(*c*) *Increased photosynthetic activity.* Since shading tends to cause an increase in *SLA* (and hence, at constant *LWR*, in **F** also), relative growth rate (**R**) can theoretically be maintained, even with falling **E**. It is generally true that *SLA* and **F** are inversely correlated with irradiance,

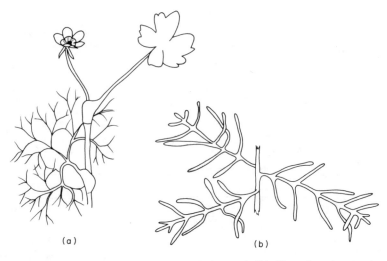

F$_{\mathrm{IG}}$. 2.6.   Leaves of (a) *Ranunculus trichophyllus* and (b) *Hottonia palustris*, showing dissection of underwater leaves.

while **E** is directly proportional to it (Blackman and Wilson, 1951; Newton, 1963; Coombe, 1966), since **E** is a manifestation of the efficiency of the photosynthetic system.

It is clear that one response open to a plant growing in shade is to increase the activity of the photosynthetic system. Accordingly, one can identify sun and shade plants with very different light response curves (Bohning and Burnside, 1956; Fig. 2.7). Shade plants are characterized by lower compensation points and light saturation levels, and by steeper angles of response. Light response curves of this type can be analysed in terms of maximum photosynthetic rate (P_{max}), the angle of response (θ), and the point of inflection (I_k) obtained by extrapolating the initial linear rise in photosynthetic rate towards P_{max}, and measuring the light intensity at the point of intersection (Talling, 1961; and see Fig. 2.4).

Generally a sun physiology has high P_{max}, low θ, and high I_k, a shade physiology the converse. The two sun plants in Fig. 2.7 have P_{max} ranging from 17–22 mg CO_2 dm^{-2} h^{-1} and I_k from 1000 to 1600 ft-candles; the two shade plants have P_{max} between 2 and 5 and I_k between 200 and 500 ft-candles. In this case there is a clear distinction between sun and shade species on physiological grounds and similar data are given for species of a beechwood ground flora by Schulze (1972).

A similar physiological distinction can be found between individual leaves on a single plant. These sun and shade leaves are morphologically

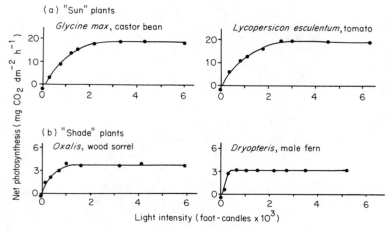

FIG. 2.7. Photosynthetic response curves for two "sun" species and two "shade" species (from Böhning and Burnside, 1956). Note the change in the vertical scale.

distinct, as shown above (cf. Table 2.6), and show parallel differences in response to light intensity (Boysen-Jensen and Muller, 1929). This plasticity can also be manifested as a temporal adaptation and as such appears to be widespread. Woledge (1971) found that leaves of plants of *Festuca arundinacea* grown previously at light intensities greater than 40 W m^{-2} had considerably faster rates of photosynthesis at high illumination (higher P_{max}) than those from plants previously grown in dim light. The same is true for *Silene alba*, a plant characteristic of sunny habitats (Wilmott and Moore, 1973); by contrast *S. dioica*, a shade plant possessing all the appropriate morphological adaptations, was much less plastic for P_{max} and for the initial slope of the photosynthesis/light intensity response curve (Table 2.7).

TABLE 2.7   Effect of light intensity during growth on two characteristics (P_{max} and k) of photosynthesis in *Silene* (Wilmott and Moore, 1973).

	Silene alba grown at		Silene dioica grown at	
		foot candles		
	400	2000	400	2000
P_{max}[a] mg CO_2 dm^{-2} h^{-1}	12·0	21·2	5·9	7·8
k[b] mg CO_2 dm^{-2} h^{-1} per 100 f.c.	0·90	1·25	0·80	0·86

[a] P_{max} is the light-saturated rate of photosynthesis.
[b] k is the slope of the linear portion of the response curve.

3. Mechanisms

Populations of plants from habitats differently illuminated, and individuals or parts of individuals similarly distinguished have differing photosynthetic responses to light intensity. Since these differences are expressed on a leaf area basis, they could have three causes:

(i) Improved access to substrate; i.e. higher CO_2 diffusion rates.
(ii) Increased light interception; i.e. more chlorophyll per unit leaf area.
(iii) Increased activity of the photosynthetic apparatus.

Changes in morphology and anatomy found in sun and shade leaves can certainly affect CO_2 diffusion (Holmgren, 1968; see p. 54). Shaded leaves, however, generally have enhanced chlorophyll levels per unit weight, though often not per unit area (Shirley, 1929). Absolute amounts of chlorophyll are usually greater in high light intensities, but it does not seem that any good generalizations can be made about the relationship between chlorophyll and light intensity.

On the other hand, consistent differences in rate of photosynthesis can be found on a leaf area basis. Björkman and his collaborators have made an extensive study of the adaptations of the photosynthetic mechanism in shaded plants. Björkman and Holmgren (1963) grew plants of *Solidago virgaurea* from shaded and exposed habitats in low $(3 \times 10^4 \text{ ergs cm}^{-2} \text{s}^{-1} = 30 \text{ W m}^{-2})$ and high $(15 \times 10^4 \text{ ergs cm}^{-2} \text{s}^{-1} = 150 \text{ W m}^{-2})$ light intensities, and found that P_{max} was generally higher in the plants from exposed habitats, an indication of genetic differentiation. In these plants P_{max} was reduced if the plants were grown in low light, showing physiological plasticity (Table 2.8). The plants from

TABLE 2.8. Differences in photosynthetic characteristics and plasticity in clones of goldenrod *Solidago virgaurea* from shaded and exposed habitats (Björkman and Holmgren, 1963).

| | Habitat of plants | |
	Shaded	Exposed
1. Light-saturated photosynthetic rate (P_{max}) plant grown at 150 W m^{-2} mg CO_2 dm^{-2} h^{-1}	17·9	25·5
2. Ratios of P_{max} for plants grown at 150 W m^{-2} to that of plants grown at 30 W m^{-2}	0·97	1·84
3. Ratios of slope of response curve for plants grown at 150 W m^{-2} to that of those grown at 30 W m^{-2}	0·64	1·04

shaded habitats, by contrast, had the same maximum photosynthetic rate, irrespective of the intensity at which they were grown; but the capacity of the process (the initial slope of the rate/intensity curve) was increased by growth in low light intensity in these shade plants, while remaining unchanged in the exposed plants. The two sets of populations are therefore physiologically distinct, but both are capable of plastic modification, which occurs by the raising of P_{max} in the sun plants and by raising the capacity, the sensitivity at low light intensities, in the shade plants. These adaptations are appropriate to the stresses likely to be encountered by the plants. Similar effects have been shown for arctic and alpine populations of *Oxyria digyna* (Mooney and Billings, 1961), and *Thalictrum alpinum* (Mooney and Johnson, 1965), and for shaded and exposed races of *Solanum dulcamara* (Gauhl, 1976). It is reasonable to suppose that they are general, although it may be that plants with a high leaf turn-over may be able to adjust by producing new leaves with altered physiology.

These responses are linked to enzymic changes. In *Solidago virgaurea* Björkman (1968) found that ribulose bis-phosphate carboxylase activity, expressed in μ mol CO_2 mg^{-1} protein min^{-1}, was 0·25 for exposed habitat plants grown in strong light and only 0·21 for those grown in weak light. The shaded habitat plants gave values of 0·15 and 0·12 for strong and weak light respectively. Once again both genetic differentiation and plasticity are apparent. On the other hand, although Hiesey *et al.* (1971), found a strong correlation between RuBP carboxylase activity and light intensity in two species of *Mimulus*, when expressed on a fresh weight basis (4·4 μ mol CO_2 min^{-1} g^{-1} at 18 W m^{-2} to 13·5 at 106 W m^{-2}), this was associated with a parallel increase in protein; all activities were around 0·5 when expressed per unit protein. The increase in RuBP carboxylase activity may not, therefore, always be specific.

RuBP carboxylase is, of course, the enzyme responsible for CO_2 fixation in most temperate plants, and in ontogeny of the chloroplast its synthesis is strongly light dependent (Walker, 1973). If maize seedlings are grown in the dark and given a brief light flash, there is a very rapid rise in RuBP carboxylase activity over the first 3 min, followed by a more gradual rise and then a slow decline. Application of chloramphenicol stops the gradual rise but not the rapid response, which appears to be due to activation of a pool of precursor and can be stopped by chloramphenicol given 3·5 h before the light flash. This enzyme is capable of both short and long-term responses to light and, being unstable, its activity slowly decays in the dark. It is probable that its photolability is responsible for much of the physiological plasticity in photosynthetic mechanisms observed in sun and shade plants.

Not all plants, however, show the same forms of adaptation. In *Solidago* the sun and shade races are clearly differentiated in their response to light intensity, but in *Solanum dulcamara* at least one shade race had a "sun" physiology and was more sensitive to water status (Gauhl, 1969, 1979), and two species of *Mimulus*, the coastal *M. cardinalis* and the subalpine *M. lewisii*, were able to grow equally well in both low (25 W m^{-2}) and high (120 W m^{-2}) light intensities (Hiesey *et al.*, 1971).

C. Effects of High Light Intensity

High light intensity is a relative term. Shade plants suffer reversible damage when grown at normal daylight intensities (Björkman and Holmgren, 1963): shade adapted plants of *Solidago virgaurea*, grown for one week at a high light intensity, had a much poorer response to light than a control plant, but after a week at low intensity this damage was repaired. The cause of the damage lies in structural malformation of the chloroplast. Similar effects have been shown for seedlings of *Quercus petraea* (Jarvis, 1964): in sun leaves, photosynthesis at 40 W m^{-2} was reduced by 12% by a prior exposure for 2 h to 400 W m^{-2}, whereas the corresponding reduction for shade leaves was 45%.

A similar distinction exists at high light intensities. In 1965 Hatch and Slack demonstrated the existence of a distinct photosynthetic pathway in sugar cane, *Saccharum officinarum*, known now as the C4 pathway, and initially thought to be quite distinct from the C3 Calvin pathway. The C4 pathway uses the enzyme PEP carboxylase for the primary fixation of CO_2, and the fixed carbon travels initially through various 4-carbon dicarboxylic acids—oxaloacetate, malate, and aspartate—but the CO_2 is eventually released and re-fixed by the universal carboxylating enzyme—RuBP carboxylase. Plants possessing this pathway are usually anatomically distinct as well, having "Krantz" anatomy, with a well-marked bundle sheath surrounding the vascular bundles and the chloroplasts concentrated in a ring of mesophyll cells radiating out from the sheath (Fig. 2.8), and in the sheath itself. There are also ultrastructural differences in the chloroplasts.

The interest of the C4 pathway lies in the very different photosynthetic physiology it confers. Black (1971) has termed plants with this pathway "high photosynthetic capacity plants", using capacity in the sense of maximum rate, on the basis of the generalizations in Table 2.9.

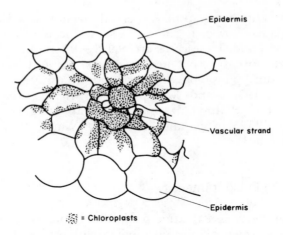

Fɪɢ. 2.8.   Cross-section of a single bundle-trace in a leaf of *Digitaria sanguinalis*, showing Krantz anatomy. Chloroplasts are stippled (redrawn from Black, 1971; × 340).

Carbon-dioxide fixation by PEP carboxylase is not in itself novel; it is well known as part of crassulacean acid metabolism (CAM), characteristic of desert succulents. In CAM, however, fixation occurs at night and CO_2 is released again in the daytime for photosynthesis; the malic acid produced by fixation is probably transported into the vacuole— concentrations achieved would depress cytoplasmic pH to around 3— and then shipped back and decarboxylated in daylight. In C4 plants,

Tᴀʙʟᴇ 2.9   Characteristics of C4 and C3 plants (based in part on Black, C.C. (1971).

Characteristic	*C4 plants*	*C3 plants*
Initial CO_2 fixing enzyme	PEP carboxylase	RuBP carboxylase
Photorespiration	Nil or low	High
Light	Not saturating at normal light intensities	Saturates at 100–200 W m^{-2}, or less in shade plants
Temperature optimum	30–40°C	10–25°C
CO_2 compensation point	less than 10 p.p.m.	about 70 p.p.m.
P_{max} in full sun ($mg\ CO_2\ dm^{-2}\ h^{-1}$)	more than 40 (field max.=85: maize; Heichel and Musgrave, 1969)	less than 30

however, the PEP carboxylase is active at the same time as RuBP carboxylase. The exact physical movements of carbon in the C4 system are unclear, for it is both biochemically and anatomically complex, but the result is a physiology with very high light saturation, high temperature optima, and the ability to reduce mesophyll space CO_2 concentrations to very low levels, so increasing CO_2 diffusion rates and alleviating one of the major limiting factors in photosynthesis at high light intensities. In addition C4 plants appear to lack photorespiration, a characteristic of C3 plants whereby light stimulates respiration, and at face value a wasteful process, particularly in view of the significance of respiration rates in adaptation to shade (see above). It has been suggested that the principal function of the C4 pathway is the re-assimilation of CO_2 produced by photorespiration (Nasyrov, 1978).

The conditions which will favour C4 plants are clearly sunny and hot—tropical—and indeed C4 photosynthesis is largely confined to plants of low latitudes. A few temperate plants are apparently C4 species, such as *Spartina anglica* (Mallot et al., 1975) and *Euphorbia peplis* (Webster et al., 1975); strikingly both are coastal species where light intensities are high. Other temperate species, such as *Jovibarba sobolifera*, *Sedum acre* and several *Sempervivum* species have CAM (Osmond et al., 1975); all are succulent.

Since C4 photosynthesis was initially discovered in and is largely confined to tropical plants, it was at first thought to be a distinct evolutionary line. More recently Björkman and his co-workers have demonstrated that both C3 and C4 species occur in *Atriplex* (Björkman et al., 1971), and the same is true in *Euphorbia* (Webster et al., 1975). Two species of *Atriplex*, *A. patula* (C3) and *A. rosea* (C4), form fertile hybrids, which are intermediate in all respects (leaf anatomy, enzyme activities, photosynthetic characteristics) between the parents. PEP carboxylase activity was closer in the hybrids to that of *A. patula*, and RuBP carboxylase activity was the same in *A. patula*, the F1, and the F2; *A. rosea* had significantly less (Björkman et al., 1971; Table 2.10). Strikingly, there was little correlation in the F2 between the anatomical characteristics of C4 plants and PEP carboxylase activity, suggesting the genetic links between the various C4 characters were easily broken. The hybrids showed poorer CO_2 assimilation rates at all light intensities than either parent, and at light saturation were operating at about 50% of the rate of *A. patula* (Table 2.10). Lacking photorespiration, *A. rosea* was not stimulated photosynthetically by low oxygen in contrast to *A. patula*; in this respect the hybrids were all characteristic of C3 plants.

All this evidence points to C3 and C4 photosynthesis being closely related in an evolutionary sense, and it is likely that the divergence has

TABLE 2.10.   Enzyme activity and photosynthetic efficiency in *Atriplex rosea* (C4), *A. patula* (C3), and their hybrids (Björkman, *et al.*, 1971).

	A. rosea	A. patula	*F1*	*F2*
PEP carboxylase activity μmol CO_2 dm^{-2} min^{-1}	66·5 (3·1)	3·6 (0·5)	14·2 (2·5)	13·6
RuBP carboxylase activity μmol CO_2 dm^{-2} min^{-1}	10·7 (1·4)	26·6 (1·5)	27·1 (2·4)	27·1 (5·2)
Light-saturated photosynthetic rate 27°C; 300 p.p.m. CO_2; 21% O_2	21·8 (1·0)	11·8 (0·6)	6·5 (0·7)	6·8 (0·7)

Figures in brackets are standard errors.

occurred frequently in response to the selective pressure of bright, hot, dry environments. Both C3 and C4 plants possess the enzymes of the other pathway (cf. Table 2.10) and in C4 plants both are simultaneously active—as was apparently true also for Björkman's F1 *Atriplex* hybrids. The classification of a plant as C3 or C4 therefore depends on the relative activity of the two carboxylating enzymes, and so, possibly, on environmental conditions. For example, of 27 epiphytic bromeliads examined for CAM by Medina and Troughton (1974), 13 showed no dark CO_2 fixation and discriminated strongly against the stable isotope ^{13}C (a characteristic of initial RuBP carboxylase fixation); these were considered to be C3 plants. A further 13 exhibited dark fixation and had low discrimination, and so were classified as C4 or CAM plants. One species, *Guzmania monostachya*, had pronounced dark fixation (accumulating 27·5 μmol malate g^{-1} in 12 h in the dark) but strong discrimination, implying that both enzyme systems were operating. CAM plants are often found in dry habitats where dark fixation is an advantage, as stomata can be closed in the daytime to conserve water; *Guzmania monostachya* grows in humid habitats but epiphytically and in high light intensities, where possibly both pathways can be valuable. As more and more carbon isotope discrimination analyses are carried out, it is increasingly clear that many species show the ability to switch from one pathway to the other, at least in part (see for example, Troughton *et al.*, 1977), and in one species *Frerea indica*, Lange and Zuber (1977) have shown that the perennial succulent stems have CAM and the seasonal leaves, only produced in the wet season, have C3 photosynthesis. Even more striking evidence of the adaptability of these various CO_2 fixation pathways is the inducibility of CAM metabolism in the succulent *Mesembryanthemum crystallinum* (Winter, 1974). Within 7 to 14 days of the onset of water stress the activity of PEP carboxylase rises and dark fixation starts, and this can be shown to be due to *de novo* synthesis of the enzyme (Von Willert *et al.*, 1976; Queiroz, 1977).

1. C4 and C3 Photosynthesis Compared

As soon as the intrinsically greater potential photosynthesis of C4 plants was recognized, much interest centred on the implications for plant productivity, for example by breeding C4 characters such as lack of photorespiration into C3 crop plants, such as wheat. The ecological implications of having plants of inherently high and low productivity also excited interest (Black, 1971).

But Gifford (1974) has shown that while C4 plants may be 60–70 times as effective as C3 plants if *in vitro* primary carboxylation is considered, this ratio declines steadily as more complex levels of organization are encountered. Thus for net photosynthesis of an intact leaf he quotes a ratio of 1·5–3, and for short-term crop growth rate a ratio of 1. Only if annual dry matter production figures are compared, with maxima of around 80 t ha^{-1} for *Pennisetum purpureum* (C4) and 30 t ha^{-1} for many C3 crops, do C4 plants again show a superiority, and this is largely due to the longer growing seasons and more favourable conditions of the climates in which they grow.

The two pathways then represent adaptations to different conditions. Although in laboratory studies C4 photosynthesis is much more effective, it would be facile to term it "better" as some have been tempted to do. The high light intensity, high temperature, long growing season conditions of the tropics have selected for activity of PEP carboxylase as a primary CO_2-fixing enzyme, whereas,·for reasons not fully clear, in most temperate climates RuBP carboxylase has been favoured. It may be significant that leaves of C3 plants are more palatable than those of C4 plants to grasshoppers (Caswell *et al.*, 1973) and to sucking insects (Kroh and Beaver, 1978), since very productive plants are normally considered most palatable to insects (Harper, 1969). Possibly herbivore pressure in the tropics has been so great that much of the extra photosynthate of C4 plants is diverted into chemical defence rather than growth (see Chapter 8). Of greater significance, however, is the effect of temperature on the two pathways. The quantum yield of C3 photosynthesis is less temperature dependent than that of C4 plants, and Ehleringer (1978) has used simulation techniques to produce predictions for the distribution of C3 and C4 grasses in prairie, desert, and shaded habitats which correspond closely to observed patterns.

D. Photosynthesis in the Community—Productivity

The productivity of a community is a reflection of the net photosynthesis of its component species, and as such will be strongly influenced by many factors other than light intensity. Nevertheless both the total irradiance over a growing season and the illumination at physiologically important times (e.g. grain filling) are important determinants of maximum photosynthetic production. To the agriculturalist, therefore, the maximization of light interception by a crop is a major goal. We need to consider again the properties of leaf canopies and, in particular, the significance of leaf area index (*LAI* or **L**).

L measures the numbers of layers of leaves above a point on the ground, and is therefore dimensionless. It is important as a measure of the intercepting capacity of a stand for light. Typical values for **L** are listed in Table 2.11, showing great variation between species. There is

TABLE 2.11   Values of leaf area index, **L**, recorded for mature stands of various species.

Species	L	Authors	Country
Trifolium subterraneum	3·75	Black (1964)	Australia
Triticum aestivum	3·0	Watson (1947)	England
	3·1–7·3	Leach and Watson (1968)	England
Solanum tuberosum	2·0	Watson (1947)	England
	1·4–3·9	Leach and Watson (1968)	England
Musanga cecropioides	3·2	Coombe and Hadfield (1962)	West Africa
Beta vulgaris	3·5–4·0	Goodman (1968)	England
	3·3–3·8	Leach and Watson (1968)	England
Hordeum vulgare	2·4–2·9	Leach and Watson (1968)	England
Brassica napus	2·4–5·4	Leach and Watson (1968)	England
Mercurialis perennis	2·3–3·5	Hutchings (1976)	England
Festuca altissima	11·2	Sheehy and Cooper (1973)	England
Dactylis glomerata	13·7–14·9	Sheehy and Cooper (1973)	England
Phleum pratense	10·4–15·5	Sheehy and Cooper (1973)	England

also variation in the distribution of **L**, some species tending to have leaves concentrated at the top of the canopy, others to have them more evenly distributed down it. Thus, radish (*Raphanus sativus*) with a rosette of leaves, has a much higher proportion of the total **L** near the base of the canopy than flax or linseed (cf. Fig. 2.3), or particularly maize (Zea), which have leaves at intervals up the stem, and similar differences exist in forage grasses (Sheehy and Cooper, 1973), though largely as a result of leaf angle variations.

As leaves absorb or reflect light, the intensity at any point in a plant stand depends upon the number of leaf layers above it. Consequently, there is often an inverse relationship between **E** for a crop and the value of **L** (Goodman, 1968); the more leaves the higher **L** will be and, as a result of mutual shading, the lower the mean value of **E**. At very high **L** some lower leaves may be below compensation point, in which case shade adaptations or self-pruning by senescence and abscission may become important. These considerations lead to the conclusion that there must be an optimum value of **L** ($\mathbf{L_{opt}}$) below which production will be lost as photosynthetically significant amounts of light will be passing unintercepted through the canopy, and above which the same result will be due to lower leaves operating below their compensation point. $\mathbf{L_{opt}}$ can be estimated by plotting crop growth rate against **L**, which gives values of 3–4 for sugar beet (Goodman, 1968) and 4–7 for *Trifolium subterraneum* (Black, 1964). Goodman's values were from different years, Black's under various light intensities; clearly the amount of incoming radiation will strongly affect $\mathbf{L_{opt}}$, as it depends on the extinction of light in the canopy (see Fig. 1.6, p. 14).

In agricultural conditions more production will be lost through supra-optimal than sub-optimal values of **L**, since the latter only occur during early growth of a sward or crop (Black, 1964). Agricultural communities are, however, essentially monospecific; in natural and semi-natural stands supra-optimal values of **L** are less likely to be important, for three reasons:

(i) Many species, most notably conifers, have self-pruning mechanisms, by which whole branches, whose leaves are below light compensation, will fall off. Senescence of lower leaves of herbaceous plants is a common phenomenon.

(ii) Where several species are involved in a community they are likely to have varying degrees of shade tolerance, and lower positions in the canopy, which may be too heavily shaded for top-canopy species, will be occupied by these species.

(iii) The action of grazing animals on a canopy so dense as to exceed $\mathbf{L_{opt}}$ is likely to be severe.

Sub-optimal values of **L** are more probable, partly for the same reason as in an agricultural sward, that at the beginning of the growing season leaves have not fully expanded, and partly because, much more than in agricultural situations, other environmental factors (water, nutrients, grazing animals) will often be limiting.

Agricultural communities have the attraction (to the physiologist or model-minded ecologist) of being monospecific, at least if the often well developed, subordinate weed and algal layers are ignored. Natural communities are almost always composed of many, more or less discrete layers (trees, shrubs, herbs, ground) and each layer may contain more than one species. Almost invariably a large part of community productivity is accounted for by the canopy, but the lower layers may be important. Even within the canopy, however, there may be several species with distinct photosynthetic characteristics, and any consideration of productivity must take this into account.

Variation in productivity between communities can be the result of environmental factors, such as temperature or the availability of water or mineral nutrients, or may be a reflection of the "age" of the community. Most successional sequences show well-marked trends in productivity (Fig. 2.9), which is very low in colonizing stands before a complex canopy architecture has developed, rises to a maximum when a many-layered canopy is established, and very often declines in climax communities. This last point has often proved a stumbling block to

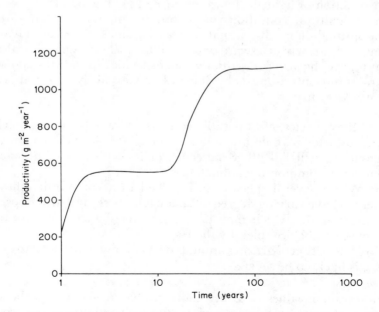

FIG. 2.9.   Productivity of the oak-pine forest at Brookhaven, New York, during the course of succession (from Whittaker, 1975).

theories of succession; Horn (1971) explains it as the result of the establishment in the canopy of monolayer trees with low productivity (due to low **L**), which let through little light and so inhibit growth beneath the canopy. An excellent example of such a situation is beech forest, which often has almost no shrub or herb layer. The explanation is attractive and underlines the interactions between species that determine community productivity.

Needless to say, little attempt has been made to model the production of complex communities, and most attempts have been with monospecific agricultural stands. Grace and Woolhouse (1974) have constructed a working model for a peat-bog community with three main species—*Calluna vulgaris*, *Rubus chamaemorus*, and *Sphagnum rubellum* at Moor House National Nature Reserve in northern England. Using physiological data obtained in laboratory studies on the effects of environmental factors such as light intensity and temperature leaf age and grazing on photosynthetic rate, and environmental data obtained from permanent records at Moor House, they were able to reconstruct the productivity pattern of the community with remarkable accuracy. This is, however, a species-poor community with a simple canopy acting as a neutral filter, and so many obvious sources of error can be minimized. It will be some time before the same predictive accuracy will be possible with more complex communities.

3. Mineral Nutrients

I. INTRODUCTION

All green plants require the same basic set of mineral nutrients and the various elements are used by different plants for essentially similar ends. One or two groups have specialized requirements, such as that for cobalt by legumes co-existing symbiotically with nitrogen-fixing *Rhizobium* bacteria, or for sodium by plants utilizing the C4 photosynthetic pathway (Brownell and Crosland, 1972), and by some salt-marsh and salt-desert plants. The amounts required do, however, vary between species, both in total and relative proportion, so that it is possible, for example to classify some plants as nitrophiles, such as *Chenopodium rubrum* which is abundant on manure heaps. The same is true for other nutrients.

All plants, therefore, possess uptake mechanisms capable of moving ions across their cell membranes, chiefly nitrate and ammonium, phosphate, potassium, calcium, sulphate, magnesium, iron, manganese, copper, boron, chlorine, zinc, and molybdenum. In addition, an enormous range of other elements, ranging from the abundant (aluminium, sodium) to the most obscure (zirconium, titanium, and similar elements) are accumulated by plants. Sometimes this accumulation is characteristic of a particular group: selenium is accumulated by some *Astragalus* species and silicon may be a major component of grass stems. As far as is known these elements have no metabolic function, though they may be ecologically important in providing support (silicon) or protection from grazing animals (selenium) for example.

There are two striking features of ion uptake by plants: one is the concentration factor—the ability of plants to accumulate ions to a concentration sometimes several orders of magnitude greater than that in the medium; the other is the quantitative differences that exist between plant species, and sometimes even within a species, in the requirements for different nutrients. To understand the basis for these

features and their ecological implications it is necessary to know something of the physiology of ion uptake by plant cells.

II. PHYSIOLOGY OF ION UPTAKE

A. Kinetics

Plant root cells generally contain much higher ionic concentrations
than their surrounding medium and are normally electrically negative
with respect to it. To maintain this potential, of the order of -60 to
-200 mV, involves energy expenditure, but as a consequence of its
existence most cations appear to be able to enter the cell passively, down
the electrochemical gradient, although usually against the chemical
concentration gradient for that ion; in some cases, certainly for Na^+,
cations are actively exported back into the medium. By contrast,
anions must be transported actively into root cells against both the
electrochemical and in most cases the concentration gradients. Whether
active or passive, however, transport is energy-dependent and so
necessarily influenced by a number of external and internal factors, in
particular the concentration of the ionic substrate and variables such as
temperature that affect respiration. When energy supply is adequate
the dominant influence on the rate of ion uptake is external concentration.

A great number of experiments have been performed on ion uptake,
some using excised roots, some whole plants, but almost all in non-
equilibrium conditions, typically using roots previously grown in $0·2$
or $0·5$ mM $CaSO_4$ and measuring uptake over very short periods. They
have shown that there is a characteristic relationship between uptake
rate and concentration which, because of its apparent similarity to that
between the rate of an enzyme-mediated reaction and its substrate
concentration, has been analysed in terms of Michaelis-Menten
kinetics. The typical hyperbolic curve is shown in Fig. 3.1 together with
two plots based on enzyme kinetics which produce linear plots. The
enzyme analogy implies that there are molecules ("carriers") in the
cell membrane, more or less specific for the ion, which can transport
ions at a particular rate (v) under given conditions, so that at high
substrate concentrations all carriers are operating at maximum rate
and saturation uptake rate (V_{max}) is reached. The Michaelis-Menten
equation can then be applied:

$$v = (V_{max} \times C_{ext}) / (K_m + C_{ext}) \tag{3.1}$$

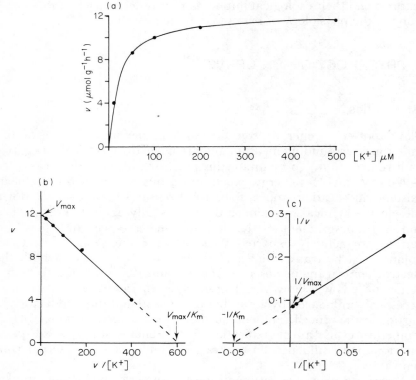

FIG. 3.1.   Absorption isotherm for potassium ions (a) and two plots to obtain linearity: (b) Hofstee plot and (c) Lineweaver-Burke plot. $V_{max} = 12\ \mu$mol g^{-1} FW h^{-1}; $K_m = 20$ μm. Hypothetical data.

where K_m represents that external concentration (C_{ext}) at which v is half V_{max}. This Michaelis coefficient, K_m, therefore describes a property we may call the "affinity" of the uptake system; a low K_m implies high affinity, the system becoming half-saturated at low concentrations.

Using these two attributes of an uptake system, K_m and V_{max}, we can obtain a good idea of its capabilities. Much controversy still surrounds the details and location of the uptake mechanism (Epstein, 1973; Higinbotham, 1973; Hodges, 1973; Clarkson, 1974) and the concept of carriers in its original form now finds less favour; fortunately this debate mostly concerns points of import to cellular biologists which only slightly affect our understanding of whole plant function. Three points are however of great significance.

B. Interactions

Typically physiological experiments are performed in very simple solutions. In their classic experiments Epstein and Hagen (1952) used single-salt (2 ion) solutions for simple uptake studies and 3 ion solutions (e.g. Na^+, Rb^+, Cl^-) for studies of interactions. Most workers have followed suit. For an understanding of the uptake mechanism this is a valid approach, but if more complex solutions are used many interactions are found, both stimulatory and inhibitory:

> (i) *Inhibition* of the uptake of one ion by another can result either in an increased K_m with no change in V_{max} (known as competitive inhibition) or in a reduction in V_{max} with no change in K_m (non-competitive inhibition). Competitive inhibition occurs for example between K^+ and Rb^+ or Ca^{2+} and Sr^{2+}, and depends on the relative frequency of the two ion species. It can therefore be overcome by raising the concentration of the test ion; this is not true of non-competitive inhibition, where the system is actually incapacitated.
>
> (ii) *Stimulation* of uptake is most often associated with changes in Ca^{2+} concentration, which appears to affect membrane function (Burstrom, 1968; Epstein, 1961).

Clearly in complex soil solutions the relationship may be radically different to that determined in experiments. Even in more realistic work using whole plants growing in nutrient culture only essential elements are normally used (Hewitt, 1967), and very little is known of the effects of non-essential ions (with the notable exception of Al^{3+} — see Chapter 6). In many soils silicate ions are dominant and these can interact with manganese (Rorison, 1971), and in calcareous soils bicarbonate ions are abundant and powerfully inhibit iron uptake by non-adapted species, such as *Deschampsia flexuosa* (Woolhouse, 1966). To complicate matters further many soil solutions contain a wide variety of organic ions, such as phenolic acids derived from the breakdown of lignin, which are present in some quantity in the rhizosphere and these have been shown dramatically to inhibit phosphate and potassium uptake by barley roots (Glass, 1973, 1974; see Fig. 6.1, p. 210).

C. Plant Demand

A further problem in interpreting physiological work in an ecological context is that the classic material for studies of ion uptake has been a short length of root tip cut from a barley plant that has been nutrient-starved by being grown in 0·2 mM $CaSO_4$ for five days (Epstein, 1961). This has the advantage of ensuring responsiveness, and the disadvantage that it is a system very far from equilibrium. Starvation may alter the uptake characteristics of a root; Leigh *et al.* (1973) showed profound differences between maize grown simply on 0·5 mM $CaCl_2$ and that grown on 7·5 mM NaCl with 2·5 mM KCl and 0·5 mM $CaCl_2$. Removing the shoot, the sink to which ions are transported and the source of fixed carbon, also has profound effects, since there is a direct relationship between K^+ transport to the shoot, for example, and shoot relative growth rate (Pitman and Cram, 1973; Fig. 3.13).

D. High Concentrations

As the external concentrations of an ion are increased, a point is reached at which saturation occurs; for most ions this is around 1·0 mM. Above this there is usually a second hyperbolic curve with similar kinetics to the first, beginning at around 10 mM. This phenomenon, first noted by Epstein and Hagen (1952), is known as the "dual isotherm", the lower curve representing System I and the upper System II (Fig. 3.2). The validity, nature, and location of System II still excite much debate, but a number of points can be made:

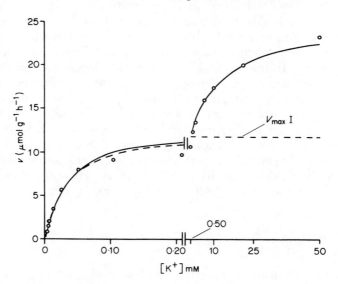

Fig. 3.2.   Dual isotherm for K^+ absorption, by barley roots from KCl with 0·5 mM $CaCl_2$. Note change of scale (from Epstein, 1973).

(i) The concentration scale on which System II is plotted is very different. If they were plotted on the same scale, the two isotherms would appear very different in form.

(ii) System II appears to represent passive absorption down a concentration gradient. Barber (1972) found the Q_{10} with respect to temperature to be about $1 \cdot 0$, whereas the Q_{10} of System I is between $2 \cdot 0$ and $3 \cdot 0$. Similarly he found that System II uptake of phosphate by barley is scarcely affected by the respiratory uncoupler DNP and later showed that thallium, which is phytotoxic above $1 \cdot 0$ mM, is taken up by barley with normal System II kinetics.

(iii) If Epstein's interpretation is correct, and both System I and System II are located at the plasmalemma (Laties (1969) believes System II to be in the tonoplast), it is difficult to see when it would operate, as soil solution concentrations rarely reach even its K_m values (Table 3.1), and when plants are grown in media maintained at such levels they show no growth response.

TABLE 3.1.   Mean values and range of soil solution concentrations for seven ions (mM).

	Ca^{2+}	Mg^{2+}	K^+	*Ion* NO_3^-	NH_4^+	$H_2PO_4^-$	SO_4^{2-}
n	9	7	9	4	3	6	5
Mean	8·9	3·7	1·7	9·1	5·7	0·02	1·6
Min	1·7	0·3	0·1	1·0	5·0	0·00	0·3
Max	19·6	10·3	6·8	27·6	6·1	0·09	3·5

Most available data are from agricultural soils. Uncultivated soils will have lower values but few data are available. These data are from ADAMS, F. (1974). The soil solution. *In* "The Plant Root and Its Environment" (Ed. E. W. Carson). University Press of Virginia, Charlottesville.

From an environmental viewpoint we may therefore safely disregard System II and consider only the active System I, but it is worth noting that some workers (Nissen, 1974) believe that uptake over all concentrations can be expressed by a single multiphasic isotherm.

III. NUTRIENTS IN THE SOIL SYSTEM

A. Concentrations

The concentrations of nutrients in solutions expressed from natural soils are typically very low (Table 3.1). Even in fertilized soils the values may be well below those that would saturate System I uptake isotherms. Nevertheless plants will grow well in solution culture at these or sometimes much lower concentrations. Asher and Loneragan (1967) found that in a group of Australian species, some such as *Erodium botrys*, *Bromus rigidus*, and *Trifolium subterraneum*, showed growth responses up to 5 μM P, while one, *Vulpia myuros*, reached a peak at 1 μM. For four species good growth was made at less than 1 μM P. It might, therefore, be a cause for surprise that conventional nutrient solution recipes recommend P levels around 1 mν apparently 3 orders of magnitude more than required. The differences are that these are for traditional static culture, whereas Asher and Loneragan used a sophisticated flowing culture system, so that the *supply* of 1 μM was maintained. This concept of supply is fundamental and is covered below briefly, and in more detail by Nye and Tinker (1977).

Ion concentrations vary greatly amongst soils and spatially within any one soil, depending on factors intimately involved in pedogenesis (parent material, climate, topography, vegetation, and the age of soil), but of more importance to the individual plant is variation in time. The process of uptake in static solution culture reduces concentration (a fact, incidentally, that often complicates the interpretation of physiological experiments) and in soil the same will occur, its extent depending upon how well the soil is buffered against depletion.

Soil buffering powers vary greatly for different ions, depending on the extent to which they are adsorbed by soil. Strongly sorbed ions such as phosphate are powerfully buffered, since the bulk of the ion is in an insoluble state and acts as a reservoir. By contrast, nitrates are very soluble and are not stored in soil to any extent; the reservoir for nitrate in soil comprises N in organic matter and adsorbed NH_4^+, both of which undergo microbial conversion to NO_3^-, and indirectly atmospheric N_2 which is fixed by various bacteria and cyanobacteria, to give NH_4^+.

B. Supply

The supply of ions in soil can be viewed in terms of mineral cycles, with inputs to and losses from the ecosystem and rates of transfer between components of the system. This approach is valuable for nitrogen, where inputs due to rainfall and fixation and losses due to leaching and denitrification represent a large proportion of the total amount being cycled through the system. For adsorbed ions, however, these inputs are usually trivial in comparison with the total amounts present, although leaching losses in fertilized soil may be important for some.

The nitrogen cycle is complex (Fig. 3.3) and the organic matter compartment is dominant. Several bacteria are involved in the conversion of NH_4^+ to NO_3^- (*Nitrobacter*, *Nitrosomonas*, and *Nitrococcus* are the most important), but both forms can in fact be taken up by most plants with equal facility. More significant is NH_4^+ production from organic matter, brought about by various fungi and bacteria. These decomposers also require N however, and if the material is low in N, it

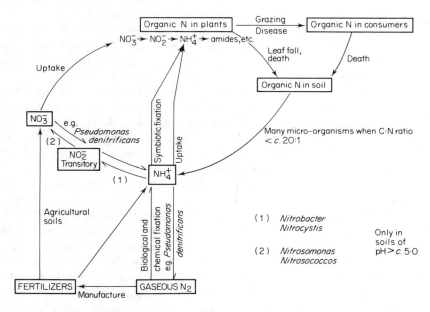

FIG. 3.3. Simplified scheme of nitrogen cycle, showing major sources and pools, and primary processes involved.

will be incorporated into their biomass and not liberated until carbon supply is reduced. There appears to be a critical value of between 1·2 and 1·8% N in litter (corresponding to C : N ratios of between 30 : 1 and 20 : 1), below which little or no NH_4^+ is released. Since most plants conserve N by recovering it before leaf-fall, and in extreme cases may short-circuit the N cycle by retaining almost all in the perennating organs (Small, 1972), freshly deposited leaves tend to have a high C:N ratio (up to or exceeding 100:1), and the more slowly N is made available to plants, the higher will be the C:N ratio of the litter, which accentuates the infertility.

Nitrogen is not the only element which cycles through the organic matter. Freshly fallen leaves contain a wide range of elements, particularly calcium, since it is immobile in the phloem and so not withdrawn from senescing leaves, unlike most other nutrient minerals. Some, such as potassium, tend to wash straight out into the soil and so enter the inorganic cycle; others, such as phosphorus, are mainly in organic compounds in the leaf, but organic P is only of indirect significance in soils, partly because to become available to plants it must be released as $H_2PO_4^-$ ions, whereupon it will be promptly adsorbed by iron, aluminium, or calcium surfaces in soil.

The supply of most cations and anions depends largely on the inorganic equilibria, best illustrated by phosphorus. A typical soil may contain anything from 0·05 to 1·0 g P per kg of soil, but the concentration in soil solution is likely to be between 0·1 and 10 μM, equivalent to less than 60 μg P per kg of a moist soil, or about 0·005% of the total amount. The remaining 99·995% is in the solid phase, in a bewildering variety of compounds, most of which are not simply characterizable chemically. Solid phase phosphate is best classified according to its relationship with the solution phase, producing a labile pool in equilibrium with the solution, and a non-labile pool.

The non-labile pool is usually much the largest (Larsen, 1964), but the distinction is empirical. The labile pool is that part that will exchange with phosphate in solution, determined experimentally with $H_2^{32}PO_4^-$. Its size depends on the time allowed for equilibration, as over long periods less labile ions will become exchangeable. Solid phase phosphate does not therefore exist as two discrete phases, but in a continuous spectrum of lability, depending on the nature of the binding to calcium, aluminium, ferric, and also organic compounds in the soil.

The value of this model is that it enables rates of supply to be quantified. A soil solution at 10^{-6}M phosphate represents about 10 g phosphate in solution per hectare; assuming crop uptake of 20 kg ha^{-1} and a growing season of 2000 h, this solution would be wholly depleted in 1 h, and long before that uptake would have been greatly reduced. Necessarily labile phosphate must come into solution to maintain the supply, and so the labile pool–solution equilibrium is of crucial importance. This equilibrium can be measured by taking advantage of the fact that if phosphate is added to soil in solution, the bulk is immediately adsorbed. By varying the amount added an adsorption isotherm can be constructed, relating the amount adsorbed to the concentration in solution after a given time, and indicating the equilibrium between labile and solution P. Equally, as phosphate is removed from solution by plant uptake or artificially, ions come into solution from the labile phase by desorption, and an analogous desorption isotherm exists. In practice such isotherms exhibit hysteresis and the desorption isotherm, which controls the supply of phosphate to absorbing roots, cannot be predicted from the adsorption isotherm.

Figure 3.4 shows three adsorption isotherms for contrasting soils, one steep, the other two more gradual. For the clay soil with a steep isotherm large changes in the quantity (Q) of adsorbed phosphate are needed to bring about a small change in solution concentration; for the sandy soil the reverse is true. For a given amount of sorbed phosphate the clay soil

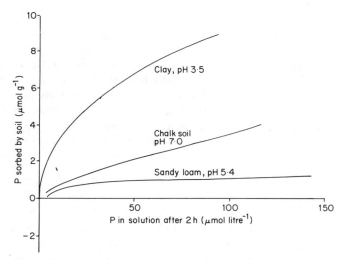

FIG. 3.4. Adsorption isotherms for phosphate of three contrasting soils (Fitter, unpublished).

will therefore show lower concentration in solution, but will maintain this concentration better against depletion; the clay soil is therefore more strongly buffered than the sandy soil.

Buffer power measurements can be used to predict fertilizer additions required to maintain plant growth (Ozanne and Shaw, 1967; Fitter and Bradshaw, 1974; Holford, 1976), but increasing the labile pool by fertilization will also alter the equilibrium between labile and non-labile pools (Fig. 3.5), and some labile will be immobilized as non-labile (Larsen, 1967). This description for phosphate applies equally to other adsorbed ions such as potassium (Beckett, 1964;

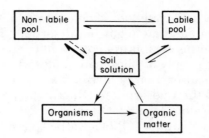

Fig. 3.5. Model of compartmentation of adsorbed ions in soil. The labile pool is the proportion of non-dissolved ion that is readily exchangeable, in the case of phosphate for ^{32}P. The thickness of the arrows indicates the balance of the equilibrium.

Fergus *et al.*, 1972), molybdenum (Barrow, 1973), manganese (Lamm *et al.*, 1969), sulphate (Fox *et al.*, 1971), and cadmium (John, 1972).

The supply of adsorbed ions in soil tends therefore to be less variable seasonally than that of ions for which organic matter is a primary source, in particular nitrate. The dynamic balance of the inorganic adsorption system provides a buffer against the fluctuations exhibited by nitrate in soil. Nevertheless, phosphate is supplied from organic matter as well, and in some soils quite marked seasonal variation can occur (Gupta and Rorison, 1975).

C. Transport

The supply parameters considered above adequately describe nutrient availability at a fixed point in soil, but absorption by a root necessarily involves movement of the ion from the soil to the root surface. Since roots are scattered in soil and even in a densely-rooted horizon are unlikely to occupy more than 10% of the space, with 1% being more usual (Dittmer, 1940), such movement must occur over considerable distances if the plant is to exploit more than a small fraction of the soil volume. The mobility of ions in soil has now been comprehensively discussed by Nye and Tinker (1977). In practice there are two ways in which an ion can move towards a plant root:

(i) by *mass flow* in the water moving through the soil toward the root, down the water potential gradient caused by transpiration. *Leaching* is a specialized form of mass flow in which the water flow is gravitational, down the soil profile. It is of great importance in agriculture but is little influenced by roots and will not be discussed here.

(ii) by *diffusion* down concentration gradients created by the uptake of ions at the root surface.

The speed at which ions can move by mass flow is vastly greater than by the very slow process of diffusion, but in practice it is only of importance for some ions. The movement of ions by mass flow can be represented as follows (Tinker, 1969):

$$F = V \cdot C_1 \qquad (3.2)$$

where F is the flux into the root in mol cm^{-2} s^{-1}, V is the water flux in g cm^{-2} s^{-1} ($= cm$ s^{-1}), C is the concentration of ions in mol cm^{-3}, and the suffix l represents liquid phase. When a single root grows into a volume of soil, the entire soil volume can in theory be exploited by mass flow; the adequacy of the supply, however, depends entirely on whether the product of water flux and bulk soil solution concentration satisfies the plant's requirements.

At the root surface uptake lowers the concentration; if the uptake rate is greater than the rate of supply by mass flow, either because of a reduction in V, as for example at night or under daytime water stress when transpiration ceases, or because of a lowering of C_1, a concentration gradient will develop between the bulk soil and the root such that diffusion will occur. Conversely, ions may arrive faster than they are taken up, so that concentrations build up at the root surface and back diffusion occurs, as may happen for calcium (Barber, 1974). The full equation for the flow of nutrient ions through soil to a plant root must therefore include both mass flow and diffusive components:

$$F = V \cdot C_1 + (-D \cdot dC/dx) \qquad (3.3)$$

where D is the diffusion coefficient in soil and dC/dx the concentration gradient.

Several predictive models have been constructed to examine the effects of mass flow and diffusion in the supply of ions to plant roots (Passioura, 1963; Nye, 1966; Olsen and Kemper, 1968; Nye and Marriott, 1969; Baldwin, 1975; see Nye and Tinker (1977) for a full discussion). Typical results are illustrated in Fig. 3.6: as the water flux increases, the zone of depletion around the root becomes a zone of accumulation. Where the line lies above the dashed line in Fig. 3.6, mass flow would be an adequate means of supply, and the same data can be plotted, alternatively, as a relationship between ion flux and water flux (Fig. 3.7). Here the line through the origin shows what would occur with mass flow only (i.e. $F = V \cdot C_1$); the dashed line represents the actual situation for magnesium—at values of V less than about 2×10^{-6} cm s^{-1} ion flux is greater than mass flow would allow, so that

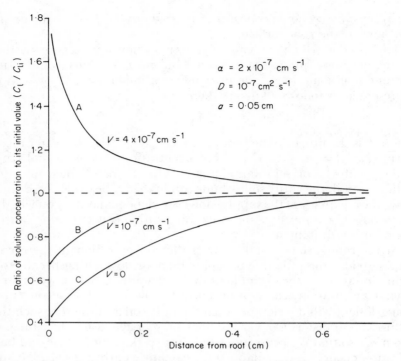

FIG. 3.6.   Changes in ion concentrations around a root after about 12 days (10^6 s) at different mass flow rates, for given conditions. (After Nye and Marriott, 1969).

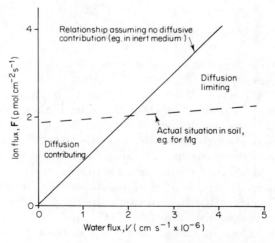

FIG. 3.7.   Relations between ion flux and water flux (from Tinker, 1969).

the diffusive contribution must be positive and a concentration gradient downwards towards the root must exist. Above this critical value of V, mass flow supplies ions faster than they are taken up and diffusion operates away from the root, lowering the flux into the root below the figure that could theoretically be supplied by mass flow (cf. A in Fig. 3.6).

Using these theoretical considerations and an increasing number of experimental confirmations, the relative importance of mass flow and diffusion for all important nutrient ions can be approximately stated. From data of available P, K, Ca, and Mg and known values of water use and nutrient uptake by a maize crop, Barber (1974) has estimated the relative contributions of mass flow, and (by difference) diffusion (Table 3.2). For potassium this suggests that 11% was supplied by mass flow, which agrees well with data obtained experimentally by Tinker (1969) by growing leek seedlings in soil and measuring water and ion uptake, ion status of the soil, and the relevant plant growth parameters. He found that $V \cdot C_1$ (the mass flow contribution to flux) represented between 4 and 13% of the total flux, F, depending on harvest interval.

TABLE 3.2. Estimated contributions of root interception, mass flow, and diffusion during one season's ion uptake by a maize crop (Barber, 1974).

Ion	Uptake by crop $(kg\ ha^{-1})$	$kg\ ha^{-1}$ supplied by	
		Mass flow	Diffusion
Ca^{2+}	45	90 (200)	negative $(-)$
Mg^{2+}	35	75 (214)	negative $(-)$
K^+	110	12 (11)	95 (89)
$H_2PO_4^-$	30	0·12 (0·4)	29 (>99)

Figures in parentheses are percentages of uptake for each ion.

1. The Contribution of Diffusion

Mass flow is a rapid process if water flux and soil solution concentrations are great enough. By contrast diffusion is a slow process in soil, measurable in mm per day. Where mass flow is insufficient to satisfy plant demand, therefore, ion concentrations at the root surface are reduced below that of the bulk soil solution, and marked zones of depletion occur. In such cases only a part of the soil volume is exploited, except for very mobile ions. The extent and development of these depletion zones are controlled partly by the plant, in creating the concentration gradient seen as a zone of depletion in autoradiographs, and partly by the soil, *via* the diffusion coefficient, D. This varies as follows (Nye, 1966):

$$D = D_1 \cdot \theta \cdot f \cdot 1/b \qquad (3.4)$$

where D_1 is the diffusion coefficient in free solution,
    θ is the volumetric water content of the soil,
    f is a tortuosity factor, and
    b is the soil buffering capacity (dC/dC_1).

The drier and the more strongly buffered the soil, the lower the diffusion coefficient will be; tortuosity is more complex. Clearly in a dry soil diffusion will be negligible and the wetter it is the nearer it approaches the free solution state. Tortuosity is a measure of the length of the diffusion path, which is affected by both moisture content and degree of compaction of the soil. The exact effect of these two interacting factors is complex (Fig. 3.8). The buffering capacity term accounts for

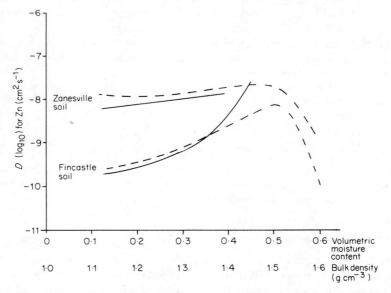

Fig. 3.8. Effect of soil moisture (continuous line) and bulk density (dotted line) on diffusion coefficient (D) of zinc in two soils. (After Barber, 1974).

sorption of ions by soil and explains why the diffusion coefficients of non-adsorbed ions are relatively little affected by soil. Typical values of D in soil are shown in Table 3.3; the extremely low values for phosphate permit negligible movement and may severely limit supply. Even in

TABLE 3.3. Range of measured values for the effective diffusion coefficient ($cm^2 s^{-1}$) of various ions in soil (summarized from several authors by Barber, 1974; Fried and Broeshart, 1967).

	Ion	Minimum	Maximum
Cations	Na^+	1×10^{-7}	1×10^{-5}
	K^+	2×10^{-7}	2×10^{-6}
	Rb	6×10^{-12}	7×10^{-6}
	NH_4^+	4×10^{-8}	1×10^{-6}
	Ca^{2+}	3×10^{-8}	3×10^{-7}
	Zn^{2+}	3×10^{-10}	2×10^{-7}
	Mn^{2+}	3×10^{-8}	2×10^{-7}
Anions	NO_3^-	5×10^{-7}	1×10^{-5}
	Cl^-	3×10^{-7}	1×10^{-5}
	$H_2PO_4^-$	1×10^{-14}	4×10^{-9}

poorly buffered soils phosphate diffusion is slow, and pronounced, though narrow, depletion zones develop (Fig. 3.9).

An important consequence of this, then, is that for ions for which the soil solution concentration is great enough to permit considerable

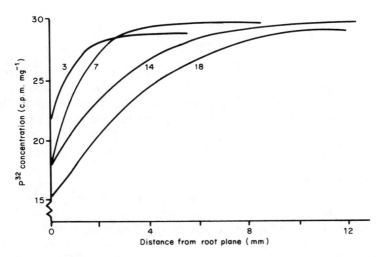

FIG. 3.9. Development of depletion zones for phosphate around an actively absorbing root (figures on curves represent days from start of the experiment). (From Bagshaw *et al.*, 1972).

movement by mass flow, little depletion occurs at the root surface, though the radius of the zone of influence is large; in contrast, ions supplied largely by diffusion typically have narrow (often less than 1 mm), but well-marked depletion zones. However, some ions with high diffusion coefficients, such as nitrate, are present at low concentrations in most soil solutions, and diffusive supply is important. Since the rate of diffusive supply is much greater for these ions than for ions such as phosphate, the depletion zones that develop will be wide and shallow, and this will mean that the whole soil volume will rapidly be exploited. In other words the entire soil pool of nitrate is available to the plant, and where several roots are involved, competition will inevitably ensue. For phosphate, on the other hand, with an effective diffusion coefficient several orders of magnitude less than that for nitrate, the immediately available amount is that within a small radius of each root, and the chances of depletion zones overlapping and so reducing the concentration gradient from bulk soil is much less at any root density. The extent of competition for ions in soil therefore depends in large measure on the diffusion coefficient, and for phosphate it will only occur at very high root densities or on soils with very low buffering capacities, and hence higher diffusion coefficients. Figure 3.10 shows that ion uptake per unit amount of root is much more sensitive to root density for K^+ (D usually between 10^{-7} and 10^{-9}) than for $H_2PO_4^-$ (D usually between 10^{-9} to 10^{-11}).

D. Variation in Nutrient Supply from Soils

The supply of nutrients from soils is complex, even if the system is limited to a single root in a large soil volume. For multiple root systems the situation is now beginning to be unravelled (Baldwin *et al.*, 1973). In evolutionary terms, however, the plant must also respond to the way in which variation in supply is controlled and this can be considered in both spatial and temporal dimensions.

1. Spatial Variation

Variation in space can always be related to its scale as shown in Chapter 1; for soils one must also consider that whereas small-scale variation will tend to be in factors controlling supply and transport, large-scale variation will additionally occur in the amounts or reserves of nutrients available. On a large scale, too, variation will be associated with pedogenic processes, which depend on five factors, viz: parent material, climate, topography, age, and vegetation.

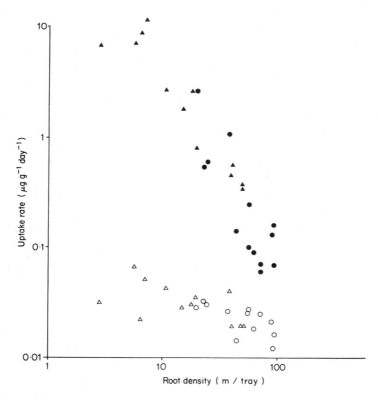

FIG. 3.10.   Effect of root density on uptake of phosphorus (open symbols) and potassium (closed symbols) by *Lolium perenne* (circles) and *Agrostis tenuis* (triangles). (From Fitter, 1976).

Parent material normally sets the upper limits on the nutrient content of soil (except for N which can enter by fixation), so that soils formed on granite are base-poor, for example. Soils formed from limestones, on the other hand, initially are very base-rich—pure chalk is 100% $CaCO_3$—and typically lose Ca^{2+} ions through the action of rainfall (*climate*), leaching out carbonates with dissolved carbon dioxide (carbonic acid), a process dependent on *topography*. Such effects are clearly time-dependent, hence the *age* factor. Topography may reverse the usual situation by allowing accumulation of base-rich water: fen peats are wholly organic, and typically have no native inorganic calcium, but are base-rich from continual flushing by ground-water. Climate, of course, has more general weathering effects and in some areas nutrient inputs in rain can be important, particularly of Na and K in coastal areas (Etherington, 1967).

The effect of *vegetation* is more complex, involving ecological succession. Soil formation does not take place without vegetation so that these two time-sequences may be considered as essentially interlinked, but at any stage in either process the vegetation both reflects existing soil conditions and influences the future course of pedogenesis, thereby secondarily determining succession. Excellent instances of this can be seen in the work of Grubb and Suter (1971) on the acidification of soil by *Ulex europaeus* and in the effect of nitrogen-fixing alders (*Alnus incana*) on glacial moraines in Alaska (Crocker and Major, 1955).

Any of the factors producing large-scale variation in soil nutrients can also be active on a small scale. Leaching can cause local acidification of hummocks in raised bogs (Pearsall, 1938) and in fens (Godwin *et al.*, 1974), outcropping of calcareous parent material in otherwise acid turf allows calcicole species to invade, and in fact the details of the vegetation mosaic of most communities can be related to variation on the appropriate scale. The mechanisms are various but the following occur:

(i) Litter fall: the litter of plant species varies greatly in nutrient content, with species of infertile soils generally returning least to the soil (Small, 1972). Most species withdraw the bulk of the N, P, and K from their leaves before abscission, but Ca concentrations normally build up (Tamm, 1951—quoted by Stålfelt, 1972). Nutrients in organic matter cycled through herbivores may be returned to the soil, for example as urea, to give even more concentrated pockets of high fertility, as a glance at a cattle field will show.

(ii) Acidification: many species produce acid litter which can have marked effects on gross soil pH. More subtle influences arise from the secretion by roots of H_3O^+ ions, normally when cation exceeds anion uptake. This occurs, for example, when NH_4^+ rather than NO_3^- is the N source (Riley and Barber, 1971), and various species differ markedly in their preference for these two ions (Gigon and Rorison, 1972). Equally the oxidation of NH_4^+ to NO_3^- in soil can cause acidification.

(iii) Depletion: plant uptake causes depletion of the soil, yet plant roots are relatively short-lived and so for immobile nutrients this will produce a mosaic of depleted, recharging, and unexploited soil zones.

(iv) Fixation: some Cyanobacteria (Cyanophyta) and bacteria such as *Azotobacter*, can fix atmospheric nitrogen to NH_4^+ either independently or symbiotically with fungi (lichens) or higher plants.

Where these organisms are active local areas of high NH_4^+ or NO_3^- concentration may occur. *Azotobacter* tends to be specifically associated with roots (Brown, 1975). In agricultural soils an analogous effect is produced by the addition of granular fertilizers.

These mechanisms will tend to produce a random patchwork of low and high nutrient concentrations, but the effects of vegetation and leaching normally interact to give a more ordered, and very widespread variation pattern—soil zonation. Except in soils where intense earthworm activity causes continuous mixing (for example brown earths), plant roots draw up minerals from deep layers which are then deposited on the surface as litter. Rainfall moves these down the profile again, but since the soil is not chemically inert, it reacts with some more than others, giving characteristic horizons. These may vary widely in pH, nutrient content, and organic matter, and provide distinct soil environments within a single soil area, with important consequences for species co-existence.

2. Variation in Time

Soil formation is itself a time-dependent process and so long-term changes may be brought about by any of the factors discussed above, but of more importance to most plants are effects on a seasonal or shorter cycle. In natural, as opposed to agricultural, soils there is well-marked seasonal nutrient variation related to the amounts passing through the organic cycle. The main input occurs as leaf-fall, in the autumn in temperate climates; in moist tropical and subarctic evergreen forests this seasonality is less clear, and in the former may be related to rainfall. In the typical temperate cycle, however, the input coincides with the slowing down of microbial activity caused by falling temperatures, and so though there may be a small autumn peak, particularly of elements easily washed out of leaves, such as potassium, the bulk of the release occurs the following spring. This spring peak is followed by a summer fall, the result of root and microbial activity, although further differences may arise from the differential uptake activity of the roots of various species.

IV. PLANT RESPONSES TO NUTRIENT SUPPLY

A. Differences between Species

Since the supply of nutrients from soils is so variable, it is not surprising to find differences in the amounts of various nutrients in plants in the field (Table 3.4). There is about a four-fold range for the major

TABLE 3.4. Contents of four major nutrient elements in dry leaf material of some widespread herbs and grasses. All values are in mg g^{-1} and represent means from more than one sample.

Grasses	N	P	K	Ca	Source
Arrhenatherum elatius	27·8	3·8	19·9	9·4	R
	23·0	2·7	27·0	7·0	A
	14·1	2·0	18·8	3·4	H
Dactylis glomerata	17·0	1·8	26·0	4·7	A
	14·7	1·8	19·1	3·7	H
	—	1·6	19·0	—	F
Deschampsia flexuosa	14·0	1·6	19·0	1·4	A[a]
	13·6	1·4	15·9	1·8	R[a]
Festuca ovina	14·0	1·5	14·3	2·0	R[a]
	13·6	1·2	13·6	3·3	R[b]
	15·0	1·7	15·0	3·7	A
Holcus lanatus	13·1	2·0	18·2	3·9	H
	17·0	1·3	21·0	8·0	A
	—	1·8	16·6	—	F
Nardus stricta	10·2	1·0	7·9	1·3	J[a]
	14·0	1·2	12·0	1·4	A[a]
Range (highest/lowest)	2·7	3·8	3·4	7·2	
Mean	15·8	1·8	17·7	—	
Herbs					
Centaurea jacea	18·7	2·0	23·9	11·5	H
Juncus squarrosus	7·9	0·9	15·0	0·6	J[a]
	13·0	1·4	16·0	0·6	A[a]
Tragopogon pratense	15·9	2·3	26·2	10·4	H
Trifolium pratense	21·3	1·8	12·1	20·6	H
	31·0	2·2	19·0	16·0	A
Urtica dioica	39·0	4·4	27·0	71·0	A
	—	6·0	17·0	—	F
Vicia sepium	36·6	2·6	17·5	8·8	H
Range (highest/lowest)	4·9	6·7	2·0	118·3	
Mean	22·9	2·6	19·3	—	

R—Rorison, 1971; A—Allen *et al.*, 1975; H—Holst, 1974; J—Jefferies and Willis, 1964; F—Fitter (unpublished).
[a] acid soil; [b] calcareous soil.

nutrients N, P, K, with the herbs tending to have high potassium contents and the legumes high nitrogen, the latter an obvious result of their symbiotic nitrogen-fixers. For Ca the range is greater, in accord with the range of soil solution concentrations encountered in the field (Table 3.1, p. 73).

Soil calcium content is one of the major determinants of soil pH, since Ca^{2+} ions occupy the exchange sites on the soil minerals and act as a buffer system, and pH is intimately involved in the availability of many nutrients. At low pH nitrification is inhibited, phosphate reacts with aluminium hydroxides (which are highly active below pH 4·5) rather than with calcium compounds, iron is available as ferric ion, molybdenum is unavailable, and so on. Many of these effects, particularly where Al^{3+} and Mn^{2+} are involved, are of toxicity rather than nutrient availability and are considered in Chapter 6, but even from its effects on the major nutrients it can be seen why pH has such a powerful influence on community composition in the field. It has long been known that limestone added to acid soils has beneficial effects on crop yield—Pliny noted that the Belgae used chalk on their fields. Where limestone is added to natural vegetation, as observed by Hope-Simpson (1938) on a partly-limed field on acid greensand, marked changes in species composition may ensue; in that case, after about 50 years and with a pH change from under 5 to over 7, 15 of the original species had been replaced by 41 new invaders.

Similarly addition of nutrients to soil can transform vegetation. The finest example of this is on the Park Grass plots at Rothamsted Experimental Station, a field that was divided up in 1856 into plots which have received, in most cases, the same controlled nutrient application ever since. On an unfertilized plot from which a hay crop has been removed each year, representing a substantial loss of nutrients, there are now about 40 species (including many herbs) present producing less than 1500 kg of hay per hectare per year. By contrast a plot receiving a complete fertilizer and limestone dressing annually has a yield about 4 times as great, but with only 10–15 species, 2 or 3 of which are clearly dominant. Other treatments produce even more extreme results: *Holcus lanatus*, for example, comprises almost 100% of the biomass on unlimed plots that have received heavy doses of ammonium, P, K, and Mg, producing a nutrient-rich but very acid (pH 4·0) soil. A similar treatment omitting P, K, and Mg, however, permits *Agrostis tenuis* to dominate, and if the soil is limed, *Alopecurus pratensis* is then the major species. Such experiments provide valuable ecological information on the nutrient requirements of individual species, and Richards (1972) points out that a micro-species of dandelion,

Taraxacum pallescens, thrives best on the Park Grass plots at a pH greater than 6·5 in soils of high potassium status.

Such effects can readily be demonstrated. Willis (1963) added a complete fertilizer (N, P, K, S, Mg, and micronutrients) to short dune turf and found that after two years the turf was completely dominated by *Festuca rubra*, with slow-growing plants such as *Thymus drucei* and short plants such as mosses being almost eliminated. Similarly, *Kobresia simpliciuscula*, a small, arctic–alpine sedge, survives in Upper Teesdale, in a small relict outpost from its main distribution, was crowded out by *Festuca ovina* if phosphate was added to the soil (Jeffrey and Pigott, 1973).

Such field experiments have the advantage of ensuring that the response measured is ecologically real, operating in natural vegetation, but suffer from the laxity of the connection between cause and effects that is their unavoidable characteristic. When phosphate, for example, is added to soil it might produce effects in several ways:

(i) stimulation of the growth of the test species;
(ii) depression by toxicity of the growth of a competitor (Foote and Howell, 1964; Green and Warder, 1973);
(iii) precipitation of Al^{3+} (toxic) or Fe^{3+} (a nutrient) at the root surface (Brown, 1972; Wright, 1943);
(iv) stimulation of N-fixing activity of associated legumes;

quite apart from any effects it may have on the soil microflora (cf. p. 107). To make the link between addition and response, one also needs results under controlled conditions, in growth room or greenhouse. Such studies as have been made tend to confirm the simple response hypothesis, particularly those of Bradshaw and co-workers on the growth of several grasses at various levels of Ca, N, and P in solution (Bradshaw et al., 1960 a, b, 1964). Figure 3.11 shows the response of four species to phosphate level; some such as *Lolium perenne* respond to the whole range from 5 to 125 p.p.m. P, while at the other extreme *Nardus stricta*, a plant of infertile, usually upland pastures, shows no response at all. Indeed *N. stricta* actually shows a decline in yield at high levels of applied nitrogen (cf. Fig. 1.1 and hypothesis (ii) above).

Such differences accord with the habitat preferences of the species, as do those examined by Clarkson (1967) for three species of *Agrostis*. At low rates of phosphate supply (33 μg $H_2PO_4^-$/plant week^{-1}) *A. setacea*, a plant of acid, nutrient-poor heaths, maintained exponential growth for ten weeks, whereas both *A. canina* and *A. stolonifera*, though initially growing faster, were slowed by phosphorus deficiency after seven weeks. The optimum rate of supply for both *A. setacea* and *A*

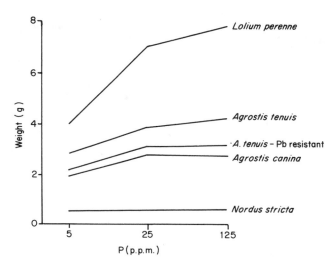

FIG. 3.11.   Responses of five grass species to phosphate applied in sand culture (from Bradshaw *et al.*, 1960a).

stolonifera was 66 μg/plant week^{-1}, when both contained about 0·3% phosphate in the shoots, so that the success of *A. setacea* at low P supply seems to lie in its ability to continue to grow, if very slowly, at low internal P concentrations.

It seems that some species utilize nutrients differently from others. Rorison (1968) found that four species from very different habitats had comparable differences in their growth response to phosphate—*Urtica dioica* giving an almost linear response, *Deschampsia flexuosa* almost none (Fig. 3.12). Two species, *Rumex acetosa* and *Scabiosa columbaria*, were intermediate and similar, though from very different habitats and of differing growth rates—$\mathbf{R}_{max}$ for *Rumex* is 1·71 week^{-1}, for *Scabiosa* 1·26 week^{-1}, according to Grime and Hunt (1975). It may be relevant that *Scabiosa* stores much of its phosphate as inorganic P (up to 80%) in the root (Nassery, 1971). Similar uptake in excess of requirements, perhaps allowing storage against times of shortage, occurs in *Banksia ornata*, growing on extremely P-deficient soils in Australia (Jeffrey, 1964).

B. Differences within Species

In Fig. 3.11 two of the lines represent populations of *Agrostis tenuis*, one taken from an acid moorland and one from the lead-contaminated

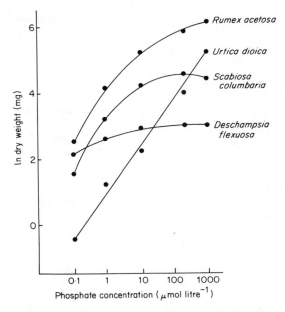

FIG. 3.12.   Response of four ecologically contrasted species to phosphate concentration in solution culture, after 6 weeks (from Rorison, 1968).

spoil of an abandoned mine. The difference in phosphate response between them was considerable; it is now evident that such intraspecific variation is widespread.

Snaydon and Bradshaw (1961, 1969) have shown for both *Festuca ovina* and *Trifolium repens* that the response of populations to a range of nutrients is related to the nutrient status of the soil on which the populations were collected, and even more strikingly, Davies and Snaydon (1973a, b, 1974) have found that plants of *Anthoxanthum odoratum* from various parts of the Park Grass plots (described above, p. 89) in some cases separated by only a few metres, show the same correlation of response to environment. These differences have arisen in some cases in less than 50 years, and have a genetic basis (Crossley and Bradshaw, 1968; Ferrari and Renosto, 1972); they are not just examples of plasticity in response to environment. That such differences in response to nutrients are hereditary should not be a surprise to anyone who considers the achievements of plant breeders in moulding the fertilizer responses of crop plants.

C. Mechanisms

1. Physiological

Thus far differences in response to nutrients have been considered in terms of yield, growth rate, and nutrient percentage in the tissue. These represent integrations by the plant of a range of processes, including uptake, demand, utilization, growth, and the interactions of environmental factors. The plant can exert control over these in several ways.

(a) *Selectivity*. Nutrient contents vary with species and the ability of plants to exploit the specificity of their uptake systems may play a large part in ecological adaptation. The serpentine endemic *Helianthus bolanderi*, which grows on soils with very high Mg/Ca ratios, is insensitive to this ratio in terms of yield, whereas *H. annuus*, the garden sunflower, fails totally at very high Mg/Ca ratios through inability to take up Ca in competition with Mg (Madhok and Walker, 1969; Fig. 6.5, p. 217). The same phenomenon occurs with serpentine and nonserpentine races of *Agrostis* species (Proctor, 1971). In serpentine soils the Mg/Ca ratio may be as high as 50, compared with under 1 in normal soils, but similar plant responses can be demonstrated over a much smaller range. Olsen (1971) measured an absorption factor, which is the ratio of Ca/Mg in the plant to Ca/Mg in solution, and so represents the selectivity of the plant; if the absorption factor is 1·0 the plant takes up the two ions in the proportions in which it encounters them, otherwise it shows selectivity. He found that mustard (*Sinapis alba*) had a constant absorption factor of 1·0, at all Ca/Mg ratios in solution, whereas rye (*Secale cereale*) had an absorption factor less than 1·0 which declined with increasing Ca/Mg in solution. Rye, which selects in favour of Ca, grew equally at all Ca/Mg ratios provided, while the unselective mustard only performed well at high Ca/Mg ratios.

(b) *Usage*. We have already noted (p. 91) that *Scabiosa columbaria* may store a large proportion of its phosphate as inorganic phosphate, presumably improving its chances of survival if the phosphate supply subsequently and temporarily declines. In some plants uptake may involve only as much of each nutrient as is being used for growth, but frequently one nutrient or some environmental factor will be limiting, causing accumulation of other nutrients, so that a typical analysis of a healthy plant does not necessarily represent the amount the plant requires (Smith, 1962). This must be allowed for when assessing the use to which the plant puts the nutrients it has gathered.

Nevertheless in experiments where the same nutrient regime has been provided to a range of species, clear differences are found in their utilization. Thus eight Australian species had dry matter production rates ranging from 1·6 (*Lupinus digitatus*) to 4·3 (*Trifolium cherleri*) g mmol P^{-1} day^{-1} (Keay *et al.*, 1970). Such differences may be explained either by variations in the amount of nutrient actually utilized or by differences in allocation to various functions. As a rule the proportion of plant phosphate that remains in inorganic form increases as P supply, and hence total plant phosphate content, increases.

Allocation is more complex. Root and shoot are effectively competing for nutrients, behaving almost as two symbiotic organisms, with the production of photosynthate by the shoots and its transport to the roots determining the ability of the roots to obtain nutrients; interactively, the supply of nutrients to the shoots controls the rate of photosynthesis. There is thus a well-balanced feedback mechanism. Barrow (1975) found that *Lolium rigidum* transports more phosphate to the shoots than *Trifolium subterraneum*, and that at the high shoot phosphate concentrations so attained, produces new photosynthate more efficiently and transports more of that to the roots to maintain high uptake rates. This combination makes the grass a successful species at high phosphate supply.

These considerations explain the storage and utilization of nutrients such as phosphate that do not show large short-term fluctuations in soil solutions. For nitrate, however, the situation is more complex. Nitrate taken into the plant is reduced to ammonium by two linked enzymes, nitrate reductase (NR, which reduces NO_3^- to NO_2^-) and nitrite reductase (NO_2^- to NH_4^+). Reduction may occur in either root or shoot, depending upon species. The ammonium so produced, along with any taken up as such from soil, is then incorporated into amino acids. Both enzymes are substrate-induced.

When a plant absorbs nitrate the level of NR in the tissue is proportional to the concentration of nitrate in the soil solution, and if the soil is fertilized with nitrate and then leached to produce rapid fluctuations in soil nitrate, the NR activity in the plant changes concomitantly in less than 24 h (Long and Woltz, 1972), since in the absence of the substrate existing enzyme is rapidly degraded by an inactivating enzyme, at least in maize roots (Wallace, 1973). The plant does not therefore retain the non-operational enzyme, but the fluctuations in NR level may, by causing fluctuations in internal nitrate levels, affect nitrate uptake (Doddema *et al.*, 1979). This is important since NR activity depends not only on nitrate concentration, but also, in leaves at least, on light to provide photosynthetic energy, and molybdenum in a co-factor. The involvement of light probably explains the evolution of rhythmic behaviour of NR activity in some plants, such as *Anthriscus sylvestris* (Janiesch, 1973), where activity peaks at mid-day. Nitrate uptake may, therefore, be controlled by several environmental factors.

The feature of major significance is, however, the response to soil nitrate. Stewart *et al.* (1972) found a 50-fold range of NR activity in plants of *Suaeda maritima* on a salt marsh which was correlated with a 3-fold range in the total N content of the plants and a 20-fold range in tissue nitrate concentrations. Later (1973) they showed that NR activity in 18 salt-marsh species ranged from a mean of 0·23 μmol NO_2^- produced g^{-1} FW h^{-1} in *Triglochin maritima* to 3·60 in *Beta vulgaris* ssp. *maritima*. The variation within each species was almost as great, however, with *Suaeda* for example ranging from 0·06 to 1·93 μmol NO_2^- g^{-1} h^{-1}, and when nitrate was added to the vegetation the NR activity of all 18 species was increased by anything up to 9-fold 72 h later.

Nevertheless, some species showed consistently high activities (*Beta*, *Atriplex hastata*) and some consistently low (*Festuca rubra*, *Triglochin maritima*), raising the possibility of ecological adaptation being based on difference in NR activity. It is in fact known that some species, particularly the Ericaceae (heaths), characteristic of acid soils where nitrification is inhibited and NH_4^+ the major nitrogen source, do not produce NR at all (Dirr *et al.*, 1973). It appears to be generally true that plants from acid sites not only have lower activities in the field than those from calcareous and neutral soils, but also in many cases show lower maximum activities after induction (Havill *et al.*, 1974). Typical NR activities for plants of a range of habitats are shown in Table 3.5, and the species seem to divide into three groups:

(i) those of high nitrate sites, characterized by flushes of nitrate availability, such as *Urtica dioica*;
(ii) an intermediate group, with calcicole species generally showing rather larger activities than calcifuges in the field, but with both having similar maximum induced activities;
(iii) those of acid peat soils, typically raised bog where soil nitrate levels are negligible, which seem to lack the enzyme altogether.

The utilization of nitrate thus illustrates both the plasticity of response conferred by an adaptive (inducible) enzyme system in fluctuating environments, and genetic differences between species exposed to stable environmental differences. The significance of the genetic component has been emphasized by the discovery that relatively small differences in NR activity between genotypes of *Lolium perenne* and *L. multiflorum* are inherited (Goodman *et al.*, 1974).

TABLE 3.5.   Nitrate reductase activity in the field before and after induction
by added nitrate, in species from various soil types (Havill *et al.*, 1974).

Soil	Species	Nitrate reductase activity (μmol NO_2^- g^{-1} FW h^{-1})	
		Before induction	After induction
Calcareous	*Poterium sanguisorba*	1·11	3·80
	Scabiosa columbaria	1·26	2·12
Neutral	*Urtica dioica*	7·93	16·10
	Poa annua	4·05	8·40
Acid	*Molinia caerulea*	0·52	1·50
	Galium saxatile	0·72	3·06
Acid peat	*Vaccinium myrtillus*	<0·1	<0·1
	Drosera rotundifolia	<0·1	<0·1

(c) *Rates*. The single most important variable controlling plant
nutrient content is rate of uptake. The relationship between rate and
concentration may be defined by the Michaelis-Menten kinetics discussed above (p. 69) and there is a clear suggestion in much of the
literature that characteristic values of K_m, the affinity coefficient, and
V_{max}, the capacity of the system, can be ascribed to various species, and
may explain differences in their response to nutrient concentration.
Jefferies *et al.* (1969) did indeed measure K_m values of 0·087 and
0·36 mM respectively for K^+ uptake for two liverworts, *Cephalozia
connivens* and *Leiocolea turbinata*, the latter collected from a habitat with
a soil solution concentration for K^+ 1000 times higher than the former.
On the other hand, Salsac (1973), comparing the calcicole *Vicia faba*
with the calcifuge *Lupinus luteus*, found K_m values for Ca uptake of
7·8 μM in each case, with only a slight difference between the two
V_{max} values.
    It may be that the apparently widespread interspecific differences in
uptake kinetics are at least in part artefactual, the result of the use of
starvation media prior to experiments (see p. 71), and of other experimental conditions. The uptake characteristics for potassium of barley
grown with and without potassium are very different (Glass, 1978).
The K_m for potassium uptake is reduced in the starved plant from
0·1 to 0·03 mM, and the same occurs for other ions, as for nitrate
(Smith, 1973) or phosphate (Cartwright, 1972), and for other species:
Doddema *et al.* (1979) show a reduction in K_m from 111 to 40 mM
NO_3^- brought about by N-starvation in *Arabidopsis thaliana*. In each

case the rate of uptake is a function of internal ion concentration and possibly also of root sugar level, which provides energy for transport and which will be affected by starvation. Root ion contents are, however, demonstrably important: for nitrate net influx ceases when an internal threshold is reached, and for potassium there is a complex control system, such that transport to the shoot does not seem to occur until such a threshold (for barley cv. Conquest 50 μmol g^{-1}) is exceeded (Glass, 1978).

The ion uptake system is not therefore genetically fixed—it exhibits plasticity, and the same plasticity occurs in response to other, interacting environmental factors. Plants collected in Alaska from tundra sites and from hot springs show pronounced differences in the maximum rate of phosphate uptake, and in the adaptability of the system (Table 3.6), and species from cold environments tend to be less temperature-sensitive in terms of P uptake than those from warm environments (Chapin, 1974).

TABLE 3.6. Maximum phosphate uptake rates ($V_{max}-\mu$M h^{-1} g^{-1} FW) at 5°C for plants from cold and warm environments grown at either 5°C or 20°C (Chapin, 1974).

Species	Habitat: July mean soil temperature (°C)	V_{max} at 5°C when grown at	
		5°C	20°C
Eriophorum angustifolium	2	0·58	0·14
Dupontia fischeri	5	0·78	0·97
Carex aquatilis	7	0·48	0·19
Scirpus microcarpus	15	0·34	0·06
Eleocharis palustris	15	0·26	0·07
Carex aquatilis	18	0·12	0·01

Any explanation for such variability depends on the model adopted. In the carrier model, the simplest proposed, changes in V_{max} can be explained simply as an increase in carrier pick-up of ions within the cell:

$$M_{ext} + \begin{matrix} membrane \\ \vdots\ k_1\quad k_3\ \vdots \\ R \rightleftharpoons MR \rightleftharpoons R\ \vdots\ + M_{int} \\ \vdots\ k_2\quad k_4\ \vdots \end{matrix} \qquad (3.5)$$

At high values of M_{int}, k_4 would become sufficiently large to slow down transport. Changes in affinity are less easily explained, perhaps requiring conformational changes in carrier molecules. Speculation on this is of little value as a simple carrier model has drawbacks and several alternatives have been proposed (see for example MacRobbie, 1970; Thellier, 1973).

(d) *Demand*. Studies on roots of different nutritional status show that internal ion concentration is as important as external in determining rates of uptake. The concentration of an ion in the root is a reflection of its utilization by the plant; if the ion is in demand by the shoot any excess will normally be transported there. This concept of demand has been quantified in a most significant way by Nye and Tinker (1969, 1977).

From the relationship between uptake rate or flux (F) per unit root surface area and the ion concentration in solution at the root surface (C_{lr}) they have defined a root absorbing power as the proportionality coefficient α:

$$F = \alpha \cdot C_{lr} \tag{3.6}$$

It follows then that:

$$\text{Uptake per unit root length} = 2\pi(\alpha a) \cdot C_{lr} \tag{3.7}$$

where a is root radius. Equation (3.7) can be summed over the whole root system to give:

$$\frac{dU}{dt} = \sum_{j=1}^{j=n} 2\pi\alpha_j a_j l_j C_{lr(j)} \tag{3.8}$$

where l is root length, and U is uptake. The root absorbing power α and the root radius a will both vary over the root system, but an average value can be defined:

$$\overline{\alpha a} = \sum \alpha_j a_j l_j / \sum l_j \tag{3.9}$$

since Σl_j can be easily measured, and $\overline{\alpha a}$ represents the root demand coefficient. We can then derive from equation (3.8):

$$\frac{dU}{dt} = 2\pi \overline{\alpha a} \cdot L \cdot C_{lr} \tag{3.10}$$

where $L = \Sigma l_j$, the total root length. Strictly this derivation requires that C_{lr} be constant which will normally be true only in flowing solution culture. The value of this derivation, however, lies in making it possible to define $\overline{\alpha a}$ in other terms, since by definition:

$$\frac{dU}{dt} = \frac{d(XW)}{dt} = \frac{X \cdot dW}{dt} + \frac{W \cdot dX}{dt} \qquad (3.11)$$

where W is plant weight and X the plant nutrient concentration (g g^{-1}). Therefore:

$$2\pi \, \overline{\alpha a} = \frac{W}{L} \cdot \frac{X}{C_{\mathrm{lr}}} \left[\frac{1}{W} \cdot \frac{dW}{dt} + \frac{1}{X} \cdot \frac{dX}{dt} \right] \qquad (3.12)$$

The significance of the root demand coefficient is that it is a measure of the ease of transport of ions across the root surface, and so analogous to a diffusion coefficient. The two coefficients are expressed in the same units (cm^2 s^{-1}) and the two processes—diffusion through soil and transport into the root—are in series, so that the slower of the two will be rate-limiting to uptake. Thus if $\overline{\alpha a}$ is less than D (see above, p. 81), as will normally be true for Ca^{2+} for example, plant uptake will limit the rate; but for H$_2$PO$_4^-$ ions, the converse is true and diffusion will be the limiting step. The value of Nye and Tinker's derivation lies in the demonstration that the root demand coefficient will be proportional to the specific root length (W/L), the internal–external concentration ratio (X/C_{lr}), the relative growth rate ($1/W \cdot dW/dt$), and an analogous term defining the rate of change of internal concentration ($1/X \cdot dX/dt$). These points merit further investigation.

Internal-external concentration ratio (X/C_{lr}). The effect of external concentration (C_{lr}) has been discussed in other contexts already; here we note that we expect the root demand coefficient to decline as this increases. Nye and Tinker used data of Loneragan and Asher (1967) and Williams (1961) and, by making certain assumptions where data was unavailable, found that $\overline{\alpha a}$ for P uptake declined from about 4×10^{-5} cm^2 s^{-1} at 0·04 μM P to 2×10^{-6} at 25 μM P, and for K uptake from 7×10^{-5} at 2·5 μM K to 2×10^{-7} at 1·25 mM. Experimentally Elgawhary and Barber (1974) have determined values of α for Ca uptake ranging from 8 to 18×10^{-5} cm^2 s^{-1}, which given a typical value of 0·05 cm gives $\overline{\alpha a}$ from 4 to 9×10^{-6} cm^2 s^{-1}; and Wild *et al.* (1974) have estimated $\overline{\alpha a}$ for K in the range 1 to 30×10^{-6} for 4 different species (Table 3.7). These last values suffer from being averaged over a 42 day growing period, but are interesting in suggesting the sort of relationship of root demand coefficient to habitat that one might intuitively predict.

Of the two grasses *Dactylis glomerata* is much more nutrient-

TABLE 3.7.   Root demand coefficients $(\bar{\alpha}\,\bar{a})$ for four species grown in flowing culture over 42 days (Wild *et al.*, 1974).

	$\bar{\alpha}\,\bar{a} \times 10^6$ cm^2 s^{-1}			
[K], μM	1	3	10	33
Species				
Dactylis glomerata	11·9	8·0[a]	3·2	1·0
Anthoxanthum odoratum	7·9[a]	4·5	1·1	0·4
Trifolium pratense	7·2	5·2[a]	2·1	0·6
Medicago lupulina	30·1	19·9[a]	6·9	2·3

[a] Concentration above which no further growth increases occurred.

demanding than *Anthoxanthum odoratum* which typically grows on very poor soils, while the high values for *Medicago lupulina* may be linked to its preference for calcareous soils. This suggests that although the demand coefficient declines with external concentration, there may be ecologically significant correlations with habitat.

The external concentration must, however, be considered in relation to that in the plant (X). This is likely to fluctuate much less than the external concentration, so that high external concentration will produce very low ratios. Christie and Moorby (1975) have shown that most of the variation in α in three Australian grasses, from 0·5 to 1096 $\times$ 10^{-6} cm^2 s^{-1}, can be accounted for by changes in the ratio.

There is also a term in equation (3.12) which allows for changes in internal concentration $1/X \cdot dX/dt$. At low values of X this will tend to be larger than at high values, reinforcing the effects already considered.

Growth rate (**R**). In physiological terms it is growth that creates demand for nutrients, and this is in accord with equation (3.12). Optimum growth requires an adequate supply of all nutrients, so that pronounced interactions occur, with N supply, for example, influencing P uptake (Blair *et al.*, 1972). Tobacco plants supplied with N and K had incorporated 40% of the N into protein after 5 h, with only 30% remaining as nitrate, whereas those supplied with N alone had put less than 20% into protein and over 40% was still present as nitrate (Koch and Mengel, 1974).

In some cases high nitrogen supply can apparently stimulate P uptake directly, without affecting growth rate. White (1973) postulated that in lucerne the effect of N was on metabolic activity in the root, permitting more rapid incorporation of P into organic compounds and discouraging the build-up of inorganic P in the root. The inorganic ion concentration in root cells is influenced by three processes. The scheme below is based on phosphate, but is applicable to other ions that undergo metabolic incorporation, symbolized here by M:

$$M_{\text{org}} \leqq = = = \gneqq M_{\text{org}}$$

$$M_{\text{inorg}} \xrightarrow{\hspace{2em}} M_{\text{inorg}} \rightleftharpoons M_{\text{inorg}}$$

$$\text{External} \qquad\qquad \text{Root} \qquad\qquad \text{Shoot}$$

If incorporation of phosphate, for example, is inhibited in the root, transport to the shoot is greatly increased (Loughman, 1969); conversely if transport to the shoot is increased, uptake is enhanced by the reduction in $(M_{\text{inorg} \cdot \text{root}})$. Such transport may depend on relative growth rate (Pitman and Cram, 1973), as shown in Fig. 3.13.

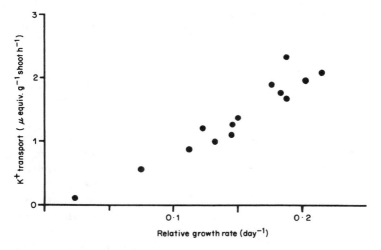

FIG. 3.13.   Transport of potassium to the shoot of barley plants as a function of shoot growth rate (from Pitman and Cram, 1973).

Transport is to some extent energy dependent, even when occurring in the transpiration stream, and the amount of transport to the shoots is a function of root sugar level, itself a function of shoot photosynthetic activity. Root sugar level also affects ion uptake from the external medium, since plants exposed to 24 h light followed by 24 h darkness take up more Rb than those given the reverse treatment (Hatrick and

Bowling, 1973); in the second case there is a lag phase during which sugar is transported to the roots. The integration of these processes may involve hormones, in particular kinetin and abscisic acid, but the evidence is far from clear. The net effect is that the rate of ion accumulation by plants, the relative growth rate of the roots, and the rate of accumulation of soluble carbohydrate by the roots are all correlated (Raper et al., 1978).

2. Morphological Mechanisms

(a) *Root:shoot ratio.* The final component of Nye and Tinker's (1969) equation that we have not yet considered is the plant mass per unit root length or root length ratio (W/L). The use of root length is a consequence of the consideration of nutrient uptake as the inflow per unit length. For this purpose root weight is of no necessary relevance, and yet because of the ease with which root weight can be measured in relation to all other root morphological parameters (length, diameter, surface area), much of the work on root systems has measured root weight and the root : shoot ratio ($W_R : W_S$).

The root:shoot ratio is a very plastic character. Generally it increases with

(i)   low water supply;
(ii) low nutrient supply (Bradshaw et al., 1964; Atkinson, 1973);
(iii) low soil oxygen;
(iv) low soil temperature (Davidson, 1969);

and may show less predictable responses to other environmental variables such as light intensity and photoperiod. Such effects are summarized by Aung (1974). On the whole, plants seem to put more of their resources into root production in stressful environments.

A corollary of this is that one might expect plants characteristic of stressful environments to have higher and less variable root:shoot ratios. Certainly three species of low growth rate associated with poor soils, *Deschampsia flexuosa*, *Carex flacca*, and *Scabiosa columbaria* examined by Hunt (1970), bore this out in contrast with species such as *Urtica dioica*. On the other hand the data of Bradshaw et al. (1964) show a clear increase with nitrogen deficiency, but no evidence of any correlation with habitat, *Nardus stricta* being the most plastic and *Lolium perenne* the least plastic of the species studied. This is confirmed by Higgs and James (1969) who also show that $W_R : W_S$ tends to be lowest in species of high growth rate.

This apparent contradiction is probably due to the complex nature of plant weight as a character. Plants in stressful conditions frequently allocate a large proportion of their photosynthate to storage organs which are often subterranean. It is easy to demonstrate, for example, that *Plantago lanceolata* growing in stressful habitats (sea-cliffs, toxic soils) has much higher root:shoot ratios than meadow plants, and that this is due to the development of a massive root stock and not to large numbers of absorbing roots. The root:shoot ratio is therefore a good guide to the stressfulness of the environment but bears little relation to nutrient absorption.

(*b*) *Root age.* Ion uptake is proportional to surface area, though not necessarily the external surface, owing to diffusion into the apoplast. Not all parts of the root system are equally active in uptake, however, since old roots may in some cases become completely suberised, and Ca^{2+} in particular is only taken up by the youngest roots in which the endodermis does not constitute a barrier (Harrison-Murray and Clarkson, 1973). Recent evidence for other ions, such as $H_2PO_4^-$ and K^+, suggests that earlier assumptions that old roots are inactive are incorrect. Phosphate is readily taken up by barley roots 50 cm from the tip and can be translocated from there to the shoot (Clarkson *et al.*, 1968). At this distance from the meristem the endodermis is massively thickened and has a pronounced suberin layer (the Casparian band); this prohibits movement of ions such as Ca^{2+} beyond the cortex, since they travel primarily in the free space of the cell walls (apoplastically), but provides no barrier to $H_2PO_4^-$ and K^+ which travel symplastically in the cortical cytoplasm, for the endodermal cells are traversed by many plasmodesmata (Clarkson *et al.*, 1971).

(*c*) *Root diameter.* All except the oldest roots do therefore possess some uptake ability. The segment behind the root tip, however, possesses a special importance by virtue of its root hairs, except in a few families (e.g. Liliaceae). The effect of root hairs is to increase the volume of soil exploited, which will have little effect on the uptake of mobile ions such as nitrate, but which one might expect to promote uptake where diffusive supply is important, as for phosphate. In the latter case depletion at the root surface will be extensive and the whole root hair zone may be depleted, as shown by autoradiographs (Bhat and Nye, 1973). Further, in field conditions where soil moisture varies greatly and the solution contact with the root may be broken, root hairs can penetrate very small pores (diameter less than 5 μm) and by secreting mucilage maintain a liquid junction between root and soil, without which both ion and water uptake would cease (Barley, 1970). Experimentally, however, the role of root hairs is unconfirmed; Barley and

Rovira (1970) showed that whereas "hairy" root zones are no more active in P uptake in stirred solution culture where transport is not limiting, in slightly compressed clay (which hairs cannot penetrate) phosphate transfer to pea roots was reduced by 78%, while transfer to anion exchange paper was increased by 29%, as compared with the uncompressed soil. On the other hand Bole (1973), using chromosome substitution lines of wheat differing in root "hairiness", could find no relationship between P uptake from soil and root-hair development. Most probably root hairs become increasingly important as the supply of an ion becomes more limited by diffusion.

The main value of root hairs is likely to be their ability to penetrate soil pores too small for roots, but root diameter itself can also vary and may be an important factor when depletion is less and the concentration in the root free space is high, so that uptake occurs into all the cortical cells, not just the epidermis. In this case uptake will be related more to root volume than to surface area, as found experimentally by Russell and Clarkson (1976) and shown theoretically by Nye (1973). Mean root diameter is certainly very variable for some plants, being lower in arctic than temperate species (Chapin, 1974) but increased by low temperature in the latter. Wild *et al.* (1974) found the radius of "coarse" roots to vary between three species, but that of the "fine" roots to be more or less constant, while Christie and Moorby (1975) subjected three Australian grasses to P concentrations ranging from 0·003 to 30 p.p.m. and recorded increases in mean root diameter of 17, 22, and 41%.

(*d*) *Root density and distribution.* When a single root grows in an unlimited volume of soil, uptake is influenced by soil factors and plant demand. In real situations, however, the depletion zones around adjacent roots will frequently overlap. There will then be interference to supply patterns by one root upon another—in other words competition for nutrients (Nye, 1969). This interference will result from the overlapping of the depletion zones resulting in the diminution of the diffusion gradient.

However, for ions of low diffusion coefficients (such as phosphate), competition will only occur at very high root densities because the depletion zones are narrow and so unlikely to overlap. Figure 3.10 shows the different effect of root density on uptake of K^+ and $H_2PO_4^-$ by monospecific stands of *Lolium perenne* and *Agrostis tenuis* (Fitter, 1976). These effects are typical and can be shown equally with a single plant (Newman and Andrews, 1973).

When the roots of more than one species (or genotype) are interacting in this way, the result may not be just a general lowering in uptake rates for all roots, for the roots of one species may be able to lower the ionic concentration at the root surface more than the other. In this case nutrient ions will move down the resulting steeper concentration gradient more rapidly to the root surface of the former species (cf. Chapter 8, Fig. 8.1), which will therefore effectively exploit a greater soil volume. There is virtually no experimental evidence on this point, though it seems certain that this is what occurs in soil and it is well established that competitive ability for nutrients varies between species, with species balance dependent on nutrient levels. Welbank (1961), for example, showed that added N had a greater effect on the growth of *Impatiens parviflora* when its roots were competing with those of *Agropyron repens* than when they were in monoculture. Similarly, van den Bergh (1969), using a de Wit competition analysis (see Chapter 8), found that at high soil fertility *Dactylis glomerata* always replaced *Alopecurus pratensis*, at pH 4·2, 6·2, or 6·7; at low fertility, however, *Alopecurus* was favoured at low pH and an equilibrium was established at the two higher pH values.

The mechanism of competition for nutrients and its interaction with competition for light and water, is discussed fully in Chapter 8, but clearly the form, extent, and distribution of the root system will be critical. All these features are plastic characters and respond to various soil environmental factors such as texture (Veihmeyer and Hendrickson, 1948; Kochenderfer, 1973) and pH (Mukerji, 1936; Fitter and Bradshaw, 1974). There are also dramatic responses to nutrient concentrations (Duncan and Ohlrogge, 1958; see review by Viets, 1965), a fact exploited in agriculture by the practice of banding fertilizer so that roots can grow preferentially in the fertile zone. Recent work has shown that such effects can be mimicked in water culture (Fig. 3.14) and that increases in root growth in response to local concentrations of, in particular, N and P, can be ascribed to the fact that lateral root growth only occurs at a point on the root if adequate external nutrient concentrations exist there (Drew *et al.*, 1973). Growth of the main root axes of cereals is not concentration-dependent in this way, so that in infertile soil these will continue to grow, but lateral production will be inhibited until a fertile zone is reached. The root system is thus adapted to explore poor soil volumes but to exploit fertile ones.

These striking and dramatic changes are not accompanied by changes in shoot growth (Drew, 1975), and nutrient uptake of the whole plant is scarcely affected in a plant only part of whose root system is exposed to high nutrient concentrations, as compared to one wholly in the high concentration, as a result of a compensatory increase in uptake in the favourably placed segment (Drew and Saker, 1975; Drew and

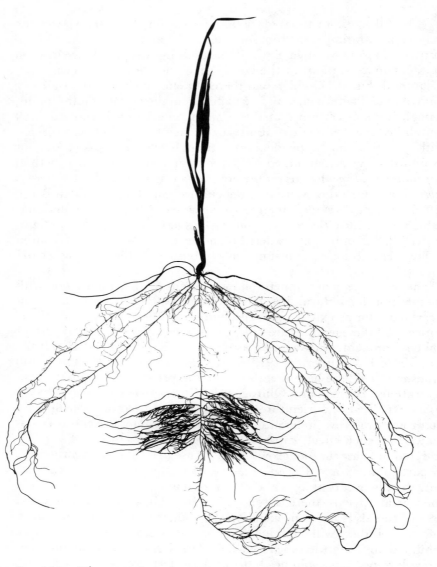

Fig. 3.14.   Silhouette of a barley plant grown with its root system in a nutrient solution containing 0·01 mM nitrate, except for the central section which received 1·0 mM nitrate. Note the proliferation of secondary laterals in this zone and their absence elsewhere. (Courtesy Dr M. C. Drew).

Nye, 1969). In other words the plasticity of uptake observed between plants by Glass (1978, see p. 96), for example, can also exist simultaneously between different parts of a root system.

Such effects also occur in soil (Fitter, 1976), with the precise distribution and growth of the root system being a response to variations in soil nutrient concentrations, so that one can assume that the highest root densities will occur in fertile soil. In this case, competition for immobile ions such as phosphate, which involves closely adjacent roots so as to obtain overlap of narrow depletion zones, will occur mostly in fertile soils or soil zones, and it may be that plants that are poor competitors for phosphate rely on exploiting less phosphate-rich soil volumes where root densities will be lower.

V. SOIL MICRO-ORGANISMS

A. Nature of the Rhizosphere

The root is not the only living component of the root-soil system; indeed soil ecosystems probably contain some of the most diverse of all temperate communities (Anderson, 1975). The supply of many nutrients depends on microbial degradation of organic matter, and soil animals play critical initial roles in this process, fragmenting the litter into pieces suitable for microbial attack. Standard procedures of sampling for soil microbes involve taking soil samples, suspending them in water, and plating them on agar to detect microbial growth. This gives a general view of the soil flora, though tending to emphasize the importance of the spore population, but more precise work shows that these microbes are not uniformly distributed; rather they are highly aggregated around energy sources, with the mineral matrix representing a microbial desert. Plant roots represent one of the major sources of energy for soil microbes and their influence on the soil microflora was first studied systematically by Starkey (1929), though the term "rhizosphere", to cover the volume of soil in which the microbial populations are influenced by the proximity of a root, was coined by Hiltner in 1904.

The most striking feature of the rhizosphere is the stimulation of bacterial numbers and activity. The effect is normally quoted in the form of an R (root):S (soil) ratio (Katznelson, 1946), and typical R:S values range from 2 to 100, though figures as high as 2000 are on record. The R:S ratio is based on the numbers in the soil adhering to the roots relative to the numbers in bulk soil, and is valuable for unicells such as bacteria (though spores cause problems), but difficult to interpret for filamentous fungi. Recently Rovira and co-workers have approached the problem directly, using scanning electron micrographs of root surfaces to examine rhizosphere (or strictly rhizoplane) populations (e.g. Rovira *et al.*, 1974), and several techniques are now available (see, for example, Polonenko and Mayfield, 1979).

The microbes in the rhizosphere are stimulated by increased concentrations of various chemicals that act as energy sources, and these arise in three main ways:

(i) By the sloughing off of root cap cells and root hairs as roots grow through soil. It is difficult to obtain figures, but this could be a major input for rapidly growing roots in mineral soil.

(ii) By exudation of compounds from intact cells. Rovira (1969) has summarized the evidence on this: in general exudation appears to amount to about 0.1% of carbon fixed by photosynthesis, but species differ in amount and type of exudate, and individuals vary with age, temperature, and nutritional status. An enormous range of compounds is exuded—from wheat alone 10 sugars, 20 amino acids, 10 organic acids and several other compounds have been reported.

(iii) By the production of mucigel by the root cap, which facilitates its passage through the soil (Juniper and Roberts, 1966; Greaves and Darbyshire, 1972).

The total effect of these losses can be considerable: Martin (1977) found that of the carbon transported to wheat roots over 23 days at $10°C$, an average of nearly 40% was lost to the soil, probably largely from the breakdown of cortical cells.

In the light of such complexity and enrichment it is not surprising that the rhizosphere flora is qualitatively as well as quantitatively different from that of the bulk soil (Rovira and Davey, 1974). Bacteria requiring amino-acids are abundant (Lochhead and Rouatt, 1955) and root-inhabiting microbes, both symbiotic bacteria (nitrogen-fixing *Rhizobium*) and pathogenic fungi (such as *Fusarium*), may show increased populations.

B. Effects on Nutrient Uptake

This immensely active microbial population might influence nutrient uptake by roots in four ways:

(i) by altering the supply at the root surface—competition;

(ii) by altering root or shoot growth, or by directly damaging the root;

(iii) by interference with nutrient uptake itself—inhibition or stimulation;

(iv) by mineralization of organic or dissolution of insoluble ions.

Evidence on all these points is conflicting, and early work which suggested that roots stimulate the activity of phosphate (apatite) dissolving bacteria and hence improve P supply, is now interpreted in terms of root growth stimulation by gibberellic acid produced by rhizosphere microbes (Gerretsen, 1948; Brown, 1975). Certainly soil microbes influence uptake. Barber *et al.* (1976) have clarified earlier reports and showed that microbes generally stimulate uptake and transport of phosphate in young plants and in short-term experiments, but depress both in older plants and over longer periods (Fig. 3.15). There appears to be a balance between the stimulation due to growth substances released by micro-organisms and only effective on young

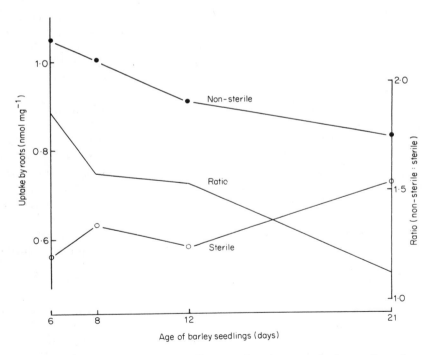

FIG. 3.15. Effect of soil micro-organisms on phosphate uptake by sterile and non-sterile roots of barley plants of different ages (from Barber *et al.*, 1976).

roots, and competition for phosphate between the microbes and the roots. In older root systems, the proportion of young root segments declines, and competition becomes the dominant force. In addition to these direct effects, soil micro-organisms may indirectly reduce the ability of roots to take up ions. Thus many fungi break down lignin in soil, releasing phenolic acids, particularly in the rhizosphere (Pareek and Gaur, 1973), and these acids markedly inhibit ion uptake (Glass, 1973).

C. Mycorrhizas

The rhizosphere is a quantitative phenomenon, defined by the increased microbial population. There is consequently a gradient of influence away from the root with the most enhanced area being the root surface, the rhizoplane. The cover and frequency of bacteria at the rhizoplane vary between species; for example *Hypochaeris radicata* may have twice as many bacteria as *Plantago lanceolata* (Rovira *et al.*, 1974). Generally the area of root covered by bacteria seems to vary rather little amongst species, but the number of bacterial cells varies greatly and can be altered by the proximity of the roots of other species (Christie *et al.*, 1974). In view of the known effects of the rhizosphere flora, discussed above, such interactions could have important implications for plant competition.

Mycorrhizas, symbiotic associations of a fungus and a plant root, can be viewed as a highly specialized development of a rhizoplane association, that has become at least partly invasive. Ectomycorrhizas (sheathing mycorrhizas) involve usually a Basidiomycete fungus and a tree; the fungus forms a mantle of hyphae around the root, a network of intercellular hyphae in the cortex and a ramifying mycelium in the soil. No intracellular connections are made and the roots are generally stunted; for a recent review refer to Marks and Kozlowski (1973). Endomycorrhizas are of three main types, two of which are very specialized, occurring respectively in the order Ericales and the family Orchidaceae, and will not be further discussed. The third type, formed with a small group of Phycomycetous fungi, is known as the vesicular-arbuscular (VA) mycorrhiza.

VA mycorrhizas occur in most families of higher plants, as well as some Bryophytes and Pteridophytes. The relationship is intracellular, the fungus producing haustoria that invaginate the plasmalemma and produce arbuscules ("little trees"), masses of minute hyphae less than 1 μm in diameter, and vesicles which are storage bodies. The fungus is of a genus known as *Endogone*, now split into several smaller genera of which the most important is *Glomus*. They are exceedingly widespread and have been reviewed by Tinker (1978).

The primary interest of both types of mycorrhizas lies in their ability to improve plant growth by enhancing P uptake. In P-deficient soils mycorrhizal plants typically grow markedly better than non-mycorrhizal ones (Fig. 3.16), but the reverse may be true in soils well supplied with phosphate (Fig. 3.17). Indeed in such soils plants normally show very low levels of infection. The advantage of the mycorrhizal

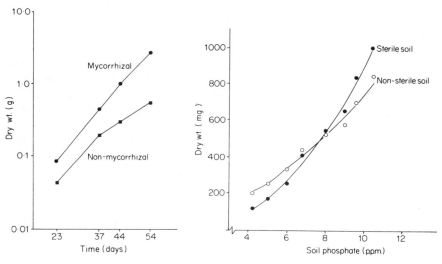

Fig. 3.16. Growth rate of mycorrhizal and non-mycorrhizal onions (data from Sanders and Tinker, 1973).

Fig. 3.17. Growth of *Lolium perenne* in sterilized and unsterilized soil at various soil phosphate concentrations. (Plumb, J., unpublished B.A. Thesis, University of York).

plants cannot be explained on the basis of root morphology, since they take up phosphate faster per unit root length than non-mycorrhizal ones (Table 3.8). In fact mycorrhizal plants have shorter root systems, visibly so in the case of ectomycorrhizas; it is possible that reported effects of rhizosphere microbes reducing root length may be due to endomycorrhizal infection, for this too has a significant effect (Crush, 1974; Fitter, 1977).

For both ectomycorrhizas (Harley and Lewis, 1969), and endomy-corrhizas (Rhodes and Gerdemann, 1975) it is well established that phosphate travels from fungus to root, so the enhanced uptake must be

TABLE 3.8.   Phosphate inflows of mycorrhizal and non-mycorrhizal onion
plants (Sanders and Tinker, 1973).

| Harvest interval | | | Inflow (pmol cm^{-1} s^{-1}) | |
No.	Duration (days)		Mycorrhizal	Non-mycorrhizal
1	14		0·17	0·050
2	7		0·22	0·016
3	10		0·13	0·042
		Means:	0·17	0·036

due to the greater ability of the fungus to obtain phosphate. It has been
suggested that the fungus might utilize sources of P not available to
plants, but when Hayman and Mosse (1972) grew VA mycorrhizal
plants on soil enriched with ^{32}P, they found that infected and uninfected plants had the same specific activity as the soil, though the
mycorrhizal plants had absorbed up to 30 times as much phosphate
(Table 3.9). If they had been using unavailable phosphate, the extra
P they took up would not have been labelled and they would have
shown lower specific activities.

An alternative explanation would therefore seem to be that the
mycorrhizal root has different phosphate uptake kinetics, perhaps a
lower K_m. This may possibly be true for ectomycorrhizas (Harley,
1971), where the root is enclosed in the fungal sheath. For VA mycorrhizas, however, Sanders and Tinker (1973) in an experiment with

TABLE 3.9.   Phosphorus content and specific activity of mycorrhizal (Myc)
and non-mycorrhizal (Non-myc) onion plants in relation to specific activity
of P in soil (Hayman and Mosse, 1972).

| Soil | P content of plants (roots and shoots (mg)) | | Specific activity of ^{32}P (c.p.m. mg^{-1} (roots)) | | (c.p.m. mg^{-1} (soil)) |
	Myc	Non-myc	Myc	Non-myc	Soil
7	1·13	0·04	4·4	3·7	6·7
8	0·33	0·26	9·7	10·1	12·9
10	0·21	0·10	24·7	20·1	24·8
11	1·33	0·13	2·1	1·9	3·0
12	1·22	0·48	2·1	2·0	3·5
15	0·14	0·08	26·1	23·8	29·5
16	1·29	1·03	1·7	1·9	2·5

onions, calculated that the maximum rate of diffusive supply, irrespective of the uptake kinetics, would be 0·035 pmol $cm^{-1} s^{-1}$, which was approximately the rate achieved by uninfected roots (Table 3.8). Mycorrhizal roots had higher rates, by a factor of about 5, an impossible result unless the effective length for uptake had been incorrectly determined; that would be true if the fungal hyphae in the soil, attached to the mycorrhizal root, were exploring unexploited soil outside the depletion zone of the root, and translocating phosphate from there to the root, and so were effectively part of the root system. They found about 80 cm of hypha per cm of root in the soil, which adequately explains the superior uptake of mycorrhizal roots. Recently Owuso-Bennoah and Wild (1979) have examined autoradiographically the depletion zones of mycorrhizal and uninfected onions, and suggest that the infection is equivalent to a zone of root hairs 0·1 cm in diameter.

It is generally accepted that VA mycorrhizas act in this way, exploring soil inaccessible to the root because of the limitations of diffusion, and Rhodes and Gerdemann (1975) have shown that mycorrhizal roots can exploit soil for phosphate up to 70 mm from the root, whereas a figure of 10 mm or less would be more typical for uninfected roots. All this has been established under laboratory conditions and the significance of VA mycorrhizas in the field is still unclear. Many strains of mycorrhizal fungi exist, and ectomycorrhizal associations may be very specific. Species of the genera *Boletus*, *Amanita*, and *Russula*, and many other Homobasidiomycetes, are normally found only under particular tree species—the fly agaric, *Amanita muscaria*, for example is characteristic of birch woods. By contrast over 100 different fungi can form associations with *Pinus sylvestris*, and these in turn with more than 700 other trees (Trappe, 1962).

Very many fewer fungal species are involved in the endomycorrhizal association, but several strains exist for which a taxonomic hierarchy has recently been suggested by Gerdemann and Trappe (1975). These strains vary greatly in their effectiveness at increasing P uptake and growth and in their behaviour on different soils (Hayman and Mosse, 1972). Table 3.10 shows that onion growth was improved by a factor of between 2 and 30 times by different strains, though heavy infection occurred in all but the two least effective, and that on two soils the order of effectiveness of 8 strains was not the same. Although, therefore, there is little or no specificity of infection, a given strain may well differentially benefit various species, depending on soil type. Indeed in the field, mycorrhizal fungi indigenous to a soil are often found to give no benefit to introduced crop plants, which require inoculation with cultured strains to show a response; this is certainly true of *Trifolium repens* in hill

TABLE 3.10.   Effect of six strains of *Endogone* on the growth of onions (dry wt. (mg)) over 12 weeks, and the influence of bacterial washings and soil type. The two soils used are selected from those in Table 3.9. (From Mosse, 1972.)

Strain	*Soil* Leachings[a]	Inoculated	*Soil* 11	*Soil* 7
Laminate	48	714	737	370
E₃	22	640	708	441
Honey-coloured	40	525	689	475
SBC	41	397	649	631
Microcarpa	31	61	151	134
Bulbous reticulate	25	43	139	153

[a] Material obtained by washing roots and filtering so as to exclude fungal spores.

pastures in New Zealand (Powell, 1976). Field studies of native communities suggest that there is a more or less uniform infection of the roots of co-existing species (Read *et al.*, 1976), so that unless a differential benefit exists, all plants would gain equally from infection. On Pennine grassland soils Sparling and Tinker (1975) could show no benefit of infection to the native grasses.

It may then be most appropriate to view VA mycorrhizal infection as a prerequisite for successful phosphate uptake, enabling plants to overcome limitations of diffusion, rather than as an advantageous adaptation achieved by certain species. In this sense it might have more in common with the putative originally symbiotic nature of some cellular organelles as a necessary part of structure, than with other classic root symbioses such as bacterial nodules.

Some plants, notably sedges and rushes (Powell, 1975), normally exhibit low levels of mycorrhizal infection. Baylis (1975) has pointed out the significance of root morphology in the development of mycotrophy. Plant families and groups which on floral characters are considered primitive, such as the Magnoliales, have very coarse root systems with all roots more than 0·5 mm in diameter; they have no root hairs and are almost obligately mycorrhizal. At the other extreme the grasses, generally accepted as an advanced family, have finely-branched roots, a dense root hair zone, and are often mycorrhizal only in soils of low P status. Rushes and sedges have similar roots but even longer root hairs. The importance of mycorrhizal infection as a means of extending the range of the root system beyond the depletion zone of the root is directly related to root morphology, and the mycorrhiza is but one of a number of approaches to root system development that plants have adopted.

VI. GENERAL PATTERNS OF RESPONSE TO SOIL NUTRIENTS

The ability of a plant to obtain nutrients from the soil depends upon a complex of factors: the rate at which the soil supplies ions to the root surface, the rate at which roots explore unexploited soil, the ability of the plant to absorb and utilize nutrient ions, and the interactions of several environmental and microbiological factors. Emerging from this, however, there is a general pattern of contrast between plants growing in habitats where growth is limited by nutrients and those of more fertile soils. These low nutrient species are typified by having:

(i) Low relative growth rate. Since the maximum uptake that can be achieved in infertile soil is restricted, it is advantageous for the plant to place a small demand on the uptake process. It cannot then be competitive for light and will tend to be overshadowed by faster growing species. Low nutrient species opt therefore for unpalatability, producing from their photosynthate not only new assimilating tissue, which tends to increase growth rate ($\mathbf{R}$, the product of $\mathbf{F}$ and $\mathbf{E}$ (see p. 12)) and which is rich in minerals and palatable to herbivores, but also supporting and fibrous tissue. Typical of this is the invasion of over-grazed, nutrient-poor grassland by *Juncus* spp., as the more palatable grasses are preferentially eaten. Higgs and James (1969), growing four grasses in fertile and infertile soil, found that *Lolium perenne* had a large plastic leaf area, whereas *Nardus stricta* and *Sieglingia decumbens*, both species of very low growth rate, had small and relatively constant leaf areas (Table 3.11).

TABLE 3.11. Maximum growth rates, leaf areas, and leaf area ratios of four grasses grown on fertile and infertile soils (Higgs and James, 1969).

Species	$\mathbf{R}_{max}$		A_L (cm^2)		A_L/W ($cm^2\ mg^{-1}$)	
	1^a	2	Fertile	Infertile	Fertile	Infertile
Lolium perenne	1·30	1·03	193·6	84·2	137·6	124·9
Agrostis tenuis	1·36	1·21	46·0	24·9	118·2	123·8
Nardus stricta	0·71	0·72	1·4	1·6	92·7	85·5
Sieglingia decumbens	0·60	0·54	2·4	1·5	113·0	97·4

[a] According to Grime and Hunt (1975).

(ii) Low saturation (V_{max}), high affinity (K_m) uptake systems. Very little work has been done on the uptake characters of wild plants, but from the work of Loneragan and Asher (1967) and Clarkson (1967) for phosphate, Jefferies *et al.* (1969) for potassium, and Clarkson (1965) for calcium, it appears that the uptake systems of low nutrient plants may have these properties, in relation to the external concentration of ions. If we accept the carrier model of ion transport, we can show that V_{max} will be proportional to the number of carrier molecules. In a low nutrient environment, maintaining a high capacity to absorb ions will therefore involve the metabolic cost of these unused carrier molecules. Even with other models some such cost will be involved, so it is significant that there is now evidence that uptake systems may be inducible (Jackson *et al.*, 1973). These physiological parameters are, however, difficult to determine in ecologically realistic conditions. A more productive approach may lie in the measurement of root demand coefficients, which relate inflow to external concentration and transport processes in soil. Wild *et al.* (1974) have already found differences between species for those, and this field will doubtless soon be more extensively investigated.

(iii) Switch of resources in favour of roots. We have noted the plasticity of root:shoot ratio as a response to stress and the correlation between growth rate and increasing root:shoot ratio. This feedback system should operate so that increased root growth will improve nutrient supply and alleviate the stress, so switching resources back to shoot growth. The differences between species can therefore be seen as the stabilization of this switching process at a value optimal to the fertility to which the species is otherwise adapted. But amounts of root are not themselves critical—morphology is more significant in many cases. The role of root hairs is still not fully defined, but it is certain that they play an important part, since it seems likely that plants with hairless roots, such as onion (*Allium cepa*), may be obligately dependent on mycorrhizas for their phosphate supply. How mycorrhizas affect plants of low nutrient soils is as yet unclear.

The differential growth of lateral roots in zones of high nutrient supply in soil, now a well-established and better understood phenomenon, may be important but nothing is known of the comparative distribution of this response. All the species used in this work are crop species which have been bred for high nutrient response. It would be valuable to know whether low nutrient plants show the same reaction.

These represent some of the ways in which plants have adapted themselves ecologically to their nutrient environment. With the exception of the mechanism by which ions are transported across the cell membrane, we now understand the operation of this system in considerable detail, but the extent to which the various mechanisms have been adapted to fit species to their environment is only recently beginning to receive attention.

4. Water

Water is the major component of green plants, accounting for 70–90% of the fresh weight of most non-woody species. Most of this water is contained in the cell contents (85–90% water) where it provides a suitable medium for many biochemical reactions. However, water has many other roles to play in the physiology of plants and it is uniquely fitted, by its physical and chemical properties, to fulfil these roles. An early, but still very useful review of these properties can be found in Henderson (1913).

I. PROPERTIES OF WATER

Because of unusually strong hydrogen bonds between its molecules, water tends to behave as if its molecules were very much larger (Bernal, 1965; Davis and Day, 1961). For example, the Melting Point (0°C) and Boiling Point (100°C) of water (molecular weight 18) are anomalously high when compared with the values (-86°C and -61°C respectively) for the closely related compound, hydrogen sulphide (H_2S, molecular weight 34). Thus, unlike all other small molecules, water normally remains as a liquid under terrestrial conditions, although problems for living organisms do result from the freezing of water. For the same reason, the Specific Heat ($4\cdot2$ J g^{-1}), the Latent Heat of Melting ($333\cdot6$ J g^{-1}) and the Latent Heat of Vapourization (2441 J g^{-1} at 25°C) of water are all unusually high, with important implications for the thermal economy of plants. The high specific heat of water buffers the plant body against rapid fluctuations in temperature, whereas the high latent heat of vapourization provides an effective means of cooling leaves by evaporation of water (Gates, 1976). The same properties are responsible for moderating the temperatures of moist soils, lakes and the ocean.

Water is an excellent solvent for three groups of biologically important solutes, namely:

(i) Organic solutes with which water can form hydrogen bonds, including amino acids and low molecular weight carbohydrates
and proteins, which contain hydroxyl, amine or carboxylic
acid functional groups. Water also forms colloidal dispersions with
higher molecular weight carbohydrates and proteins (e.g. the cytoplasm itself).

(ii) Charged ions such as the major nutrient ions (K^+, Ca^{2+},
$H_2PO_4^-$, NO_3^- etc.). Water molecules, which carry partial charges,
orientate themselves round ions to give larger, but highly soluble,
hydrated ions. In the same way, water molecules become attached
to fixed charges on the surface of plant cell walls, cell membranes and
soil particles, giving tightly bound layers of water a few molecules
thick (Bernal, 1965).

(iii) Small molecules, like the atmospheric gases (O_2, N_2), which
presumably can fit into holes in the rather open structure of liquid
water (Crafts, 1968a).

Thus, as well as being an ideal solvent for many biochemical reactions, water is also a suitable medium for the transport of organic
molecules (e.g. sucrose in the phloem), inorganic ions (e.g. nutrients
from root to leaf in the xylem) and atmospheric gases (e.g. movement
of oxygen to sites of respiration).

Two other physical properties, Tensile Strength and Viscosity, are
highly important in the long distance transport of water and dissolved
solutes. In particular, the high tensile strength (cohesion) of liquid
water columns in the fine conduits of the xylem (Table 4.6) means that
water can be drawn to the tops of tall trees by transpirational pull alone
(Oertli, 1971). This cohesion is again due to the strength of hydrogen
bonds amongst water molecules; however, in spite of these bonds,
water has a moderate viscosity (Meidner and Sheriff, 1976). This
results in rapid flow in, for example, soil macropores, but may not be
important in soil capillaries and in xylem conduits where the ratio of
surface-bound to bulk water is high.

Water can move from the soil, through root and stem, to a transpiring
leaf only if there is continuity of liquid throughout the pathway. Thus,
in addition to continuous columns of water in the xylem, the plant also
requires continuity of water in the capillaries of the soil and the
apoplasts of both root and leaf. That this continuity does exist is due to
two properties of water. First, as explained above, continuous thin
films form on the hydrophilic surfaces of soil and cell wall capillaries.
Secondly, since the Surface Tension of water is very high ($73.5 \times
10^{-3}$ kg s^{-2} at 15°C, i.e. two to three times the value for most laboratory

solvents), the filling of capillaries with water results in a large reduction
in the energy (and increase in stability) of the capillary/water system
due to the reduction of water surface in contact with air. These two
forces retaining water in capillaries constitute the Matric Forces. For
example, after the gravitational water has drained from a water-
saturated soil, all the soil capillaries of diameter less than 60 μm are
filled with water retained by matric forces (Russell, 1973).

Both the distribution and the morphology of green plants are influenced by the fact that water absorbs specifically in the infra-red but
is relatively transparent to short-wave radiation. Thus, aquatic plants
can absorb photosynthetically active radiation at considerable depths
in clear water; on the other hand, in terrestrial plants, these optical
properties have permitted the development of leaves in which the
colourless outer layer of cells (the epidermis) permits the passage of
light to the underlying layers of light-harvesting cells (mesophyll). However, there is no evidence that the epidermis acts as a heat filter, protecting the mesophyll; on the contrary, Sheriff (1977a) has demonstrated that, under moderate light intensities, the epidermis can be cooler
than underlying tissues due to heat loss by transpiration.

As well as being a useful solvent, water is also an important biochemical reagent in, for example, photosynthesis and hydrolysis reactions. Much of the chemical activity of water is due to its dissociation
to give highly reactive hydronium and hydroxide ions:

$$2H_2O \rightleftharpoons H_3O^+ + OH^-, \text{ where } K_w = 10^{-14} \qquad (4.1)$$

Thus even pure water is a 10^{-7} M solution of hydronium ions.

II. THE WATER RELATIONS OF PLANTS AND SOILS

A. Water Potential

Water flowing down a hillside can turn a water wheel, yielding useful
work. The water at the bottom of the slope has lost part of its capacity
to do work and has a lower free energy content than the water at the
top. Thus we have a flow of water whose driving force is the difference
in free energy between the top and bottom of the slope.

In a similar way, water movement in the soil–plant–atmosphere
system is due to differences in the free energy content (capacity to do
work) of water in different parts of the system. For example, in a well-

watered transpiring plant, the free energy content of water decreases progressively as we pass from the soil, *via* the xylem and the leaf, to the free atmosphere; consequently, water flows from the soil through the plant to the air in response to this gradient in free energy.

In plant physiology, it is customary to express the free energy content of water in the form of Water Potential (Ψ). Derivations of water potential from strict thermodynamic principles can be found in Slatyer (1967) and Meidner and Sheriff (1976); however, for the present purposes, it is sufficient to define water potential as the free energy per unit volume of water, assuming the potential of pure water to be zero under standard conditions (usually ambient temperature and atmospheric pressure). Since energy per unit volume has the same dimensions as pressure, plant and soil water potentials are expressed in pressure units, either bars or Pascals (Pa), where 1 bar $= 10^5$ Pa.

Because water potential increases with temperature, it is important to maintain constant temperature during a series of measurements. In contrast, water potential is lowered below that of pure water by dissolved solutes and also by the binding of water to surfaces by matric forces. Since these effects are considered to be mutually independent, the water potential of a solution (Ψ) can be expressed as

$$\Psi = \psi_s + \psi_m \tag{4.2}$$

where ψ_s, the Solute Potential, is the reduction in water potential due to dissolved solutes (negative), ψ_m, the Matric Potential, is the reduction in water potential due to matric forces (negative) and Ψ will be negative, since the water potential of pure water is defined as zero.

Consequently, in the soil–plant–atmosphere system, water potentials are usually negative, and water flows towards regions with more negative values. For example, in rapidly transpiring Sitka spruce trees, 10 m high, water was flowing upwards, but down a water potential gradient, from the soil (-0.4 bar) to the terminal shoots at the top of the trees (-15 bar) (Hellkvist, Richards and Jarvis, 1974).

In plant tissues, water potentials may be increased by hydrostatic pressure and, therefore, equation 4.2 must be modified to give

$$\Psi = \psi_s + \psi_m + \psi_p \tag{4.3}$$

where ψ_p, the Pressure Potential, is the increase in water potential due to hydrostatic pressure (positive). Since ψ_p is positive, the resulting water potential is less negative than would be expected if only the solute and matric effects were considered. Occasionally, hydrostatic pressure in plants can result in zero, or even positive, water potential values; in particular the xylem water potential in guttating plants will be positive (Crafts, 1968b).

Methods for measuring water potential, and its separate components, are described in detail in Slavik (1974).

B. The Water Relations of Plant Cells

Most of the cells involved in plant–water relations are fully mature, with a large fraction of the cell water contained in a central vacuole. The thin layer of cytoplasm, together with its associated plasmalemma and tonoplast, can be considered to be a complex semi-permeable membrane separating the vacuolar contents from the external medium.

In a leaf, the external medium is the water in the cell walls and intercellular spaces (the apoplast) which is subjected to atmospheric pressure (i.e. $\psi_p = 0$). Since the solute concentration of this water is normally very low, ψ_s is small and, therefore, the water potential in the apoplast is determined by the matric forces exerted by the cell walls. Thus

$$\Psi_{apoplast} = \psi_m \qquad (4.4)$$

where ψ_m will normally be high (> -1 bar) in a leaf well supplied with water but not actively transpiring (e.g. at night).

Matric forces are considered to be unimportant in vacuolar sap and, therefore, water potential is determined largely by the solute potential. Thus

$$\Psi_{vacuole} = \psi_s \qquad (4.5)$$

where ψ_s may vary from -5 to -30 bar according to the solute concentration in the vacuolar sap.

Since Ψ_{vac} is lower than Ψ_{apo}, water tends to flow inwards across the cytoplasm, raising the vacuolar water potential but also increasing the volume of the vacuole. In a plant cell lacking cell walls, this flow of water would continue until either the cell burst or the difference in water potential was abolished by dilution of the vacuolar sap. However, in a leaf, cell volume is limited by the cell walls and only a relatively small inflow of water can be accommodated by the elasticity of the cell walls. Consequently, hydrostatic pressure (turgor pressure) develops in the vacuole, pressing the cytoplasm against the inner surface of the cell walls, and raising the vacuolar water potential. As turgor pressure rises, adjacent cells press against one another, with the result that a leaf, originally in a wilted, flaccid condition, becomes increasingly turgid. At equilibrium, turgor pressure has reached its maximum value, and there is no tendency for water to flow from apoplast to vacuole. Thus

$$\Psi_{apo} = \Psi_{vac} \tag{4.6}$$

$$\text{i.e. } (\psi_m)_{apo} = (\psi_s + \psi_p)_{vac} \tag{4.7}$$

The continuous and progressive development of turgor pressure (pressure potential) caused by water influx into plant cells can be illustrated by modern versions of Höfler's diagram. For example, Fig. 4.1 shows a typical Höfler plot for leaf cells, in which, for clarity, the

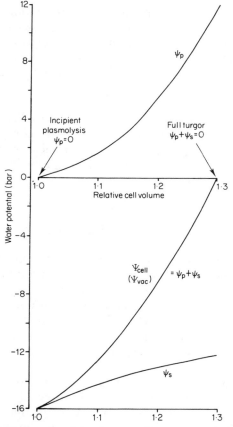

FIG. 4.1.   "Höfler" diagram for an idealized leaf cell showing the relationship between vacuolar water potential (Ψ_{vac}) and its components, pressure potential (ψ_p) and solute potential (ψ_s), at different cell volumes (after Meidner and Sheriff, 1976).

water potential of the bathing medium is fixed at zero. In this figure, a plant cell with a relative cell volume of 1·0 and a ψ_s of -16 bar will absorb water from the bathing medium, thus increasing cell volume and raising ψ_s by sap dilution. However, since the cell wall resists expansion, ψ_p rises at an increasing rate until maximum turgor pressure is achieved when $\psi_p = 12$ bar whereas ψ_s has risen to -12 bar. At this point, since $\Psi_{vac} = \psi_p + \psi_s = 0$, the driving force for the entry of water has declined to zero and the cell has reached its maximum volume (1·3).

In the discussion so far, we have concentrated upon the water relations of cell vacuoles. Since virtually all the biochemical and physiological processes in a plant take place in the cytoplasm or cytoplasmic organelles, the water relations of the cytoplasm are of much greater interest. It is customary to assume that the cytoplasmic water is in thermodynamic equilibrium with the vacuolar water. Consequently, under most conditions, water potential in the cytoplasm (Ψ_{cyt}) will be identical to that in vacuole, (Ψ_{vac}), and we can simplify subsequent discussion by using the term cell water potential (Ψ_{cell}), where

$$\Psi_{cell} = \Psi_{cyt} = \Psi_{vac} \qquad (4.8)$$

However, it must be stressed that although cytoplasmic and vacuolar potentials are equal, the relative sizes of the components of water potential may not be the same. In particular because of high concentrations of colloidal particles there must be a significant matric potential component in the cytoplasm.

C. The Influence of Water Stress on Plant Cells

The rate of growth of plant cells and the efficiency of their physiological processes are highest when the cells are at maximum turgor. However, the absorption of carbon dioxide through moist cell walls exposed to the atmosphere, which is essential for photosynthesis, is associated with the loss of water from leaf tissues. In a photosynthesizing plant there will, therefore, be a tendency for water to be withdrawn from leaf cells, with resulting reductions in cell turgor pressure and in cell water potential.

Plant cells which have lost water, and are at a turgor pressure lower than the maximum value, are said to be suffering from Water Stress. This is a misleading term since stress has a precise definition in mechanics and can easily be measured. Water stress is a much more imprecise term indicating that the water content of cells has fallen below the optimum value, causing some degree of metabolic disturbance. Cell water potential is a convenient index of water stress and Hsiao (1973) has attempted to describe water stress a little more precisely by defining three classes of stress (in a typical cell):

Mild Stress—Ψ_{cell} lowered by a few bars.
Moderate Stress—Ψ_{cell} lowered by more than a few bars but less than 12–15 bars.
Severe Stress—Ψ_{cell} lowered by more than 15 bars.

In Fig. 4.1, mild stress in a typical leaf cell corresponds to a small loss of turgor whereas moderate stress is associated with more complete loss of turgor and the wilting of leaves. If more water is withdrawn from wilted leaves, the cells are exposed to severe water stress. As the volume of the cell contents decreases, there is a tendency for the plasmalemma to shrink away from the cell wall (plasmolysis); however, according to Meidner and Sheriff (1976), plasmolysis of leaf cells is a rare event in nature since it is difficult for water or air to move inwards through the cell walls to fill the space vacated between plasmalemma and cell wall. Severe stress is thus associated with serious dehydration and mechanical stresses in the cytoplasm and vacuole.

It is difficult to determine the effects of each of these classes of water stress on individual cells because water stress may have a large effect on the physiology of the tissue as a whole. In particular, mild to moderate stress causes the closure of stomata in the leaves of many species, thereby cutting off carbon dioxide supplies to mesophyll cells. Thus it is possible that the rate of photosynthesis in these cells may be reduced significantly by levels of water stress which would have a much smaller influence upon the photosynthetic apparatus of isolated cells.

In spite of this difficulty, there are many reports of the effects of varying degrees of water stress on cell growth and physiology and these have been reviewed by Hsiao et al. (1976) in diagrammatic form (Fig. 4.2). Cell and leaf growth are highly sensitive to water stress because cell expansion is caused by the action of turgor pressure upon "softened" cell walls (Greacen and Oh, 1972). Thus, even under mild stress when turgor pressure is reduced by only a few bars, there is a significant decrease in growth; since turgor is essential for cell enlargement, cell and leaf growth cease at zero turgor pressure or, more likely, at a threshold turgor before leaf wilting (moderate to severe water stress) (Hsiao, 1973).

Figure 4.2 indicates that as water stress increases from mild to moderate, cell biochemical processes are increasingly affected. Thus, protein and chlorophyll biosynthesis are sensitive to rather mild stress whereas, under conditions of moderate stress, nitrate reductase level,

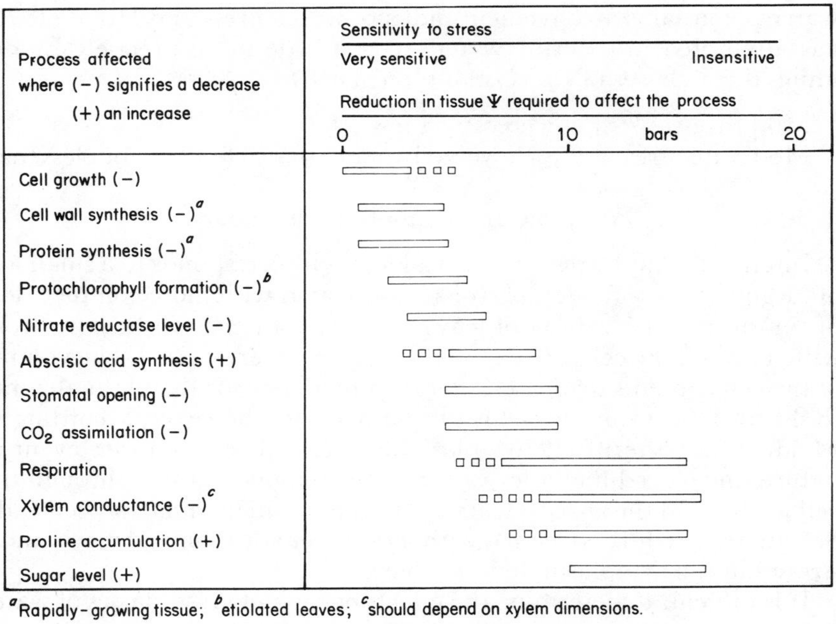

Process affected where ($-$) signifies a decrease ($+$) an increase	Sensitivity to stress		
	Very sensitive Insensitive		
	Reduction in tissue Ψ required to affect the process		
	0 10 bars 20		
Cell growth ($-$)			
Cell wall synthesis ($-$)[a]			
Protein synthesis ($-$)[a]			
Protochlorophyll formation ($-$)[b]			
Nitrate reductase level ($-$)			
Abscisic acid synthesis ($+$)			
Stomatal opening ($-$)			
CO_2 assimilation ($-$)			
Respiration			
Xylem conductance ($-$)[c]			
Proline accumulation ($+$)			
Sugar level ($+$)			

[a]Rapidly-growing tissue; [b]etiolated leaves; [c]should depend on xylem dimensions.

FIG. 4.2. The influence of water stress on the physiology of mesophytic plants. The continuous horizontal bars indicate the range of stress levels within which a process is *first* affected, whereas the broken bars refer to effects which have not yet been firmly established. The reductions in tissue Ψ used are in relation to the Ψ of well-watered plants under mild evaporative demand (after Hsiao *et al.*, 1976).

growth hormone metabolism and carbon dioxide assimilation begin to be affected. Moderate to severe stress is associated with serious disruption of cell metabolism as indicated by increases in respiration and the accumulation of proline and sugars (see Chapter 6, p. 223).

Throughout the preceding treatment of cell water relations, attention has been concentrated upon the behaviour of "typical" leaf cells with a solute potential of about -15 bar and a response to water loss similar to that shown in Fig. 4.1. This has simplified the discussion of water stress and permitted the use of Hsiao's (1973) water potential classification to explain the effects of stress on cell growth and metabolism. However, there is considerable variation in vacuolar solute potential amongst plant species (normally within a range of -5 to -30 bar) and also, the response to water loss in the cells of some plant species may be different from that shown in the Höfler diagram. For example, the cells of some drought-resistant species avoid loss of turgor and the resultant cessation of growth by secreting solutes into the vacuole, thereby lowering the solute potential (e.g. Osonubi and Davies, 1978). Consequently, some authors prefer to indicate the severity of water stress in a tissue by the fraction of cell water lost rather than the depression of water potential. Thus, Bannister (1976) uses the terms

$$\text{Relative water content, } W_R = \frac{100 \ (w_f - w_d)}{(w_s - w_d)} \qquad (4.9)$$

$$\text{and Water deficit, } W_D = \frac{100 \ (w_s - w_f)}{(w_s - w_d)} = 100 - W_R \qquad (4.10)$$

where w_f and w_d are the fresh and dry weights of the water stressed tissue, and w_s is the weight of the tissue after it has become completely resaturated with water. These terms are of very limited application. Since a given water deficit will result in different degrees of water stress in the cells of different species. W_R and W_D should be used only as indices of water stress in plants of the same, or closely related species (e.g. Bannister, 1976).

Overall, it can be seen from Fig. 4.2 that even mild water stress in the leaves of a plant can result in a reduction in growth rate and the disruption of several metabolic processes. Depending upon their severity, these effects may reduce the ability of the plant to survive and reproduce. Consequently, it is crucially important for plants of all species either to *avoid* water stress or to evolve anatomical, morphological and biochemical adaptations to *ameliorate* or *tolerate* water stress. Much of the remainder of this chapter will describe these adaptations.

D. The Supply of Water by the Soil

As we shall see later, the absorption of dew and rain by leaves may be an important factor in the survival of some plant species in arid regions. However, in most terrestrial plants, this mechanism is of negligible importance compared with the absorption of soil water through the root system.

The quantity of water held by a soil depends primarily on the climate and, in particular, on the excess of precipitation over evapotranspiration (P–E). Thus, in "extremely humid" areas like the northern and western parts of the UK (Geiger, 1965), where annual precipitation is at least twice evapotranspiration, it is unusual for the availability of soil water to be a factor in the survival and distribution of plant species. Exceptions to this rule occur in unusually dry habitats, for example on shallow or sandy soils. In contrast, in "extremely arid" regions, where potential evapotranspiration is more than twice precipitation, soil moisture levels are so low that vegetation is generally very sparse.

Between these extremes, there is a spectrum of humid and arid climates, clearly illustrated by Walter and Lieth (1960), where the availability of soil water depends not only on the annual P–E but also on the distribution of rainfall within each year. Many of the features of drier climates, where the risk of water stress in plants is high, can be illustrated by Fig. 4.3 which compares the rainfall distribution for two contrasting, but not extreme, years in a tropical savanna region where virtually all of the annual rainfall is received during the months November to April. In 1970/71, the "wet season" began and ended decisively on 25 November and 8 March respectively, with a few scattered days of rain in early November, late March and April. During the wet season there were no prolonged dry spells when significant depletion of soil moisture could occur. On the other hand, in 1971/72, both the beginning and end of the wet season were ill-defined and a higher proportion of the annual precipitation fell in the first half of November and in April. In addition, there were at least two mid-season dry periods (26 December to 4 January and 26 January to 8 February) during which, according to agrometeorological calculations, there was a risk of serious water stress in annual crop plants (Hay, 1981).

To be successful under such conditions, a natural plant species must possess several characteristics, including the following abilities:

(i) To survive a long period without rain every year (here six months).

(ii) To make use of the maximum period of soil water availability to complete its annual growth cycle without incurring serious water stress at the beginning and end of the wet season. Since the date of the beginning of the growing season is highly variable, the plant requires a timing mechanism to signal the earliest "safe" date for the resumption of growth. (Such mechanisms will be discussed briefly when considering the timing of germination of dormant seeds and leaf production in deciduous perennials.)

(iii) To avoid, ameliorate or tolerate short periods of severe water stress at different stages of growth (see p. 24).

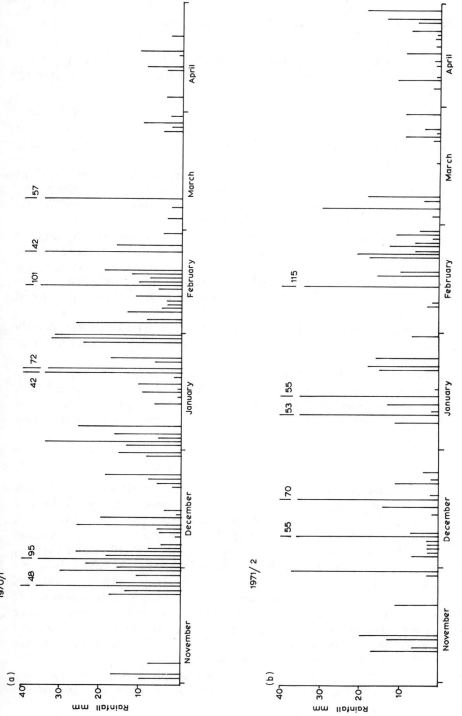

FIG. 4.3.   The distribution of daily rainfall in a savanna region (Bunda College of Agriculture, Malawi, C. Africa) in (a) 1970/71 and (b) 1971/72. There was virtually no rainfall during the remaining months of each year.

(iv) To survive occasional years of drought when either the total amount of precipitation or the length of the wet season is greatly reduced.

In more humid and more temperate regions, where rainfall is less seasonal, (i) and (ii) become less important but (iii) and (iv) remain essential characteristics for plant species growing in all but extremely humid climates.

Within a given climatic region, the availability of water for plant growth and function depends on the water storing properties of the soil. Soils consist of mineral particles of varying diameter (sand 2–0·06 mm, silt 0·06–0·002 mm and clay <0·002 mm, Soil Survey of England and Wales classification), bound together into aggregates by organic matter and clay particles. Within and between these aggregates there is a network of interconnected pores of diameter ranging from a few cm (drying cracks, earthworm or termite channels) through a few mm (pores between aggregates) down to a few μm or tenths of a μm (finest pores within aggregates). When a soil is saturated with water after prolonged rainfall, this interconnected pore space becomes temporarily water filled. However, a free-draining soil can not hold all of this water for plant use.

Since the solute concentration of soil water is usually very low, the major forces retaining water in soil pores are the matric forces which increase as pore diameter (d) decreases. Consequently, the water potential in a water-filled pore is inversely related to pore diameter by the expression

$$\Psi_{\text{pore water}} = \psi_m = -3/d \qquad (4.11)$$

where water potential is in bars and d is in μm (Russell, 1973). For example, pure water held in soil pores of diameter 10 μm will be at a potential of $-0·3$ bar; to withdraw water from these pores requires a suction of at least 0·3 bar. Similarly, since gravity exerts a suction equivalent to about 0·05 bar in temperate areas (Webster and Beckett, 1972), all pores wider than 60 μm will tend to drain spontaneously after a soil has been saturated with water. In a freely-draining field soil, this drainage may take 2 to 3 days and once it is complete, the soil is at *field capacity*. At field capacity, the soil contains the maximum amount of water water (normally expressed in g/100 g oven dry soil) that it can hold against gravity. The gravitational water normally lost in drainage is not available to plants unless soil drainage is impeded.

As indicated in an earlier section, the transpiration of water from the leaves of a plant causes the establishment of a gradient of water potential in the plant/soil system. If the water potential in the xylem of a root axis is thereby lowered below the water potential in the soil pores surrounding the root, then water will flow into the root and pass *via* the xylem to the site of transpiration. Soil water is therefore available to plants only if the root xylem water potential can be lowered below the pore water potential. Water is retained in soil pores at potentials down to about − 30 bar but few mesophytic species can tolerate the lowering of xylem water potential required to absorb all of this water, especially as this would mean leaf water potentials lower than − 30 bar.

The majority of plant species that have been studied (mostly crop plants) can withdraw water from pores wider than about 0·2 μm (− 15 bar); once all the water in these pores is exhausted, no more can be transported to the leaf and the plant will wilt permanently and eventually die, unless the soil is recharged with water. Consequently, the property *permanent wilting point* has been defined as the soil moisture content (g/100 g oven dry soil) after the soil has been subjected to a suction of 15 bar. The "available water content" of the soil is then the difference between field capacity and permanent wilting point. Although this standard method of determining permanent wilting point and available water is useful in comparing the water relations of different soils, it is no more than a laboratory convenience. In reality, a given soil will release differing quantities of water to different species according to the maximum suction their roots can exert on the water in the pores of the soil.

The amount of soil water available to a given species depends primarily upon the size distribution of the soil pores. This size distribution, in turn, is dependent upon both soil texture and structure (degree and type of aggregation) but, in general, medium to fine textured soils tend to hold more water for plant use than coarse textured soils (Fig. 4.4). Temperature also influences soil water availability through its effect upon the viscosity of water. In the foregoing discussion of field capacity, the conventional assumption has been made that only those pores wider than 60 μm drain under the influence of gravity. However, this assumption is based on field investigations of soils in winter and spring in the U.K. (e.g. Webster and Beckett, 1972). Russell (1973) estimates that in subtropical regions, the lowering of water viscosity under warmer conditions coupled with very free drainage may permit the drainage of pores as narrow as 10 μm. Depending upon pore size distribution, this may cause a significant reduction in available water. Finally, any increase in the solute concentration of soil water will result in a lowering of soil water potential and a reduction of the amount of water available for plant use. This effect is particularly important in

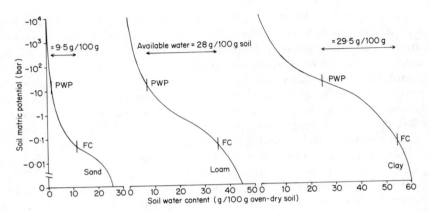

Fig. 4.4. Typical soil water release curves for coarse (sand), medium (loam) and fine (clay) soils. Note that although the available water contents of the loam and clay soils are very similar, a larger proportion of this water is held at matric potentials above −1 bar (i.e. in wider pores) in the loam soil (redrawn from Brady, 1974).

saline soils where soluble salts can give a lowering in osmotic pressure of several bars.

Plants do not draw water only from the immediate vicinity of their actively-absorbing roots. As depletion of the nearest pores proceeds, a gradient of water potential is set up between the root and the bulk soil causing water to flow towards the root from at least a few mm from the root surface (Newman, 1974). However, at the same time, the withdrawal of water from the larger pores both reduces the volume of soil through which flow can take place and increases the "tortuosity" of the pathway between the moist bulk soil and root. These effects combine to give a drastic reduction in the hydraulic conductivity of a soil as it dries. For example, a Pachappa sandy loam soil had a conductivity of 6 cm/day at a matric potential of −0·05 bar (field capacity) compared with less than 10^{-6} cm/day at −15 bar (permanent wilting point) (Gardner, 1960). Consequently, maintenance of a steady flow of water into a root from a drying soil requires:

(i) a progressive lowering of root xylem water potential to maintain a gradient in potential between the xylem and the remaining soil water, and
(ii) a progressive increase in the *steepness* of the gradient to overcome the increasing resistance to water flow offered by the soil (Ohm's Law analogy, see section F below). The increase in this gradient ($\Psi_{soil} - \Psi_{root\ xylem}$) is clearly illustrated in Fig. 4.7.

This rapid lowering of $\Psi_{\text{root xylem}}$ (and Ψ_{leaf}) explains the unexpectedly dramatic effects on leaf growth which may accompany a modest lowering of soil water potential (e.g. 1–2 bar in various species, Jarvis (1963)). Overall, it is clear that the supply of water frequently does not meet demand during rapid transpiration, with the result that temporary wilting and leaf water stress may occur long before the soil permanent wilting point has been reached (see following section).

E. The Loss of Water from Transpiring Leaves

Within a leaf, the walls of the mesophyll cells adjacent to substomatal cavities (Fig. 4.5) must remain moist to permit the dissolution and uptake of carbon dioxide for photosynthesis. Consequently, as long as the stomata are fully closed, and the temperature is not changing rapidly, the air contained in the leaf will tend to be saturated with water vapour. Under such conditions, water can escape from the leaf to surrounding unsaturated air only by diffusing across the hydrophobic cuticle covering the epidermal cells. The rate of cuticular transpiration depends upon the thickness, continuity and composition of the cuticle, being low in all plants and particularly low in young leaves with undamaged cuticles and in drought-resistant species.

When stomata begin to open in response to environmental conditions, the air outside the leaf is normally not saturated with water vapour. As a result of this difference in water vapour concentration, water molecules diffuse out of the leaf air spaces into the bulk air *via* the stomatal pores. It is possible to express the driving force for this outward diffusion of water molecules rigorously as a gradient in air water potential, but it is convenient and customary to use differences in percentage saturation (or water vapour density) when discussing transpiration (Meidner and Sheriff, 1976).

In a leaf with a plentiful water supply the rate of water loss by stomatal transpiration at a given level of saturation of bulk air depends upon the resistance to the diffusion of water molecules offered by the pathway between the leaf air space and the bulk air (the leaf diffusive resistance). This pathway can be resolved into a number of components in series, namely, the distance moved within the leaf air space; entry into, passage through, and exit from the stomatal pores; and passage through the boundary layer outside the leaf. However, in most species, stomatal transpiration rate is controlled by resistance to diffusion through the stomata and through the boundary layer, the other components being of negligible resistance (Meidner and Mansfield, 1968).

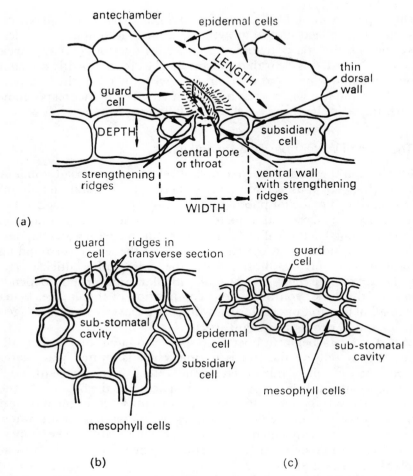

FIG. 4.5. The structure of stomata (a) section through a typical elliptical stoma shown as a perspective diagram; (b) transverse section of an elliptical stoma and sub-stomatal cavity; (c) longitudinal section through one guard cell and the sub-stomatal cavity of an elliptical stoma (after Meidner and Mansfield, 1968).

1. Stomatal Resistance

The resistance to the diffusion of water vapour through stomata is inversely proportional to the diameter of the stomatal aperture which, in turn, is dependent in a complex manner on a number of environmental factors. Since the most important function of stomata is to admit carbon dioxide to the leaf mesophyll, periods of stomatal opening normally coincide with conditions favouring photosynthesis. Thus the stomata of most species open in the light and close in the dark, often under the control of endogenous circadian rhythms (Meidner and Mansfield, 1968). Stomata also tend to open if the carbon dioxide concentration in the substomatal cavities falls below a critical level; this is, presumably, a mechanism to ensure adequate supplies for carbon dioxide fixation (Raschke, 1975).

Because of the experimental difficulties encountered in studying guard cells, the complex processes leading to stomatal opening are poorly understood. However, it is known that both light and lowered carbon dioxide concentrations cause a depression in the solute potential (ψ_s) of guard cells by the accumulation of potassium, chloride and/ or organic acid ions in guard cell sap. Water is therefore drawn into the guard cells, their turgor pressure rises above that of surrounding epidermal cells and the stomata open due to the mechanical effects of this difference in turgor pressure (Meidner and Mansfield, 1968). The size of the stomatal aperture, and therefore the resistance to diffusion, depends upon the magnitude of this difference in turgor pressure. Some examples of stomatal aperture size are given in Table 4.1.

The fundamental response of stomata to light is modified by several other factors. In particular, the increases in cell respiration rate, which accompany water stress or high temperatures, result in high carbon dioxide levels in the leaf air spaces and the closure of stomata. This closing of stomata in water-stressed leaves, which is a valuable strategy in water conservation, is not fully reversible even if an adequate water supply is provided. It may take several days before such stomata respond normally to environmental conditions. As Meidner and Mansfield (1968) point out, this delay in stomatal opening is particularly useful to mesophytes which experience short periods of stress only. By the time normal stomatal responses are re-established it is likely that rain will have recharged the soil water.

Experimental evidence is accumulating that stomatal closure leading to the conservation of water and the avoidance of severe stress can be caused by factors other than enhanced carbon dioxide levels. For example, the stomatal aperture of several species can respond directly to changes in the water saturation of the air before changes in leaf water potential have had time to occur (Hall et al., 1976). Such a response to humidity permits the leaf to control its water content very accurately. A further control of stomatal aperture is exercised by growth substances in the leaf (Hiron and Wright, 1973; Mansfield and Davies, 1981); in particular, it has been established that abscisic acid, which is synthesized in the chloroplasts during water stress, can cause stomatal closure and delayed opening.

TABLE 4.1. Stomatal frequencies, dimensions and pore areas on the upper and lower surfaces of fully-expanded leaves of a selection of plant species (from Meidner and Mansfield, 1968).

Species	Frequencies (per mm²)		Dimensions of stomatal apparatus (μm)[a]		Length of stomatal pore (μm)		Pore[b] area
	Upper	Lower	Upper	Lower	Upper	Lower	
Tradescantia virginiana	7	23	67 × 38	70 × 42	49	52	0·35
Larix decidua	14	16	42 × 26	42 × 26	20	20	0·15
Nicotiana tabacum	50	190	31 × 25	31 × 25	14	14	0·8
Vicia faba	65	75	46 × 25	46 × 25	28	28	1·0
Pteridium aquilinum	—	85	—	46 × 28	—	21	0·45
Zea mays	98	108	38 × 19	43 × 24	12	16	0·7
Pinus sylvestris	120	120	28 × 28	28 × 28	20	20	1·2
Carpinus betulus	—	170	—	32 × 24	—	13	0·6
Xanthium strumarium	173	177	39 × 25	39 × 25	17	17	1·5
Allium cepa	175	175	42 × 38	42 × 38	24	24	2·0
Quercus robur	—	340	—	28 × 18	—	10	0·8
Tilia europea	—	370	—	25 × 18	—	10	0·9

[a] I.e. length × width in Fig. 4.5.
[b] Expressed as a percentage of total leaf area; pore width taken as 6 μm.

Stomatal resistance is therefore determined by the interplay of a complex array of factors—light, carbon-dioxide level, water stress, temperature, humidity, wind, growth substances, endogenous rhythms —and it is not surprising that some authors consider stomata to be "miniature sense organs" (Mansfield and Davies, 1981). The success of a plant species in a given environment depends upon control of the responses to these factors to give a favourable balance between photo-synthesis and water conservation.

2. Boundary Layer Resistance

Even in the absence of wind, the bulk air surrounding a leaf is turbulent due to convective heat exchange. Consequently the air is thoroughly mixed, and water molecules move rapidly from the transpiring leaf into uniform unsaturated air by mass flow rather than, much more slowly, by diffusion. However, at the leaf surface, there is a relatively un-disturbed layer of air, the boundary layer, through which water vapour must diffuse before entering the turbulent bulk air (see Chapters 2 and 7). The thickness of the boundary layer depends upon wind speed and upon leaf shape and size but a typical value would be 1 mm thick at 1 m s^{-1} bulk wind speed.

Using data from Holmgren et al. (1965) and Meidner and Sheriff (1976) it is possible to compare the magnitudes of the resistances to the diffusion of water vapour across the cuticle, through stomata and across the boundary layer, in typical mesophytes (the origin of the unit, s cm^{-1}, is fully explained in Meidner and Mansfield, 1968):

Cuticle (r_c) 20–80 s cm^{-1} (with much higher values for some tree species).
Stomata (r_s) 0·8 s cm^{-1} to 16 s cm^{-1} (value dependent upon degree of stomatal opening).
Boundary Layer (r_a) 3·0 s cm^{-1} (at 0·1 m s^{-1} wind, Beaufort Scale Force 0); 0·35 s cm^{-1} (at 10 m s^{-1}, Beaufort Scale Force 6).

Note that r_s is of the same magnitude as r_c when stomata are fully closed.

Since the stomatal and cuticular pathways are in parallel, these high values of r_c indicate that cuticular transpiration will be a negligible fraction of total transpiration as long as the stomata are open. The leaf diffusive resistance (R_1) of a transpiring plant is the sum of r_a and r_s; under most conditions, r_s is the dominant component of R_1 and there-fore, stomatal aperture controls transpiration rate. However, as wind speed falls, the thickness of the boundary layer increases and r_a becomes a larger fraction of R_1. At very low wind speeds or in still air (which are relatively uncommon occurrences), the boundary layer resistance may control transpiration rate over a range of stomatal apertures, as shown in the classic experiment of Bange (1953).

F. Water Movement in Whole Plants

In a freely-transpiring plant, water evaporates from the moist walls of epidermal and mesophyll cells in the interior of the leaves and is lost to the atmosphere through the stomata. As water loss proceeds, the water potential in the leaf apoplast falls below that of the leaf cells and also below the water potential in the xylem and the soil. This results in the rapid withdrawal of water from leaf cells and a lowering of cell water potential. In contrast, although there is continuity of liquid water between leaf and soil *via* the xylem, equalization of water potential throughout the plant by upward water movement can not occur very rapidly because there is a resistance to hydraulic flow in the plant/soil system. Consequently, transpiration establishes a water potential gradient in the plant down which water tends to flow from the soil to the leaf.

The path of water movement from the root surface to the site of evaporation in the leaf is considered by most workers (Spanswick, 1976), to be predominantly extracellular. Many observations and theoretical calculations are consistent with the hypothesis that in the apical 10–20 cm of young roots, water flows radially inwards through the cell walls and intercellular spaces of the root epidermis and cortex up to the endodermis, where further apoplastic movement is blocked by Casparian strips in fully differentiated regions. Thereafter, water is thought to pass through the cells of the endodermis before entering the lumina of the xylem vessels by way of the stelar parenchyma apoplast (Anderson, 1976). The pathway then follows the stem xylem vessels into the leaf where bundle sheaths and branching networks of veins deliver water to the apoplast within a few cells of the sites of evaporation. Throughout its length, this pathway appears to cross membranes and pass through living cells only at the root endodermis (and, possibly, at the mestome sheath in the leaf bundles of some species). The pathway is less clear for older and less permeable roots covered with a suberized exodermis or in roots which have undergone secondary thickening; it may be that water enters the apoplast of such roots through cracks or lenticels.

Following van der Honert (1948), it is possible to describe the flow of water to a transpiring leaf in response to a water potential gradient by an expression analogous to Ohm's Law (which describes the flow of electric current in response to an electric potential difference). Thus

$$F = \frac{\Psi_{rs} - \Psi_{leaf}}{R} \qquad (4.12)$$

where F is the quantity of water moving from soil to leaf in unit time.

Ψ_{leaf} is the water potential of the *transpiring leaf*, as measured by one of the standard techniques (psychrometry or pressure bomb). Strictly, the matric potential at the site of evaporation in the leaf apoplast ($\psi_{m\ apo}$) should be used here, but it is impossible to measure this value. (Ψ_{leaf} will be equal to $\psi_{m\ apo}$ if the leaf cells and cell walls are in equilibrium; if they are not, for example at high transpiration rates, then Ψ_{leaf} will be intermediate between $\psi_{m\ apo}$ and $\Psi_{leaf\ cell}$):

Ψ_{rs} is the water potential of the soil at the root surface; and
R is the resistance to hydraulic flow between the root surface and the site of evaporation.

For a simple plant (e.g. a seedling), it is possible to divide this resistance, R, into a series of component resistances within the plant:

$$R = r_{root} + r_{stem} + r_{leaf} \qquad (4.13)$$

where r_{root} is the resistance to flow between the root surface and the lumen of the xylem; r_{stem} is the resistance to flow in the xylem (root, stem and leaf); and r_{leaf} is the resistance to flow across the leaf to the site of evaporation.

In the few cases where all three have been measured for the same plant under the same conditions, it has been found that the largest resistance resides in the root. This is consistent with the theory that the pathway of water movement crosses membranes only in the root. For example, Jensen *et al.* (1961) found the following ratios:

$$r_{root} : r_{stem} : r_{leaf} = 1 : 0 \cdot 42 : 0 \cdot 42 \text{ (sunflower)}$$
$$1 : 0 \cdot 42 : 0 \cdot 21 \text{ (tomato)}$$

Thus, in these species, no single component of the plant resistance exercises overall control over water flow; the root resistance is the largest but it accounts for no more than 54–61% of the total hydraulic resistance. More recent work has suggested that, in some species, either the root or the leaf resistance may control the rate of water flow.

If the rate of water uptake from the soil is equal to the transpiration rate, then steady-state flow has been established and it is possible to extend equation 4.12 to describe water movement in the soil/plant/atmosphere system as a flow through a catena of resistances:

$$F = \frac{\Psi_{soil} - \Psi_{rs}}{R_{soil}} = \frac{\Psi_{rs} - \Psi_{leaf}}{R_{plant}} = \frac{\Psi_{leaf} - \Psi_{air}}{R_{leaf}} \qquad (4.14)$$

where Ψ_{soil} is the water potential of the bulk soil; R_{soil} is the resistance of the soil to water movement towards the root (the reciprocal of the soil hydraulic conductivity); Ψ_{air} is the water potential of the bulk air; and R_{leaf} is the leaf diffusive resistance.

When a plant is transpiring rapidly $(\Psi_{soil} - \Psi_{rs})$ and $(\Psi_{rs} - \Psi_{leaf})$ cannot exceed values of 10–30 bar whereas $(\Psi_{leaf} - \Psi_{air})$ varies between 100 and 2000 bar (Milthorpe and Moorby, 1974). Therefore, according to equation 4.14, leaf diffusive resistance is by far the largest resistance in the catena, and *as long as steady state flow is maintained, R_{leaf} controls the rate of water flow throughout the soil/plant/atmosphere system* as well as transpiration rate.

Great care must be exercised in applying this model to the behaviour of plants in the field. Most plants do not consist of a single root, stem and leaf in series; they should rather be considered as a number of root axes, branches and leaves attached in parallel to a single (or multiple) stem. Thus, for example, the resistance of a complete root system can be evaluated by the expression

$$\frac{1}{r_{root}} = \frac{1}{r_{x1}} + \frac{1}{r_{x2}} + \frac{1}{r_{x3}} + \ldots \qquad (4.15)$$

where r_{x1}, r_{x2} etc. are the resistances of individual root axes. Similar calculations can be performed for branches and leaves.

Another difficulty with the Ohm's Law analogy is that water can be withdrawn into, or released from, storage at different points along the pathway, thus altering the flow rate. For example, we have already seen that, although leaf cells do not fall on the direct route of water movement from soil to air, they supply water to the leaf apoplast at the beginning of rapid transpiration (see p. 138). In a similar way, the cells bordering the xylem in the stem and root system may lose water during periods of water stress during the day and absorb water during the night. The extent of this exchange can be assessed by measuring diurnal fluctuations in leaf thickness, stem diameter and root diameter (Kozlowski, 1972). This problem can be overcome by extending the electrical analogy to include capacitance, as well as resistance, in the soil, stem and leaves; the exchange of water with storage is then likened to the charging and discharge of electrons stored on the plates of a condensor. The complex array of resistances and capacitances required to describe a plant with only four leaves is shown in Fig. 4.6.

However, the most serious defect in the catenary model is the fact that steady-state water flow is a rare occurrence because most environmental variables (light intensity, temperature, humidity, wind

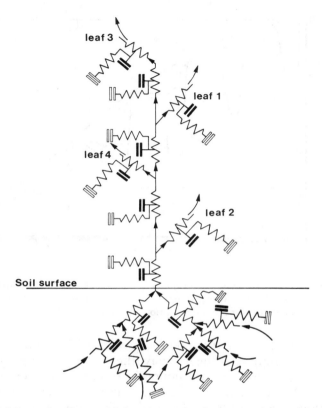

Fig. 4.6.   Schematic diagram of the system of resistances and capacitances required in the description of water movement through a simple plant with four leaves and a branched root system. The filled capacitor symbols represent the capacitance of the "main path" of water movement and the unfilled capacitor symbols, that of the "secondary path". For example, the "main path" capacitance in a leaf is the water stored in the cell walls, whereas the "secondary path" capacitance is the water within the mesophyll cells. Water flow between these two capacitances is controlled by the resistance of the cell plasmalemma, cytoplasm and tonoplast (from Meidner and Sheriff, 1976).

etc.) are continually changing, both in a regular diurnal pattern and in an irregular fashion from one minute to the next. Both leaf diffusive resistance and transpiration rate vary continually in response to these changes and, therefore, equation 4.14 does not generally hold. Under such conditions plant and soil resistances fulfil more important roles in the movement of water through the soil/plant/atmosphere system.

   The importance of plant and soil resistances may be illustrated by Fig. 4.7 which shows changes in leaf, root (surface) and soil water

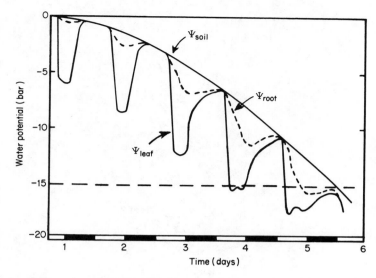

Fig. 4.7. Schematic representation of the changes in leaf, root surface and bulk soil water potentials associated with the exhaustion of the available water in a soil by a transpiring plant. See text for a full description (from Slatyer, 1967).

potential during a six day period of soil water depletion by an "ideal" plant. At the beginning of the first day, the stomata open progressively wider over a period of several hours, in response to external stimuli (light, etc.) or endogenous rhythms, causing a progressive rise in transpiration rate. Because of the hydraulic resistances in the plant and the soil, water will begin to move from the soil to the leaf only after a gradient in water potential has been established (see p. 138). Since the soil is at field capacity ($\Psi_{soil}=0$), an adequate flow of water can be maintained without lowering leaf water potential below −6 bar. This would cause only mild water stress in the leaves for a few hours. The low resistance of the wet soil means that water flows to the root in response to a very small difference in water potential (< 1 bar).

In the evening, transpiration rate diminishes with stomatal closure and the upward movement of water to the leaf begins to exceed the rate of loss. Consequently, the leaf apoplast and cells are rehydrated and the differences in water potential between soil, root and leaf are abolished overnight. However, due to the lowering of soil matric potential by uptake during day 1, the leaves begin transpiration on the second day at a water potential of about −1 bar.

Plant/water relations on the second day are essentially similar to those of the first except that it is now necessary to lower leaf water potential to about −9 bar to maintain the necessary gradient to ensure upward water movement. In addition, the soil hydraulic resistance is beginning to rise with soil drying and a water potential difference of 1 to 2 bar is now required to maintain water flow towards the root.

At the beginning of the third day, the equilibrium water potential in the soil, root and leaf has fallen to −4 bar and it becomes necessary during the course of the day to lower leaf water potential to about −12 bar. The progressive increase in soil resistance with drying has two effects: first, the potential difference between the root and soil has increased to about 3 bar but, more important, the slow movement of water through the soil is now delaying the rate of overnight equilibration of water potential. Consequently, the leaves experience mild to moderate water stress during most of the day. These developments become more serious on day 4 when leaf water potential falls to below −15 bar and the stomata close due to water stress. Finally, by the end of day 5 when soil water potential has fallen to −15 bar (PWP), there is no available water left, the plant wilts and eventually dies if the soil is not rewatered.

Figure 4.7 gives an idealized account of the responses of a plant to soil drying, stressing the importance of plant and soil resistances in determining leaf water potential and water stress. However, by indicating that stomata respond in a consistent daily pattern, broken only by severe water stress, it underestimates the complex role that stomata play in the water economy of plants (pp. 134–138). In particular, it is likely that the stomata would close for a few hours around midday on days 2 and 3, in response to high temperature and low air humidity. This "midday closure", which is a common feature of species growing in dry areas, reduces water loss from the leaf and permits partial recovery from water stress before the stomata open in the afternoon.

III. ADAPTATIONS TO ENSURE SUCCESSFUL GERMINATION AND SEEDLING ESTABLISHMENT

Where an environmental factor (such as temperature or water supply) is favourable for plant growth during a limited part of each year, it is important for a plant species to use the maximum period of favourability for vegetative and reproductive growth. Because of this, seeds or other propagules are often shed at the end of the growing season when conditions may still be favourable for germination but will rapidly become very unfavourable for the subsequent growth of seedlings (which tend to be highly susceptible to environmental stresses). In response to this risk of seedling death, which is a particularly serious threat to the survival of annual plants, many species have adapted to produce seeds which are dormant when shed and do not germinate until the beginning of the next prolonged period of favourable conditions. (As we shall see in Chapter 5, such adaptations ensure that the seeds of temperate species, when they are shed in autumn, do not normally germinate until the onset of growing weather in spring.)

For example, in tropical savanna regions, water is available for rapid growth and development from the beginning of the wet season up to 20–30 days after the main rains have ceased (e.g. Fig. 4.3). Thereafter water becomes increasingly unavailable as the soil profile dries. Seeds dispersed over the dry soil surface at the end of this period of favourable water supply may experience good conditions for germination during isolated periods of rain (e.g. in April 1972, Fig. 4.3) but seedlings resulting from the germination of non-dormant seeds would soon die due to drought. Similarly, in deserts, where rainfall is less predictable, it is essential that seeds of ephemeral species do not germinate until the soil contains enough water to enable the resulting plants to complete their life-cycles.

Species which overcome these risks by producing dormant propagules face the further problem of how the seeds are to recognize the onset of conditions permitting seedling establishment. Some species, especially the legumes, avoid this problem by releasing "soft", non-dormant seeds and "hard" seeds whose coats are impermeable to water (Villiers, 1972). In a given generation of seeds, the non-dormant seeds will germinate whenever rainfall permits, whether subsequent conditions are favourable for seedling establishment or not. The production of the dormant seeds can also be considered to be a "random strategy", well adapted to areas of irregular rainfall, because the breakdown of the impermeable seed coat, presumably by soil microorganisms, may take from a few months up to several years; consequently seeds from a single generation become ready for germination over a long period and it is likely that at least a few will germinate and establish successfully (Koller and Negbi, 1966). Another method of avoiding seedling loss, without the need to recognize favourable conditions, is employed by some tropical grasses whose seeds are dormant only during a period of after-ripening (e.g. Longman, 1969). In areas of seasonal rainfall (e.g. Fig. 4.3), such seeds normally lose their dormancy in the second half of the dry season, after the risk of late rain has passed, and are therefore ready to germinate at the beginning of the next wet season.

A much more precise control of germination is required in those arid regions where both the amount and distribution of precipitation are highly unpredictable. For example, the amount of water-soluble germination inhibitor in the seeds of several desert annuals appears to be correlated with the volume of water required for the completion of the life cycle (Koller, 1972). As a result of rainfall, dormant seeds become imbibed with water and inhibitor molecules begin to dissolve and diffuse out of the seed into the soil. If the rainfall is prolonged, the concentration of inhibitor outside the seed remains at a low level, due to vertical drainage of soil water, and therefore the inhibitor continues to diffuse outwards into the soil. After a critical quantity of rain has fallen, the inhibitor concentration in the seed falls below a threshold value and germination begins. However, if there is a break in the rainfall before the critical amount has been received, the inhibitor will be resynthesized and the process of leaching must begin anew. Thus the inhibitor appears to "measure" the amount of soil water present and does not permit germination to proceed until enough water is present for successful growth and reproduction.

An alternative mechanism is adopted by *Hildegardia* spp. in dry areas of West Africa (Longman, 1969). Once the seed coat of these trees has dried, it becomes impermeable to water and this change can be reversed only by prolonged wetting as would occur at the beginning of the rainy season.

In some species, the existence of an adequate water supply is not in itself a sufficient condition for germination and another environmental factor must also be favourable. Thus, for example, annual grasses predominate after summer rain in certain arid regions of Australia whereas annual dicotyledons are much more abundant after winter rain, although seeds of both groups are present in the topsoil throughout the year (Mott, 1972); laboratory work has shown that this difference is due to differences in temperature between the two seasons. Similarly, the seeds of some desert plants require a specific light regime, in addition to an abundant water supply, before they can germinate (Koller and Negbi, 1966).

With a few notable exceptions such as the groundnut (*Arachis hypogea* L.), the seeds or fruits of most terrestrial species are scattered over the soil surface, with the result that germination normally takes place within the surface layers of soil. These layers are subject to frequent and rapid cycles of wetting and drying, even in humid climates, and it is therefore important for seeds to lodge in "safe sites" where soil moisture remains adequate throughout germination and seedling establishment. This is particularly important in those species which colonize disturbed areas (burned or cultivated), where bare soil is not protected from desiccation by vegetation. Many of these species have adopted seed characteristics favouring germination in "safe sites".

In particular, many temperate weeds produce very small seeds which are able to lodge in cracks in the soil surface where better contact can be made with soil moisture, and evaporative loss from the seed surface is reduced by an undisturbed, humid boundary layer (Harper *et al.*, 1965). In a number of other species from several families (e.g. Gramineae, Geraniaceae, Ranunculaceae, etc.), each dispersal unit is equipped with a hygroscopic awn (Fig. 4.8) whose twisting movements

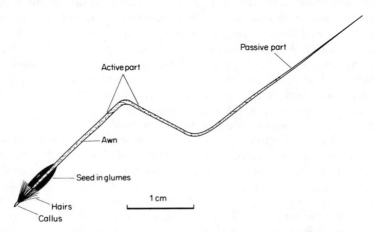

FIG. 4.8.   The dispersal unit of *Themeda triandra*, a perennial grass species native to savanna regions in sub-tropical Africa, Arabia and India. The "active part" of the awn twists and untwists in response to changes in humidity, thereby driving the seed into the soil surface (from Lock and Milburn, 1971).

drive the seed into the soil during periods of alternating low and high humidity (Darwin, 1876; Koller, 1972). Thus in *Avena fatua*, a common weed of temperate cereal crops, the awn first acts as a flight, enabling the seed to lodge upright in the soil, and then screws the seed into the soil where the water supply is less variable and evaporation is reduced (Thurston, 1960). In the tropics, this mechanism may have the additional role of placing seeds at a depth where they can not be damaged by grassland fires (Lock and Milburn, 1971).

In a study of several composites, Sheldon (1974) found that the pappus ("parachute") attached to the fruit not only aids the wind dispersal of the fruit but also ensures that it lands, in soil cracks and crevices, with the attachment scar downwards. Consequently good contact is made between soil moisture and the micropile which is adjacent to the scar and through which water enters the fruit. In other species, contact between seed and soil water is promoted by the secretion of mucilage (van der Pijl, 1969) and by smooth seed coats (Harper and Benton, 1966).

There are, therefore, a number of known modifications of seed morphology favouring the uptake of water from the surface layers of soil. However, physiological adaptations are not so well documented, although Mott (1974) has shown that the seeds of certain grasses and composites from arid parts of West Australia can undergo at least two cycles of imbibition and dehydration without loss of viability.

The ability of seeds to extract water at different soil matric potentials has been investigated by a number of authors but their results are difficult to interpret. For example, it is known that the rate of germination in several species is significantly reduced if soil is dried from saturation or field capacity to a matric potential of -1 bar (e.g. Harper and Benton, 1966) and that the germination of different crop seeds ceases at soil matric potentials ($\leq -12\cdot5$ bar, Table 4.2) which are rather modest when compared with the matric potential of dry

TABLE 4.2.   Minimum soil water potentials at which the seeds of selected agricultural crops can germinate (from Hunter and Erickson, 1952).

Species	Minimum water potential (bar)[a] at 25°C
Sugar beet	$-3\cdot5$
Soybean	$-6\cdot6$
Rice	$-7\cdot9$
Maize	$-12\cdot5$

[a] Similar values for each species were obtained from five different soils including one silt loam, two clay loam and two clay soils.

seeds (about -500 bar, Hillel, 1972). At such values of soil matric potential there is still an enormous difference in water potential, between seed and soil, which would be expected to drive water into the seed.

This anomaly may be explained by the work of Owen (1952) who found that wheat seeds could absorb water and germinate in a gaseous environment corresponding to a water potential at least as low as -32 bar (note that below this value of matric potential there is little capillary water left in most soils; Fig. 4.4). This value is much lower than those in Table 4.2 for two reasons. First, Owen's wheat seeds had access to an unlimited quantity of water whereas, in soil, the moisture content falls rapidly with matric potential. Secondly, the resistance to the flow of water through the boundary layer round each seed in Owen's experiment would have been lower than the resistance offered to the movement of water through a drying soil (see p. 132). Overall, it is likely that the rate of movement of water into seeds in the soil is governed by the resistance to hydraulic flow and by the amount of water available in the soil; it is, therefore, surprising to find that pronounced differences in the ability to extract water do exist amongst cultivated species (Table 4.2) and presumably, amongst natural species. These differences may be, in part, due to the increased mechanical resistance to root and shoot expansion offered by drying soils (Russell, 1977).

IV. ADAPTATIONS TO ENSURE SURVIVAL AND REPRODUCTION UNDER CONDITIONS OF WATER SHORTAGE

In order to develop and reproduce successfully in all but the most humid climates, plants must be able to survive periods of water stress varying in length from hours to months (see p. 128). For example, xerophytic species, from the driest climatic zones, may experience many months without rainfall but with very high levels of solar radiation; they can normally be distinguished by their unusual morphology— succulence, sclerophylly or leaflessness, etc. Mesophytes, the typical plants of more humid areas, do not exhibit such extremes of morphology, but they may also have to endure prolonged periods (hours, days) of water stress during drought, and in dry habitats such as shallow soils over rock and sand dunes. Note, however, that the terms xerophyte and mesophyte are not precisely defined and that, for example, there is no sharp discontinuity between mesophytic and xerophytic vegetation as we move from rainforest through savanna grassland to desert. In addition, xerophytic characteristics turn up in some unexpected habitats, e.g. in bog species (see Chapter 7).

The tactics adopted by xerophytes and mesophytes to ensure survival under conditions of water shortage can be grouped into three classes:

(i) Adaptations leading to the acquisition of the maximum amount of water (principally the *amelioration* of water stress).

(ii) Adaptations to ensure the conservation and efficient use of acquired water (involving the *amelioration* and *tolerance* of water stress, but also *avoidance* in those species which restrict their activities to periods of water availability).

(iii) Adaptations (mainly biochemical and ultrastructural) protecting cells and tissues from damage and death during severe desiccation (*tolerance* of water stress). See Chapter 1 for a full discussion of the terms avoidance, amelioration, and tolerance.

Although it is convenient to discuss classes (i), (ii) and (iii) separately in the following three sections, it must be stressed that many xerophytes exhibit all three types of adaptation.

A. Acquisition of Water

In humid areas, plants do not require deep and widely spreading root systems for water uptake because soil water is plentiful and all the moisture required for transpiration can be supplied by a relatively small volume of soil. Consequently, root:shoot ratios are low; for example, it is estimated that roots account for only 21–25% of the total phytomass in coniferous forests (Lange *et al.*, 1976). In drier, tropical savanna woodland, the proportion rises to 30–40% whereas in desert species the root systems, which grow to great depths, may represent as much as 90% of the phytomass.

These measurements are valuable in stressing the variation between climatic zones in the overall amounts of photosynthate invested in roots. However, since a variable fraction of root systems is active in water absorption (Kramer, 1969), root:shoot ratios are not particularly useful in detailed comparisons of the water relations of different species at the same site. The ratio

$$\frac{\text{length (or surface area) of absorbing roots}}{\text{area of transpiring leaf}}$$

would be much more useful but it is not practicable at present to discriminate between absorbing and non-absorbing roots in the field.

In contrast, there exists a wealth of qualitative and semi-quantitative information on the distribution of plant roots in soil profiles, in relation to soil water availability. For example, much of the rain falling in deserts accumulates in depressions before draining into the soil to a depth of several metres (Walter, 1963). Annual or ephemeral species are able to flourish briefly in such moist depressions using short, poorly developed root systems, whereas the perennial species growing at low density have extremely deep, unbranched root systems tapping the groundwater. Walter (1963) quotes rooting depths of perennial species near Cairo varying between 1·2 m (*Fagonia arabica*) and 5·0 m (*Pitu-*

ranthus tortuosus); other authors give much more extreme depths such as 18 m for *Welwitschia mirabilis* in South African deserts (cited by Kozlowski, 1964) and 30 m for a species of *Acacia* near the Suez Canal (cited by Parker, 1968). The ability of such deep roots to conduct water to the shoot at a reasonable rate must depend upon the diameter of their xylem vessels (Passioura, 1972).

In the North American prairies, where precipitation is higher, more seasonal and more readily accepted by the soil, the root systems of native grassland species tend to be deep but with profuse branching in the top 0·8–1·0 m of soil. For example, the maximum rooting depth of the dominant species *Agropyron smithii* varies from 1·5 to 3·6 m in the USA, and from 0·6 to 1·5 m in the moister Saskatchewan prairies (various authors, reviewed by Coupland and Johnson, 1965). This pattern of root growth, which is also common in tropical savanna grasslands (Taerum, 1970), encourages rapid and efficient absorption of moisture (and nutrients) in the top 1 m of soil during wet periods, as well as the extraction of water from deeper horizons during drought. Genera such as *Agropyron* maintain their dominance by absorbing water from horizons below the maximum rooting depth of competing grasses; in contrast, some shrubs and herbs adopt a morphology similar to that of desert species with long unbranched tap roots absorbing groundwater below the grass roots (e.g. at 1–3 m in Saskatchewan).

Another important feature of prairie species is the morphological plasticity of their root systems in response to differences in soil conditions. Figure 4.9 illustrates variations in the spread and maximum depth of the roots of *Agropyron smithii* associated mainly with changes in soil moisture status. However, such results should be treated with caution since they may also reflect differences in above-ground growth. A much more remarkable example of root system plasticity is provided by the herb *Artemisia frigida* which develops a deep tap root if the surface layers of soil are dry; in contrast, under more moist conditions, the tap root disappears, to be replaced by a mass of fibrous roots in the top metre of soil (Coupland and Johnson, 1965; Weaver, 1958; and cf. Chapter 1, p. 20).

Deep rooting is clearly an important feature of established perennial plants in desert, prairie and savanna regions as well as in other dry environments, such as sand dunes (Salisbury, 1952), where groundwater is a major source of moisture. However, as pointed out by Parker (1968), it is difficult to understand how such species can become established. In some cases, this may be achieved by vegetative reproduction, producing rhizomes which can depend upon the parent root system until their own roots have developed fully. Alternatively, these

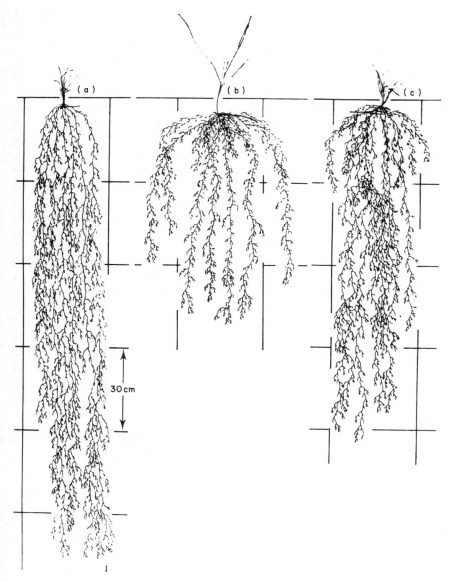

Fig. 4.9. Root systems of *Agropyron smithii* growing in the Saskatchewan Great Plains. Within the dark brown soil zone, rooting tends to be deeper on more xeric, south-facing slopes (a) than on level sites (b); rooting is also deeper in the drier climate of the brown soil zone (c) (from Coupland and Johnson, 1965).

plants may release very large quantities of seed, a very few of which will germinate under appropriate soil moisture conditions. Even with such an adaptation, it is essential that the first roots produced after germination extend rapidly in order to make contact with groundwater while the surface layers remain moist. This explains the very high rates of root growth which may be encountered in dry regions; for example, Parker (1968) reported that seedlings of *Quercus macrocarpa*, from the prairie/forest transition zone, can produce a tap root 0·9–1·5 m long during their first season. Rapid root elongation at the start of the growing season can also give a competitive advantage to annual plants. In particular, since the seminal roots of *Bromus tectorum* and *Taeniatherum asperum* can grow at lower temperatures than the roots of competing species in the western rangelands of the USA, these grasses absorb a large proportion of the limited supply of available water in early spring by sending new roots into successive horizons ahead of their competitors (Harris and Wilson, 1970).

Under conditions of low or irregular rainfall, the leaf structure of certain plant species has evolved to favour the absorption of dew or rain directly into the shoot. Thus *Chaetacme aristata* from Natal deserts has specialized cells in the leaf epidermis for the absorption of liquid water adhering to the leaf surface (Meidner, 1954). However, it should be stressed that the collection of liquid water by leaves is not restricted to plants from arid regions; for example, the blade and sheath structure of the Gramineae, both temperate and tropical, leads to the accumulation of water in the leaf sheath (e.g. Glover and Gwynne, 1962). Although there is considerable debate over the contribution of dew to the water economy and distribution of xerophytes (e.g. Stone, 1957a), it does appear to prolong survival in certain cases, probably due to the suppression of transpiration (Stone, 1957b; Slatyer, 1967).

In addition to these morphological adaptations, plant species also vary in the ability of their roots to extract water from soils. Most agricultural crops are able to dry soils down to a matric potential between − 10 and − 20 bar, and this has led to the widespread use of the moisture content at − 15 bar as the standard measure of permanent wilting point (see p. 131). However, by increased water loss from the leaf and/or by accumulation of solutes in the leaf and in the root xylem vessels (Hsiao *et al.*, 1976; Osonubi and Davies, 1978), some species growing in drier climates can absorb more water from the soil, giving permanent wilting point values corresponding to − 20 to − 30 bar (Larcher, 1975). Attempts to increase water supply in this way can be successful only as long as the necessary depression in leaf water potential is not in itself damaging to the leaf tissue; its effectiveness, therefore, depends upon the relationship between leaf water potential and water content (see below).

There is no advantage, in water absorption, to be gained from lowering plant water potentials much below -30 bar because there is very little capillary water left in a soil at a matric potential of -30 bar. Where very low leaf water potentials do occur (e.g. down to -163 bar in the xerophyte *Artemisia herba-alba*, Richter, 1976) they are the consequence of severe desiccation and, frequently, of salinity and are not an adaptation for the absorption of more water from the soil. In contrast, certain herbs can absorb much less soil moisture, having permanent wilting points corresponding to soil matric potentials above -10 bar (Larcher, 1975).

B. Conservation and Use of Water

As we have noted earlier, the assimilation of carbon dioxide is inevitably associated with loss of water to the atmosphere through open stomata. However, this is not a simple exchange of one CO_2 molecule for one molecule of water; since the diffusion pathway for water is shorter and the concentration gradient driving water out of the leaf is steeper than that driving CO_2 inwards, the amount of water transpired is greatly in excess of the amount of CO_2 fixed. For example, Raschke (1976) has estimated, for an idealized leaf, that at least 20 water molecules are lost for each molecule of CO_2 taken up (20°C, 70% R.H.) rising to 430 at 50°C and 10% R.H. Losses from real leaves will be many times higher.

Since photosynthesis is essential for growth and reproduction, xerophytes and many mesophytes must possess adaptations minimizing transpiration during photosynthesis, even though this may result in slow growth rates. Thus if the water use efficiencies (expressed as g of water transpired/g dry matter produced) of several species are compared (Table 4.3) it is clear that there is some degree of correlation between water loss during photosynthesis and the water supply in the natural range of the species. For example, C4 species, which originated mainly in the drier tropics, are much more efficient in using water than are the predominantly temperate C3 species; as a particular example, the choice of millet rather than maize as the staple crop for the drier areas in Africa is explained by its more economic water use. These large variations in efficiency do not result from a single adaptation but from a variety of (commonly interrelated) anatomical, morphological and biochemical adaptations. A number of these adaptations for conservation and use of water are examined in the remainder of this section

TABLE 4.3. The water use efficiency of selected plant species expressed as g of water transpired g^{-1} of dry matter produced (data compiled by Larcher, 1975).

Herbaceous plants		Trees	
C4 plants		Deciduous trees	
Maize	370	Oak	340
Millet	300	Birch	320
Amaranthus	300	Beech	170
Portulaca	280		
C3 plants		Conifers	
Rice	680	Pine	300
Rye	630	Larch	260
Oats	580	Spruce	230
Wheat	540	Douglas Fir	170
Barley	520		
Alfalfa	840		
Bean	700		
Crimson clover	640		
Potato	640		
Sunflower	600		
Watermelon	580		
Cotton	570		

Many species from drier habitats develop deep and extensive root systems giving high values of the ratio:

$$\frac{\text{length of absorbing root}}{\text{area of transpiring leaf}}$$

The alternative approach—the reduction of leaf area—is also widely adopted. In particular it is common for such species to have smaller, thicker and more dissected leaves than those of mesophytes, resulting in a higher ratio of photosynthetic mesophyll to transpiring leaf area. This ratio is expressed most clearly by the specific leaf area (dm^2 of leaf area g^{-1} of leaf dry weight—see Chapter 2); thus as we pass from the extremely arid Sahel zone to the humid regions of Central Europe, the mean specific leaf area of trees and shrubs rises from 0·36 (Sahel) through 0·70 (N. Sahara) to 1·10 for Central Europe, which is very similar to the value of 1·03 measured in the Ivory Coast rainforests (Stocker, 1976). Similarly Larcher (1975) tabulates values greater than 1·5 for some species growing in mesic conditions (*Fagus sylvatica*, 1·4–1·6; *Oxalis acetosella*, 1·8; *Impatiens noli-tangere*, 2·2) but much lower values for xerophytes (*Sedum maximum*, 0·12, *Opuntia camanchica*, 0·026). However, these values must be treated with caution since they are, in part, a response to light conditions (Chapter 2) and in xerophytes, a result of extreme succulence which is discussed later.

Although reduced specific leaf area and increased leaf dissection give reductions in transpiring leaf area, they are also associated with a thinning of the leaf boundary layer (Lewis, 1972) and commonly with a higher density of stomata. Consequently, both the stomatal and boundary layer components of the leaf diffusive resistance will tend to be reduced rather than increased, giving a potential *increase* rather than a reduction in water loss by transpiration. This effect may be slightly counteracted by increased mesophyll resistance (normally negligible but more important in thick leaves); however, it appears that changes in specific leaf area and dissection are more important in the thermal economy of the leaf than the water economy.

Lewis's (1972) work on *Geranium sanguineum* from a variety of European habitats is an unusually well-documented account of the effects of leaf characteristics on the temperature and water relations of leaves. As we move from wetter woodland sites to the more xeric steppe and limestone (Alvar) sites, the leaves of this species become smaller, thicker and more dissected. In parallel with these changes, the stomatal frequency rises and the leaf boundary layer becomes thinner, giving large, but not statistically significant, reductions in leaf diffusive resistance when the stomata are open (Table 4.4).

This variation in leaf morphology does not, therefore, appear to be an adaptation to reduce water loss at dry sites. However, since the lowering of the boundary layer resistance to the diffusion of water vapour also increases heat flow from the leaf surface, the more xeric leaf form may be an adaptation to give protection against the higher solar radiation levels and temperatures experienced in drier zones. For example, it can be calculated (Lewis, 1972) that the "woodland leaf" will be at a temperature several degrees higher than the "Alvar leaf" over a range of irradiance levels, when the stomata are open. This could reduce the photosynthetic efficiency of the woodland leaf at high irradiance. More important, when the stomata are closed and heat can be lost only by convection, the larger, less-dissected, woodland leaf could be exposed to temperatures above the thermal death-zone of this species (47–50°C), if grown in the open.

Under more arid conditions, woody perennial plants tend to bear leaves only when the supply of water is adequate for transpiration; at

TABLE 4.4. Differences in leaf anatomy and diffusive resistances to water vapour movement, between eight populations of *Geranium sanguineum* from contrasting European habitats. Components of the leaf diffusive resistance (R) are indicated by r_a (boundary layer at 0·15 m s^{-1}), r_c (cuticle) and r_s (stomata) (from Lewis, 1972).

Habitat type	Leaf anatomy		Diffusive resistances (s cm^{-1})				
	Thickness (μm)	Stomatal frequency[a] (per mm²)	r_a	r_c	r_s	R open stomata	R closed stomata
Alvar 1[b]	313	281	0·19	12	0·8	1·1	12·7
Alvar 2	305	277	0·21	14	1·0	1·2	14·4
Steppe	276	308	0·19	58	1·4	1·7	58·0
Woodsteppe 1	240	275	0·29	23	3·4	3·5	23·8
Woodsteppe 2	264	235	0·32	31	1·3	1·8	31·0
Coastal	240	318	0·37	10	3·3	3·9	10·1
Woodland 1	230	179	0·48	16	2·5	2·9	16·0
Woodland 2	243	195	0·42	12	3·5	3·7	12·7
Probability[c]	†	*	‡	‡	‡	n.s.	n.s.

[a] Compare with the range of stomatal frequencies for mesophytes in Table 4.1.
[b] Alvar is a dry limestone pavement site in E. Sweden.
[c] Probability of significant difference between habitat types estimated by analysis of variance (* = 5%, † = 1%, ‡ = 0·1%, n.s. = differences not statistically significant).

the onset of prolonged drought, water loss is reduced dramatically by leaf abscission. This is a widespread adaptation, observed in deserts, the Mediterranean region, Central Asia and also in the eastern United States where drought can cause premature, and damaging, autumn defoliation (Parker, 1968). In tropical savanna regions, trees and shrubs tend to show a regular seasonal pattern of abscission, shedding leaves soon after the beginning of the dry season (e.g. Fig. 4.3) but reforming the canopy several weeks before the main rains begin. Since differences in daylength are small in these regions, it is thought that these woody species leaf out in response to increasing temperature and are therefore able to make full use of the entire wet season for growth and reproduction. However, seasonal dimorphism (large leaves during the wetter winter period replaced by smaller leaves in the dry summer months), which is a feature of dominant shrubs in plant communities of the Middle East (Orshan, 1963), would seem to be a more effective adaptation, since photosynthesis can continue throughout the year. Alternatively a photosynthetic rachis can be retained, as in *Parkinsonia aculeata*.

Without doubt, stomatal closure is the most important factor in the protection of mesophytes against severe water stress. In particular, it is possible to consider the rapid responses of stomata to changes in the humidity of the air to be a "first line of defence", protecting the leaf from rapid transpiration and tissue desiccation, even before low leaf water potentials have developed (Mansfield and Davies, 1981). However, not all species respond to humidity in this way and it has not been possible to relate such stomatal behaviour to the dryness of the habitat (Sheriff, 1977b).

Where necessary, the "second line of defence", i.e. the closing of stomata in response to lowered leaf water potential, can come into play. According to a number of workers, stomata remain fully open until a threshold value of leaf water potential is reached; at this value the aperture begins to narrow and closure is normally complete (causing the cessation of photosynthesis) within 5 bar of the threshold (Hsiao, 1973). Considerable variation in this threshold potential exists both amongst species and treatments; for example cotton in the greenhouse has given values of -14 to -16 bar compared with at least -27 bar in the field (Jordan and Ritchie, 1971). However, Hsiao et al. (1976) were able to give generalized values of -5 to -10 bar for mesophytes (Fig. 4.2) and -10 to -20 bar (and lower) for xerophytes. Thus mesophytes use stomata to conserve water and avoid moderate to severe water stress (see p. 125); in addition, since partial closure has a greater influence on water loss than CO_2 uptake (Raschke, 1976), the water use efficiency of mesophytes is improved at leaf water potentials just below the threshold.

Paradoxically, it seems that xerophytes, growing under conditions of water shortage, are less well adapted to conserve water by stomatal closure. However, part of this apparent paradox stems from the use of water potential values as indices of water stress, because there is no unique relationship between leaf water potential and leaf water content. For example, Bannister (1971, 1976) found that the threshold leaf water potential values in *Erica cinerea* (from dry heathland) and *Calluna vulgaris* (from wetter areas) were very similar (-18 to -20 bar) but that at this water potential, the leaves of the two species had very different relative water contents (88% for *Erica*, 75% for *Calluna*). Thus in *Erica*, as in many other species from dry and xeric sites, rapid lowering of leaf water potential is associated with modest losses of water from the leaf tissue.

In a photosynthesizing leaf, carbon dioxide molecules must traverse the leaf boundary layer and the stomatal pore before diffusing through the cell walls and plasmalemma membranes of mesophyll cells to the site of fixation. In contrast there is no mesophyll component in the pathway of water vapour loss by transpiration. Consequently, the diffusive resistance presented to CO_2 molecules by a leaf is greater than that offered to H_2O molecules and any change in the resistance of the common part of the pathway (stomata and boundary layer) will have a greater influence upon transpirational loss of water than upon carbon dioxide absorption.

For example, we have already noted that partial closure of stomata, by increasing stomatal resistance, improves the efficiency of water use in photosynthesis. In addition to this universal, but temporary effect, many species exhibit permanent structural adaptations favouring photosynthesis over transpiration by increasing the diffusive resistance of stomata. In particular, stomata may be (a) situated at the bottom of depressions in the epidermis (e.g. *Canna indica*); (b) situated at the bottom of a deeply sunken pore, below an "antechamber" (*Allium cepa*, *Pinus sylvestris*); or (c) surrounded by a "chimney" of cutin (*Euphorbia tirucalli*) (Meidner and Mansfield, 1968). Jeffree *et al.* (1971) have shown that stomatal resistance in conifers is further increased by the occlusion of the antechamber by loosely packed wax plugs. However, it must be stressed that such stomatal adaptations do reduce the diffusion rate of CO_2 and therefore any improvements in water use efficiency are gained at the cost of the rate of production of photosynthate.

Once stomata have closed completely, photosynthesis and stomatal transpiration cease, but water loss continues, at a lower rate, through the cuticle. Consequently, it is important for plants growing on limited water supplies that cuticular transpiration be kept to a minimum. Thus xerophytes have cuticular resistance values of 60–400 s cm^{-1} compared with typical values of 20–60 s cm^{-1} in mesophytes (Cowan and Milthorpe, 1968); without such high resistances, which are achieved by laying down thick layers of cutin, often with additional coatings of wax (Martin and Juniper, 1970), desert species could not survive many months of drought.

Other morphological features which are thought to favour the survival of plants in dry climates include:

Hairs on leaves, especially round stomata, giving increases in the thickness and, therefore, the resistance to water loss of the leaf boundary layer. Pubescence, leading to increased reflectance of light, can also affect photosynthesis in two mutually antagonistic ways. For example, Ehleringer and Mooney (1978) found that leaf hairs on the desert shrub *Encelia farinosa* tended to reduce photosynthesis by reducing the input of photosynthetically active radiation. However at high air temperatures ($>40°C$) the same effect enabled the leaves to remain within the optimum temperature range for photosynthesis (20–30°C— (35°C)) without substantial loss of water in transpirational cooling. The balance between these effects is clearly crucial for plant survival, and it may alter with the seasons. Overall, hairs can fulfil at least two roles in arid climates (water conservation and cooling) and they may also be important in repelling herbivores (Johnson 1975; see p. 283).

Leaf rolling in some grass species, reducing the transpiration of one surface of the leaf (Parker, 1968), and *leaf angle*, which influences the amount of radiation received, and which is continuously adjustable in some species.

The storage of water in *bulbs*, *tubers* or *swollen roots*. For example, many species in tropical savanna regions survive the dry season as leafless buried tubers (e.g. African arrowroot, *Tacca leontopetaloides*).

It has frequently been observed (Lange *et al.*, 1976; Kozlowski, 1964; Parker, 1968) that a large proportion of the successful perennial species in arid and semi-arid regions belong to four classes of plant:

(i) Shallow-rooted succulents fixing carbon dioxide by crassulacean acid metabolism (CAM). (Succulent leaves have very high water contents, predominantly located in large cell vacuoles, and low proportions of cell wall and cytoplasmic materials. Thus succulents have low leaf dry matter contents and small leaf areas due to leaf size and shape.)

(ii) Plants, especially grasses, with a characteristic "Kranz" leaf anatomy (Chapter 2), fixing carbon dioxide by the C4 or Hatch/Slack pathway.

(iii) Sclerophylls, i.e. woody plants with small thick evergreen leaves protected by a thick cuticle and containing a high proportion of cell wall in which water is stored.

(iv) Leafless plants (e.g. brooms) and plants shedding their leaves, but which are able to assimilate CO_2 by photosynthetic stems and thorns.

Many of the remaining perennials are more mesophytic species which avoid dry periods by leaf abscission or as bulbs or tubers.

Classes (i) and (ii) are particularly interesting because they display inter-relationships between leaf organization, physiology and metabolism which lead to conservation of water and maximum photosynthesis under arid conditions. In particular, the stomata of CAM plants are unusual in opening at night (when transpirational demand is low) to admit CO_2 which is fixed by PEP carboxylase and stored in leaf vacuoles as malate and other organic acids. During most of the daylight hours, the stomata remain closed, reducing water loss to cuticular transpiration only. In most plants this would cause the rapid cessation of photosynthesis, but in succulents, prefixed CO_2 is steadily released from malate stores into the leaf air spaces and can be assimilated by the normal C3 or Calvin pathway (Chapter 2; Kluge, 1976).

Under arid conditions, the productivity of succulent plants is very low and CAM is normally considered to be a mechanism for maintaining a positive carbon balance under severe stress (high irradiance, high temperatures, drought, salinity—Kluge, 1976). However, under less extreme conditions, CAM plants can switch to a more conventional metabolism, opening their stomata during the day and assimilating CO_2 by the C3 pathway. Thus CAM plants are particularly well adapted to survive the alternating climate of the semi-arid tropics.

The success of C4 plants is probably as much due to their high temperature optima for growth and photosynthesis (30–45°C as compared with 10–25°C for C3 plants; Huber and Sankhla, 1976) as to their tolerance of water stress. These plants carry out similar reactions to those in CAM plants but here the two fixation processes are separated spatially rather than in time. The preliminary fixation of CO_2 by

PEP carboxylase is carried out in the mesophyll and much of the resulting malate and aspartate passes through plasmodesmata into the thick-walled collenchymatous tissue of the bundle sheaths where CO_2 can be released and refixed by the Calvin cycle. The great advantage of this apparently cumbersome process is that PEP carboxylase has a much higher affinity for CO_2 than RuBP carboxylase (see Chapter 2 for comparison of C3 and C4 plants) and therefore, CO_2 levels in the mesophyll are kept at a very low level. Furthermore, the diffusion pathway for CO_2 is shorter than in C3 plants because PEP carboxylase is a cytoplasmic (rather than a chloroplastic) enzyme. These factors ensure a steep gradient of CO_2 concentration under high irradiance when CO_2 supply is limiting photosynthesis, and at high temperatures, keep CO_2 levels in the sub-stomatal cavity low so that the stomata remain open (see p. 135). Consequently, photosynthesis is favoured at high irradiance and temperature. However, C4 grasses do also show some strictly xerophytic features; for example, young leaves of some C4 grasses can withstand water potentials as low as -1000 bar and recover unaffected when rewatered (Ludlow, 1976). The relative productivities of C3 and C4 grasses are discussed in Chapter 2.

The ability of plants to use water efficiently and avoid the damaging effects of water stress depends upon the stage of development. For example, in many investigations, plants have been found to be most sensitive to water stress at the beginning of the reproductive phase of development but relatively insensitive during vegetative growth (Kaufmann, 1972). Reasons for this phenomenon include the very large leaf areas carried by plants at the end of vegetative development, the diversion of photosynthate from roots to developing fruit at the onset of flowering and, in the Gramineae, the temporary, but severe, disruption of the vascular system of the stem during rapid internode elongation (Hay, 1978). It is difficult to recognize plant adaptations which have evolved to overcome water stress at flowering, but the rapid growth and early maturation of desert ephemerals and some C4 plants in arid climates could be interpreted as adaptations favouring the completion of reproduction before water supplies run out. Passioura (1976) considers that the distinct seminal and nodal root systems of temperate cereals are an adaptation to ensure favourable water relations during ear filling, thus maximizing grain yield.

C. Tolerance of Desiccation

Under very dry conditions, many of the adaptations discussed in the previous two sections serve only to delay the onset of serious dehydration of plant tissues and cells, and therefore the survival of plants may ultimately depend upon the ability of their tissues to tolerate desiccation. This is generally true of the most arid, desert regions but it may also hold in more xeric habitats within humid areas, e.g. shallow rendzina soils during a prolonged summer drought.

The desiccation of plants has been less thoroughly investigated than the acquisition and conservation of water, principally because it is less important agriculturally; in addition, it is intrinsically a most difficult subject for research since it should involve the simultaneous study of whole plant physiology, cell ultrastructure and many biochemical pathways. However, it has been established for a number of species (Parker, 1968) that serious loss of cell water is accompanied by the disruption of all major metabolic pathways (notably carbohydrate and nitrogen metabolism) and the denaturation of macromolecules (proteins, nucleic acids), presumably due to changes in the amounts of water bound to hydrophilic surfaces. In addition, it has been suggested that the shrinking and swelling of cell contents during dehydration and rehydration can cause irreversible mechanical damage to cell membranes and/or plasmodesmata between cells.

Although it is clear that differences in resistance to desiccation damage do exist amongst plant species, it is difficult to quantify such differences because of uncertainties in establishing suitable indices of "stress" (level of cell or tissue dehydration) and the resulting "strain" (changes in cell metabolism and ultrastructure, or cell death) (Parker, 1972). Barrs (1968) indicates that the level of dehydration in a plant may be best expressed by a *combination* of Ψ_{leaf} and W_R of the leaves (see p. 127), whereas Parker (1972) suggests that cell survival should be monitored using tetrazolium dyes. However, detailed studies of both stress and strain are rare and, therefore, it becomes necessary to fall back on minimum recorded leaf water potential values (Ψ_{min}) in order to establish differences in desiccation resistance between groups of species. For example, Table 4.5 shows that species from xeric sites are exposed to, and can survive, much lower values of Ψ_{min} than those from more mesic sites.

As yet, the mechanisms of such resistance are rather obscure but may involve changes in the viscosity of the cytoplasm during drought hardening and the protection of membrane properties by the release of simple sugars, polyhydroxyalcohols and proteins.

One problem that is common to plants exposed to different types of stress (drought, high and low temperature, salinity, etc.) is the need to preserve the three dimensional tertiary structures of enzymes as the

TABLE 4.5.   Minimum recorded water potential values in the leaves of plants from a range of habitats (from Richter, 1976).

	Ψ_{min} (bar)
Desert plants	−18 to −163 (mainly −60 to −100)
Plants from sites with pronounced drought periods	−32 to −70
Woody plants at mesic sites	−15 to −26
Mesophilic herbs	−14 to −43

cytoplasm is desiccated. The formation of disulphide bonds between neighbouring protein molecules appears to be an important step in the destruction of these tertiary structures, and Levitt (1972) has demonstrated that hardening may reduce such condensation reactions by causing reductions in the number and reactivity of protein thiol groups (see Fig. 5.8). However, it seems clear that this is only one facet of the hardening of plants to drought. Overall, younger tissues appear to be more tolerant than more mature, presumably due to the higher ratio of non-vacuolated to vacuolated cells (Parker, 1968, 1972).

The creosote bush, *Larrea tridentata* provides a particularly good example of the importance of desiccation resistance. In spite of being widespread over the deserts of California, Arizona and Mexico (Woodell *et al.*, 1969; Yang, 1967), its moderate leaf size, numerous unprotected stomata and shallow root system are more typical of a mesophyte than a xerophyte (Chew and Chew, 1965). However, as the dry season proceeds, this shrub sheds its mature leaves, twigs and branches, retaining only the smaller, younger leaves which can lose water down to a moisture content of 50% of leaf dry weight without significant damage. (Mabry *et al.* (1977) quote Ψ_{min} values as low as −115 bar in New Mexico, with positive net photosynthesis at leaf water potentials as low as −80 bar.) Full recovery from such dehydration can be complete in a few days after rain.

V. SOME SPECIAL PROBLEMS IN TREE/WATER RELATIONS

Because of their great height and the structure of their leaf canopies, tall trees face unique difficulties in maintaining favourable leaf water relations; as a result, tall forest (e.g. tropical and temperate rainforest; northern deciduous and coniferous forest) is the characteristic vegetation of only the most humid areas of the world.

For example, due to the normal increase in wind velocity with height, tree leaves tend to transpire more rapidly than do the leaves of shorter plants. An even more serious problem is that the "sun" leaves at the top of a tree canopy (up to 100 m above the ground surface) are exposed to greater water and thermal stresses than leaves lower down, or shaded within the canopy. Thus the leaves which require the most water are furthest from the point of supply, the soil. A third feature of tree physiology is that although the leaf area index of forests or plantations tends to be similar to that of agricultural crops (values between 2·5 and 8·5, reviewed by Rutter, 1968), a very large leaf area is supplied by a single trunk rather than a number of small stems; thus the water relations of an enormous number of leaves depend upon the health and normal function of the vascular system of a single trunk.

In addition to such physiological difficulties, there is also the fundamental physical problem that work must be performed to raise water against the force of gravity. In short vegetation this effect can be neglected; however, when considering water potential in tall trees, a gravitational component must be included. Thus (cf. equation 4.3)

$$\Psi = \psi_s + \psi_m + \psi_p + \psi_g \qquad (4.16)$$

where ψ_g, the gravitational potential, falls by 0·1 bar for each metre increase in height. Thus, in the absence of differences in solute, matric or pressure potential between root and leaf, there should exist a permanent gradient in stem water potential of 0·1 bar m^{-1}. This has been confirmed by measuring the water potential in branches from tall trees at dawn, after equilibration with the soil water had presumably been achieved (e.g. Connor et al., 1977). Consequently, it appears that the water potential in leaves at 50 m, for example, can never be higher than -4 bar, a value at which leaf growth is significantly reduced in many plant species (Fig. 4.2) assuming ψ_g to be $+1$ bar at the soil surface (Zimmerman and Brown, 1971).

Trees therefore require:

(i) A vascular system of high capacity which can deliver water rapidly and preferentially to those parts of the canopy which are most active in transpiration. The system must also be highly resistant to environmental stresses, especially frost and pathogenic attack.
(ii) Leaves designed not only to use water efficiently but also to continue growth and assimilation at low water potentials.

A. Vascular System

As in all higher plants, the conduction of water in the trunks and branches of trees takes place in the lumina of dead xylem elements; in trees, of course, the lignified xylem is also important in providing the mechanical strength necessary to support the leaf canopy. The structure of the vascular system differs markedly amongst groups of trees (Esau, 1965). For example, in ring-porous trees (including many north-temperate deciduous species), water moves predominantly in an outer ring of large tracheids (60–400 μm in diameter, Table 4.6) laid down in the current season. Most of the older vessels in these trees are gas-filled. In contrast, the functional xylem in diffuse-porous deciduous trees and in conifers is not restricted to the outer ring of xylem and is composed of finer and shorter elements (Table 4.6) (Zimmermann and Brown, 1971).

Because of the high hydraulic conductivity of wide tracheids, ring-porous trees are able to transport water at much greater velocities (normally between 15 and 45 m h^{-1}—Table 4.6) than diffuse-porous (1–6 m h^{-1}) or coniferous trees (up to 2 m h^{-1}). However, this does not necessarily mean that ring-porous trees can support faster transpiration rates, because the rate of flow of water to the canopy also depends upon the total cross-sectional area of functional xylem. For example, Jordan and Kline (1977) demonstrated that the transpiration rate of tropical rainforest trees and of Douglas Fir is highly correlated with the sap-wood area of the trunk, but independent of species and soil type.

In temperate and boreal regions, tracheid geometry is probably more important in ensuring xylem function in spring after a severe winter. In ring-porous trees, new xylem elements are laid down just before the development of the leaf canopy; during the subsequent growing season, a relatively small number of these wide and long vessels can provide sufficient conduit volume to supply the transpiration of the tree canopy. However, in a severe winter, after leaf-fall, the contents of the xylem may freeze and then melt, leading to the release of many small bubbles of previously dissolved gases; in the long vertical files of wide tracheids in ring-porous trees, these bubbles are able to merge together into large bubbles of air which eventually lodge at the constrictions between xylem elements. Since the continuity of water in these files of tracheids is now broken they can no longer contain water columns under tension and, therefore, they cease to function as water conduits and must be replaced by fresh water-filled xylem (Zimmermann and Brown, 1971).

Although they achieve an efficient functional relationship between

TABLE 4.6. Vessel diameters of selected tree species and the midday peak velocities of water movement which have been observed through such vessels (data measured at breast height, compiled by Zimmermann and Brown, 1971).

Tree species	Vessel diameter (μm)	Velocity (m h^{-1})
Ring-porous		
Quercus robur	200–300	43·6
Robinia pseudacacia	160–400	28·8
Quercus rubra	250	27·7
Fraxinus excelsior	120–350	25·7
Castanea vesca	300–350	24·0
Ailanthus glandulosa	170–250	22·2
Carya alba	180–300	19·2
Rhus glabra	—	16·0
Ulmus effusa	130–340	6·0
Laburnum anagyroides	60–250	3·9
Diffuse porous		
Populus balsamifera	80–120	6·25
Juglans regia	120–160	4·12
Juglans cinerea	—	3·79
Tilia tomentosa	25–90	3·43
Salix viridis	80–120	3·00
Liriodendron tulipifera	50–120	2·62
Acer pseudoplatanus	30–110	2·40
Magnolia acuminata	—	2·06
Alnus glutinosa	20–90	2·00
Betula pendula	30–130	1·60
Carpinus betulus	16–80	1·25
Pyrus communis	50–80	1·11
Fagus sylvatica	16–80	1·07
Aesculus hippocastanum	30–60	0·96
Conifers		
Larix decidua	up to 55	2·1
Pinus strobus	up to 45	1·7
Picea excelsa	up to 45	1·2
Tsuga canadensis	up to 45	1·0

xylem development and leaf production, ring-porous trees are faced with other serious problems. For example, mechanical damage (e.g. the effects of wind) can also cause tracheid embolism and, as the recent spread of Dutch Elm disease has shown, their xylem is peculiarly susceptible to pathogenic organisms (Zimmermann and McDonough, 1978).

In contrast, conifers are much more resistant to environmental stress. In particular, small gas bubbles released in the xylem tend to be trapped within the fine tracheids and therefore only a small proportion of the conducting volume is lost. Similarly, since the functional xylem is not restricted to the periphery of the trunk and since successive tracheids are arranged in a complex, often spiral fashion, the vascular system is less susceptible to mechanical damage and to pathogens (Zimmermann and Brown, 1971; Zimmermann and McDonough, 1978). These features presumably contribute to the wider prevalence of coniferous species in more extreme boreal regions.

Several authors have used the Huber Value $(mm^2 \ g^{-1})$

$$\frac{\text{transverse section xylem area } (mm^2) \text{ of a stem or branch}}{\text{fresh weight of leaves (g) supplied with water by that stem or branch}}$$

to show that the upper branches of a tree have a better water supply than the lower branches. For example, Huber (1928) (discussed in Zimmermann, 1978) obtained values of $0.5 \ mm^2 \ g^{-1}$ in the lower stem and lateral branches, and $4.26 \ mm^2 \ g^{-1}$ in the terminal shoot of *Abies concolor*. Such values have been subject to criticism because the measurement does not discriminate between functional and non-functional xylem. However, by measuring leaf specific conductance rather than the Huber value, Zimmermann (1978) has recently confirmed this phenomenon in three diffuse-porous deciduous tree species; due to constrictions in the xylem of lateral branches, the hydraulic resistance of the pathway supplying water to the "sun" leaves at the top of the canopy is lower than that supplying lower and more shaded leaves.

B. Leaves

Because the resistance to water flow in the stem and branches of a tree is high, considerable gradients in stem water potential (of the order of $0.1 \ bar \ m^{-1}$ irrespective of xylem type) must be set up to ensure a supply of water to the canopy sufficient for maximum transpiration rates (Zimmermann and Brown, 1971). Consequently the total gradient (including the gravity component) will be up to $0.2 \ bar \ m^{-1}$

giving leaf water potentials of −9 bar at 50 m. It is therefore imperative that tree leaves use water efficiently so as to minimize further lowering of leaf water potential. Many of the mechanisms adopted by tree leaves (sunken stomata, thick cuticles, leaf abscission, etc.) have already been discussed in detail above and are reviewed in Kozlowski (1976).

Under certain circumstances, measured gradients in water potential in tall trees are not consistent with these theoretical gradients and to explain this, it has been suggested that tree leaves are capable of absorbing significant amounts of liquid water from their surfaces, thereby raising leaf water potential (Connor *et al.*, 1977). In this connection it should be noted that tree canopies are able to intercept up to 80% of the rain falling on a forest area (Penman, 1963). Nevertheless, it appears that tree leaves must be able to grow and develop at leaf water potentials substantially lower than −10 bar; in such cases growth must take place principally at night and turgor maintained by the depression of leaf solute potential (Hsiao *et al.*, 1976; Osonubi and Davies, 1978).

In conclusion, it should be noted that tree species growing in cold regions are probably most at risk from water stress during the early spring when transpiration (in evergreens) is beginning to rise in response to seasonal increases in irradiance and air temperature. At the same time the roots may be unable to absorb water if the soil is frozen or if low soil temperatures have caused a serious lowering in root permeability to water (Kramer, 1969). However the leaves (needles) of most of the typical coniferous species of these areas are equipped with xerophytic features (especially, small size; sunken, occluded stomata; thick waxy cuticle) to deal with the resulting leaf water stress. Other species (larches) avoid the hazards of winter and early spring by leaf abscission.

Part III

Responses to Environmental Stress

5. Temperature

I. THE TEMPERATURE RELATIONS OF PLANTS

Unlike homeothermic animals, higher plants are unable to maintain their cells and tissues at a constant optimum temperature and therefore their leaves, stems and roots are normally within a few degrees of the temperature of the surrounding air or soil. Because of this, the growth and metabolism of plants are profoundly affected by changes in environmental temperature.

However, it is difficult to establish precise relationships between plant processes and environmental temperature because of the extreme variability of soil and air temperatures. For example, the temperature of a leaf depends upon:

   (i) time of day (regular diurnal variation);
  (ii) month of the year (regular seasonal variation);
 (iii) cloudiness and wind speed (irregular, short-term variation);
 (iv) position in the canopy (e.g. "sun" or "shade" leaves);
  (v) height above the soil surface;
 (vi) leaf dimensions;

whereas, root temperature depends mainly upon (i) and (ii) but also upon:

(vii) depth below the soil surface;
(viii) soil properties determining the absorption and transmission of heat (principally soil moisture, bulk density and the nature of the soil surface).

Consequently, the leaf canopy (and the soil profile) is a complex mosaic of rapidly fluctuating thermal regimes such that each group of leaves (or roots) is responding to a unique pattern of temperature fluctuation. This variability makes it very difficult to carry out field studies on the effects of temperature on processes such as photosynthesis.

It causes even greater difficulty in long-term investigations where plant growth rate (and, ultimately, plant distribution) can depend upon one or more of a number of thermal parameters; these include mean, minimum and maximum temperature and the amount of heat accumulated (degree hours, degree days) above a threshold during the whole year, or a shorter critical period (e.g. Pigott, 1975; Wassink, 1972).

In addition to these problems of variability, it has been found that different stages of plant development, and different physiological processes, may have different temperature optima. For example, in *Tulipa* spp., the temperature optima for the various stages of flower development vary between 8°C and 23°C, these optima being synchronized with seasonal temperature changes in the native range of these species (Pisek *et al.*, 1973). Furthermore, the reproductive development of certain species is controlled by night, rather than day, temperatures (Went, 1953; Leopold and Kriedemann, 1975) and many processes, especially germination, are enhanced by alternating temperatures (Thompson *et al.*, 1977). Even more important, it may be difficult to establish the relative importance of soil and air temperatures for plant processes; this is particularly true during the vegetative development of many monocotyledonous plants where leaf extension takes place from stem apices below the soil surface (controlled by soil temperature — Peacock, 1975; Watts, 1973), whereas the mature photosynthesizing leaves are subject to air temperature.

Because of these problems, most investigations of plant response to temperature have been carried out under controlled conditions with root and shoot at the same constant temperature or, more rarely, with soil and air at different, but still constant, temperatures (Precht *et al.*, 1973; Cooper, 1973). It is clear that extrapolation of such data to the field should be carried out with caution.

The response of plant growth rate to a wide range of (constant) temperatures can commonly be represented by an asymmetric bell-shaped curve as shown in Fig. 5.1(a) (Pisek *et al.*, 1973; Cooper, 1973; Sutcliffe, 1977). From such a curve, it is possible to read off the three classic cardinal temperatures i.e. the *minimum* and *maximum* temperatures, at which growth ceases entirely, and the *optimum range* of temperature over which the highest growth rate can be maintained, assuming that temperature is the factor limiting growth. In practice, the optimum range normally covers the range of temperatures over which the rate of growth or of a metabolic process, is within (say) 10% of the maximum rate (e.g. Fig. 5.5). The cardinal temperatures of higher plant processes vary widely within the range − 10°C to 60°C and are normally related

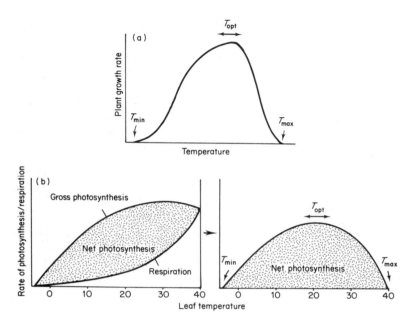

FIG. 5.1. Schematic representations of plant responses to temperature. (a) A generalized diagram of the response of plant growth rate to temperature, illustrating the three cardinal temperatures, i.e. the minimum (T_{min}) and maximum (T_{max}) temperatures, and the optimum temperature range (T_{opt}) for growth. (b) The influence of temperature on photosynthesis and respiration in a typical plant (see text for full description) (adapted from Pisek et al., 1973).

to the temperature regime in the natural range of the species (Table 5.1).

This characteristic response of plant growth to temperature arises because increase in temperature affects biochemical processes in two mutually antagonistic ways. First, as the temperature of a plant cell rises, the velocity of movement (vibrational, rotational and translational) of the reacting molecules increases, leading to more frequent intermolecular collisions and more rapid reaction rates; this effect is common to most chemical reactions. However, virtually all the reactions occurring in cells are catalyzed by enzymes whose activities depend upon the maintenance of precise tertiary structures (three-dimensional shapes) into which reagents must fit exactly in order to react. As the temperature rises, increased molecular agitation tends to damage tertiary structures, leading to reduced enzyme activity and reaction rates. Overall, at sub-optimal temperatures, thermal inactivation of enzymes is slight and the response to increases in temperature is therefore positive. In the optimal range, temperature changes

TABLE 5.1.　Cardinal temperatures for net photosynthesis at light saturation in different groups of plant species (data compiled by Larcher, 1975).

	T_{min}	T_{opt}	T_{max} °C
Herbaceous plants			
Tropical C4 plants	5–7	35–45	50–60
C3 Crop plants	−2 to over 0	20–30	40–50
Sun plants	−2 to 0	20–30	40–50
Shade plants	−2 to 0	10–20	*c.* 40
Spring-flowering and alpine plants	−7 to −2	10–20	30–40
Woody plants			
Tropical evergreens	0–5	25–30	45–50
Trees and shrubs from arid regions	−5 to −1	15–35	42–55
Temperate deciduous trees	−3 to −1	15–25	40–45
Evergreen conifers	−5 to −3	10–25	35–42
Dwarf shrubs of heath and tundra	*c.* −3	15–25	40–45

have little effect upon the process because the two antagonistic effects are balanced i.e. the acceleration in reaction rate due to increased thermal agitation is matched by the reduction in the rate due to enzyme damage. However, above the optimum, thermal denaturation rapidly destroys the enzyme, leading to a rapid cessation of the reaction. Thus the asymmetry of the curve is a result of a gradual, sigmoid pattern of increase in metabolic rate mainly caused by increases in collision frequency, followed by an abrupt fall in rate due to thermal inactivation of enzymes (Sutcliffe, 1977).

The individual processes contributing to plant growth do not all respond to temperature in the same way. For example, gross photosynthesis in many temperate species ceases at temperatures just below 0°C (minimum) and well above 40°C (maximum), with optimum rates in the range 20–35°C (Fig. 5.1 (b)). In contrast, respiration rate tends to be slow below 20°C but due to the thermal disruption of metabolism (disruption of fine control of reaction rates, breakdown of compartmentation etc.), at higher temperatures it accelerates rapidly up to the compensation temperature where the rate of respiration equals the rate of gross photosynthesis, and there can be no net assimilation (Fig. 5.1(b)). Consequently, the response of net photosynthesis (gross photosynthesis—respiration) to temperature is broadly similar to that of overall growth (Fig. 5.1(a), (b)).

Since the exact pattern of response to temperature varies amongst species and amongst processes, it is necessary to have a quantitative expression of these responses, especially at sub-optimal temperatures. Most commonly, Q_{10} or Q_5 values are used, where

$$Q_{10} = \frac{\text{rate at temperature } T + 10°C}{\text{rate at temperature } T}$$

similarly for Q_5

Because it has been found that Q_{10} values for chemical reactions *in vitro* usually fall around 2, it is normally assumed that measured Q_{10} values in excess of 2 indicate a plant process under metabolic control, whereas values below 2 are taken to indicate that the rate of the process under study is limited by a purely physical process such as diffusion or by a photochemical reaction (Sutcliffe, 1977). However, although these assumptions are generally useful, Q values for plant processes should be treated with caution because they are themselves temperature-dependent since plant response to temperature is not strictly exponential (Fig. 5.1); for example the Q_5 value for the respiration of maize root systems fell from 1·85 to 1·35 over the temperature range 10–30°C (Wassink, 1972). Some typical Q_{10} values for plant processes are given in Table 5.2.

Recently, the finding that plant growth in the field can respond linearly (rather than exponentially) to environmental temperature has suggested that the asymmetric bell-shaped response to temperature (Fig. 5.1) may not be as widely applicable as was formerly considered.

TABLE 5.2. Temperature Coefficients (Q_{10}) for selected plant processes, measured at varying intervals within the range 0–30°C. (Compiled from Barber, 1979; Barber, 1972; Franck and Loomis, 1949; Miller, 1938; Street, 1963; Yudkin and Offord, 1973).

Process	Q_{10}
Diffusion of small molecules in water	1·2–1·5
Water flow through the seed coat of *Arachis hypogea*	1·3–1·6
Water movements into germinating seeds, various species	1·5–1·8
Hydrolysis reactions catalysed by enzymes	1·5–2·3
Respiration	2·1–2·6
Photosynthesis (light reactions)	$\simeq 1$
(dark reactions)	2–3
Phosphate uptake into beetroot discs	$0·8^a$–3^b
Potassium uptake into maize seedlings	2–5

[a] At high external concentrations (50 mM) where uptake is largely by passive diffusion.
[b] Active uptake at low external concentrations (0·1 mM) (see p. 73).

For example, Gallagher and Biscoe (1979) have demonstrated that, in the absence of water stress, the extension rate of barley leaves is directly proportional to the temperature of the stem apex. It remains to be seen what the theoretical interpretation of such linear responses can be.

As well as influencing the *rate* of plant growth and metabolism, environmental temperature also plays a part in controlling the *development* of certain plant species. For example, many species (e.g. those forming bulbs or rosettes at the end of the first growing season, and winter cereals) are unable to flower until they have been "vernalized" by a period of low temperature; this adaptation improves the chances of successful reproduction by ensuring that flowering and seed production do not begin until the beginning of the second growing season. Similarly, dormancy of seeds, shown by a wide variety of temperate plants, which prevents premature germination in autumn, can be broken only by exposure to low temperatures (stratification) similar to winter temperatures. In the same way, the annual development and abscission of the leaf canopy in autumn-deciduous trees and shrubs are largely under thermoperiodic control (Went, 1953; Addicott and Lyon, 1973).

However, few developmental processes are controlled by temperature alone and responses to temperature can in many cases be modified by other factors, particularly the light environment. This is clearly illustrated by the finding that tuber initiation in the potato (*Solanum tuberosum*) depends upon the interplay of temperature, photoperiod, light intensity and nutrient supply (Milthorpe and Moorby, 1975; Hay and Allen, 1978).

As a further complication, the thermal regime during growth and development can influence the morphology and dimensions of the resulting plant parts. For example, root diameter has been found to be inversely correlated with growth temperature in a number of contrasting species (reviewed by Cooper, 1973); this is presumably because more photosynthate is available for radial expansion of cortical cells at lower apical growth rates (Rovira and Bowen, 1973). Growth temperature can also influence the branching of roots (Cooper, 1973) and the dimensions and shapes of leaves (e.g. in lettuce—Bensink, 1971).

In summary, it appears that the complexity of the thermal regime of plants in their natural environment is matched by the complexity of plant responses to temperature. In the present chapter, we shall concentrate upon those adaptations of plants which allow them to survive in areas where extremes of temperature are commonly experienced.

A. The Energy Budget of a Plant Leaf

When a leaf is illuminated, it absorbs between 20 and 95% of the incident radiation, depending upon the wavelength (Fig. 2.1). However, only a small fraction of this absorbed energy is required for photosynthesis; the remainder is transformed into heat energy and unless the leaf can lose this heat, its temperature will rise rapidly, leading to death by thermal stress. In a well-watered plant, there are three major processes acting to remove heat from leaves i.e. re-radiation (long-wave), convection of heat, and transpiration. Consequently, if the leaf is to remain at a constant temperature, its Energy Budget must balance:

$$Q_{abs} = Q_{rad} + Q_{conv} + Q_{trans}$$

| energy absorbed by leaf | energy lost by radiation | energy lost by convection of heat | energy lost by transpiration of water | (5.1) |

Therefore, if

$$Q_{rad} + Q_{conv} + Q_{trans} > Q_{abs} \qquad (5.2)$$

the leaf will be cooled; whereas, if

$$Q_{rad} + Q_{conv} + Q_{trans} < Q_{abs} \qquad (5.3)$$

leaf temperature will rise.

In a series of theoretical papers (reviewed in Gates and Papian, 1971; Gates, 1976), Gates has expanded equation 5.1 to give the precise form:

$$Q_{abs} = \varepsilon \sigma T_1^4 + k_1 (V/D)^{1/2} (T_1 - T_a) + \frac{L \cdot d_1^s(T_1) - rh \cdot d_a^s(T_a)}{R_1} \qquad (5.4)$$

$$(Q_{rad}) \qquad\qquad (Q_{conv}) \qquad\qquad (Q_{trans})$$

where ε is the emissivity of the leaf (long-wave radiation);

σ, k_1 are constants;

T_1 and T_a are the temperatures of leaf and bulk air, respectively;

V is wind velocity;

D is leaf width;

L is the latent heat of vapourization of water (dependent upon leaf temperature);

$d_1^s(T_1)$, $d_a^s(T_a)$ are the saturation water vapour densities in the leaf and in the air, respectively;

rh is the relative humidity of the bulk air;

R_1 is leaf diffusive resistance (see chapter 4).

Therefore, it can be concluded from equations 5.2 and 5.4 that the following effects will tend to cause leaf cooling:

(i) high wind velocity and/or narrow (and dissected) leaves (increased convection);

(ii) low relative humidity and/or low diffusive resistance (increased transpiration);

whereas, from equations 5.3 and 5.4, leaf heating will result from low wind velocity, wide (and entire) leaves, high relative humidity, high diffusive resistance (e.g. due to stomatal closure).

Leaf temperature also depends upon the radiative properties of the leaf (both the reflection coefficient and the emissivity—Gates and Papian, 1971) which, in turn, are dependent upon the nature of the leaf surface (waxiness, hairiness, etc.) as well as the leaf angle in relation to the direction of illumination.

As we shall see in later sections, many plant species have become adapted to conditions of extreme temperature by the modification of leaf characteristics (dimensions, degree of dissection, diffusive resistance, leaf angle, reflection coefficient, pubescence, etc.) leading to heating or cooling, where appropriate, thereby permitting net photosynthesis to continue.

II. PLANT ADAPTATIONS AND RESISTANCE TO LOW TEMPERATURE

A. The Influence of Low Temperature upon Plants

The primary effect of cooling plants below their optimum temperature range is the reduction of rates of growth and of metabolic processes (Fig. 5.1). Consequently, the length of time required for completion of the annual growth cycle increases as the climate becomes cooler and there may be a critical mean temperature below which the plants of a given species cannot reproduce successfully. Such an effect is responsible for the distribution of *Juncus squarrosus* in upland Britain. This perennial rush produces fertile seed, and is widely distributed, at altitudes up to 760–840 m in north-west England; however, above 840 m, the mean temperature is normally too low to permit completion of reproductive development and fertile fruit are produced only in unusually warm years. Consequently, plants of *J. squarrosus* are sparsely distributed above this altitude, occurring only where viable seed has been dropped by sheep or birds (Pearsall, 1968).

Cooling subtropical and tropical plants down to temperatures in the range of 0–10°C tends to cause a very rapid fall in the activity of metabolic processes (especially respiration) and may result in severe damage and death within a few hours or days (Larcher *et al.*, 1973). The available evidence suggests that the chilling of these species causes a phase change ("liquid" to "solid") in membrane lipids resulting in the inactivation of membrane-bound enzymes, such as the respiratory enzymes attached to mitochondrial membranes. It is thought that higher proportions of unsaturated fatty acids in the membrane lipids of temperate species lead to more stable ("liquid") membranes and less risk of chilling injury (Lyons, 1973).

In general, temperate plants are not susceptible to chilling injury at temperatures above 0°C and tend to show signs of damage only after ice has formed within their tissues. For example, it has been demonstrated that photosynthesis in several tree species does not cease completely until extracellular ice has formed (normally at -3 to -5°C) and even then the initial cessation of activity may be due to a purely physical effect—the blocking of CO_2 diffusion by ice (Larcher *et al.*, 1973). Under relatively low cooling rates (< 1°C h^{-1}), ice tends to form preferentially in the apoplast of plant tissues because of higher solute concentrations in cytoplasm and vacuoles. As long as such periods of freezing are not prolonged and the rate of thawing is not too rapid, the formation of extracellular ice may not cause significant tissue damage in hardened plants (see below).

However, if extracellular ice persists, the gradient of water vapour pressure between the apoplast and the cells causes water to migrate out of the cells and into the apoplast, where it freezes, thereby increasing the amount of ice in the plant tissue. As well as causing mechanical damage to plant tissues this process results in the progressive dehydration of the cell contents and an increase in the concentration of the cell sap (similar phenomena occur in water stress, see Chapter 4). Consequently, the biochemistry of the cytoplasm is seriously disturbed; proteins, including enzymes, are denatured, various components are precipitated, compartmented substances such as hydrolytic enzymes are released into the cytoplasm, the buffer system becomes unable to control the pH, and there may be a tendency for macromolecules to condense when forced together by the dehydration of the cytoplasm. In many species, these effects lead inevitably to cell death (Burke *et al.*, 1976). Rapid thawing may also have a lethal effect upon frozen plants due to further disruption of cell metabolism and water relations.

As we shall see in a later section, hardened plants of many species can survive prolonged periods of very low temperatures and high levels of cell desiccation, due to the resistant nature of their cytoplasm. However, it appears that the cells of even the most resistant plants cannot tolerate intracellular freezing caused by very rapid cooling (rates of several degrees per hour). Overall, much of the literature on frost resistance is highly confusing because

(i) it has not yet been established that intracellular ice formation does occur in nature—outside the laboratory (Levitt, 1978); and
(ii) difficulties are experienced in discriminating between damage caused by intra- and extra-cellular freezing in the laboratory (Habeshaw, 1973).

B. The Characteristic Features of Cold Climates—Arctic and Alpine Environments, Temperate Winters

In subsequent sections, we shall examine plant adaptations favouring survival in cold environments, especially arctic and alpine areas but also in temperate regions during the winter months. However, it should be stressed that low temperature is only one of a number of unfavourable environmental factors in these areas, and plant distribution may not be determined by temperature alone.

Although it can not be defined precisely, the term arctic is generally used in ecology to describe regions stretching from the limit of tree growth (the treeline or timberline) into higher latitudes; it therefore includes tundra areas in both the Arctic and Antarctic. Many of the characteristic features of the arctic environment (with particular reference to plants) can be summarized as follows:

(i) Temperature (air and soil). Very low temperatures during the winter; low (and frequently sub-zero) temperatures in summer (Table 5.3).
(ii) Light. Very long photoperiod in summer (continuous light for several weeks) associated with relatively low light intensities. Light received by plants may also be reduced by snow cover.
Note that (i) and (ii) combine to give a very short growing season (maximum length 3–4 months).
(iii) Wind. Arctic regions are subject to persistent high winds throughout the year which are in themselves damaging and which cause severe abrasion of plant tissues by sand particles and sharp snow and ice crystals, especially in winter.
(iv) Water relations. In spite of the presence of large quantities of snow and ice, arctic plants are exposed to drought in summer

1968).

	Arctic tundra[a]	Alpine tundra[b]	Temperate forest[c]
Solar radiation			
Mean July intensity (W m^{-2})	209	391	405
Quality	Low in short wavelengths, particularly short UV	High in short UV	—
Maximum photoperiod	84 days	15 h	15 h
Air temperature (1 m, °C)			
Annual mean	−12·4	−3·3	8·3
January mean	−26·7	−12·8	−1·7
July mean	3·9	8·3	20·6
Absolute min.	−48·9	−36·6	−33·8
Soil temperature (15 cm, °C)			
Annual mean	−6·2	−1·7	8·3
Absolute min.	−15·5	−20·0	−10·0
Precipitation (mm)			
Annual mean	107	634	533
Wind (km h^{-1})			
Annual mean	19·3	29·6	10·3
Air composition			
CO_2 (mg l^{-1})	0·57	0·36	0·44
O_2 (partial pressure, mm)	160	100	122
Depth of soil thaw	20–100 cm	>30 cm	—

[a] Barrow, Alaska (altitude 7 m, latitude 71° 20′N).
[b] Niwot Ridge, Colorado (altitude 3749 m, latitude 40° N).
[c] Bummer's Gulch, Colorado (altitude 2195 m, latitude 40° N).

due to frozen soil moisture, low precipitation, high transpiration rates caused by high winds and the direct sublimation of snow into dry air. In addition since pedogenesis is very slow, many arctic soils are unstructured sands and gravels with very low water holding capacities.

(v) Inorganic nutrients. Due to the inhibition of soil microbial activity (nitrogen fixation, mineralization of organic nitrogen) by low soil temperatures and the virtual absence of legumes in the tundra flora, inorganic nitrogen levels are low in arctic soils. The supply of phosphate may also be low due to poor root development.

(vi) Mechanical effects. Frost heaving of soils due to cycles of freezing and thawing may cause the uprooting of plants, especially seedlings during early stages of establishment.

(vii) Reproductive problems. Because of the scarcity of insects and the relatively sparse vegetative cover in many tundra areas, cross-pollination may be impossible. In addition, low population densities of mammals and birds rule out several temperate seed-dispersal mechanisms.

In summary, it can be seen that the arctic environment is an extremely hostile and variable environment (Ives and Barry, 1974; Kevan, 1972; Rosswall and Heal, 1975; Savile, 1972). Details of environmental conditions at a typical arctic site are given in Table 5.3.

The alpine zone in mountainous regions is normally defined as those areas above the treeline. The altitude of the treeline boundary in this definition is extremely variable, depending upon latitude, exposure and distance from the sea (Manley, 1952; Wardle, 1974); extreme examples include regions in the Arctic where the treeline is at sea level, and northern Chile where forest is found up to an altitude of 4900m (Wardle, 1974).

Alpine conditions are similar to those in the arctic environment (Table 5.3) and this is reflected in the number of plant species that are common to both regions (e.g. *Trisetum spicatum, Oxyria digyna, Silene acaulis*—Billings and Mooney, 1968). However, the two environments do differ in several important ways (Table 5.3) i.e.:

(i) Light. Light intensity and photoperiod depend upon latitude, season and snow-cover. For example, levels of irradiance can be very high in the Alps in clear weather, leading to very high soil temperatures (Tranquillini, 1964). Furthermore the amount of ultra-violet radiation received increases with altitude (see Chapter 2).

(ii) Composition of the Atmosphere. Due to decreasing atmospheric pressure, the partial pressures of O_2 and CO_2 in the atmosphere fall with altitude.

(iii) Variability. The alpine environment is exceptionally variable. For example, there are large differences in temperature and in radiation received between north- and south-facing slopes at the same altitude (Tranquillini (1964) quotes a measured difference in soil surface temperature of 57°C); such variations are matched by variations with altitude in a number of environmental factors (see (i) and (ii) above; wind velocity, etc.).

Together, arctic and alpine regions account for a significant area of the earth's surface—23·6 million km² in the Northern Hemisphere and 1·3 million km² in the Southern Hemisphere (Good, 1964).

It is not possible to describe a typical temperate winter climate because conditions vary widely according to altitude and the warming effects of the sea. For example, in the lowlands of the British Isles, soil and air temperatures vary in frequent irregular cycles between − 5 and 10°C, according to whether the prevailing air flow originates in the arctic or the sub-tropics (e.g. Hay, 1977). In contrast, the winter climate of central North America tends to be much more severe, with sub-zero temperatures persisting through several months (i.e. approaching an arctic climate).

The most important difference between arctic/alpine areas and temperate regions is therefore the length and quality of the growing season. In temperate climates, the growing season normally exceeds six months per year and native species are able to use this period of favourable conditions to grow vigorously and complete their annual growth cycle; most species are able to *avoid* the following winter period in dormant form, although some "opportunist" species continue to grow whenever conditions permit (e.g. members of the Gramineae whose growing points below the soil surface are insulated from the extremes of air temperature). In contrast, the growing season in arctic/alpine regions is short, conditions are generally unfavourable for plant growth during this growing season and severe weather may occur at any stage of growth. In order to survive such conditions, plants must be adapted to grow *rapidly* under *unfavourable* conditions and to survive and recover quickly from periods of severe temperature stress during growth.

C. Adaptations Favouring Plant Growth and Development in Arctic and Alpine Regions

According to Savile (1972), the primary factor limiting the full development of trees beyond the arctic treeline is the level of leaf abrasion caused by wind-blown snow crystals; the resulting loss of photosynthetic tissue, coupled with the short and unfavourable growing season, means that there is very little surplus assimilate to be invested in woody tissues (Elkington and Jones, 1974). The influence of snow abrasion on tree growth can be illustrated by the morphology of isolated spruce trees (*Picea glauca* and *P. mariana*) growing at the treeline (Fig. 5.2). The

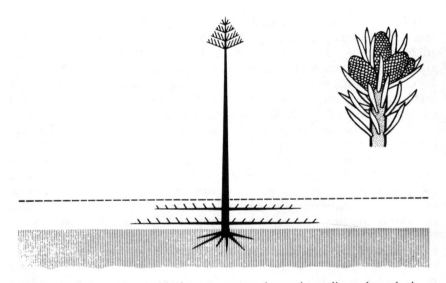

FIG. 5.2.   The form of an isolated spruce tree at the arctic treeline, where the lower branches are protected from abrasion in winter by a covering of snow. Above the level of intense abrasion, the terminal bud survives, protected by a "mop-head" of branches and a whorl of lateral buds (inset) (from Savile, 1972).

lowest branches of these trees, up to about 30 cm from the soil surface, tend to be well developed because they are protected from severe winter abrasion by a covering of early snow. Since snow abrasion kills most buds above this height, many trees are severely stunted and those that do continue to grow have bare trunks stripped of branches. However, very little snow is carried by the wind at heights greater than 1–2 m, and therefore if trees do achieve sufficient height, abrasion is reduced and normal development can be resumed; thus we have the "mop-head" effect in Fig. 5.2 (Savile, 1972).

In response to severe snow abrasion in winter, most arctic and alpine species have evolved a dwarfed habit, either as a permanent feature of the genotype or as a plastic response. Consequently, tundra plants are generally protected by layers of snow during winter, except on exposed ridges. For example, arctic shrubs (e.g. *Betula nana*, *Salix* spp.) are rarely more than 15 cm tall, and tend to exceed this height only when growing amongst large boulders (Savile, 1972). Similarly, arctic and alpine herbs occur as rosettes, cushions or leafy, short-stemmed plants (dicots), or as short monocotyledons (grasses, sedges and rushes) whose apical meristems are insulated by soil and vegetation. Other morpho-logical features which protect young and growing tissues from wind and abrasion include the clustering of twigs around the buds of de-ciduous shrubs, the formation of dense grass tussocks, and the protection of the growing points of herbs like *Saxifraga tricuspidata* by dead leaves and fruiting stems (Savile, 1972). Because of the low level of bacterial activity (Baross and Morita, 1978), wind-breaks composed of dead tissues can persist for several years.

Dwarfing confers other advantages on arctic and alpine species. In particular, it ensures that in summer, plant growth and metabolism occur in the warmest zone, just above the soil surface. This zone is clearly illustrated by Bliss (1975) and Roswall et al. (1975); and Bliss (1962) has reviewed a number of earlier reports confirming that maxi-mum air temperatures immediately above stands of arctic plants can be several degrees higher than at screen height. Dwarfing also tends to ensure that a substantial fraction of annual production is invested in reproductive development; this important adaptation is common in hostile environments.

A characteristic feature of alpine species is the high level of antho-cyanin pigments in their leaves (Billings and Mooney, 1968; Klein, 1978). The combined effect of these red pigments with the green of chlorophyll can give dark purple to black leaves which absorb a higher proportion of the incident solar radiation than corresponding green leaves (i.e. the reflection coefficient and/or transmission of light in the dark leaves is lower), leading to leaf temperatures substantially higher than ambient air temperature. Leaf-heating has been confirmed experi-mentally by a number of authors in alpine (Tranquillini, 1964) and in arctic regions (Bliss, 1975). Where heavy pigmentation is associated with a cushion life form in which pockets of warm air can be trapped, high tissue temperatures can be achieved; for example, cushion plants at 3800 m in Colorado were between 1 and 12°C warmer than the surrounding air (Fig. 5.3). Because of these elevated temperatures, the growing season is extended and growth and development are accelerated. It may even be possible for deeply-pigmented plants to absorb enough solar radiation to begin growing when still covered with snow at the beginning of the season (Billings and Bliss, 1959; Kimball *et al.*, 1973). In different species, the level of pigmentation appears to be genetically determined or environmentally induced. However, it must be stressed that synthesis of anthocyanin pigments is not a feature which is restricted to arctic and alpine plants; it is also a common response to other stresses such as drought and high temperature.

The level of pigmentation in the corolla of flowering plants also varies amongst arctic and alpine species and it has been demonstrated that on sunny days in Siberia, blue flowers can be 3–4°C warmer than the surrounding air compared with up to 2°C warmer for white flowers (Russian work quoted by Bliss, 1962). This warming of flowers, which should hasten reproductive development, has reached a high stage of development in species like *Dryas integrifolia* and *Papaver radicatum* whose flowers "track" the sun across the sky (see Chapter 2). The

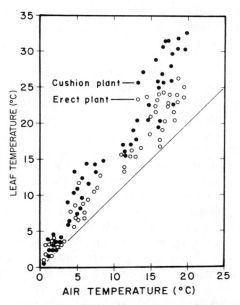

FIG. 5.3.   Leaf temperatures in alpine cushion (*Arenaria obtusiloba*) and more erect, rosette (*Geum turbinatum*) plants at 3800 m in Colorado. The data include measurements from both cloudy and clear conditions and the line indicates equal air and plant temperatures (from Salisbury and Spomer, 1964).

resulting increases in temperature (up to 10°C at low wind speeds) are not only of benefit to the plants themselves but also to insects which bask in these warm flowers for prolonged periods (Hocking and Sharplin, 1965; Kevan, 1975). The remarkable increases in temperature (15–25°C) measured at the surfaces of the catkins of arctic willow species appear to be due to a "greenhouse" effect, with the profuse hairs of the catkins blocking the emission of long-wave radiation (Krog, 1955).

Up to this point, it has been assumed that deep pigmentation is beneficial to alpine plants due to the warming of illuminated tissues. However, in addition to improving absorption of radiation, dark leaves are also more efficient at emitting long-wave radiation. Consequently, the accumulation of pigment molecules in leaves may lead to very low temperatures and the risk of frost damage during long alpine nights in the growing season (Tranquillini, 1964). This has led to the suggestion (Klein, 1978), that high levels of anthocyanins, flavonoids and epidermal waxes serve to protect leaf tissues from damage by ultra-violet radiation. This conclusion is the subject of some debate but it has become clear from controlled experiments that not only are alpine plants more resistant to UV damage, but also that their morphology and development may be partly controlled by the level of ultra-violet radiation (Klein, 1978; Caldwell, 1968; cf. Chapter 2, p. 38).

A further characteristic feature of the morphology of perennial species in arctic and alpine regions is the development of large storage organs for carbohydrates below the soil surface (swollen roots, rhizomes, corms, bulbs) containing a large proportion of the plant biomass (e.g. Bliss, 1975). In other species, lipids are stored above ground in old leaves and stems. Investigations using arctic/alpine species like *Oxyria digyna* (Fig. 5.4) have shown that these reserves play a crucial role in enabling plants to make the best use of very short growing seasons. The rapid translocation of reserve carbohydrate from root to shoot at the beginning of the season supports a rapid rate of leaf and stem growth at a time when low temperatures are holding the rate of photosynthesis below its optimum (see below). Thus, for a few weeks, the carbohydrate content of the plant tends to fall; however, as conditions improve, net assimilation becomes positive and surplus assimilate is partitioned between developing reproductive organs and recharging storage organs. This pattern of carbohydrate cycling coupled with the widespread occurrence of preformed flower buds (developed one or two seasons earlier) increases the probability of successful reproduction and survival (Billings and Mooney, 1968; Billings, 1974). A similar

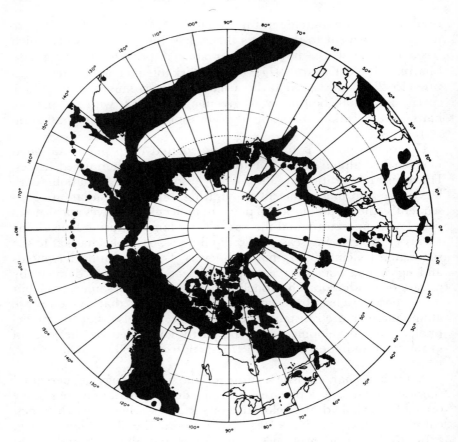

Fig. 5.4. Geographical distribution of the arctic/alpine species *Oxyria digyna* south-wards to 40°N (simplified from Hultén, 1962; and Billings, 1974).

phenology is employed by woodland species like the bluebell which need to flower early in the year before the tree canopy has formed (see Chapter 2).

However, in spite of such adaptations, the growing season may only rarely be long enough for the production of mature viable seed and even if the growing season is adequate there may be problems in ensuring successful pollination (see above). Furthermore, seedlings attempting to establish themselves in these hostile environments cannot fall back on substantial carbohydrate reserves, and they are at great risk from frost heaving. Consequently, reproduction by seed is rarely successful and this accounts for the scarcity of annual tundra species,

especially in the arctic. In many perennials, these difficulties have been
overcome by adopting vegetative reproduction (by rhizomes, layering
of branches, bulbils, viviparity etc.) and, in some cases this may confer
a distinct advantage in dispersal since large propagules are more easily
carried by the wind (Billings and Mooney, 1968; Savile, 1972).

However, the survival and reproduction of plants growing in arctic
and alpine environments depends ultimately upon their ability to
maintain a positive carbon balance at low temperatures around 0°C.
This ability has been demonstrated for a variety of species and locations
(reviewed by Pisek *et al.*, 1973; Billings, 1974); for example, with some
notable exceptions, the optimum temperature range for photosynthesis
in species growing in the Alps falls with altitude (Fig. 5.5). The exceptions include valley evergreens (e.g. *Abies alba*) whose low optima permit

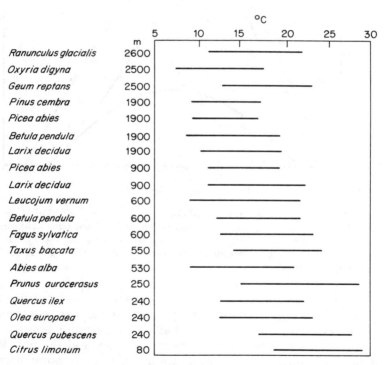

Fig. 5.5.   Optimum temperature ranges for net photosynthesis at low light intensity
(70 W m^{-2}), in species originating from warm temperate lowland (80–250 m), mountain valley (530–900 m) treeline (1900 m) and high mountain (2500–2600 m) regions
of the Alps. At higher light intensities, each optimum temperature range tends to move
upwards by several degrees (redrawn from Pisek *et al.*, 1973).

photosynthesis to proceed during the greater part of the year (Neilson *et al.*, 1972). They also include the high-altitude dwarf perennials *Ranunculus glacialis* and *Geum reptans*; the relatively high optima for these species may reflect the high day temperatures in their natural habitat—sheltered rock crevices subject to intense insolation.

It can be seen from Figs 5.5 and 5.6 that the photosynthetic apparatus of *Oxyria digyna* is particularly well adapted to the temperatures prevailing beyond the treeline at least at low light levels. Not only is the

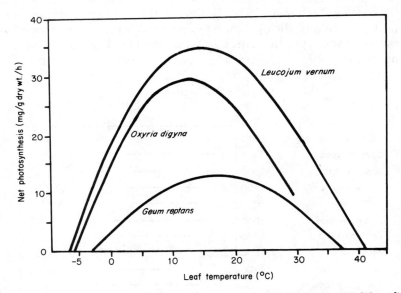

FIG. 5.6.   The response of net photosynthesis at low light intensity (70 W m^{-2}) to temperature in three alpine species (from Pisek *et al.*, 1973). Increasing light intensity tends to give increases in the rate of net photosynthesis and an upward shift in the optimum temperature range apparently without significant alteration in the minimum cardinal temperature (Pisek *et al.*, 1969).

maximum photosynthetic rate attained at relatively low positive temperatures (7–10°C), but also net photosynthesis can continue at temperatures down to −6°C with half the maximum possible rate achieved at 0°C. In other investigations (Mooney and Billings, 1961; Mooney and Johnson, 1965) it was found that arctic populations of *Oxyria digyna* and *Thalictrum alpinum* have lower optimum temperatures for photosynthesis than alpine populations, possibly reflecting the higher temperatures experienced during the alpine summer. The anatomical and biochemical adaptations which favour photosynthesis at low temperatures remain obscure; however, there are a number of research areas in which progress is being made. For example, it has been shown that the low temperature activities of isolated mitochondria and chloroplasts from a number of widely distributed species are positively correlated with the altitude of origin of the populations studied (Klikoff, 1969; May and Villareal, 1974—but note that the "low temperatures" employed were 10°C and 15°C respectively). This tends to confirm the generally held view that low temperature respiration rates are unusually high in arctic and alpine species (Billings, 1974) but it does not help in the understanding of the low temperature optima for net photosynthesis because it indicates that rates of gross photosynthesis at low temperature must be particularly high to make up respiratory losses. Taking an alternative approach, Neama, Bryant and Woodward (personal communication, 1979) have shown that in cold-adapted *Salix herbacea* the decrease in net photosynthesis at higher temperatures is caused, not by a decrease in CO_2 fixation, but by increased rates of photo-respiration and respiration.

There is also some experimental evidence of the adaptation of the photosynthetic apparatus to the light regime in arctic and alpine regions. For example, Mooney and Billings (1961) and Clebsch (1960) found that arctic populations of *Oxyria* and *Trisetum* reached light saturation at lower light intensities than alpine populations. However, it appears that there is an important interaction between light intensity and temperature. Several authors have found that photosynthesis in arctic and alpine species is saturated by lower light intensities at low temperatures rather than at higher (Billings, 1974). According to Wilson (1966) this effect is caused by lower demand for assimilate at low temperatures resulting in the accumulation of sugars and the suppression of photosynthesis by product inhibition.

As yet there are few experimental data on the adaptation of arctic and alpine species to other environmental factors such as drought, low partial pressures of CO_2 and O_2, and low soil nutrient levels. However there are many reports of profuse plant growth around animal and bird excreta, presumably in response to increases in soil fertility (e.g. Russell, 1940).

D. Adaptations Favouring Survival of Cold Winters—Dormancy

As noted earlier, temperate plant species face different problems from those of arctic and alpine species. Because climatic conditions are favourable for vegetative and reproductive development for at least six months in each year, temperate plants are normally able to complete their annual growth cycles successfully; however, in order to make use of the next growing season, they must be able to survive the intervening cold winter without sustaining substantial damage. This problem, which is particularly acute in north-temperate and boreal regions, is commonly overcome by the adoption of winter dormancy.

For example, the seeds of many species, annual and perennial, are dormant when shed in the autumn and will germinate only after they have experienced a period of low temperature (stratification). In many cases, the temperature need not fall below 1–8°C and the cold period required for successful stratification may vary between a few days and a few months (Pisek *et al.*, 1973). A particularly clear example of this adaptation is provided by *Betula pubescens*. When the seeds of this birch species are shed in the autumn (short daylength), they are dormant and can be induced to germinate only when exposed to unseasonable long days. However, after a period of chilling, dormancy is broken and the seeds begin to germinate whenever the temperature permits, even in continuous darkness (Black and Wareing, 1955). Thus under natural conditions, autumn germination is suppressed by daylength but once the winter is over, birch seeds can germinate and become established early in the spring.

In the same way, the growing points of perennial species can cease growth and pass into a resting phase in autumn. For example, shoot growth in most temperate woody plants ceases in autumn and dormant terminal buds are formed, under the influence of short days; as with seed dormancy, bud dormancy is naturally broken by chilling in winter. In addition to developing dormant buds, deciduous woody plants avoid frost damage by autumn leaf abscission which is stimulated by a combination of short daylength and low temperatures. Winter-dormant buds are also found in the bulbs, corms, rhizomes and tubers of herbaceous perennials (Wareing, 1969).

Arctic and alpine plants also have to survive very severe winters. However, because of the shortness and irregularity of the growing season, it is essential that growth be resumed at the earliest possible date and continue to the end of the growing season (compare with temperate perennials which produce dormant buds in early autumn before the light and temperature regimes have deteriorated seriously). Consequently, dormancy is less common in these regions and growth is generally resumed whenever temperature permits. For example, of 60 alpine species considered by Amen (1966), only 19 possessed seed dormancy and in many of these (eight), dormancy was due to a hard, impermeable seed coat. This last seed characteristic, which is common to several dominant alpine species, may be an adaptation to spread germination over several years in soils where freeze/thaw cycles can cause abrasion of seed surfaces (Amen, 1966; see Chapter 4).

In tundra perennials, the onset of winter, bringing reduced day-length and lower temperatures, causes a progressive slowing of metabolism, the "hardening" of plant tissues (see below) and the enforcement of dormancy in leaves and in perennating buds. Since this dormancy is relieved in spring, whenever temperatures rise to about 0°C, it is important that such dormant buds be able to respond rapidly to changes in temperature. Thus, unlike their temperate counterparts, the buds of arctic perennials are not enclosed in heavy bud scales which would insulate the contents against changes in air temperature (Savile, 1972).

Dormancy, whether innate or enforced, is clearly a widely adopted method of avoiding severe conditions in winter. However, the survival of plant tissues, even in the form of dormant buds, depends ultimately upon the ability of the cells to avoid freezing injuries.

E. Adaptations Favouring Survival of Cold Winters—Plant Resistance to Freezing Injury

Much of the existing literature on frost resistance deals with temperate species of economic importance, especially field and horticultural crops. and timber trees. However, where natural species have been studied, the degree of frost resistance in their tissues is broadly related to the temperature regime in their natural range. For example, Sakai and Weiser (1973) found that the freezing resistance of dormant twigs from a number of N. American tree species was dependent upon the winter minimum temperature regime in their area of origin. Exceptions to this rule include the tolerance of very low sub-zero temperatures (− 30 to − 50°C, after hardening) in *Salix* species originating in the lowland tropics (Sakai, 1970).

Plant resistance to freezing injury, which is primarily resistance to the formation of intracellular ice, can be seen as a series of successive "lines of resistance". In general, as the winter climate becomes more severe, the possession of more of these lines becomes necessary for plant survival. The first line of defence in herbaceous and woody species is simply the depression of the freezing point of the water in the vacuole and cytoplasm due to the soluble solute content of the cell sap. Thus, even before hardening, the tissues of most temperate plants can be cooled to a few degrees below zero (typically − 1 to − 5°C) before ice forms; similarly, halophytes can have freezing point depressions as great as 14°C below zero (Burke *et al.*, 1976). This colligative property of cell sap gives complete protection from frost damage in warm areas, such as Mediterranean regions, with a low incidence of frost.

It has been suggested by several authors (reviewed by Larcher *et al.*, 1973) that the accumulation of soluble solutes (sugars, organic acids, amino acids or proteins) in plant cell sap in autumn (e.g. Grace and Marks, 1978) may give increased frost resistance due to further depression of the freezing point of cell water. However, this additional depression cannot be more than a few degrees and therefore cannot be responsible for the tolerance of extremely cold temperatures discussed below. It may be that the accumulation of solutes, possibly resulting from the suppression of photosynthesis by low temperatures (Wilson, 1966—see above), plays a more important role in protecting cytoplasmic macromolecules and membranes from the effects of severe desiccation (Larcher *et al.*, 1973).

The second line of defence, protecting critically important tissues (dormant buds and xylem ray parenchyma cells) of woody plants from freezing at temperatures down to about −40°C, can come into operation only after growth has ceased, dormancy has been established and the plant tissues have been "hardened" by exposure to temperatures below 5°C for several days (Langridge and McWilliam, 1967; Burke *et al.*, 1976). This protection is therefore induced by autumn conditions, in preparation for severe conditions in winter. Tissues conditioned in this way tend to behave as if they contained ultrapure water, lacking any nucleating sites where ice formation can begin; thus they can undergo deep supercooling down to about −38°C (the spontaneous nucleation temperature of water) before ice forms. Although the reasons for this deep supercooling are not clear, the effect has been observed in the twigs of several tree species (intracellular freezing occurring at −38 to −47°C; George *et al.*, 1977). However, in other cases, supercooling gives protection only to −20 or −30°C. It is important to stress that whereas these critically important tissues are protected by deep supercooling, the remaining tissues survive by accommodating intercellular ice and tolerating cell dehydration.

In other woody species, hardened tissues can be cooled slowly to temperatures far below −40°C without serious damage (third line of defence, required only in the most severe climates). For example, Sakai (1970) found that dormant twigs of *Salix* species from a number of provenances could be cooled to the temperature of liquid nitrogen (−196°C) without impairing subsequent growth; in these cases it may be that intracellular ice formation is prevented because all of the "freezeable" water in the cell has been withdrawn into the apoplast, leaving thin layers of tightly bound water molecules round macro-molecules and cell inclusions (Burke *et al.*, 1976). There is no evidence that deeply supercooled plant tissues can survive intracellular freezing.

However, this rather simple account of frost resistance as a series of lines of defence must be modified in several ways. In particular, as noted earlier, rapid cooling rates in the laboratory (several degrees per hour) tend to cause intracellular freezing and cell death even in hard-ened plants. This occurs, presumably, because the permeability of the cell membranes is not high enough to permit the rate of water efflux necessary for intercellular ice formation. Thus the rapid changes of temperature and the frequent cycles of freezing and thawing character-istic of the Alps in spring, lead to tissue damage even in highly resistant species such as *Pinus cembra* (Tranquillini, 1964). Secondly, the tissues of a given species are not uniformly resistant to frost injury; this is clearly illustrated in Fig. 5.7 which stresses that below-ground organs which are normally insulated from the extremes of temperature ex-perienced by aerial parts, are much more susceptible than stems and leaves.

Plants which tolerate very low temperatures must be able to accom-modate large volumes of ice in the apoplast without causing serious disruption of their tissues; for example in woody species like *Buxus* and *Camellia*, ice is formed between readily separated layers of leaf tissue (Sutcliffe, 1977). They must also be able to survive severe desiccation of the cytoplasm and the accompanying mechanical and biochemical stresses. The mechanisms of desiccation resistance are not clear but it is known that hardening causes an increase in cytoplasmic viscosity such that the cytoplasm may be more resistant to mechanical damage during the withdrawal of water into the apoplast. Another, untested, hypothesis suggests that hardening involves an increase in the amount of water bound tightly to macromolecules and membranes. Levitt (1972) considers that the denaturation of proteins, and cell death following freezing and desiccation are caused primarily by formation of disulphide bonds ($-S-S-$) between neighbouring protein mole-cules (Fig. 5.8) and he suggests that stress resistance (freezing, drought, high temperature) is related to a low incidence and reactivity of thiol ($-SH$) groups.

The relatively sparse amount of evidence available indicates that arctic and alpine plants, like temperate plants, undergo a period of hardening before the onset of winter and can then survive very low temperatures by deep supercooling and extracellular ice formation. However, unlike temperate species, they must also be able to tolerate freezing at any time during the growing season and recommence active

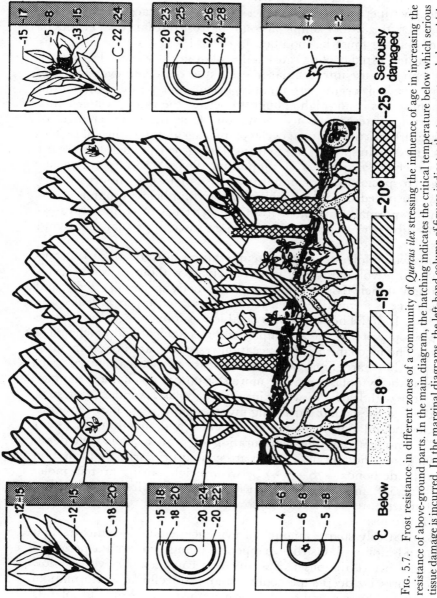

FIG. 5.7. Frost resistance in different zones of a community of *Quercus ilex* stressing the influence of age in increasing the resistance of above-ground parts. In the main diagram, the hatching indicates the critical temperature below which serious tissue damage is incurred. In the marginal diagrams, the left-hand column of figures indicates the temperature below which initial damage is caused, whereas the temperatures in the right-hand column (shaded) refer to 50% damage. C indicates cambium. Note that a whole year's crop of germinating acorns will be wiped out by soil temperatures below −4°C (from Larcher, 1975).

°C Below -8° -15° -20° -25° Seriously damaged

growth and metabolism as soon as possible (Savile, 1972). This combination of frost resistance and active growth is unknown in temperate regions and its mechanism remains unexplored.

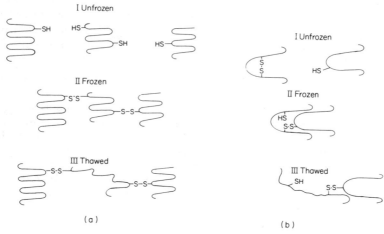

FIG. 5.8.   Schematic diagrams of the disulphide bond theory of freezing injury to the tertiary structures of proteins. In scheme (a), the cytoplasmic dehydration associated with freezing forces three protein molecules together, with the result that they become linked together by disulphide bonds. On rehydration of the cytoplasm, the tertiary structure of the central molecule (determined largely by weak hydrogen bonds) is destroyed as the outer molecules regain their former positions. Alternatively, the shape of a protein molecule can be changed by the breaking and reforming of disulphide bonds (scheme (b)). Similar phenomena are thought to occur during periods of drought, high temperature and salinity stress (after Levitt, 1972).

III. PLANT ADAPTATION AND RESISTANCE TO HIGH TEMPERATURES

As we noted earlier, plant tissues dissipate heat by three main processes (emission of long-wave radiation, convection of heat, transpiration) of which transpiration is the most effective in many natural situations (Gates, 1976). Consequently, high plant temperatures ($>40°C$) are almost invariably due to the cessation of transpirational cooling, caused by stomatal closure in response to leaf water stress. A combination of water stress and thermal stress is therefore commonly experienced by the vegetation of drier areas in the tropics and subtropics; it can also occur in xeric habitats (e.g. sand dunes, shallow soils) in temperate zones during periods of high irradiance.

Because of this close association between water stress and high temperature, it is difficult to disentangle the effects of each stress on plants growing in the field. To do this, it is necessary to consider the stresses separately under controlled conditions, for example by studying the influence of high temperatures on plants which are adequately supplied with water. The results of such experiments indicate that exposure to temperatures over 45°C for as little as 30 min can cause severe damage to the leaves of plants from a wide range of climatic regions (Table 5.4). This rapid development of tissue damage suggests that the primary effect of high temperature is the disruption of cell metabolism, possibly

TABLE 5.4.   Resistance to extremes of temperature in plant species from a range of climatic regions. The temperatures quoted are for 50% injury after exposure to low temperature for 2 h or more, or after exposure to high temperature for 0·5 h (compiled by Larcher, 1975).

	°C for cold injury in winter	°C for heat injury in summer
Tropics		
Ferns and herbaceous flowering plants	+5 to −2	45–48
Trees	+5 to −2	45–55
Subtropics		
Succulents		50–55
Sclerophyllous woody plants	−8 to −12	50–60
Temperate zone		
Evergreen woody plants of coastal regions with mild winters	−6 to −15	50–55
Dwarf shrubs of Atlantic heaths	c. −20	45–50
Deciduous trees and shrubs with broad distribution[a]	−25 to −40	c. 50
Herbs		
Sunny habitats	−10 to −20	48–52
Shady habitats		40–45
Water plants	c. −10	38–42
Cold-winter areas		
Evergreen conifers	−40 or lower	44–50
Alpine dwarf shrubs	−20 to −70	48–54
Herbs of the high mountains and the arctic[a]	−30 to −196	44–54

[a] Leaf primordia in vegetative buds.

by protein denaturation, production of toxic substances or membrane damage (Levitt, 1972).

As we saw in Chapter 4, certain species (e.g. *Geranium sanguineum*) growing in xeric habitats have evolved small, dissected leaves, thus reducing the risk of thermal damage by increasing the rate of convective heat loss (see equation 5.4). However, in addition to this widely adopted adaptation, some plants avoid thermal stress by reducing the amount of solar radiation absorbed by their leaves. Thus the leaves and stems of *Helichrysum newii* growing under intense insolation at 4200 m on Kilimanjaro have high reflection coefficients due to a covering of thick white pubescence (Hedberg, 1964). Similarly, the desert shrub *Encelia farinosa* exhibits seasonal leaf dimorphism, with white pubescent leaves which promote cooling in summer being succeeded under moister conditions by greener, less hairy leaves which favour photosynthesis (Ehleringer and Mooney, 1978; see p. 159). Alternative adaptations are shown by tropical perennials which reduce the amount of energy received by altering leaf angle, folding leaves together or by leaf abscission during periods of drought (Longman and Jenik, 1974).

In addition to displaying morphological features favouring leaf cooling, plant species from hot, dry climates are also physiologically adapted to high tissue temperatures. A particularly good example of this adaptation (more fully discussed in Chapters 2 and 4) is provided by the C4 grasses of the dry tropics and subtropics; due to the high affinity of PEP carboxylase for CO_2, stomatal closure at high temperatures (and high respiration rates) is prevented, and these species can continue to assimilate up to 45–60°C compared with 35–45°C for C3 plants (Ludlow, 1976).

A large proportion of the successful plant species in the hottest and dryest parts of the world have survived by adopting a succulent growth form or as evergreen sclerophylls. However, the low rates of transpiration, associated with efficient water conservation, and the bulky shapes of these plants mean that cooling by water loss and convection will be negligible. Consequently, these species can survive only because they are able to tolerate very high temperatures (Table 5.4); for example, the highest recorded plant temperature is 65°C, measured on the succulent, *Opuntia* (Levitt, 1972). As with frost and drought resistance, the mechanisms of heat resistance are not yet clear but resistance can be induced by "thermal hardening", and it appears to be related to the stability of protein structure (Levitt, 1972).

6. Ionic Toxicity

I. THE NATURE OF TOXICITY

In the tangled environmental web that controls the growth of a plant, it is possible to identify chemical factors that are toxic. For almost all such factors there is a concentration range at which no injurious effects are suffered by any species, and one at which all species are susceptible; in between lies the area of interest to the ecologist, where only a few adapted or resistant species are able to survive. Classic examples are the halophytes of saline soils, calcifuges on acid soils, flood-tolerant plants on waterlogged soils, and, more topically, plants resistant to air pollution. The exception to this are radionuclides, where defined chemical substances (the radioactive elements) are involved, but the actual cause of the toxicity lies in the destructive power of the particles emitted. Consequently, the toxic effect is simply statistical, depending on the number of cells killed by impact of α or β particles, or γ rays, and there is no definable lower threshold below which no toxicity occurs. Although plants can adapt to radiation stress—*Andropogon filifolius* growing on uraniferous soil has more resistant seeds than other populations (Mewissen *et al.*, 1959)—we will not deal with this stress here. This chapter deals only with ionic toxicity; toxicity caused by gases, whether in soil or air, is covered in the next chapter. The ecological situations in which toxicities of 20 elements occur are shown in Table 6.1.

Ionic toxicity can be classified on the basis of two important distinctions:

(i) the concentration at which toxicity occurs;
(ii) whether or not the element is essential to plant growth—can a deficiency occur?

If an ion is toxic only at high concentrations, it may bring with it the problem of low soil water potential; in this case the simplest resistance mechanism, straightforward exclusion of the toxic compound from the plant, would make it impossible for the plant to take up water. Similarly if an ion is both an essential micronutrient and yet toxic at very low concentrations (Zn^{2+}, Cu^{2+}), exclusion may again be inappropriate, unless uptake can be precisely controlled. These two considerations greatly influence both the physiological and ecological responses of plants adapted to resist toxicity.

TABLE 6.1. Ecological situations in which ions of various elements can cause toxicity.

Element	Essential (E) or not (N)	Situation
N	E	NH_4^+ toxic to calcicoles (Rorison, 1975).
P	E	Only under agricultural conditions of very high fertilizer applications (Green and Warder, 1973).
K	E	May compete with Na^+ in obligate halophytes (Austenfeld, 1974).
Ca	E	Toxic to some calcifuges, particularly bog plants.
Mg	E	Toxic on serpentine soils with high Mg:Ca ratios (Proctor, 1971).
S	E	Soils containing sulphide oxidize to produce sulphuric acid and give pH values below 3. Arid zone soils may accumulate Na_2SO_4 by evaporating.
B	E	Occurs at toxic levels in pulverized fuel ash (Hodgson and Buckley, 1975).
Cu, Zn	E ⎫	In natural ore deposits and mine spoil heaps; occasionally by aerial deposition.
Pb, Cd, Cr, Ni	N ⎭	
Fe	E	High concentrations of Fe^{3+} occur in soils of pH below 3·5. Fe^{2+} occurs in waterlogged soils.
Mo	E	As molybdate, in highly calcareous soils.
Na	(E)	In saline and sodic soils.
Cl	(E)	In saline soils.
Mn	E	Usually on acid soils.
Al	N	In soils below pH 4.
H	—	H_3O^+ ions are directly toxic at concentrations above 1 mM (pH below 3).

A. Saline and Sodic Soils

Soils affected by large concentrations of sodium salts arise in two main ways. Most simply, coastal soils that are tidally inundated by sea water at least once a year, are ionically dominated by Na^+ and Cl^- and are characteristically wet (*salt marshes*). Alternatively, in very dry inland areas where evaporation exceeds precipitation, the influx of water containing dissolved salts at very low concentrations may, over long periods, cause the massive accumulation of salt in the upper soil layers, since soil water movement will be predominantly upwards and leaching minimal (*salt deserts*). In these soils Na^+ and SO_4^{2-} are typically most abundant. More rarely soils rich in Na_2CO_3, produced volcanically, or gypsum ($CaSO_4$) are found. A full treatment is given by Chapman (1977). Salt marshes are normally coastal, although they may be found in inland areas where the surface water is saline. Coastal marshes occur in sheltered sites (frequently estuaries) where wave action is slight and deposition of silt allows higher plants to root. No angiosperms have managed to adapt to growing by the sea where wave action is severe, that niche being occupied by seaweeds, with holdfasts rather than roots. In sheltered conditions, the establishment of plants accelerates the deposition of silt and so salt marshes are characteristically sites where successional processes are highly active, since raising of the shore surface reduces the frequency of flooding by salt water and so permits the invasion of differently adapted species. The upper reaches of salt marshes are thus less frequently flooded and so show greater fluctuations in soil NaCl levels, since after flooding they may be leached by rain or concentrated by evaporation. Salt deserts, on the other hand, tend to be highly stable communities, though where salt input is prolonged there may be salination to such a degree as to eliminate all organisms. Salt deserts cover huge areas of the world where evaporation greatly exceeds precipitation, or where inland basins are served by rivers that simply dry up without reaching the sea. The same process is involved when irrigated land becomes useless through build-up of salt, as happened in ancient Sumer, after a thousand years of irrigation (Hyams, 1952; Jacobsen and Adams, 1958). Careful husbandry can avoid such damaging consequences, as in Mexico (Coe, 1964). The consequences for the development of civilization are immense; where irrigation is by the natural flooding of a river, as in the Nile valley, the annual rinsing of the soil by low-salt water prevents salination.

Plants that can grow on soils of high salt content are termed *halophytes*. To survive they have to overcome several problems:

(i) Osmotic effects—the solute potential (ψ_s, cf. Chapter 4) of sea water (c. 3% NaCl) is -20 bar and even 0·5% NaCl has a potential of $-4\cdot2$ bar. To take in water from such solutions a resistant plant must achieve an even lower intracellular potential.

(ii) Specific ion effects—high concentrations of Na^+ and Cl^- are toxic to most cells and Mg^{2+}, SO_4^{2-}, and many others can also be lethal.

(iii) Habitat effects—soils affected by salt tend to be extreme areas in other respects. Salt deserts are of course dry, whereas salt marshes tend to be waterlogged, and the high Na^+ content causes deflocculation of soil clay particles and loss of air-filled pore space. This occurs because the monovalent sodium ions are only half as attractive to individual clay particles as are the divalent calcium ions, the more usual dominant soil cation. Thus, the electrical double layer around Na-saturated clay particles is wider than in a Ca-system, and the repulsion between similarly charged Na-particles acts at a much greater distance than between Ca-particles. Therefore, aggregation of soil particles fails to occur, pore space is low, and the soil acts like a cement.

B. Calcareous and Acid Soils

One of the first things that any field botanist learns is the importance of limestone as a determinant of vegetation. Soils formed over parent materials containing a high proportion of $CaCO_3$ (limestones, chalks, and many other rocks and glacial deposits) tend to have pH values around or above 7, although during soil formation Ca^{2+} ions will be leached out, gradually reducing pH. Nevertheless, limestone soils are well-buffered by the reservoir of $CaCO_3$ and only in extreme conditions will the pH fall below 5. On the other hand soils formed on parent materials such as granite or base-poor sands are typically dominated by Al^{3+} as the major cation; such soils are strongly acid, their pH controlled by a complex hydrated aluminium ion buffer system, which, however, also sets a lower limit to pH. Al-based soils seldom have pH values below about 3·5 to 4·0. Lower pH values are encountered, but usually in soils with very little aluminium—e.g. ombrotrophic peat—or where soil sulphides are oxidized to sulphate, producing in effect sulphuric acid. This occurs in polders reclaimed from the sea (van Beers, 1962), mangrove swamps (Hart, 1963), and in pyrites-containing mine spoils, where pH values may rarely fall as low as 1·0. At such extremes no plants can survive.

The distribution of acid and calcareous soils is therefore a function of the standard soil formation relationship (see Chapter 3, pp. 84–85). Wide areas may be characterized by calcareous or acid soils, determined by appropriate parent material and climatic conditions; local patches may differ due to topographic effects or the deposition of acid litter by vegetation, such as gorse (Grubb and Suter, 1971); and different vertical horizons within soil often vary greatly, due to movement of Ca^{2+} ions within the profile, caused by leaching or evaporation.

The differences between calcareous and acid soils are not just those of pH, nor only of Ca^{2+} and Al^{3+} ion concentrations. H^+ ions are toxic to most plants at pH values below 3, and below pH 4·0 to 4·5 mineral soils contain so much soluble Al^{3+} as to be severely toxic. But pH controls the solubility of Mn^{2+}, Fe^{3+}, and many other cations as well. Both Mn and Fe are essential nutrient elements which may be present at toxic concentrations in acid soils and below deficiency levels in calcareous areas. Of the major nutrients, K^+ is displaced from exchange sites at low pH and lost by leaching, P availability varies in a most complex fashion with pH, but tends to be least at extreme values, and N availability is very low in acid soils because of impaired microbiological activity. Overall, therefore, plants of calcareous soils (*calcicoles*), must contend with deficiencies and plants of acidic soils (*calcifuges*) with toxicities, though there are important exceptions to this generalization. Table 6.2 summarizes these relationships.

C. Metal-contaminated Soils

Few elements reach toxic concentrations in soils at all frequently. Some such as selenium and arsenic can naturally reach toxic levels, but the most important are all heavy metals, principally copper (Cu), zinc (Zn) and lead (Pb), and more rarely cadmium (Cd), chromium (Cr), cobalt (Co), and nickel (Ni). Ores of all these metals occur naturally, often in veins in rocks, and local high concentrations can occur. Such outcrops can be very small, or cover several hectares, as is often the case where ultrabasic rocks such as serpentine, variously rich in Ni, Cr, or other metals, are involved.

Although such natural contamination provides certain fascinating problems, the type of metal-affected soil that has attracted most attention is where the soil is artificially contaminated—polluted by metals. Typically this occurs where waste from mining or smelting operations has been dumped. Such waste varies greatly in metal content, but older extraction methods were often very inefficient and it is not un-

TABLE 6.2. Ionic relationships of calcareous and acid soils.

Ion	Calcifuges on acid soils (pH < 5)	Calcicoles on calcareous soils (pH > 6·5)
H^+	High: may become toxic to non-adapted plants	Low: not required
OH^-	Low: not required	High: may compete with anions for uptake
HCO_3^-	Low: not required	High: may compete with anions for uptake
Ca^{2+}	Low: if very deficient may disrupt membrane function	High: may cause phosphate precipitation at root surface, and compete with other cations for uptake
Al^{3+}	High: not required and may cause precipitation of ions (e.g. $H_2PO_4^-$) at root surface, inhibition of Ca^{2+} uptake and transport, and interfere with DNA metabolism, *inter alia*	Low: not required
Fe^{3+}	High: acts similarly to Al^{3+} in phosphate precipitation	Low: deficiency a major problem
Mn^{2+}	High: toxicity relatively unimportant in relation to Al^{3+}	Low: deficiency common in agricultural conditions
MoO_4^{n-}	Low: deficiency may interfere with N fixation	High: occasionally produces toxicity symptoms
NO_3^- / NH_4^+	Balance in favour of NH_4^+; nitrification inhibited	Balance in favour of NO_3^-; nitrifying bacteria active
$H_2PO_4^-$ / HPO_4^{2-}	$H_2PO_4^-$ dominant species; adsorbed by Fe and Al	HPO_4^{2-} increases; adsorbed by Ca
K^+	Displaced from exchange sites by H^+; leached	Ca^{2+} ions may interfere with uptake

usual to find mining wastes containing 2–3% by weight of metal. Alternatively soil can become contaminated by metals deposited from the air, typically in the neighbourhood of large smelters, but also from such improbable sources as galvanized fences.

Where mineral deposits are the source of contamination, release of the metal ions is usually facilitated by low pH. Copper for example,

TABLE 6.3.   A simple classification of the effects of toxins on plants.

A. Effects on the ability to acquire resources
   (i) acquisition of water: (a) osmotic effects arising from excess solute concentrations
                                      (b) inhibition of cell division, reducing root growth

   (ii) acquisition of nutrients:
                                        (a) competition between ions
                                        (b) damage to membranes
                                        (c) effects on symbionts
                                        (d) inhibition of cell division

   (iii) acquisition of CO_2 and light energy: (a) stomatal malfunction caused by toxic gases[a]
                                        (b) chlorophyll bleaching[a]

B. Effects on the ability to utilize resources
   (i) inhibition of enzyme action
   (ii) inhibition of cell division
   (iii) loss of respiratory substrates; O_2 deficiency[a]

[a] See Chapter 7.

typically occurs as the sulphide or carbonate ores, the latter being obviously more labile in acid conditions. Copper sulphide reacts with ferric sulphate, formed by the natural oxidation of ferric sulphide, to release soluble copper and sulphate ions (Peterson and Nielsen, 1978). The activity of oxidizing bacteria, particularly *Thiobacillus* and *Ferrobacillus* species, upon iron sulphide can indirectly release copper, nickel, zinc, arsenic, and even molybdenum from their native minerals (Firth, 1978). Almost the only important exception to the greater availability of toxic heavy metals in acid soils is molybdenum: in rather exceptional situations, molybdenum toxicity can occur on calcareous soils, as for example in parts of Derbyshire, where carboniferous limestone deposits have high native Mo levels.

II. EFFECTS OF TOXINS ON PLANTS

The range of substances capable of adversely affecting plant growth is enormous, and inevitably the specific effects of these toxins are too numerous to document. For instance Foy *et al.* (1978) suggest that aluminium alone may fix phosphate on root surfaces, and decrease root respiration, cell division, cell wall rigidity and the uptake and utilization of Ca, Mg, P, K, and H_2O. It is possible to classify these effects according to whether they exert their influence on the acquisition of resources by the plant or on the utilization of those resources (Table 6.3). In the former case the toxins can be seen as in some sense acting by exacerbating unfavourability of a second factor (cf. Chapter 1, p. 4), rather than by a direct toxicity. Thus, a plant growing in an already phosphate-deficient soil may appear to suffer from toxicity through the precipitation of phosphate by aluminium at the root surface—what the plant experiences is in effect phosphate deficiency rather than aluminium toxicity.

A. Acquisition of Resources

1. Water

Only three ions commonly reach solution concentrations sufficient to cause plants osmotic problems, without first having lethal specific toxicity. They are chloride (usually in wet saline soils) and sulphate (in dry sodic soils), both typically associated with sodium as the cation, though magnesium and, rarely, calcium may also be involved.

If the roots of a plant are placed in a solution of lower water potential than the xylem of the roots, then water uptake ceases. It was for a long time considered that this was the major cause of salt toxicity, but two pieces of evidence clearly show that this is not normally the case. First, the osmotic potential of the sap of such plants is normally found to be much greater than that of unstressed plants; in other words osmotic adjustment has occurred so that water uptake is still possible.

The second line of evidence derives from the use of large, inert, organic molecules (such as mannitol) to reduce water potentials without producing any "chemical" toxicity. Manohar (1966) used glycerol, which is readily taken up by plants, and mannitol (to which plants are relatively impermeable) to show that a water potential of -15 bar induced by glycerol caused only a short delay (24 h) in pea seed germination whereas the same potential induced by mannitol delayed germination by about ten days. Clearly some osmotic adjustment had occurred, and the low water potential was not inhibitory, but until it had adjusted the seed was unable to rehydrate. Similar effects were shown for root extension, respiration, glucose uptake, and the synthesis of methanol-insoluble compounds by Greenway and Leahy (1970).

Low water potentials are, therefore, not normally damaging even to non-halophytes unless the ions are excluded because they are toxic and adjustment cannot occur. In such a case the plant must either tolerate a water deficit, as discussed in Chapter 4, or else reduce its water potential by internal synthesis of inert metabolites. These mechanisms are of considerable importance. There are, however, no halophytic trees taller than mangroves, which rarely exceed 10–15 m; almost certainly this is because the requirement for a water potential gradient from roots to leaves, coupled with the inevitable reduction in potential due to gravity, would mean that a tree of any size, growing in salt water, would have to endure normal leaf water potentials of −40 bar or lower (cf. Chapter 4).

2. *Nutrients*

In contrast to the physiological experiment, plant roots in soil absorb ions from a complex medium, containing not only the dozen or so essential nutrient ions, but also a range of non-essential ions and organic compounds. If severe imbalances arise in this supply, the plant may not be able to take up nutrients efficiently, either because of direct effects of the toxic ions on root metabolism or function, or simply by competition or other interactions with nutrient ions. As a result even essential ions can become toxic (e.g. magnesium, see below), and plant species show great differences in the extent to which they can tolerate variation in ionic ratios.

The simplest effects are those where interactions occur outside the root. The process of transpiration causes accumulation of some ions at the root surface, if their rate of arrival exceeds their rate of uptake (see Chapter 3), and calcium can certainly accumulate in calcareous soils in this way. Since many calcium salts are insoluble, this may markedly inhibit diffusive supply of these anions, such as sulphate and phosphate. In acid soils, aluminium may accumulate and aluminium phosphate deposits certainly occur on the rhizoplane (McCormick and Bowden, 1972). This Al-bound phosphate may, however, be exchangeable and so still in some measure be available to the plant (Andrew and vanden Berg, 1973).

Damage to the plasmalemma, the selective boundary, may also occur. Calcium, as a plant nutrient, is largely involved in maintaining membrane function (Burstrom, 1968; van Steveninck, 1965), and one of the effects of aluminium toxicity is a reduction in Ca uptake (Clarkson and Sanderson, 1971). It is therefore striking that Lance and Pearson (1969) found that exposure of cotton roots to Al concentrations between 0·15 and 0·30 p.p.m. had identical effects in reducing uptake of Ca, Mg, K, P, nitrate, and water. The generality of the effect suggests that aluminium was causing some fundamental damage to the cell membranes. This is also reflected in increased leakage of K^+ ions across Al^{3+}-treated plasmalemmas, an effect also produced by Cu (Wainwright and Woolhouse, 1975); Zn^{2+} on the other hand does not increase K^+ loss and does not appear to damage the plasmalemma.

More specific effects, however, occur without actual membrane damage, where ions interfere directly with each other's uptake. Generally such interactions may be competitive, where closely related ions compete for the same uptake sites, or non-competitive, where the toxic ion simply inactivates the uptake mechanism. The latter clearly grade into the general membrane disruption phenomena already discussed.

Competitive and non-competitive inhibition can be distinguished by their effect on uptake kinetics. In non-competitive cases, the actual uptake mechanism is incapacitated and so the maximum rate attainable (V_{max}) is reduced, whereas competitive inhibition manifests itself as a raised K_m, or uptake affinity, and unchanged V_{max}, since the inhibition depends on the relative concentrations of the two ions. Competition occurs usually between chemically related ions, such as the alkali metals (Na^+, K^+, Rb^+) or alkali earths (Ca^{2+}, Mg^{2+}, Sr^{2+}). Thus, saline soils may be toxic partly due to competitive inhibition of K^+ uptake, and Mg^{2+} certainly inhibits Ca^{2+} uptake on some serpentine soils with high Mg:Ca ratios (Proctor, 1971).

Such interactions have received surprisingly little attention if one bears in mind the complexity of natural soil solutions. These bear little relation to the artificial nutrient solutions in which ion uptake is normally studied, which have been designed to maximize plant growth or to simplify interpretation. Soil solutions are not only qualitatively and quantitatively different in their inorganic components, but also contain a range of organic compounds, some of which, such as phenolic acids, can profoundly alter ion uptake (Glass, 1973; Fig. 6.1).

It should also be remembered that nutrient supply in soil may be heavily dependent on microbial symbionts, most obviously N-fixing bacteria and P-supplying mycorrhizas (see Chapter 3). Any adverse effects on these symbionts will severely reduce the nutrient supply. Thus most *Rhizobium* strains are more or less inactive below pH 5, though *Myrica gale* (bog myrtle), with an actinomycete symbiont can continue to utilize atmospheric N at a pH as low as 3·3 (Bond, 1951).

B. Utilization of Resources

1. Enzymes
All metabolic behaviour ultimately involves enzymes, which typically operate optimally in well-defined ionic environments. Ions may be in-

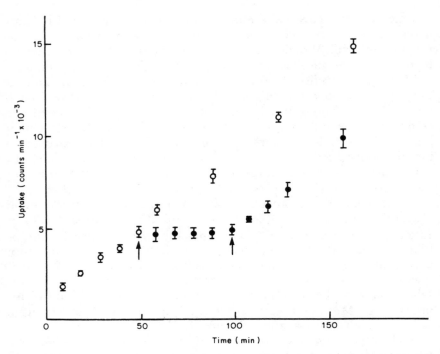

FIG. 6.1.   The effect of p-hydroxybenzoic acid on potassium uptake by excised barley roots. Arrows indicate application and removal respectively of the acid (from Glass, 1974).   Control   (no   inhibitor) $\bigcirc—\bigcirc$;   and $2{\cdot}5 \times 10^{-4}$ M p-hydroxybenzoic acid $\bullet—\bullet$. The first arrow indicates the time when the p-hydroxybenzoic acid was added to the root samples. At the time indicated by the second arrow roots were rinsed briefly and returned to inhibitor-free solutions. Each point (with standard error) is the mean of ten (prior to addition of inhibitor) or five (after addition of inhibitor) replicates.

volved in enzyme functions as structural components of the enzyme molecule (Fe in cytochromes), chelated by an essential co-factor (Mo in nitrate reductase) or simply as an activator (K in pyruvate kinase). Ionic imbalances, therefore, are peculiarly capable of disrupting enzyme action, but the results may be identified at three levels: the enzymic reaction itself, the metabolic process, or some measure of growth.

The direct effects of ions on enzymes depend on both the ion and the plant species. Some, for example Cl^-, tend to have rather general inhibitory effects at high concentrations (Porath and Poljakoff-Mayber, 1964), presumably the result of conformational changes. In contrast ions such as Cu^{2+}, Zn^{2+}, and Ni^{2+} may have specific reactions with particular enzymes at rather low concentration, often by complexing with chemical groups such as sulphydryl. Thus, cadmium ions cause almost total inhibition of nitrate reductase extracted from leaves of *Silene vulgaris* at 0·01 mM but have no effect on iso-citrate dehydrogenase at concentrations as high as 1·0 mM (Fig. 6.2; Mathys, 1975).

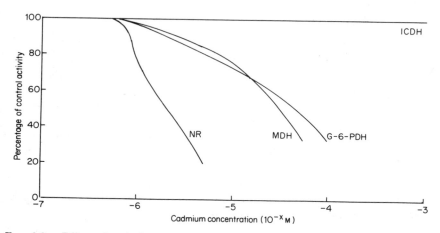

FIG. 6.2.   Effect of cadmium on four enzymes from leaves of *Silene vulgaris*. NR, Nitrate reductase; ICDH, Isocitrate dehydrogenase; MDH, malate dehydrogenase; G-6-PDH, Glucose-6-phosphate dehydrogenase (after Mathys, 1975).

2. Cell Division and Elongation

One of the characteristic symptoms of metal toxicity is the stunting of roots, often accompanied by browning and death of the meristem. This is particularly noticeable if roots of an aluminium-sensitive plant are exposed to low Al concentrations. Using a radioactive scandium isotope ([46]Sc) as an analogue, Clarkson and Sanderson (1969) showed that primary cell walls on the root tip have a very low resistance to Al^{3+} movement, apparently owing to low exchange capacity, so that Al ions rapidly penetrate to the meristematic cells and inhibit DNA synthesis. Sainfoin (*Onobrychis viciifolia*) roots exposed to 20 p.p.m. Al^{3+} were able to incorporate only one third as much ^{32}P in nucleotides as were control roots (Rorison, 1965). In older root segments the primary effect of Al^{3+} and of many other di- and tri-valent cations, appears to be on elongation (cf. Fig. 6.6, p. 218). The elongation of plant cell walls involves the orderly creation and breakage of cross-linkages within the pectic fraction. One of the major functions of Ca^{2+} ions is to regulate this process. Many polyvalent cations can interfere with this, including

Al (Rorison, 1958) and Pb (Lane *et al.*, 1978). In the latter case, lead was found to be bound specifically to the pectinic acid fraction. It is not surprising, therefore, that levels of Ca^{2+} are critical in experiments on metal ion toxicity.

III. RESISTANCE TO TOXICITY

Some plants can grow in soils that contain levels of toxic ions lethal to other species. Four main mechanisms can achieve this:

(i) Phenological escape—where the stress is seasonal the plant may adjust its life-cycle so as to grow in the most favourable season.
(ii) Exclusion—the plant may be able to recognize the toxic ion and prevent its uptake, and so not experience the toxicity.
(iii) Amelioration—the plant may absorb the ion but act upon it in such a way as to minimize its effects. Variously this may involve chelation, dilution, localization, or even excretion.
(iv) Tolerance—the plant may have evolved a metabolic system which can function at potentially toxic concentrations, possibly by means of distinct enzyme molecules.

Those species most able to resist toxic ions are found to employ more than one such mechanism, but the adoption of any one or any combination imposes important physiological and ecological constraints.

A. Escape Mechanisms

1. Phenology
Stresses that vary over a sufficiently long-term and predictable time scale—typically seasonally—permit the adjustment of the life-cycle so that growth occurs at the most favourable time. This is particularly clear in the early spring growth of herbs in temperate deciduous forest (Chapter 2, p. 47) and in the rain-triggered growth of desert ephemerals (Chapter 4, p. 145). There is little evidence as to the seasonality of toxic ion concentrations in soil, though where bacterial transformations of heavy metal ores are involved, one might expect spring levels to be low, since low winter temperatures should inhibit bacterial activity and high rainfall promote leaching. Saline soils, however, do fluctuate considerably. The upper reaches of salt marshes are inundated by sea water only rarely, and at that time the soil water will be 3% NaCl. Subsequently, rainfall may reduce, or evaporation increase that

concentration. As a habitat this zone is therefore subject to large, but mainly unpredictable fluctuations, and is typically characterized by few species. One such is *Juncus maritimus*, which strikingly, and in contrast to other *Juncus* species, shows little osmotic adjustment over a range of external NaCl concentrations from 0–300 mM, since its osmotic potential at zero NaCl concentration can be as low as −18·8 bar (Rozema, 1976).

Unlike the other species studied—*J. gerardi* (a lower salt marsh plant), *J. bufonius* (a plant of wet, non saline soils), and *J. alpino-articulatus* ssp. *atricapillus* (normally an alpine plant, exceptionally found near salt marshes)—*J. maritimus* was unaffected by salinity in terms of growth rate, which was always low, and solute potential, which is maintained at low external salt concentrations by high internal potassium levels (Fig. 6.3). *J. maritimus* apparently manages to survive by a

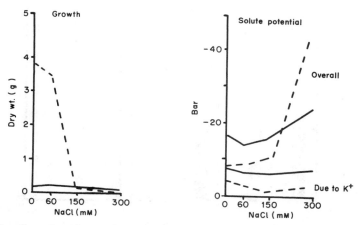

FIG. 6.3.   Growth and osmotic potential of *Juncus maritimus* (solid line) and *J. bufonius* (dotted line) over a range of NaCl concentrations. Note the association between the growth decrease in *J. bufonius* and the increase in solute potential, caused by ions other than K⁺ (from Rozema, 1976).

pre-adaptation to the most severe states of the environment, important because these are unpredictable. In contrast, inland saline areas tend to show a predictable rise in salinity due to evaporation as the summer progresses. Certainly salt concentrations in leaves of halophytes near the Neusiedlersee in Austria do rise during the season (Albert, 1975), but little critical work has been done on phenology in such habitats.

Escape may not, however, require cessation of growth but rather the timing of the most sensitive stage—typically seedling establishment—to coincide with the most favourable period. Dumbroff and Cooper (1974) showed that tomato plants were very sensitive to salt stress (−6 bar) in the first eight days of growth, and suffered irreversible damage. Thereafter both their resistance and their ability to recover from the stress increased. It is probably the need to protect seedlings from salinities that explains the germination responses of *Limonium vulgare*, a common salt-marsh plant. Sea water inhibits germination, which is low even in fresh water; but if seeds are transferred from sea water to fresh water, there is a pronounced stimulation (Boorman, 1967; Fig. 6.4). Clearly

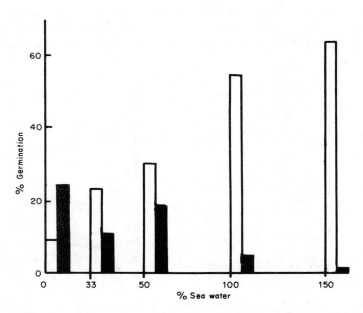

FIG. 6.4.   Effect of varying concentrations of sea water on germination of the seeds of the halophyte *Limonium vulgare*. Solid bars indicate germination in the stated medium; open bars germination in fresh water after 25 days at the stated salinity. Note the inhibitory effect of sea water and its potentiation of subsequent germination in fresh water (from Boorman, 1967).

for the seed, the transfer from sea water to fresh water would signal the onset of temporarily favourable conditions for seedling growth. Similarly, soil pH fluctuates seasonally in many soils, particularly on waterlogged soils as redox potentials change. Gupta and Rorison (1975) found changes of the order of 1 pH unit in a podzol, and regular seasonal changes of 2·0 to 2·5 units may occur in waterlogged peat (Fitter *et al.*, 1980). In mineral soils such changes will have dramatic effects on Al^{3+} concentrations, so that it may be significant that in some species, mature plants can grow in Al^{3+} concentrations that are lethal to seedlings (Rorison *et al.*, 1958).

2. Direct Environmental Modification

More rarely a plant may have the power to alter the environment, so as to reduce the toxicity. Where NO_3^- is the main N-source, anion uptake exceeds cation uptake and OH^- ions are extruded to maintain the electrochemical potential; NH_4^+ uptake requires the loss of H^+ ions with consequent acidification. Riley and Barber (1971) found that soybeans fertilized with NO_3^--N raised rhizosphere pH by 1.4 units; NH_4^+-N fertilizer caused a reduction of 0·5 units. They were able to explain variation in P uptake by this means. Such effects can readily explain the deleterious effect of low pH on *Rumex acetosa* and *Scabiosa columbaria*, a neutrophile and a calcicole respectively, that occurred in the presence of NH_4^+ but not if NO_3^- was supplied. In contrast the calcifuge *Deschampsia flexuosa* was inhibited by high pH in the presence of NO_3^- but insensitive to pH if NH_4^+ was the N-source (Gigon and Rorison, 1972). Somewhat less intuitively obvious is the finding that *Holcus lanatus* grown at low pH is susceptible to Al-toxicity if nitrate is the N-source, but not if NH_4^+ is supplied (Rorison, 1975). The interaction here must be presumed to be more complex.

A further example of environmental modification can be observed in waterlogged soils. For example rice plants can oxidize Fe^{2+} to Fe^{3+} by O_2 excretion from the roots, so avoiding Fe^{2+}-toxicity (Tadano, 1975; cf. Chapter 7).

B. Exclusion

Prima facie, exclusion of a toxic ion would seem to be the ideal resistance mechanism, but it presents a number of problems, both in respect of the ability of the plant to exclude the ion (recognition, damage to external structures), and of the consequences of exclusion (if the ion is either present at osmotically damaging concentrations, or required by the plant in small quantities).

1. Recognition

Plants typically have highly selective uptake systems, capable of distinguishing chemically similar ions, but a number of ion pairs cause problems, particularly K^+ and Na^+, and Ca^{2+} and Mg^{2+}. In saline soils, the otherwise non-functional System II of the uptake isotherm (cf. Chapter 3, p. 72) may be important. At K^+ concentrations appropriate to System I (around 0·5 mM), the K^+/Na^+ selectivity of barley roots is high, but at high concentrations of K^+ and Na^+, this selectivity is found only in halophytes (Epstein, 1969). Potassium is of significance in maintaining osmotic potentials in halophytes subject to fluctuating external salinity (Rozema, 1976; see p. 213), and a mechanism conferring some degree of stability of K^+ uptake over a wide range of NaCl concentrations is therefore necessary.

A similar situation occurs with Ca^{2+} and Mg^{2+}, between which most plants discriminate poorly, so that at very low Ca:Mg ratios in soil, excess Mg accumulates in plant tissue, with toxic effects (Proctor, 1971). Such conditions exist on many serpentine (ultra-basic) soils, and may account for the general paucity of vegetation there. Those plants that do grow on such soils, such as ecotypes of *Agrostis stolonifera* or *A. canina*, appear to take up the two ions to a greater extent in proportion to the external concentrations than do susceptible genotypes, so that their resistance mechanism must be internal. By contrast Olsen (1971; see p. 93) showed that the ability of rye (*Secale*) to withstand low Ca:Mg ratios lay in its ability to discriminate in favour of Ca, and the same is true of the serpentine endemic *Helianthus bolanderi*, when compared with the sunflower *H. annuus* (Madhok and Walker, 1969; Fig. 6.5).

2. External Structures

Even if the plant can recognize the toxic ion and so exclude it, there are still metabolically active structures which cannot be protected in this way. Clearly, all cell membranes in contact with the external solution are potentially at risk, and if the ion can move in the apoplast this may include all cells as far in as the endodermis. As already mentioned (p. 209), copper ions, in contrast to zinc ions, cause leakage of potassium from cells, presumably by membrane damage. Wainwright and Woolhouse (1975) showed that a Cu-resistant race of *Agrostis tenuis* was only half as susceptible to such K^+ leakage as a Zn-resistant or a normal race.

In addition, all plant roots have surface enzymes, of which the best known and studied are the acid phosphatases. The function of these enzymes is not clear; it is widely assumed that they are involved with the breakdown of organic phosphate in soil, but there is no evidence that plants are able to utilize directly soil organic P (Abeyakoon and Pigott, 1975). Nevertheless, acid phosphatases are widespread and are inhibited by toxic ions in soil. Wainwright and Woolhouse (1975)

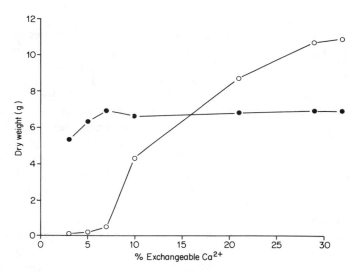

FIG. 6.5. Growth of two species of *Helianthus* in response to increasing Ca supply. *H. annus* (○) is the common garden sunflower; *H. bolanderi* (●) is an endemic Californian serpentine species, adapted to growth in soils of high Mg : Ca ratios. The serpentine species is almost insensitive to Ca (from Madhok and Walker, 1964).

found differential responses to Al^{3+} and Cu^{2+} of enzymes from different ecotypes of *A. tenuis*. In the case of Cu, kinetic analysis indicated a non-competitive inhibition, with the presumed adaptive differences resting in a difference in inhibitor constant (k_i) between the two ecotypes. The k_i for copper-resistant plants was 1·50 mM Cu^{2+}, and for the susceptible enzyme 0·54 mM Cu^{2+}; the smaller value indicates that the susceptible enzyme has a greater affinity for copper, which presumably forms an ineffective complex with it.

Such results suggest a change in the molecular properties of the enzyme as a basis for resistance to toxicity. However, the preparation used was of cell-wall fragments rather than purified enzyme, which leaves open the possibility that the enzyme was in some way protected from free copper ions in the resistant ecotype. This is certainly more consistent with work on other systems exhibiting enzyme "tolerance" (see pp. 222–225). Nevertheless, cell walls, both inside and outside the plant, are liable to experience higher concentrations of toxic ions than other parts of the plant, and there are many active molecules in or adjacent to these walls, most conspicuously the uptake systems for other ions. Whether or not these show a direct resistance to ionic toxicity is not yet known.

3. Deficiencies: Ionic Imbalance

As a resistance mechanism, exclusion obviously provides problems where the toxic ion is metabolically essential at low concentrations, such as Cu, Zn, or Fe. Is resistance to these ions, therefore, less often achieved by exclusion than is the case for Pb, Cd, Cr, and other non-essential toxins? The evidence is far from clear, and although it was possible for Antonovics *et al.* (1971) to state that "nowhere . . . is there any evidence for (tolerant) plants having an exclusion mechanism", Mathys (1973) clearly demonstrated exclusion of zinc in *Agrostis tenuis*, whereas Wu and Antonovics (1975) found accumulation of Zn in resistant ecotypes of *Agrostis stolonifera*.

At present it is not possible to make firm generalizations on this point, but it is likely that the stimulatory effects on growth and root elongation produced by low concentrations of Al^{3+} in calcifuge species (Clarkson, 1967; Fig. 6.6) are due to the presence of Al-binding sites on the root surface. When these are unoccupied by Al^{3+} ions they tend to bind the similar Fe^{3+} ions, and may thus cause Fe deficiency. Grime and Hodgson (1969) showed that growth responses to Al tend to be diphasic, with an initial decline at very low concentrations, due to the toxic effect of Al on cell division, and then a minor peak at slightly higher concentrations, apparently resulting from the liberation of Fe

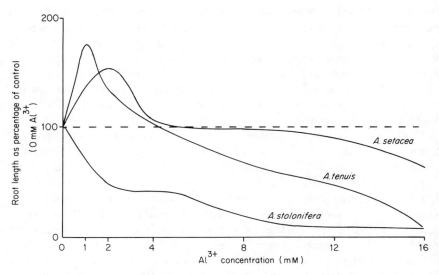

Fig. 6.6.   Effect of Al^{3+} ions on root length growth in one week of three species of *Agrostis*. *A. setacea*, calcifuge; *A. tenuis*, mildly calcifuge; *A. stolonifera*, mildly calcicole (from Clarkson, 1966).

from binding sites on the cell wall. Finally, at high Al concentrations, growth falls off again. The position of the peak of growth varied according to the pH-tolerance of the species or ecotype, falling at around 20–30 μM Al^{3+} in calcifuges such as *Nardus stricta* and *Ulex europaeus*, and nearer 5 μM in calcicoles (*Bromus erectus, Scabiosa columbaria*).

In those experiments the position of the initial growth depression also altered—from around 1 μM in calcicoles to as high as 10 μM in calcifuges—and there is evidence (Foy *et al.*, 1978) that some Al-resistance may be due to an ability to prevent Al^{3+} migrating through the free space to the meristem, so protecting cell division. Hemming (quoted by Foy *et al.*, 1978) found that a resistant wheat variety could withstand a hundred-fold increase in external Al concentration before Al entered the root meristem, as compared with a sensitive variety. This again suggests a binding mechanism in the cell wall.

4. Osmotic Imbalance

There is little evidence that low water potentials are inherently damaging, even to mesophytes, until extremely low values (less than -20 bar) are reached. As long as the xylem water potential is lower than that of the soil water, uptake will continue. If such osmotic adjustment does not take place, water stress will occur. Tal (1971) found that cultivated tomatoes (*Lycopersicon esculentum*) took up less Na and Cl when subjected to high salinity than the wild *L. peruvianum*, with adverse effects on both relative water content and growth rate. In contrast, Greenway (1962) using barley and Gates *et al.* (1970) with soybean varieties found precisely the opposite: it was the sensitive varieties that took up most salt. Presumably there osmotic adjustment was achieved at the expense of a toxic effect of the salt itself.

Generally, agricultural species achieve resistance by exclusion (Greenway, 1973) and the same is true for a number of wild plants. Tiku and Snaydon (1971) found that salt-marsh populations of *Agrostis stolonifera* had lower leaf Na concentrations than normal plants at the same salinity. It is dangerous to draw conclusions from leaf analyses (see below, p. 220), but this conforms with the observations of Ahmad and Wainwright (1976) that the leaves of the salt-marsh *A. stolonifera* were less wettable and retained only 1/16th as much NaCl after immersion in sea water as leaves of inland plants: apparently the exclusion mechanism here is in part physical.

Cultivated plants, however, rarely experience severe salt stress, and appear to be able to make good the osmotic deficit created by salt exclusion, by internal synthesis of solutes. Arid saline habitats, in contrast, present much lower soil water potentials, and halophytes there appear to carry out much of their osmotic adjustment by NaCl uptake. When this occurs, other problems arise, as salt is generally highly toxic at such concentrations.

A fuller discussion of the significance of water potentials is given in Chapter 4.

C. Amelioration

For a variety of reasons it may not be possible for a plant to exclude a toxic ion. If high internal concentrations must be withstood, the ions will either have to be removed from circulation in some way, or tolerated within the cytoplasm. The former process is here termed amelioration. Four approaches are apparent:

(i) Localization, either intra- or extracellularly, and usually in the roots;
(ii) Excretion, either actively through glands on shoots or by the roots; or passively by accumulation in old leaves followed by abscission;
(iii) Dilution, which is of primary significance in relation to salinity;
(iv) Chemical inactivation, so that the ion is present in a combined form of reduced toxicity.

1. Localization

Analyses of both roots and shoots of a plant are rather rarely carried out, but data compiled by Tyler (1976) and summarized in Table 6.4 suggest that for *Anemone nemorosa* metals can be divided into four groups:

(i) Those more or less equally distributed throughout the plant, in-including the essential major nutrients K, Ca, and Mg. Rb behaves as K in most plants.
(ii) Those showing some accumulation in the root, including the three important micro-nutrients Cu, Zn, and Mn.
(iii) Non-essential, toxic ions such as Al and Cd, which are primarily stored in the root. Fe, a micronutrient, also falls into this class, presumably because of its high availability in soil, in contrast to Cu, Zn, and Mn.
(iv) Pb is clearly exceptional, in that the root content is grossly higher than that of the shoots. It is possibly significant, however, that its actual concentration in the shoots is the same as that for Cd.

Accumulation of toxic ions by roots is a widespread phenomenon. In

TABLE 6.4. Shoot concentrations and ratios of root concentration to shoot concentration for 12 elements in *Anemone nemorosa* (from Tyler, 1976).

		Shoot concentration (p.p.m.)	root : shoot ratio
Widely distributed	Ca	7180	0·8
	Mg	2970	1·3
	K	11,400	1·3
	Rb	35	1·6
Slight root storage	Mn	405	2·3
	Cu	10·5	2·4
	Zn	113	3·6
Major root storage	Al	260	10·7
	Cd	1·24	11·7
	Fe	217	12·4
	Na	242	16·7
Shoot exclusion	Pb	1·04	62·6

all but one of the examples quoted in Table 6.4, concentrations in the roots were higher than in the shoots. Even if roots have an inherently higher tolerance to toxins than shoots, this clearly implies some form of localization.

Turner (1969) showed that zinc resistance in *Agrostis tenuis* was associated with the accumulation of the element in cell wall fractions. In both resistant and normal plants 70–80% of Zn in the root cell walls was in the pectic fraction; the distinction lay in the proportion of root Zn that was in the cell walls as opposed to the soluble fraction—two-thirds in the resistant, one-third in the sensitive plants (Peterson, 1969). Recently a very specific association has been shown between Pb^{2+} ions and the pectinic acid fraction of the cell wall (Lane *et al.*, 1978). The pectic fractions of the cell wall have a considerable cation exchange capacity and the ability to form cross-linked structures—hence one of the major roles of Ca in plant metabolism—and so are well suited to the binding of polyvalent cations. However, several limitations must be borne in mind. First, the toxicity due to NaCl will not be amenable to this solution, as both ions are monovalent; secondly cell walls are not inert, but contain active enzymes (cf. p. 216); and thirdly any such system is likely to be saturable, and so have a threshold effectiveness.

There are two possible escapes from the last problem. It is possible that binding sites could be continually synthesized within each cell wall, but this would certainly require enzyme action, and these enzymes would then be exposed to the toxic ion. Alternatively, continued growth could provide new sites for chelation. In the latter case the maintenance of a healthy meristem is critical, and, particularly in the case of Al, therefore, it seems probable that the ability to protect the meristem from damage may be central to the resistance mechanism.

(a) *Intracellular*. If very much higher concentrations of an ion are found in the roots than the shoots, it is strong evidence for extra-cellular localization, possibly by binding to the pectic fractions of the cell walls. Once ions have crossed the plasmalemma, there is no general reason for their restriction to the roots. If the ion is to be kept out of general circulation, it must be accumulated in some particular compartment within the cell. Lead appears to accumulate in dictyosome vesicles in the corn *Zea*, with mitochondria, plastids and nuclei remaining Pb-free (Malone *et al.*, 1974). Isolated mitochondria are capable of accumulating Pb^{2+} *in vitro*, so that clearly some specific affinity is exhibited by the dictyosomes.

The intracellular distribution of NaCl is more complex. The chloroplasts of the halophyte *Limonium vulgare* appear to accumulate Cl^- (Larkum, 1968). More generally, however, salt accumulated by plants to maintain osmotic integrity appears largely in the vacuole. Direct evidence for this is limited, although Hall *et al.* (1974) showed Rb^+ accumulation there, but convincing indirect evidence comes from the total lack of specific tolerance to toxic ions exhibited by higher plant enzymes active within the cell (cf. p. 223).

Enzymes from halophytic bacteria, which of course have extremely limited intracellular compartmentation, can operate *in vitro* at very high NaCl concentrations (Ingram, 1957). In those eukaryotes that have been examined, from fungi (e.g. *Dunaliella parva*, Heimer (1973)) to higher plants, no intracellular enzymes have been shown convincingly to exhibit any resistance to high concentrations of NaCl. Occasionally stimulations of enzyme activity are reported at low NaCl concentrations, usually less than 100 μM, but these can be found equally in glycophytes and halophytes.

The explanation appears to be that NaCl is isolated in the vacuole and so is not in the same compartment as the enzymes. However, this implies an osmotic imbalance between cytoplasm and vacuole: the concentration of Cl^- for example, in the vacuoles of the alga *Tolypella intricata* was five times that in the cytoplasm (Larkum, 1968). The cytoplasm must be at the same water potential as the vacuole, and this is achieved using organic solutes. Thus, the halophilic fungus *Dunaliella parva* contains large quantities of glycerol (Ben-Amotz and Avron, 1973); its nitrate reductase is unaffected *in vitro* by glycerol concentrations greater than 3 M, but although it can grow in 2 M NaCl (4 times sea water), nitrate reductase activity is reduced by 50% in 0·4 M NaCl. The alga *Ochromonas malhamensis* also uses glycerol for osmotic balancing (Kraus, 1969).

It appears to be a fairly general observation that the enzymes and organelles of halophytes are not tolerant of high NaCl concentrations, but can withstand the low water potentials of isosmotic solutions of organic solutes. Von Willert (1974) found that malate dehydrogenase in several halophytes was in fact more inhibited by sucrose than by NaCl, but Stewart and Lee (1974) have found evidence that the amino acid proline is used by many halophytes for osmotic balance. In a wide range of plant species, they found proline to comprise on average 54·6% of the amino-acid pool in halophytes, as compared to 2·9, 2·4, and 4·0% respectively in calcicoles, calcifuges, and ruderals. Proline accumulation was directly related to the salinity of the medium and was found to have no effect on the activity of nine enzymes extracted from *Triglochin maritima*, at concentrations where NaCl was extremely inhibitory (Fig. 6.7). Since the concentrations used (up to 700 mM) were comparable to measured internal NaCl levels, and since Treichel (1975) found that the ratio of proline to Na^+ and Cl^- in the vacuole was maintained constant in three halophytes, the suggested role for proline is very attractive. Stewart and Lee were also able to show that inland races of *Armeria maritima* had a much lesser tendency to ac-

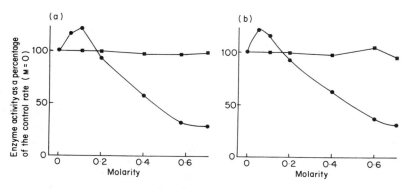

FIG. 6.7.   The effect of proline (■) and NaCl (●) on the activity of two enzymes extracted from *Triglochin maritima*. (a) glutamate dehydrogenase; (b) nitrate reductase (from Stewart and Lee, 1974).

cumulate proline than maritime ones, when subjected to NaCl concentrations above 100 mM.

Of the eleven halophytes tested by Stewart and Lee, one, *Plantago maritima*, showed no proline accumulation; presumably it achieved osmo-regulation by other means. Indeed Storey *et al.* (1977) have found that another amino-acid, glycine-betaine, is of greater significance than proline in many species, and it is established that different, though analogous, mechanisms, operate in relation to heavy metals. Here there is no osmotic problem and zinc for example may be localized in the vacuole. The problem here is the electrochemical balance, and this is solved by complexing the Zn^{2+} ions with malate, so avoiding disturbance of the electrochemical equilibrium (Mathys, 1977).

As with halophytes, there is no evidence for actual tolerance by intracellular enzymes to high concentrations of ions, but the resistant ecotypes maintain full enzyme function *in vivo* by means of compartmentation. Indeed, zinc-resistant *Silene vulgaris* appears to have an increased zinc requirement, presumably because of an active chelating system: the activity of nitrate reductase in its leaves is increased by growing the plant in 0·4 mM Zn, whereas even 0·1 mM is inhibitory to the non-resistant ecotype (Mathys, 1975; Fig. 6.8).

(*b*) *Chemical inactivation.* Zinc resistance is a multiple phenomenon, partly involving exclusion in the root cell walls and partly localization in the cell vacuoles, where the ion is complexed with malate. Such complexes are probably widespread—copper, for example, is normally translocated chelated with polyamino-polycarboxylic acids (Tiffin,

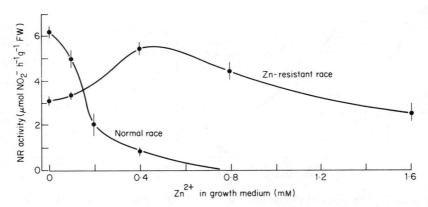

FIG. 6.8. *In vivo* activity of nitrate reductase in leaves of *Silene vulgaris* cultivated for four weeks at various levels of Zn^{2+} (from Schiller, 1974).

1972)—and may even allow the plant to retain the toxic ion in the metabolic compartment, but in an inactive form.

When interest in the calcicole-calcifuge problem first appeared in experimental form much stress was laid on Ca levels. It is now generally accepted that the effects found on strongly acid or calcareous soils are better explained in terms of Al toxicity and Fe deficiency, amongst others. Nevertheless Ca is one of the most variable elements in different soils and its significance in less extreme conditions has perhaps been overlooked. Horak and Kinzel (1971) have attempted to classify plants in respect of their K:Ca ratios and the form in which Ca occurs in the plant. Using standard diagrams (Fig. 6.9), they suggest the existence of three distinct forms of cation nutrition:

(i) oxalate plants, which take up Ca but remove it from circulation as oxalate, such as Polygonaceae, Chenopodiaceae, most Caryophyllaceae, and Violaceae (e.g. *Silene inflata*, Fig. 6.9);

(ii) calciotrophes, which require high concentrations of free calcium, such as the Crassulaceae, and most of the Cruciferae and Leguminosae (e.g. *Coronilla vaginalis*, Fig. 6.9);

(iii) potassium plants, which have large amounts of K and little free Ca, and are found in the Umbelliferae, Campanulaceae, and Compositae (e.g. *Achillea clavenae*, Fig. 6.9).

The ecological significance of this metabolic diversity is unclear, since the ability to tolerate calcareous or acid soils follows no such clear taxonomic pattern. It may influence the ability of plants to colonize unusual habitats, such as serpentine soils with high Mg:Ca ratios. Serpentine-adapted plants do not generally exclude Mg (Proctor, 1971), but may bind it as oxalate (e.g. *Petrorhagia saxifraga*, Caryophyllaceae—Ritter-Studnicka, 1971) or, in calciotrophe species, simply allow it to accumulate in the cell sap (*Sedum album*, *Biscutella laevigata*—Horak and Kinzel, 1971).

It is perhaps necessary to gain a wider perspective on cation utilization. Austenfeld (1974b) subjected *Salicornia europaea*, a characteristic salt-marsh plant, to a range of salinities, and found that the Na^+ content of the plant responded in a simple fashion to a range of NaCl concentrations from 0 to 250 mM. The bulk of the Na^+ was water-soluble, whereas the level of water-soluble Ca^{2+} was low and constant. The acid-soluble Ca^{2+} level, however, declined with increasing salinity, as did acid-soluble oxalate, whereas the water-soluble oxalate increased dramatically (Fig. 6.10). Possibly *Salicornia* uses oxalate to inactivate Ca^{2+} when grown at low salinity, and Na^+ at high salinities. If *Halimione portulacoides*, another salt-marsh plant, is grown at high NaCl

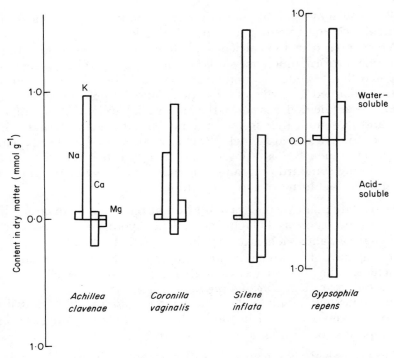

Fɪɢ. 6.9. Diagrams to illustrate nutritional differences in response to soil pH. Each histogram shows the proportions of water- and acid-soluble Na, K, Ca, and Mg. The scale of Na is enlarged 10-fold relative to the others (from Kinzel, 1969).

levels, again water-soluble oxalate increases, and at high $CaCl_2$ concentrations, it is the water-insoluble fraction that accumulates.

2. Excretion

Animals faced with excessive ion loads typically excrete them. Plants generally rely more on controls in uptake—simpler because their food is taken up in its component parts, not as a package—but are capable of excretion. A major disadvantage of excretion for plants, however is that, because they are stationary, the excreted substances will be returned to the root zone and may eventually lead to a build-up of toxin. This does not apply, of course, to plants growing in water.

The simplest form of excretion is the loss of an organ which has become saturated with the toxin. It is generally true that old leaves have much higher salt or heavy metal contents than young leaves and buds.

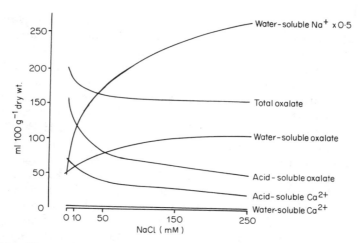

FIG. 6.10. Changes in amounts and extractability of Ca, Na, and oxalate in *Salicornia europaea* in response to salinity. Note the increase of water-soluble oxalate as internal Na rises and the correlation between acid-soluble Ca and acid-soluble oxalate (from Austenfeld, 1974).

Indeed old leaves of tea may contain up to 30,000 p.p.m. (3%) Al, most of which is in the epidermis (Matsumoto *et al.*, 1976). Plants which accumulate Al in the shoots in this fashion are generally found in the more primitive, woody families (Chenery and Sporne, 1976), suggesting that this technique was adopted early on in Angiosperm evolution. It is noticeable that localization may also occur within a leaf: yellow margins of mustard leaves contained 2300 p.p.m. Mn, while the green parts had only 570 p.p.m. (Williams *et al.*, 1971). What appears at first sight to be a toxicity symptom, may be a part of the plants resistance mechanism.

The relationship between toxin accumulation and abscission may be complex, for high salt levels may hasten senescence (Prisco and O'Leary, 1972). The same is almost certainly true of toxic heavy metals, as copper induces leaf chlorosis even in the very resistant *Becium homblei* (Reilly and Reilly, 1973). In halophytes, abscission is most significant in rosette plants, which continually produce new leaves as the old ones senesce (Albert, 1975).

More active excretion also occurs, at least for salt. Salt is apparently actively withdrawn from the xylem back into the xylem parenchyma (Yeo *et al.*, 1977) and then possibly extruded from the roots back into the medium; certainly a potassium-stimulated Na^+ efflux can be shown to occur across root plasmalemmas (Jeschke, 1973). The most important route, however, is certainly through the glands found on leaves of mangroves, *Atriplex* species, and *Halimione portulacoides*, amongst others. In *Halimione* the glands are bicellular, the distal cell being highly vacuolated. When the plants are grown in high salt media the glands always contain much higher concentrations of Na^+ and Cl^- than the sap from the leaves (Baumeister and Kloos, 1974). The glands are highly selective, K^+, Na^+, Cl^- and HCO_3^- being secreted against a concentration gradient and Ca^{2+}, NO_3^-, SO_4^-, and $H_2PO_4^-$ being retained against a concentration gradient.

The activity of these glands, at least in *Limonium vulgare*, is not constitutive but is induced by growth in NaCl (Hill and Hill, 1973). A Cl^--stimulated ATPase in these glands shows a 300% increase in activity if incubated *in vitro* with NaCl, as compared with water or even Na_2SO_4. Such a flexible system could be of great significance in environments showing wide fluctuations. A further advantage of inducibility is in the metabolic cost of an energy-consuming process such as salt excretion: in *Tamarix ramosissima* 65% of leaf Na^+, 82% of leaf Cl^- (and strikingly 90% of leaf Al^{3+} and 88% of leaf Si) could be removed by washing (Kleinkopf and Wallace, 1974); no other elemental losses exceeded 40%. Although net photosynthesis was actually stimulated by up to 200 meq litre^{-1} of NaCl, growth declined even at 10 meq litre^{-1} and was reduced to 32% of the control at 200 meq litre^{-1}. The growth decrease was apparently due to energy losses through increased respiration maintaining salt excretion.

3. Dilution

Toxic metals, such as zinc and copper, have rather specific affinities for particular biochemical groups. Thus copper reacts with sulphydryl groups, and nitrate reductase, an SH-enzyme, is particularly susceptible to Cu-poisoning; zinc reacts primarily with carboxyl groups. For these toxins, dilution by increasing cell water content is not a practicable resistance mechanism. Against salinity, with its osmotic and non-specific toxic effects (cf. p. 203), dilution is widespread and effective.

In many halophytes succulence, an increase in the water content per unit dry weight, is specifically stimulated by NaCl. Both Na^+ and Cl^- ions can produce succulence and there is an intriguing link between succulence and CAM metabolism (cf. Chapters 2 and 4). In *Mesembryanthemum crystallinum* high salt levels induce both succulence and CAM, and the malate produced by CAM appears to have an additional role in balancing charge discrepancy between Na^+ and Cl^-.

D. Tolerance

Resistant prokaryotes and some simple eukaryotes, such as yeasts, show true tolerance of their metabolic systems. Enzymes extracted from them operate *in vitro* in the presence of toxin concentrations lethal to the enzymes of eukaryotes. The membranes of halophilic bacteria are astonishingly permeable. *Halobacterium* admits molecules up to a molecular weight of 40,000 (Ginzburg, 1969).

Eukaryotes have much more complex intracellular compartmentation, and rely on this to ensure that their metabolic systems do not experience high concentrations of toxins. Nevertheless, such stress may induce enzymic changes. Salt induces the synthesis of a new isozyme of malate dehydrogenase in peas (Hassan-Porath and Poljakoff-Mayber, 1979), which may be better equipped to operate at low potentials.

If one examines plants under mild stress, it is apparent that enzyme adaptation can occur. Cultivated oat is a calcifuge and has an Mg^{2+}-activated ATPase system in the roots; under low-Ca conditions it operates adequately. By contrast the calcicolous wheat has a Ca^{2+}-activated ATPase inhibited by Mg^{2+}: if grown under low-salt conditions, however, ATPase activity is equally stimulated by Ca^{2+} and Mg^{2+} (Kylin and Kahr, 1973). Clearly some enzymic changes have occurred.

There are some enzymes, however, which cannot be protected by compartmentalization—those in the plasmalemmas and cell walls. In some cases cell wall enzymes, particularly acid phosphatases, have been shown to be tolerant of much higher levels of toxic ions (Cu^{2+}, Zn^{2+}) in resistant than in normal plants (Wainwright and Woolhouse, 1975). Unfortunately, rather little is known of the function of these enzymes.

IV. THE ORIGIN OF RESISTANCE

Some forms of resistance to toxic ions are ancient. Saline habitats are certainly as old as the Angiosperms and the high proportion of halophytes in some families, in particular the Chenopodiaceae, including the genera *Chenopodium*, *Atriplex*, *Halimione*, *Salicornia*, *Suaeda* and *Salsola*, is strongly indicative of an ancient origin. Similarly Al accumulators, plants containing more than 1000 p.p.m. Al in their shoots, tend to be primitive on taxonomic grounds (Chenery and Sporne, 1968), suggesting that this physiologically crude method of excretion is also in evolutionary terms a first attempt.

It seems likely that the more sophisticated mechanisms have evolved more recently, and particularly the combinations of resistance mechan-

isms that characterize most specialist toxicity-resistant species. In many
cases resistance is found to be multi-layered—an exclusion mechanism
at the root reducing the intensity, and the ions that do penetrate being
localized, inactivated, or excreted.

In the case of heavy-metal resistance at least, it has been clearly demonstrated by Bradshaw and others that individuals with a measure of
resistance exist in normal populations not previously exposed to toxicity
(Walley *et al.*, 1974). Table 6.5 shows that plants of *Agrostis tenuis*

TABLE 6.5.   Selection for Cu and Zn resistance in *Agrostis tenuis* (Walley
et al., 1974). Plants were grown for four months in soil, Copper-mine waste,
or Zinc-mine waste, and the resistance of survivors measured by rooting
tillers in 0.5 g litre^{-1} Ca $(NO_3)_2$, containing the appropriate metal. Resistance
is measured on a 0–100 scale, with 100 representing insensitivity to the toxin.

| Population | Treatment | Mean and (maximum) tolerance of survivors to | |
		Zn	Cu
Pasture	Direct measurement	0·6 (1·7)	2·0 (8·6)
Commercial	Grown on soil	N.D.	5·6 (8·5)
	Grown on Cu-waste	N.D.	48·0 (77·5)
	Grown on Zn-waste	31·8 (41·3)	0·3 (0·9)
Copper mine	Direct measurement	0·8 (0·8)	79·0 (87·5)
	Grown on soil	17·6 (20·2)	85·3 (93·5)
	Grown on Zn-waste	36·4 (47·8)	52·1 (66·9)
Zinc mine	Direct measurement	93·0 (93·0)	3·8 (3·8)

growing on zinc- or copper-waste from old mines have high resistance
to the appropriate metal, and to that metal only. It is possible, however, by growing commercial seed on contaminated soil to select for a
few individuals (1–2%) which have Cu-resistance indices as high as the
naturally occurring populations. Zinc-resistance appears to be more
complex, since the most resistant individual selected was only about
half as resistant as the mine population.

If such effects can be produced in a population in one generation,
one would naturally expect to observe them occurring in the wild.
Zinc-resistance has been observed under a galvanized fence after 30
years (Bradshaw *et al.*, 1965), and progressive increases in Cu-resistance
in lawns established at different times around a copper refinery were
found by Wu and Bradshaw (1972; Fig. 6.11).

The dramatic effects of heavy metal toxicity on plants and the consequently massive selection pressures have highlighted the ease with

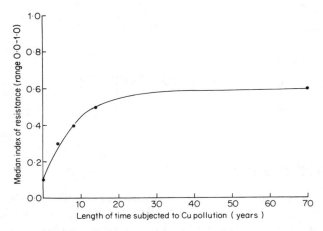

Fig. 6.11. Rate of increase of copper resistance in a population of *Agrostis tenuis* around a copper smelter. (Data from Wu and Bradshaw, 1972).

which physiological attributes of plants can be altered. Recently it has been shown that the adaptation of plants to many other environmental variables exhibits a similar small-scale pattern. *Anthoxanthum odoratum* grows in many of the Park Grass plots at Rothamsted which have received different fertilizer treatments for over 120 years. Plants from closely adjacent plots are clearly distinct in their responses to Ca, Al, P, and Mg (see, for example, Davies and Snaydon, 1974).

Typically, such adaptation involves ecotypic differentiation, that is the evolution of distinctly adapted genotypes. More rarely, resistance is explained by phenotypic plasticity, as appears to be true for the resistance of *Typha latifolia* to zinc, although possibly *Typha* is physiologically inherently Zn-resistant (MacNaughton *et al.*, 1974). Nevertheless it seems likely that investigation of plastic responses to mild toxicity would be amply repaid.

7. Gaseous Toxicity

I. ANAEROBIOSIS IN SOILS

As we saw in Chapter 4, freely draining soils cannot retain water in pores wider than 10–60 μm and therefore, even at field capacity they tend to contain substantial air-filled pore spaces (normally in the range 10–30% of soil volume) which become even more extensive as water is withdrawn from the capillary pores by plant roots. Consequently, the oxygen content of the soil air is usually maintained at 15–20% by gaseous diffusion, giving adequate supplies of oxygen for root growth and metabolism (Russell, 1973).

However, in the many "wetlands" (marshes, mires, swamps) of the world, soil drainage is impeded by the low permeability of the underlying subsoil or rock, or by high groundwater levels, giving seasonal or permanent waterlogging when the soil pore space is almost entirely occupied by water. Under these conditions, the oxygen in trapped pockets of air is rapidly exhausted by soil and root respiration, and further supplies of oxygen from the free atmosphere are effectively cut off by the very low rate of oxygen diffusion through water (10^{-4} times the rate in air). Thus waterlogged soils rapidly become anaerobic and aerobic respiration rates fall to a very low level.

However, in the absence of oxygen, facultative and obligate anaerobic organisms are able to maintain soil respiration by transferring electrons from the respiratory chain to a range of electron acceptors other than oxygen. Thus, in contrast to the normal aerobic reaction which yields water:

$$O_2 + 4H^+ + 4 \text{ electrons} \rightarrow 2H_2O \tag{7.1}$$

anaerobic reactions such as:

$$NO_3^- + 2H^+ + 2 \text{ electrons} \rightarrow H_2O + NO_2^- \tag{7.2}$$
$$\text{(further reduced to } N_2O \text{ or } N_2\text{)}$$
$$MnO_2 + 4H^+ + 2 \text{ electrons} \rightarrow Mn^{2+} + 2H_2O \tag{7.3}$$
$$Fe(OH)_3 + 3H^+ + 1 \text{ electron} \rightarrow Fe^{2+} + 3H_2O \tag{7.4}$$

$$SO_4^{2-} + 10H^+ + 8 \text{ electrons} \rightarrow H_2S + 4H_2O \qquad (7.5)$$
$$CO_2 + 8H^+ + 8 \text{ electrons} \rightarrow CH_4 + 2H_2O \qquad (7.6)$$

result in the loss of nitrate from the soil as gaseous N_2O or N_2 (denitrification) and the accumulation of phytotoxic substances such as H_2S and high concentrations of soluble Fe^{2+} and Mn^{2+} ions. The anaerobic decomposition of soil organic matter also releases a variety of toxic organic chemicals (especially carboxylic acids) and a number of hydrocarbons including the gaseous plant growth regulator, ethylene (Russell, 1977; Ponnamperuma, 1972).

A. The Effects of Anoxia on Plant Roots

In plant cells receiving an adequate supply of oxygen, the oxidation of carbohydrate to yield energy for growth and metabolism normally takes place in three stages. In the first stage (the Embden-Meyerhof-Parnas Pathway or Glycolysis; Fig. 7.1(a)), the conversion of 1 mol of glucose to 2 mol of pyruvate is associated with the net synthesis of 2 mol of the high-energy intermediate, ATP (which is the main form in which energy is transported and utilized in plants) and 2 mol of $NADH_2$. In the second stage, the complete oxidation of each mol of pyruvate to carbon dioxide by the Krebs or Tricarboxylic Acid Cycle (Fig. 7.1(b)) is accompanied by the synthesis of 1 mol of ATP and a further 5 mol of $NADH_2$ (or reduced flavoprotein). Finally, the energy stored in each mol of $NADH_2$ is used for the synthesis of 3 mol of ATP (2 for FPH_2), by means of the mitochondrial respiratory chain (Fig. 7.1(c)); in this process, electrons and protons are transferred, via the cytochrome chain, from $NADH_2$ to oxygen, giving water. Overall, the complete aerobic respiration of 1 mol of glucose yields 38 mol of ATP (Lehninger, 1965).

When a soil in which plants are growing becomes waterlogged, the cytochrome chain in the root cells ceases to function in the absence of molecular oxygen and this, in turn, leads to the accumulation of $NADH_2$ and the suppression of the Krebs cycle. The resulting build-up of acetaldehyde, the end product of anaerobic glycolysis (fermentation, Fig. 7.1), induces the synthesis of the enzyme alcohol dehydrogenase (ADH) which catalyses the transformation of acetaldehyde to ethanol. Because this transformation uses up the $NADH_2$ generated by fermentation, the reactions involved in fermentation can continue to generate ATP and pyruvate under anaerobic conditions.

However, dependence on this pathway for energy supplies has two serious drawbacks. First, the final end-products of anaerobic fermentation (acetaldehyde, ethanol and lactic acid, the last especially in seeds,

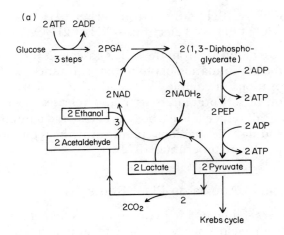

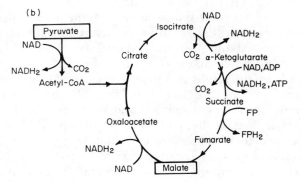

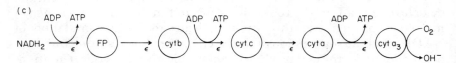

Fig. 7.1. The oxidation of glucose by plant cells. (a) The Embden-Meyerhof-Parnas Pathway. Under anaerobic conditions, reaction 1 is catalysed by Lactic dehydrogenase, reaction 2 by Pyruvic decarboxylase and reaction 3 by Alcohol dehydrogenase. (b) The Krebs Cycle, and (c) The Respiratory (Cytochrome) Chain, showing the transport of electrons (ε) from $NADH_2$ to molecular oxygen. Boxed compounds are discussed at length in the text. (Where ATP and ADP are adenosine tri- and diphosphate respectively; NAD and $NADH_2$ are the oxidized and reduced forms of nicotinamide adenine dinucleotide; PGA is phosphoglyceraldehyde; PEP, phosphoenol pyruvate; Acetyl-CoA Acetyl coenzyme A; FP, flavoprotein; and cyt, cytochrome).

Fig. 7.1) are phytotoxic; their rapid accumulation in plant cells leads to the disruption of cell organization and eventually to cell death. In particular, due to its high lipid solubility, ethanol may damage cell and organelle membranes (Kiyosawa, 1975). Secondly, the yield of useful energy, at 2 mol of ATP per mol of glucose, is much less than that obtained in aerobic respiration (38 mol per mol of glucose). Consequently, when anaerobic conditions are imposed, the rate of glycolysis (now fermentation) must increase sharply if the cell is to maintain energy supplies near to the aerobic level. This "Tasteur Effect" leads to the rapid and inefficient exhaustion of available carbohydrate, a rapid build-up of toxic metabolites and, eventually, to the death of both root and shoot, if anoxia is prolonged (Vartapetian, 1978).

In addition to these effects, there is evidence to suggest that anaerobic soil conditions cause changes in the balance of growth substances exported from root to shoot, presumably in response to exogenous ethylene in the soil (see below); thus certain above-ground symptoms of waterlogging, such as the inhibition of stem elongation in sensitive species, may be secondary effects of hypoxia (e.g. Reid and Crozier, 1971).

In summary, it is clear that wetlands are very hostile environments for higher plants. Their roots are exposed not only to very low oxygen and high carbon dioxide levels but also to a wide range of inorganic and organic toxins, and to varying levels of salinity in coastal areas. However, in spite of this formidable array of unfavourable factors, many wetland areas are richly vegetated. In the following section, we shall explore some of the many adaptations which permit the colonization of waterlogged soils.

B. Plant Adaptations Favouring Survival and Growth in Waterlogged Soils

Of the many physical and chemical characteristics of waterlogged soils which can limit plant growth, lack of oxygen is the primary, but not neccessarily the most important, problem. This is because many wetland species appear to be able to avoid anoxia in their root cells by transporting oxygen from shoot to root (e.g. in British bog plants—Armstrong, 1964; in *Spartina alterniflora*—Teal and Kanwisher, 1966; in the swamp tupelo, *Nyssa sylvatica*—Hook et al., 1971; Keeley and Franz, 1979). In these species, oxygen diffusion through roots is facilitated by the presence of large, continuous air spaces in the cortex (aerenchyma), which may be a permanent anatomical feature of the roots (e.g. in rice—John, 1977) or induced in new roots by flooding (e.g. in maize—Fig. 7.2); this movement of oxygen through stomata, stem lenticels and root aerenchyma may be great enough to cause the oxidation of the rhizosphere soil round the roots (Philipson and Coutts, 1978; Hook and Scholtens, 1978) as clearly shown by the deposits of red ferric hydroxide commonly found on the roots of wetland species (e.g. Armstrong, 1967). In addition, the development of aerenchyma may improve root aeration by reducing the volume of respiring tissue (i.e. the root demand for oxygen).

Other morphological features favouring oxygen supply to roots include superficial root mats (as in rice—Alberda, 1954) which, in trees, are normally associated with more vertical "sinker" roots 'e.g. in *Pinus contorta*—Boggie, 1972), and the aerial roots of mangroves whose lenticels above the water level give oxygen direct access to the aerenchyma of submerged portions (e.g. Scholander *et al.*, 1955). In general, trees growing on waterlogged soils are shallow-rooted and subject to "wind throw" (Armstrong *et al.*, 1976).

Much of the evidence for oxygen transport from shoot to root and for the leakage of oxygen from the apical portions of roots has come from laboratory experiments on seedlings and young plants. Consequently, when Greenwood (1967) demonstrated that oxygen transport is also a feature of the seedlings of several flood-sensitive vegetable species, it was suggested by several workers (e.g. Crawford, 1972) that this ability might be a characteristic of seedlings in general rather than of flood-tolerant species in particular. Whether this is true or not, it has been shown clearly in the field that older, more established, bog plants are able to oxidize the rhizosphere (e.g. Armstrong and Boatman, 1967) and therefore, if we are to understand the significance of this process for plant survival and distribution, it is essential to have quantitative information about the capacity of root aerenchyma to supply oxygen to roots growing in anaerobic soils i.e. how quickly and how far can oxygen move to supply root respiration?

Unfortunately, experimental data on this subject are scarce. Armstrong and Gaynard (1976) have shown that for rice and *Eriophorum angustifolium* plants whose roots are immersed in anoxic media, maximum rates of whole root respiration can be maintained at oxygen pressures in the cortical air spaces down to 0·02–0·04 bar (2–4% O_2). In other words, the critical oxygen pressure for respiration in the roots of these species is 0·02–0·04 bar. These authors suggest that since aerenchyma oxygen pressures of this magnitude (or greater) have commonly been found in the roots of wetland plants, root respiration will not normally be restricted by anaerobic soil conditions. However, it is not possible to discover from this, and most other investigations

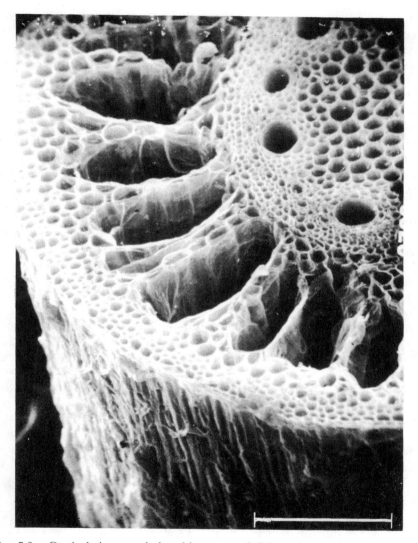

Fig. 7.2. Cortical air spaces induced by oxygen deficiency in a nodal root of maize. The parent maize plant was grown in aerated culture solution before being transferred to unaerated culture solution, which rapidly became oxygen deficient. The original root system died but, within 9 days, was replaced by new nodal roots, up to 15 cm long, with well-developed aerenchyma (cortical tissue containing large air spaces) due to the collapse of cortical cells. (Scanning electron micrograph of a transverse section 10 cm from the root tip, where the bar = 200 μm; from Drew, 1979 and personal communication).

how *far* oxygen can move through the root aerenchyma to maintain respiration, but it seems likely that the maximum distance will be of the order of 20–30 cm in the roots of herbaceous species, the actual distance depending upon root diameter, the level of aerenchyma development (i.e. the porosity), the rate of leakage of oxygen to the rhizosphere and the respiratory demand for oxygen (Armstrong, 1978 and personal comunication). In some cases, the problems involved in conducting oxygen down long, fine roots appear to have been overcome by the adoption of large underground stolons supplying a network of shorter fine roots. For example, an aerenchyma oxygen content of 8% was maintained in the distal end of a 75 cm stolon of *Menyanthes trifoliata* immersed in anoxic medium (Coult and Vallance, 1958).

However, in many cases, deep-rooting species cannot depend upon oxygen movement through the roots alone to enable them to avoid the effects of anoxia; similarly, oxygen transport will not be particularly effective in plants growing in normally well-aerated soils (and therefore lacking well-developed root aerenchyma) which are subjected to seasonal or irregular periods of waterlogging (for example, on lake margins and river banks). In such cases it is likely that survival involves tolerance of prolonged fermentation, although there is some experimental evidence to show that some flood tolerant species may be able to continue respiration by transferring electrons from the respiratory chain to other electron acceptors such as nitrate (e.g. Garcia-Novo and Crawford, 1973). Overall, the wide range of metabolic adaptations to fermentation found in wetland species testifies to the inability of their roots to maintain aerobic respiration when growing in waterlogged soils.

When exposed to hypoxia, the tissues of many flood-tolerant species do not show the Pasteur effect (acceleration of glycolysis/fermentation), thereby avoiding the rapid depletion of carbohydrate stores and the accumulation of large quantities of toxic metabolites. According to Crawford (1978), this lack of response is due to the fact that

(i) ADH is not induced by anaerobiosis, and may in some cases even be inhibited (e.g. in *Iris pseudacorus, Phalaris arundinacea*— Crawford and McManmon, 1968; Fig. 7.3).

(ii) ADH isoenzymes in flood-tolerant species have much higher K_m values (and therefore much lower affinities for acetaldehyde) than the ADH isoenzymes in flood-sensitive species (McManmon and Crawford, 1971).

Consequently, acetaldehyde and pyruvate will tend to build up, eventually causing the rate of glycolysis to be reduced (Fig. 7.1).

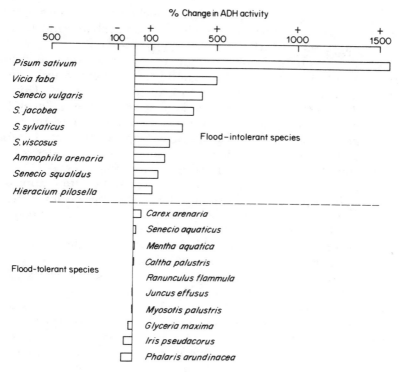

Fig. 7.3.   Changes in alcohol dehydrogenase activity (ADH, expressed on a soluble protein basis) in the roots of 19 species after flooding in sand culture for one month, as compared with unflooded controls (redrawn from Crawford, 1978).

Crawford's theory is supported by the work of Marshall *et al.* (1973) and Brown *et al.* (1976) who demonstrated that the level of flood tolerance in cultivars of maize and in populations of *Bromus mollis* is related to the properties of the ADH isoenzyme(s) present in the root. However, there are a number of serious difficulties associated with the use of ADH activity in the roots as an index of flood-tolerance. For example, at least one flood-sensitive species (maize) has shown a peak of ADH activity at intermediate oxygen levels (8–13%—Wignarajah and Greenway, 1976) with lower levels at 20% and under anoxic conditions, and there are indications that ADH levels may respond to a number of other factors including rooting density. Furthermore, excised rice roots have shown increases in ADH level in response to anoxia without any Pasteur effect; these findings, and other results from rice, barley and maize, have led John and Greenway (1976)

to suggest that levels of pyruvate decarboxylase (catalysing the transformation of pyruvate to acetaldehyde) may give a better indication of
flood tolerance than ADH.

The suppression of fermentation may be a valuable adaptation
during short periods of anaerobiosis and in soils where waterlogging is
confined to the winter months, when growth is suspended. However
there is abundant evidence that wetland species can grow rapidly in
permanently waterlogged soils and in many of these cases, the energy
for root growth and metabolism must be supplied by fermentation.
Consequently, it is essential for these plants to excrete or detoxify the
accumulating products of continued fermentation.

The excretion of ethanol from roots into the soil solution appears to
be possible in both flood-tolerant and flood-sensitive species, although
it has been found to be particularly effective in some wetland species
(e.g. in rice—Chirkova, 1978). The root aerenchyma/stem lenticel
system also provides a route for the diffusion of volatile acetaldehyde
and ethanol out of the root and into the air.

In addition to excreting ethanol, some flood-tolerant species appear
to be able to suppress the synthesis of ethanol and to divert fermentation
into producing a variety of less harmful substances, principally carboxylic acids, alcohols and amino acids. For example, it has been proposed
that in a wide range of species from waterlogged sites (e.g. *Betula
pubescens*, *Veronica peregrina*, *Glyceria maxima*, *Juncus effusus*—reviewed by
Crawford, 1978), phosphoenol pyruvate is transformed into malate
(Fig. 7.4), which cannot be converted to pyruvate and ethanol because,
in these plants, malic enzyme is either absent or inhibited by flooding
(McManmon and Crawford, 1971). The accumulating malate can be
stored in the vacuoles of root cells until aerobic conditions are resumed
or transported in the vascular system to the shoot (e.g. in *Betula
pubescens*—Crawford, 1972) where it may take part in normal aerobic
metabolism. Thus, the roots are able to use the limited energy released
by fermentation without the wasteful loss of energy and carbon involved in the excretion of ethanol; indeed the transformation of phosphoenol pyruvate to oxaloacetate (Fig. 7.4) results in the net fixation
of 1 mol of carbon dioxide which could subsequently be contributed
to the metabolism of the shoot (Crawford, 1972).

Amongst the flood-tolerant plant species which have been studied,
malate appears to be the most widespread non-toxic product of
fermentation; other less common metabolites which accumulate under
anaerobic conditions include glycerol in flooded *Alnus incana* roots
(Crawford, 1972), and the amino acids alanine, glutamic acid and
γ-aminobutyric acid in *Salix cinerea* roots (Dubinina, 1961). In a num-

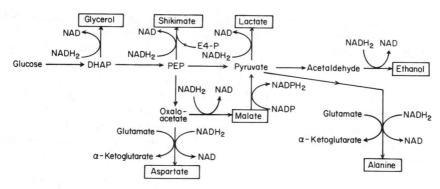

FIG. 7.4. Metabolic pathways, proposed by Crawford (1978), for the disposal of NADH$_2$ and the generation of non-toxic products of fermentation, in flood-tolerant plants. (Where DHAP is Dihydroxyacetone phosphate; PEP is Phosphoenolpyruvate; and E4-P is Erythrose 4-phosphate; the other abbreviations as in Fig. 7.1.) (From Crawford, 1978).

ber of rhizomatous wetland species, phosphoenol pyruvate from gly-colysis can condense with erythrose 4-phosphate, produced by the pentose phosphate pathway, to give another non-toxic metabolite, shikimic acid, which may be stored in cell vacuoles or used up in the biosynthesis of amino acids or lignin (Tyler and Crawford, 1970). The proposed pathways leading to the synthesis of these end-products of fermentation are shown in Fig. 7.4. A great deal remains to be dis-covered about these pathways, particularly their energy yields. For example, Crawford (1978) has suggested that the synthesis of malate by fermentation may be accompanied by no net synthesis of ATP; the value to a plant of fermentation without the production of useful energy is not clear.

   Under natural conditions in many environments, the energy re-quired for the initial stages of seed germination is supplied by fermenta-tion (Mayer and Poljakoff-Mayber, 1975). This is particularly true of those species whose seed coat has a low permeability to gases, and in wet soils where oxygen diffusion is restricted (e.g. Sherwin and Simon, 1969). However, once the radicle has ruptured the seed coat and an adequate supply of gaseous oxygen has been established, the products of fermentation (lactate initially but ethanol later—Davies et al., 1974), will be oxidized to CO$_2$ by aerobic respiration.

   In contrast, seeds in permanently waterlogged soils must rely upon fermentation throughout germination and therefore face two serious problems:

(i) Energy conservation. The carbohydrate or lipid stores in the seed are finite and cannot be renewed before germination has been completed and photosynthesis has begun. Consequently, since fermentation releases less than 10% of the useful energy of carbohydrates, its rate must be strictly controlled to avoid wasteful use of these stores. Thus flood-tolerant seeds (rice, lettuce) showed only a small Pasteur effect after 72 h of soaking, possibly due to a lack of ADH induction (Crawford, 1977). This conservation of energy which will tend to give slow rates of germination under anaerobic conditions, should also lead to natural selection for larger seeds.

(ii) Disposal of Toxic Metabolites. Unlike whole plants, seeds have very limited vacuolar volumes in which to store the products of fermentation and they are unable to transport these metabolites to the shoot. In spite of this, the seeds of a large number of species can germinate very successfully under waterlogged conditions (e.g. Lazenby, 1955; Mayer and Poljakoff-Mayber, 1975) and it is still not clear how they dispose of lactic acid (which alters the pH of the cell contents) and ethanol (which may damage cell membranes). It may be that disposal is primarily by excretion of ethanol, although Crawford (1977) suggests that the more tolerant species tend to produce lactic acid rather than ethanol for as long as possible.

In hostile environments in general, where unfavourable conditions such as low temperature or drought inhibit germination, there is a tendency for plants to adopt vegetative reproduction as a more certain method of propagation (see Chapters 4 and 5). This tendency towards vegetative reproduction is also evident amongst rhizomatous marsh plants. Since these plants die back each autumn, the rhizome, like a seed, must produce an aerial shoot in spring before photosynthesis can recommence and before there can be any transport of oxygen from the atmosphere into the roots and rhizomes. However, their large storage capacities both for carbohydrate and for the products of fermentation (here shikimic acid) may make rhizomes much more successful propagules than seeds (Tyler and Crawford, 1970).

Overall, the significance of metabolic adaptations for flood-tolerance in plants and seeds is the subject of some controversy. Although there can be no doubt that populations and species do vary in their ability to control the rate, and the nature of the products, of fermentation, it is difficult to assess how widespread a given adaptation may be. Furthermore, since most of the published work on flood-tolerance has involved relatively short periods of hypoxia (typically from a few days up to a month), the findings and conclusions may not apply to permanent wetlands. For example, Keeley (1978) has shown that for *Nyssa sylvatica* roots, the fermentation rate rose during the first month of flooding but thereafter it fell, over a year, to a value below that of control seedlings growing in drained soil. These changes in fermentation rate did not correlate with root malate content, making it very difficult to reconcile this flooding response with Crawford's theories outlined above. Instead Keeley (1978) and Keeley and Franz (1979) propose that the acceleration of fermentation in the early weeks of flooding serves as an "emergency" measure to support the metabolism of the existing root system, while a fresh system of roots, rich in aerenchyma and able to support a predominantly aerobic respiration, is developed. Further criticism of Crawford's metabolic theory has come from Smith and ap Rees (1979) who failed to find malate accumulation in apical segments of the roots of three wetland species (*Ranunculus sceleratus*, *Senecio aquaticus*, and *Glyceria maxima*).

However, it is important to stress that metabolic adaptations leading to the tolerance of prolonged fermentation will be of little use to wetland species which are not able to deal with the high concentrations of toxins (e.g. Fe^{2+} ions, H_2S) generated by anaerobic soils. Thus, it has been found that in the British Isles, the plant species occupying the wettest sites in woodlands (Martin, 1968), dune and slack areas (e.g. Jones, 1972) and moorlands (e.g. Jones and Etherington, 1970) are the most efficient at excluding toxic Fe^{2+} ions from the shoot. Although the mechanism of this exclusion has not been formally established, the high iron content of resistant roots and the clearly visible deposits of ferric hydroxide on the root surfaces of wetland plants (e.g. Armstrong and Boatman, 1967) indicate that soluble ferrous (Fe^{2+}) ions are oxidized to insoluble ferric (Fe^{3+}) ions in the rhizosphere and in the intercellular spaces of the cortex. The relative ability to exclude iron from the shoot will therefore depend upon the degree of oxygen movement from shoot to root (Green and Etherington, 1977). In the case of *Erica tetralix*, there is the additional suggestion (Jones, 1971) that its xerophytic growth habit, apparently ill-adapted to its wet moorland habitat, gives reduced transpiration rates which, in turn, reduce the mass flow of soluble Fe^{2+} ions to the root surface and their accumulation in the rhizosphere (see Chapter 3).

Plant responses to the two other important toxins in anaerobic soils, Mn^{2+} and H_2S, are not clearly defined. Manganese levels in most soils are much lower than those of iron, and plant adaptations which exclude Fe^{2+} ions will also prevent uptake of Mn^{2+} ions. Sulphate ions are reduced to H_2S only under the most reducing conditions when all of the iron in a soil has been converted to Fe^{2+}, and even then, according to Ponnamperuma (1972), the sulphide concentration in the soil solution should be very low due to precipitation as FeS. In spite of this, Armstrong and Boatman (1967) measured H_2S concentrations as high as 8 mg litre^{-1} round the roots of *Menyanthes trifoliata*, in a Yorkshire bog, whereas *Molinia caerulea* was found to be absent wherever H_2S was detectable in the soil. This difference in distribution may reflect differences in ability to oxidize H_2S in the rhizosphere. An outstanding example of an adaptation protecting plant roots against the toxicity of H_2S is provided by the relationship between the bacterium *Beggiatoa* and rice roots in Louisiana paddy fields. The bacterium is able to oxidize H_2S to sulphur intracellularly, thus removing the toxin from the rhizosphere, but the reaction also produces hydrogen peroxide which is potentially harmful to the micro-organism. However, the rice roots release the enzyme catalase which catalyses the breakdown of peroxide. This is an excellent example of symbiosis since neither partner could survive without the other (Pitts, 1969; Hollis, 1967—cited by Armstrong, 1975).

Amongst other unfavourable characteristics of waterlogged soils, high carbon dioxide concentrations are normally considered to be of minor importance compared with low oxygen levels (Armstrong, 1975). Although the growth regulator ethylene does occur in anaerobic soils at physiologically active levels, especially during the early stages of waterlogging, its occurrence is probably more characteristic of imperfectly drained soils and therefore its effects on plants are discussed in subsequent sections.

In conclusion it seems clear that plants cannot colonize wetlands unless they possess a *range* of anatomical, biochemical and physiological adaptations leading to the *avoidance* or *amelioration* of the many unfavourable features of anaerobic soils. In most cases, this range will include

(i) anatomical and morphological features improving oxygen transport to respiring roots, *and*
(ii) biochemical features, permitting prolonged anaerobic glycolysis (fermentation) in roots, *and*
(iii) mechanisms for the exclusion of phytotoxic substances in the rhizosphere.

Furthermore, if (iii) is not fully effective, it will be necessary for such plants to be *tolerant* of toxins within their tissues e.g by compartmentation in the vacuole (see Chapter 6).

C. Imperfectly-drained Soils and Soils with Anaerobic Microsites

So far in this chapter, we have considered only the extreme cases of soil aeration. On the one hand, we have seen that in freely draining soils with large air-filled pore spaces, the oxygen content of the soil air in the rooting zone may be maintained at a high level (e.g. 15–20%) by gaseous diffusion; on the other hand, waterlogged soils rapidly become anaerobic. However, the aeration status of many undisturbed and agricultural soils is intermediate between these extremes. For example, throughout western parts of the British Isles, where soil drainage tends to be imperfect because of high rainfall coupled with fine soil texture, temporary anaerobiosis is widespread, especially during the winter.

The overall influence of poor soil drainage on vegetation depends upon the extent and seasonal distribution of anaerobic soil conditions, but at any given time, plant growth and survival will be controlled by the same factors as in permanently waterlogged soils i.e. oxygen supply and levels of inorganic toxins and ethylene. There exists a great wealth of literature documenting the preference of certain plant species for poorly drained, rather than drier, soils (e.g. Harper and Sagar, 1953) but there is a serious lack of information on the physiological and biochemical adaptations involved. For example, it would be valuable to have values of critical oxygen pressure for respiration in the roots of a range of species colonizing sites of differing drainage status; however, few measurements have been made and even these, according to Armstrong and Gaynard (1976) are generally unreliable because excised roots rather than roots attached to whole plants were used.

In concentrating upon the oxygen status of soils, we have seriously underestimated the extent of anaerobiosis in better-drained soils. For example, in moderate to freely draining agricultural soils, ethylene has been detected at levels varying between 0·1 and 10 p.p.m. (v/v) in soil air samples containing 5–20% oxygen (e.g. Smith and Dowdell, 1974). Here a product of anaerobic soil respiration is accumulating in soils which would be considered to be well-aerated.

This apparent paradox can be resolved if soil structure is taken into account. In medium to fine-textured soils at field capacity, most of the air filled macropores (>60 μm diameter) are *between* soil aggregates whereas the narrower, water-filled pores are *within* aggregates. Thus, oxygen can move rapidly through the macropore space, but since its diffusion to the centre of a water-saturated aggregate will be very much slower, the oxygen content in the aggregate will fall rapidly with distance from the aggregate surface. Using simple diffusion theory, it is possible to predict that the smallest (spherical) aggregate to have an anaerobic volume at its centre will have a radius given by

$$r_c = \left(\frac{6 \, D_a \cdot C \cdot S}{Q} \right)^{1/2} \quad \text{Smith (1977)} \qquad (7.7)$$

where D_a is the diffusion coefficient of oxygen within the aggregate; C is the concentration of oxygen just outside the aggregate; S is the solubility of oxygen in water; and Q is the rate of uptake of oxygen by soil respiration within the aggregate.

Using data from a number of sources, Russell (1973) has estimated that this critical radius (r_c), for an agricultural soil at Rothamsted, will be about 1 cm in summer and 2 cm in winter; the conclusion that the critical radius is higher in winter underlines the fact that anaerobic conditions at the centre of an aggregate are due to oxygen demand by soil respiration, which is reduced by lower winter temperatures. It seems likely that these values of r_c will prove to be overestimates when more precise determinations of D_a, C and Q become available.

Clearly, r_c will vary widely with soil conditions and the values quoted do no more than indicate the magnitudes of aggregates containing anaerobic volumes. However, this diffusion analysis is very valuable in providing a visual model of soil aeration i.e. a mosaic of anaerobic microsites set in an aerobic matrix (Fig. 7.5). This alternation of aerobic and anaerobic soil appears to provide an ideal environment for the generation of ethylene by (aerobic) saprophytic fungi. For example, studies on pure cultures of *Mucor hiemalis* (reviewed by Lynch, 1975a) have shown that:

(i) Evolution of ethylene (in aerobic and substrate-deficient anaerobic soils) is enhanced many fold by the addition of glucose and methionine, the latter being considered to be a precursor in the biosynthesis of ethylene. These substrates appear to be supplied naturally in the soil by periods of anaerobiosis.

(ii) Evolution of ethylene is most effective when fungal growth is restricted by unfavourable soil conditions. In particular, ethylene production is maximal at an oxygen content of 1% in the soil atmosphere.

(iii) Evolution of ethylene can be stimulated by ferrous ions, which are formed under anaerobic conditions.

In general, the production of ethylene by anaerobic soils is dependent upon temperature, organic matter content, pH and the

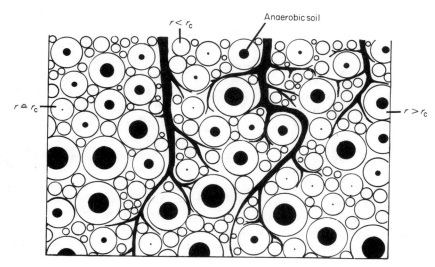

FIG. 7.5.   Schematic profile of a well-drained soil whose macropore space between aggregates is aerobic but whose water-saturated aggregates (drawn as circles of varying radius) contain anaerobic microsites if their radius is greater than the critical value, r_c (see text). Note that roots are confined to aerobic zones.

wetting/drying history of the soil, but it is virtually independent of the nitrate status (Goodlass and Smith, 1978).

Consequently, when a soil atmosphere sampling probe (e.g. Dowdell *et al.*, 1972) is inserted into a soil, it collects gas predominantly from the aerobic macropore space, enriched with ethylene diffusing out of anaerobic microsites and from the poorly aerated volumes surrounding these microsites. Since plant roots are, by their size, virtually confined to the macropores, the soil atmosphere composition obtained using such sampling probes will give a reasonable estimate of their gaseous environment.

D. Plant Responses to Exogenous Ethylene in the Soil Atmosphere

Ethylene is produced normally by most plant tissues and it appears to be involved, in association with other growth substances, in the regulation of a wide range of developmental processes including renewal of growth after dormancy (seeds, buds, etc.), root growth, stem extension, leaf expansion, flowering, fruit ripening, and tissue senescence (Abeles, 1973). Endogenous ethylene production by plants may also be stimulated by damage or disease, giving rise to morphological distortions such as "coiled sprout" in mechanically impeded potato shoots.

Certain species exhibit atypical responses to endogenous ethylene which may be of benefit in their natural environment. For example, in contrast to the inhibition normally observed, stem extension in several wetland species (e.g. rice, *Ranunculus sceleratus*, *Callitriche platycarpa*) is promoted by ethylene, especially at low oxygen and high carbon dioxide levels, which are normally antagonistic to the action of ethylene. When a young shoot of one of these species is submerged under water, the ethylene naturally produced by the tissues, which is normally dissipated by gaseous diffusion, tends to accumulate in the apoplast. Once the threshold for promotion of cell extension (0.01 nl ml^{-1} of tissue in *R. sceleratus*) has been exceeded, the stems and petioles will extend until the leaves have been returned to the aerial environment where normal rates of photosynthesis and dissipation of ethylene can be resumed. Exogenous ethylene from the underlying soil may also contribute to this effect (Ku *et al.*, 1970; Musgrave *et al.*, 1972; Musgrave and Walters, 1973).

Due to the great heterogeneity of the soil environment and the difficulties involved in studying roots *in situ*, the effects of exogenous ethylene in the soil atmosphere upon root development in undisturbed soils are not clear. In fact, much of the information available comes from experiments in which young root axes, growing down filter papers moistened with culture solution, are exposed to different gas mixtures (e.g. Smith and Robertson, 1971). These experiments, on a variety of crop species, have shown that levels of ethylene above 1 p.p.m. cause the inhibition of root apex extension coupled with increases in axis diameter and the proliferation of lateral roots; in contrast to other effects of ethylene, the inhibition of root extension is not affected by carbon dioxide concentrations up to 20%, and is essentially reversible if exposure to ethylene is not prolonged. The sensitivity of the species examined:

Tomato > Tobacco > Barley > Rye > Rice

correlates well with their sensitivity to waterlogging (Smith and Jackson, 1974; Fig. 7.6). At lower levels of ethylene (< 1 p.p.m. for rice, <0.15 p.p.m. for pea and <0.02 p.p.m. for tomato, the value depending upon the rate of *endogenous* production of ethylene), root extension is stimulated (Konings and Jackson, 1975).

The ecological implications of these findings remain largely unexplored, partly because of lack of information about the composition of the soil atmosphere in natural ecosystems. It has been suggested that shallow, highly branched root systems, formed under the influence of

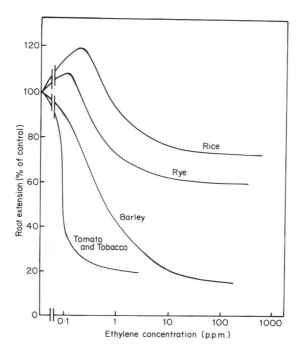

Fɪɢ. 7.6.   The influence of ethylene on the extension of seedling root axes during three days at 20–25°C in water culture. The ethylene concentrations used in the figure are the concentrations in the air which was in equilibrium with the culture solution (from Smith and Jackson, 1974).

ethylene in poorly drained soils, might be well placed to exploit the nutrient-rich surface layers of undisturbed soils (Smith and Jackson, 1974; Smith, 1976). However, such root systems would render plants highly susceptible to drought in seasonally fluctuating environments.

Evidence that ethylene in the soil atmosphere can also affect the shoot is provided by the observation that the short-term effects of waterlogging on sensitive species (e.g. epinasty, leaf wilting and senescence, formation of adventitious roots) can be induced by treating aerated roots with ethylene (Smith and Jackson, 1974). However, although these effects are associated with increases in leaf ethylene content, not all of this ethylene has been transported from the soil atmosphere *via* the root; recent work with tomato has suggested that a proportion of this enhanced ethylene content is synthesized in the leaf in response to a factor exported from roots exposed to low oxygen levels (Jackson and Campbell, 1975, 1976).

In view of the involvement of ethylene in most developmental processes and its mobility in soils and plants, exogenous ethylene may play a number of important, and as yet unappreciated, roles in the regulation of plant communities. For example, although it has been demonstrated in the laboratory that exogenous ethylene stimulates the germination of dormant seeds (Mayer and Poljakoff-Mayber, 1975) but inhibits root nodulation in legumes (Grobbelaar *et al.*, 1971), it is not known whether these effects can be produced by ethylene in the soil atmosphere. However, the proposed role of ethylene as an agent in soil fungistasis (Smith, 1976) appears to be restricted to the suppression of pathogenic fungi only (e.g. Lynch, 1975b; Smith, 1978).

II. AERIAL POLLUTION

Up to this point, we have considered the effects on plants of naturally generated phytotoxic gases. However, it has been clear for many years that pollutant gases, originating from urban and industrial areas and from the internal combustion engine, have a profound and increasing influence upon the composition, biomass and distribution of natural vegetation.

A. Sources and Levels of Pollutant Gases

Gaseous pollutants originate from a variety of sources. For example, sulphur dioxide, SO_2, is a primary product of the combustion of sulphur-containing fossil fuels whereas nitrogen oxides, commonly written as NO_x, are by-products of combustion, arising out of the thermally induced combination of atmospheric nitrogen and oxygen. The initial product of this reaction, NO, is slowly oxidized to NO_2 in the atmosphere. The burning of fuels also gives rise to a number of hydrocarbon gases including ethylene, C_2H_4; thus, for example, motor vehicle exhaust contains varying proportions of CO_2, H_2O, CO, SO_2, NO_x and C_2H_4.

When NO_2 is released into the atmosphere, it can take part in a series of photochemical reactions leading to the synthesis of ozone, O_3. These reactions occur most rapidly in warm sunny regions and the resulting "photochemical smog", as in California, can be very damaging to plants, animals and humans. However, recent evidence has established that even in a cool area like the UK, phytotoxic levels of ozone can occur frequently during clear weather in summer (Bell and Cox, 1975).

Other important sources of pollutants include the chemical industry, which releases varying quantities and mixtures of gases (especially SO_2, NO_2, NH_3 and HCl), and brickworks and metal smelters, which produce localized enhancement of SO_2, HF and particulate fluoride levels in the atmosphere.

In spite of the economic importance of aerial pollution, there is still a scarcity of precise information on the levels of phytotoxic gases in polluted atmospheres. However, analysis of the air over the British Isles indicates that levels of the most important pollutants experienced by plants will normally fall within the ranges presented in Table 7.1.

TABLE 7.1. Representative concentration levels of selected gaseous pollutants in the air over the British Isles (5 min averaging period), all values p.p.m.

Pollutant	Rural areas	Urban areas	Industrial areas
SO_2	< 0·001–0·05	0·02–0·5	< 0·001–1
NO_x	0·005–0·05[a]	0·02–0·2[a]	up to 1[b]
O_3	0·02–0·06[c]		0·08–0·25[d]
C_2H_4	< 0·001–0·01	0·005–0·05	< 0·001–0·5

[a] Primarily as NO_2.
[b] About 1:1 $NO:NO_2$.
[c] Natural background.
[d] Photochemical pollution.
Data compiled for 1979 by Dr R. Harrison, Department of Environmental Sciences, University of Lancaster.

At a given site, the concentration (within these ranges) will depend upon a large number of environmental factors including distance from the source of pollution, topography, altitude, rainfall, solar radiation, wind direction, and velocity. There are also considerable seasonal variations, with O_3 levels rising in clear weather in summer, whereas SO_2 and NO_x concentrations tend to be highest in winter due to increased domestic fuel use.

B. The Influence of Aerial Pollution on Plants

Although the effects on plants of pollutant gases (especially SO_2) have been studied for nearly a century, much of the information collected is of doubtful value because of deficiencies in experimental procedure and in the interpretation of results. In particular:

(i) In the majority of experiments where plants have been fumigated with pollutants in controlled environments, the air has been inadequately stirred. Consequently, the boundary layer over each leaf has offered a high resistance to the entry of the pollutant gas molecules into the leaf tissue (see Chapter 4 and below), and therefore the effects recorded for a given level of pollutant have been much milder than would have been observed in the field (Ashenden and Mansfield, 1977). Such confusion can be avoided in the future if all reports include details of the dose (concentration of pollutant and period of exposure) and windspeed employed.

(ii) Inadequate attention has been paid to variations in the susceptibility of plants at different stages of development and at different times of the year. For example, there is recent evidence that ryegrass runs the greatest risk of SO_2 damage in winter when atmospheric levels of SO_2 are high, but plant recovery and regrowth are limited by low temperatures (Bell and Mudd, 1976).

(iii) It is likely that the rather mild effects of SO_2 fumigation on plants found in some experiments may have been due to the low sulphur status of the soils used; under these conditions, atmospheric SO_2 can act as a fertilizer giving a stimulation rather than a reduction in growth (e.g. Cowling et al., 1973).

(iv) In spite of the fact that polluted air invariably contains a mixture of gaseous pollutants, most of the experimental work reported in the literature has involved exposure of plants to varying levels of a single pollutant. This accumulated information is of limited value in the explanation or prediction of damage in the field because the effects of different pollutants in combination are not simply additive. For example, Ashenden and Mansfield (1978) found that low concentrations (0·068 p.p.m.) of SO_2 and NO_2 in combination, suppressed the dry matter yield and leaf area of pasture grasses more than would have been predicted by the sum of their individual effects (Table 7.2). Other synergistic responses are reviewed by Reinert et al. (1975).

(v) A major factor hindering progress in air pollution research has been the tenet, widely held until recently in North America, that gaseous pollutants (and SO_2 in particular) do not have a significant influence upon plant growth and physiology until tissue lesions are visible (e.g. Thomas, 1951). This theory which arose partly out of the experimental deficiencies noted above, has now been generally discarded. More recent work, starting with the pioneering investigation of Bleasdale (1973) has established that "hidden" or "invisible" injuries (such as reduction in photosynthetic rate and dry matter

TABLE 7.2. Percentage changes (relative to control) in total dry weights and leaf areas of grass plants exposed to atmospheres containing SO_2 or NO_2 alone, or in combination, for 20 weeks (Ashenden and Mansfield, 1978).

	$SO_2{}^a$	$NO_2{}^a$	$SO_2+NO_2{}^a$	*Effect*
		Dry weights[b]		
Dactylis glomerata	−40‡	−22*	−78‡	Synergistic
Lolium multiflorum	−5	+10	−52†	Synergistic
Phleum pratense	−51‡	+1	−86‡	Synergistic
Poa pratensis	−46‡	−38‡	−84‡	Additive
		Leaf areas[b]		
Dactylis glomerata	−20	+1	−76‡	Synergistic
Lolium multiflorum	−22	+1	−43*	Synergistic
Phleum pratense	−11	+30	−82‡	Synergistic
Poa pratensis	−28*	−17	−84‡	Synergistic

[a] All concentrations 0·068 p.p.m.
[b] Levels of significance of difference from control, established by analysis of variance— *=$p<0·05$; **=$p<0·01$; ***=$p<0·001$. All other differences are not significant.

yield, disruption of water relations and cell biochemistry) occur commonly in plant tissues exposed to doses of pollutants which do not cause visible injury (e.g. Table 7.2). The most important consequence of this misconception is that the concentrations of pollutants used in most experiments before 1960 were unreasonably high.

Overall, improvements in experimental techniques and in the theoretical foundation of the subject have resulted in such an expansion in air pollution research that only a few salient topics can be discussed here.

1. Gas Exchange between Leaves and Polluted Atmospheres

It is unfortunate for plants growing in polluted air that adaptations favouring CO_2 assimilation tend also to favour the uptake of other gases into the leaf mesophyll. Thus, for example, many plant species are more sensitive to SO_2 during the day, when the stomata are open, than during the night; an exception to this observation is the potato, whose stomata remain open at night (Mansfield, 1976).

According to the conventional resistance analysis (Chapter 4), the diffusive flux of CO_2 or of pollutant molecules to the site of assimilation or damage in the leaf mesophyll is controlled by the leaf diffusive resistance, which is made up of a series of component resistances:

r_a—boundary layer resistance, outside the leaf surface
r_s—stomatal resistance $\left.\vphantom{\begin{array}{c}1\\1\end{array}}\right\}$ in parallel
r_c—cuticular resistance
r_m—mesophyll resistance (resistance of the pathway through the mesophyll apoplast and cells to the site of assimilation of damage, together with the "resistance" of the enzyme systems involved in assimilation or damage)

where r_a and r_s (at least) are dependent upon the molecular weight of the diffusing molecules (Unsworth et al., 1976).

In still air or at low windspeeds, r_a will be the dominant resistance of the series, over a range of stomatal apertures (see Chapter 4). Consequently, as noted above, inadequate ventilation during experimental fumigation may result in unexpectedly low rates of pollutant uptake and damage at dose levels which are clearly phytotoxic in the field (e.g. Ashenden and Mansfield, 1977).

It is much more difficult to discover which section of the diffusion pathway is limiting uptake of pollutant gases at higher windspeeds (low r_a) because there is, as yet, no technique for measuring the appropriate r_m (see below). In spite of this, there are a number of reports (e.g. Spedding, 1969) showing large increases in SO_2 uptake accompanying stomatal opening. These findings would seem to suggest that under field conditions, SO_2 absorption (like CO_2 uptake) will normally be limited by stomatal aperture, with the leaf cuticle offering a very high resistance.

Despite these similarities between CO_2 and SO_2 uptake, the processes involved in the exchange of pollutant molecules between air and leaf are much more complex. First, some phytotoxic gases are able to override the plant's control of stomatal aperture; in particular, SO_2 can cause stomatal opening, even when the leaf is water-stressed, leading to increased SO_2 absorption and water loss (Mansfield, 1976). For example, Biscoe et al. (1973) found that stomatal resistance in leaves of Vicia faba fell by 20% at levels of SO_2 of 140 μg m^{-3} and above, although more recent work suggests that stomatal response is highly dependent upon the humidity of the air (Black and Unsworth, 1979). In contrast, O_3 tends to cause stomatal closure (Mansfield, 1976).

Secondly, the cuticle appears to be relatively permeable to HF and HCl and may form the major pathway from air to mesophyll for these gases (Guderian, 1977). Thirdly, when leaves have been moistened by dew or rain, a significant proportion of the SO_2 absorbed will be dissolved in the water films coating their *outer* surfaces (Fowler and Unsworth, 1974); it remains to be seen whether this fraction can gain access to the mesophyll.

Since there is uncertainty about the primary sites of action of pollutant molecules in the mesophyll (see below), the meaning and size of the mesophyll resistance remain obscure. Unsworth *et al.* (1976) argue that SO_2 dissolves and is oxidized to sulphite (and sulphate) on the walls of the substomatal cavity; subsequently, it can be absorbed into mesophyll cells where it can take part in normal sulphur metabolism. Consequently, r_m for SO_2 will be zero at the beginning of a period of exposure, but this value will presumably rise considerably as the cell walls become saturated with sulphur-containing anions. On the other hand, HF molecules appear to move long distances within leaves to give lesions preferentially at leaf margins (Guderian, 1977). This would suggest a high r_m for HF.

It is clear that an enormous amount remains to be discovered about the exchange of pollutant gas molecules between bulk air and leaf tissues.

2. Primary Sites of Attack

It is reasonable to assume that once pollutants have been absorbed into mesophyll cells, their primary effects will be at the molecular or ultra-structural level. This assumption is supported by a large number of short-term experiments showing significant alterations of (for example) enzyme activities, levels of metabolic intermediates and membrane permeabilities (Horsman and Wellburn, 1976), but the true significance of these findings for the whole plant is unclear because of the multi-plicity of effects recorded for each pollutant. However, several primary sites do seem to have been identified by a number of investigators, namely:

(i) Stomata. As indicated earlier, SO_2, NO_x and O_3 have a rapid influence upon stomatal aperture, although the mechanism is not understood (Mansfield, 1976). Thus in the case of SO_2, tissue damage may sometimes be due to severe water stress rather than the action of the pollutant.

(ii) Chloroplasts. Exposure of plant leaves to low doses of SO_2, NO_2, or O_3 which do not give visible lesions have been found to cause gross disruption of the thylakoid membrane systems in chloroplasts (e.g. Wellburn *et al.*, 1972). Ozone also causes the breakdown of plas-malemma membranes (Thomson *et al.*, 1966) and it has been suggested that it acts directly upon membranes by reacting with the double bonds of unsaturated lipid molecules (Heath, 1975).

(iii) CO_2 fixation. Exposure of leaves to SO_2 commonly causes a rapid fall in the rate of CO_2 fixation. Experiments with sub-cellular fractions have indicated that at least part of this inhibition is due to competition between sulphite and bicarbonate ions for the CO_2-fixing sites on RuBP carboxylase and PEP carboxylase (e.g. Ziegler, 1972).

Other authors suggest that SO_2 causes primary damage by blocking sulphydryl groups or by a direct effect upon cell pH, and that NO_x (as nitrite) interferes with the redox systems within chloroplasts (Bleasdale, 1973; Capron and Mansfield, 1976; Mudd and Kozlowski, 1975).

3. Photosynthesis and Dry Matter Accumulation

Since the major pollutants have been shown to cause changes in stomatal responses, chloroplast structure, CO_2 fixation and photosynthetic electron transport systems, it is not surprising to find that short-term doses of air pollution cause rapid (but reversible) depressions in the rate of photosynthesis. Some of the work of Bennett and Hill (1974) in this field is summarized in Fig. 7.7 which indicates that the effects of single pollutants on photosynthesis (in oat, barley and lucerne) follow the series

$$\text{HF} \quad > \quad \text{O}_3 \quad > \quad \text{SO}_2 \quad > \quad \text{NO}_x$$
$$\left(\begin{array}{c} 0\cdot01 \\ \text{p.p.m.} \end{array}\right) \quad \left(\begin{array}{c} 0\cdot05 \\ \text{p.p.m.} \end{array}\right) \quad \left(\begin{array}{c} 0\cdot2 \\ \text{p.p.m.} \end{array}\right) \quad \left(\begin{array}{c} 0\cdot4-0\cdot6 \\ \text{p.p.m.} \end{array}\right)$$

where the figures in brackets indicate the minimum pollutant level at which depression in the apparent rate of photosynthesis could be detected. Similar work in the UK indicates that photosynthesis in pea and tomato is susceptible to slightly lower levels ($>0\cdot1$ p.p.m.) of SO_2 and NO_x (Bull and Mansfield, 1974; Capron and Mansfield, 1976). Comparison of these minima with the concentrations in Table 7.1 confirms the serious risk of "hidden injury" run by plants growing in urban and industrial areas of the British Isles. However, this type of analysis underestimates the risk of damage in many cases caused by the synergistic effects of pollutant combinations, and overestimates the hazards to tolerant populations (see below).

Where plants are exposed to such levels of pollutants over a prolonged period, these reductions in photosynthesis (along with other effects) cause significant depressions in dry matter accumulation, often without visible injury, as shown by a number of authors (e.g. in various grass species—Ashenden, 1978, 1979; Ashenden and Mansfield, 1977,

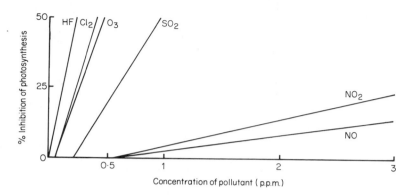

Fig. 7.7.   The inhibition of photosynthesis (as measured by CO_2 uptake) in 3–5 week old canopies of barley and oats when exposed to varying levels of gaseous pollutants for two hours. During the treatments, the plants were maintained at 24°C, a wind velocity of $1·2$–$1·6$ m s^{-1}, low humidity (45% RH) and high light (40–50 Klux $\simeq$ 280–350 W m^{-2}) (adapted from Bennett and Hill, 1974).

1978 and Table 7.2; Bell and Clough, 1973). This lowering of dry matter yield is normally associated with reductions in the components of yield (number of tillers and leaves, leaf area etc.) and with accelerated tissue senescence (e.g. Table 7.3).

4. Symptoms of Acute Toxicity

Chronic exposure of plants to low concentrations of pollutants can cause progressive leaf chlorosis and accelerated senescence, which may be difficult to recognize as symptoms of air pollution. In contrast, high concentrations generally cause visible lesions due to the death, drying out and bleaching of localized areas of leaf tissue. In some cases, the causative agent can be identified from the characteristic injuries produced; e.g.,

SO_2—interveinal chlorosis;
NO_x—irregular brown or black spots, interveinal or marginal;
O_3—white, yellow or brown flecks ($0·1$–1 mm) on the upper leaf surfaces, associated with stomata.
HF—"tip burn" or marginal necrosis (Mudd and Kozlowski, 1975).

In practice, it is not feasible to define widely-applicable concentration thresholds for the appearance of such visible symptoms because of the interactions between pollutants and environmental factors, and the great variation in resistance to damage within and between species. In addition, exposure of plants to combinations of pollutants will change

TABLE 7.3. Components of the yield of S23 *Lolium perenne* grown for 26 weeks in 191 μg m^{-3} SO$_2$ (SO$_2$ plants) or in 9 μg m^{-3} SO$_2$ (control plants), expressed as means per plant (from Bell and Clough, 1973).

	No. of tillers	No. of living leaves	No. of dead leaves	Dry weight of living leaves (g)	Dry weight of "stubble" (g)	Dry weight of dead leaves (g)	Leaf area (cm²)
SO$_2$ plants	14·84	47·31	12·02	0·388	0·217	0·047	203·6
Control plants	25·18	85·61	6·39	0·791	0·478	0·027	417·2
Difference in productivity between SO$_2$ and control plants[a]	−41·1%	−44·7%	+88·1%	−50·9%	−54·6%	+77·7%	−51·2%

[a] All differences significant at p < 0·001.

both thresholds and symptoms. However, as a single example, Bennett and Hill (1974) found that, under the conditions of the experiments illustrated in Fig. 7.7, foliar lesions were caused by 0·15 p.p.m. HF, 0·2 p.p.m. O_3, 0·8 p.p.m. SO_2 and by more than 5 p.p.m. of NO_2.

5. Ethylene as an Air Pollutant

Although included in Table 7.1, ethylene has been entirely ignored in the preceding discussion, mainly because its influence on plants as an air pollutant has been largely neglected. Its great importance for plants growing in polluted areas is underlined by the difficulties experienced (in laboratories in urban areas) in establishing ethylene-free atmospheres as controls for growth-substances experiments (Abeles, 1973).

C. Plant Resistance to Air Pollution

Although it is not possible for plants to be resistant to pollutant gases at all concentrations experienced in the atmosphere, there is ample evidence of species, and populations within species, which are unusually resistant to damage. Many of the published reports of resistance originate from rather short-term experiments; for example, Taylor *et al.* (1975) have reviewed a number of reports of inter-specific variation in resistance to nitrogen dioxide based on fumigation treatments at very high pollutant concentrations lasting only a few hours, for example 8, 16 and 32 p.p.m. NO_2 for a single hour (note that a level of 1 p.p.m. is representative of the most polluted atmospheres in the UK, Table 7.1). However, other authors have succeeded in establishing differences in resistance at more reasonable dose levels; for example, Taylor and Murdy (1975) demonstrated variation in resistance to SO_2 lesions amongst natural populations of *Geranium carolinianum* using 0·8 p.p.m. SO_2 for 12 h.

Studies of the mechanism of resistance are severely handicapped by uncertainties about the primary sites of pollutant action. Where progress has been made has been in the study of stomatal characteristics leading to the avoidance of mesophyll damage. For example, it has been found that the stomata of several resistant field crops are particularly sensitive to O_3, closing rapidly and remaining closed during a period of fumigation, thereby denying the gas access to the mesophyll (e.g. onion—Engel and Gabelman, 1966). Exclusion may also be facilitated by low stomatal density (e.g. in tobacco—Dean, 1972).

However, in most cases, resistance is not related to the amount of pollutant absorbed; for example, SO_2-resistant perennial ryegrass from a polluted site in Lancashire actually absorbed more SO_2 than the sensitive S23 cultivar (Bell and Mudd, 1976). For these plants resistance does not involve the exclusion of the pollutant but rather, the tolerance of high levels of the pollutant in the cells and organelles. The biochemical adaptations leading to such tolerance are unknown, although Bell and Mudd (1976) have shown variability in the ability of chlorophyll to resist denaturation in the presence of SO_2.

8. Interactions between Organisms

I. INTRODUCTION

All previous chapters have considered physical or chemical aspects of the environment and their effects on plants. In axenic culture such a description of plant–environment interactions might be adequate, but even in the simplest ecological systems other organisms form part of the environment. The effects of these organisms may be of three kinds:

(i) direct influence on the supply or stock of resources;
(ii) indirect effects achieved by alteration of the physical or, more usually, the chemical environment;
(iii) dispersal, as in pollination or seed dispersal.

In this way it is clear that many of the effects of one organism on another can be viewed in terms of the physico-chemical factors discussed in previous chapters. The first category covers situations where organisms compete for resources, where symbiotic associations exist (whether parasitic or mutualistic), or where predation, typically by grazing, occurs; the physiological responses elicited in the plant will be those appropriate to an increase or decrease in the supply or stock of the resource in question. By contrast, alterations to the microclimate or to soil structure, or most strikingly the addition to the environment of toxic or growth-controlling chemicals are of the second type. Again, however, explanations of the effect of one plant on another can be described wholly in terms of physical and chemical characteristics of the environment. Some other plant–plant interactions cannot be explained in this way, such as pollination and reproduction; these fall outside the scope of this book.

Most interactions between plants and other organisms (microbes, fungi, other plants, animals) can, then, be explained in terms of changes in the physical or chemical environment of the affected plant. That is not to imply that such interactions do not involve peculiar ecological and physiological effects and have profound evolutionary implications. Indeed it would be true to say that for most plants the responses shown towards environmental factors can only be understood in the light of the complex interactions that result from the acquisition of the same resources by competing plants, fungi, and microbes, and the modification of other environmental parameters by co-habiting species. It is for example of limited value merely to calculate the phosphate supplying power of a soil and to catalogue in detail the responses of a plant growing on that soil to phosphate supply, if what is required is an understanding of the factors controlling phosphate supply to that plant in the field. The effects of rhizosphere microorganisms and competing plants, of temperature and moisture on root growth and distribution, of grazing by the soil fauna and of many other factors would also be involved.

This chapter attempts to examine some of the influences of other organisms on plants, regarding them purely as additional environmental factors, and considers in detail four types of interaction:

(i) competition for resources,
(ii) predation and parasitism,
(iii) mutualistic association,
(iv) allelopathic chemicals.

II. COMPETITION

The definition of competition is one of the longest-running semantic debates in biology. A basic division exists between those who wish to define it in terms of population dynamics (e.g. Williamson, 1972) and those who use mechanistic definitions (Milne, 1961; Harper, 1961). The former definitions are based on the mutual depression of population numbers and tend to work best with microbes and animals where population numbers are easily counted. The latter can again be subdivided into those who include all deleterious effects on individuals, whatever the cause, and those who confine competition to the situation where the supply of a resource is less than the joint requirements of two organisms—in other words, competition has to be "for something". It is in this last sense that the word is used here, since it is both clearly defined and appropriate in this context.

Clearly, no two species can have identical requirements—this would imply a greater degree of affinity than is found within many species. Nevertheless, all species have some potential competitors when they are exploiting a resource, and their success depends therefore either on partitioning of the resource in some way, thereby avoiding competition, or on the establishment of competitive superiority. Resource partitioning is relatively simple to visualize in animals, where food items, for example, can be categorized on the basis of size, but all autotrophic green plants require roughly similar quantities of CO_2, light, water, and 15 or so inorganic ions. Clearly partitioning, if possible for such resources, must rely on different criteria. If one species possesses competitive superiority over others with respect to all resources, then one might expect that species to eliminate the others in all appropriate habitats. In practice one finds that communities of plants are very diverse and mono-specific stands are rather rare in nature, and many species (e.g. *Pteridium aquilinum, Urtica dioica*) only manage such dominance as a result of human activity. Clearly then, where species are competing for resources there are processes acting to reduce the intensity of that competition.

A. Competitive Superiority

The simplest competitive situation is one where species A has some advantage over B. This is frequently true in laboratory and greenhouse environments where only one factor is varied. In the oft-quoted experiments of Gause (1934) where two *Paramecium* species competed for food in an otherwise homogeneous environment, one was always competitively superior. Similarly when Idris and Milthorpe (1966) grew barley (*Hordeum vulgare* cv. Union BN) and charlock (*Sinapis arvensis*) in pots in an experimental garden, barley showed increased growth rates, net assimilation rates, root growth and nitrogen uptake rates, as its proportion in the mixture decreased. In other words the individual barley plants grew better if their neighbours were charlock than if they were other barleys. This implies that barley was the competitive dominant under these conditions, though under others the situation must be modified, as charlock is an acknowledged weed of barley crops.

The characteristics of plants that convey this superiority are different in the case of competition for light, from that of competition for water or nutrients. Where two plants compete for light, height and size of photosynthetic organs are critical (Fig. 8.1a) and physiological adaptation is only of significance to a subordinate species to compensate for growing in low light intensity. This occurs because light is directional; in contrast the supply of nutrients, and to some extent of water, in soil is diffuse and positional effects of the roots are less important. In this case it is the relative quantities of the root systems and most importantly the ability to lower soil water potential or ionic concentrations at the root

surface which determine competitive superiority. The exception to this
is where the surface soil is dry and water is rising from deeper layers—in
that case a deep-rooted plant will intercept the now directional supply
of water (Fig. 8.1b).

1. Competition for Water and Ions

There is, however, an important distinction between the uptake of
water and that of nutrients in the mechanism by which plants lower
soil water potential on the one hand and ionic concentration on the
other. Water flows into roots and up stems along a catena of declining
water potential, created by evaporation from the leaves (cf. Chapter 4).
The lowering of water potential at the root surface is therefore, a function of the rate of transpiration and hence of leaf area. In fact, ignoring

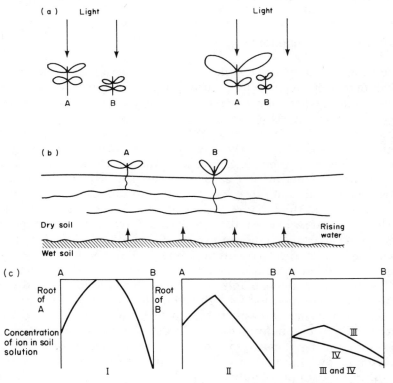

FIG. 8.1(a–c). Diagrammatic representation of plant factors controlling the development of competition for light, nutrient ions, and water. In (c) I–IV represent successive
time intervals, with plant B attaining the greater supply due to its lower root surface
concentration.

other variables such as stomatal conductance and differences in the leaf water potential at which stomata close, it is likely to be the leaf:root surface area ratio which determines relative rates of water uptake in competition. Some ions arrive at the root surface in the consequent mass flow of water in sufficient quantities to satisfy plant demand; this is certainly true of Ca^{2+} in calcareous and for Fe^{3+} in very acid soils (cf. Chapter 3).

For other ions, notably $H_2PO_4^-$, mass flow is quite inadequate to satisfy requirements, and concentration gradients are set up. For these ions, the situation in Fig. 8.1(c) arises and the controlling factor is the physiological ability to lower the concentration at the root surface. The lower the diffusion coefficient for the ion the narrower and steeper will be the depletion zones around the roots. Ions with relatively high diffusion coefficients, such as NO_3^-, are characterized by wide but shallow depletion zones. Clearly the higher the diffusion coefficient, the more likely competition is to ensue since depletion zones are wide; since solution concentrations tend to be higher for such ions, facilitating mass flow, shoot characteristics controlling transpiration will be more important in determining uptake in competition.

For competition for an ion to occur, two conditions must be satisfied —the ions must not arrive by mass flow at the root surface faster than they are required by the plant, and depletion zones must be wide enough to overlap between adjacent roots. To some extent these conditions counteract one another, since there is a general correlation between ion mobility in soil and the contribution of mass flow to uptake (cf. p. 84). They can also be quantified into two dimensionless mathematical expressions which are fully explored by Baldwin and Nye (1974) and Baldwin (1975):

(i) The relationship between mass flow ($V=$ the water flux at the root surface, in $cm^3 cm^{-2} s^{-1}$) and plant demand ($\alpha=$ root absorbing power, $cm s^{-1}$—see Nye and Tinker (1969) and p. 98) is simply given by the ratio $V:\alpha$. If $V<\alpha$, uptake is greater than supply by mass flow, depletion occurs at the root surface, and competition may ensue. α is itself of course highly dependent on the concentration of the ion at the root surface. The extent of depletion, both in terms of concentration at the root surface and radial spread from the root, depends on D, the diffusion coefficient.

(ii) Where depletion occurs, the extent and occurrence of overlap is controlled by the dimensionless function DtL_v where D is the diffusion coefficient ($cm^2 s^{-1}$), t is time (s), and L_v is root density ($cm cm^{-3}$). Baldwin (1975) shows that as DtL_v falls below $2\cdot5$ towards zero, the ion becomes increasingly immobile with respect to that particular root system. Uptake of $H_2PO_4^-$ and K^+ in typical soils will in fact be directly related to this function, and for these ions high values of L_v (the only term in the expression which the plant can control) will be advantageous.

There emerge from such an analysis, then, four critical parameters— water flux (V), plant demand (α), root density (L_v), and diffusion co-efficients (D)—of the soil–plant system that control uptake in competition. The situation is greatly complicated, however, by the interactions of these as shown in Figure 8.2.

2. Competition for Light

In contrast to the complexity of competition for nutrients and water, that for light is governed simply by the directional and transitory nature of the photon as an energy source. If a photon strikes a leaf it may be absorbed, transmitted, or reflected, but both the latter have selective effects, producing light of altered spectral quality (see p. 34) and of little photosynthetic value. Competitive superiority for light therefore resides in the ability to place leaves in illuminated rather than shaded positions, and will be determined by plant characteristics determining foliage height and the rate at which that height is attained.

Where, as in annual crops and their weeds, both competitors start simultaneously from seed, the critical factors determining rate of growth are seed size, relative growth rate, and elongation rate. Black (1958) sowed together small (4 mg) and large (10 mg) seeds of *Trifolium subterraneum*, which in monoculture produced identical yields, and found that plants developed from large seeds made up almost the entire sward (92%) after 115 days. This advantage was manifested from the very start, as the large seeds produced larger cotyledons, producing a positive feedback, for these captured more light and so grew faster. Similarly, where the two cultivars Yarloop and Bacchus Marsh, which in monoculture produced equal yields and had modal petiole lengths of 18 and 14 cm, were grown together, Yarloop produced 80% of the final combined yield (Black, 1960).

It is in such circumstances that the significance of etiolation becomes apparent, as a means of growing out of shade, and the importance of the sensitivity of etiolation to far-red light, the dominant wavelength of transmitted light, is then obvious. McLaren and Smith (1978) have shown that *Rumex obtusifolius* shows greater etiolation if FR increases in proportion to the red flux after germination. Thus seeds germinating under an established canopy, with a high FR:R ratio, will respond less than those where the canopy is growing up, gradually increasing the

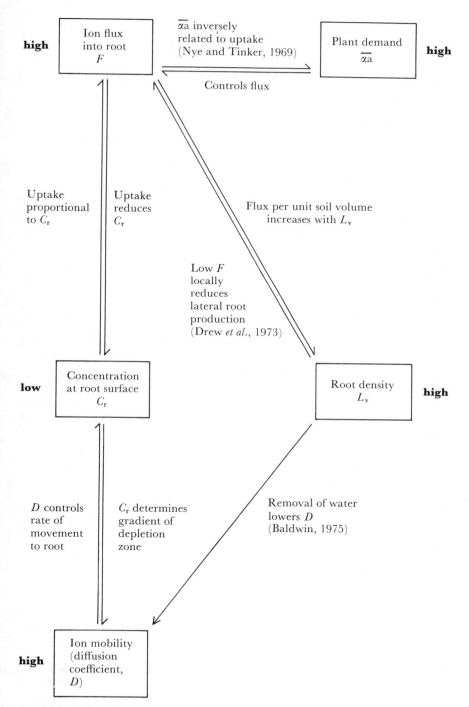

FIG. 8.2. Schematic representation of interactions of major soil and plant variables controlling uptake. **Bold** type indicates conditions conducive to the onset of competition.

ratio. In the latter situation elongation is likely to bring the plant to the top of the canopy, in the former it would probably be suicidal.

What then of the suppressed plant, confined to sub-canopy layers, or of the suppressed leaf on an otherwise well-illuminated plant? The various adaptations for shade resistance described in Chapter 2 permit survival—namely, decreases in leaf thickness, abscission of leaves below the compensation point (as long as some are above it), and the phenomenon described by Chippindale (1932) as "inanition". In the latter case plants of *Festuca pratensis* survived for over a year without growth beneath a canopy of *Lolium italicum*; when the canopy was removed and nutrients applied, the *Festuca* resumed growth. Similarly Mahmoud and Grime (1974) have ascribed the ability of *Deschampsia flexuosa* to survive deep shade to its low negative growth rate at very low light intensities.

Clearly adaptations within the better illuminated portions of the canopy will be important. It is widely found that the early, and therefore lower leaves of a plant are entire and the higher, most recent leaves dissected (Fig. 8.3). Certainly cotyledons are nearly always entire and serve to maximize light interception and cast shade on seedling competitors. The significance of dissected leaves in full sunlight is discussed on pp. 53 and 155. In addition to changes in leaf morphology there may be changes in leaf angle, such that lower leaves are more nearly horizontal and upper ones more erect. The latter are still at light saturation in full sunlight, but intercept less and allow more to pass to the lower leaves. This explains why the optimum light intensity for a complex canopy is always greater than that for an individual leaf.

A parallel situation can be observed in a mixed pasture, which has a high canopy of rather vertical grass leaves, and a lower one of herbs with horizontal leaves. The critical factor here is grazing. Clearly the higher, erect grass leaves are more vulnerable but their basal meristems enable them to recover. The dicotyledons cannot so readily risk grazing damage, but compensate for this by greater light interception.

Finally, one should not ignore the role of solar angle, which varies continually and may make it difficult for any one plant to place its leaves in such a position as to shade others, allowing the environmental heterogeneity to permit avoidance of competition and so co-existence.

3. *Interactions in Competition*

Following the lead of Donald (1958) a number of workers have attempted to disentangle the effects of competition for light and nutrients. Using dividers to separate the shoot and root systems independently,

FIG. 8.3. Silhouettes of successive leaves from base to top of a stem of musk mallow *Malva moschata*, showing the progressive increase in leaf dissection.

TABLE 8.1. Growth of two grasses (*Lolium rigidum* and *Phalaris tuberosa*) with all combinations of root and shoot competition and at two nitrogen levels (Donald, 1958).

| | \multicolumn{8}{c}{*Yield (105 days from planting) (g dry matter)*} |
| | \multicolumn{4}{c}{Lolium} | \multicolumn{4}{c}{Phalaris} |

	NC	SC	RC	FC	NC	SC	RC	FC
Low N	2·45	2·71	2·12	2·77	2·00	1·63	0·35	0·18
High N	4·71	4·19	4·13	4·72	4·67	3·19	1·17	0·32

| | \multicolumn{6}{c}{*Yield as %age of non-competition yield*} |
| | \multicolumn{3}{c}{Lolium} | \multicolumn{3}{c}{Phalaris} |

	SC	RC	FC	SC	RC	FC
Low N	111	87	113	82	18	9 (15)
High N	89	92	100	68	25	7 (17)

NC, SC, RC, FC—no, shoot, root and full competition respectively.
Figures in parenthesis represent expected FC values obtained by multiplying SC and RC.

Donald examined the effects of shoot and root competition on the inter-action between *Lolium perenne* and *Phalaris tuberosa*. The figures in Table 8.1 are derived from his paper and show that *P. tuberosa* was clearly the subordinate species, both under shoot and root competition, but particularly in the latter case. Root competition, therefore, appeared to be a more severe treatment. When full competition was permitted (shoot and root—no dividers) yield was further reduced and more so than would be expected by combining the shoot and root competitive effects. The figures in the last column of Table 8.1 represent predicted full competition yields on the assumption that root and shoot effects were simply additive. They are clearly higher than those actually obtained for *P. tuberosa*.

There is here a clear implication of a synergism between the effects of root and shoot competition, that is not unexpected. The root and shoot perform distinct but almost symbiotic functions. Reduction in nutrient supply to the shoots caused by root competition will lower the efficiency of the shoots and hence the plant's ability to compete for light; this in turn will reduce the flow of assimilate to the roots, dam-aging root function, and so on.

Such interactions have led to the suggestion that competitive superiority is largely a function of overshadowing of the leaves of one plant by another, which in turn reduces the competitive ability of the subordinate species for nutrients giving a "snowball" effect (Newman, 1973). Thus Idris and Milthorpe (1966) sowed barley and charlock in pure stands and in mixtures with either species in excess. The larger-seeded barley quickly over-shadowed the charlock which was pro-gressively suppressed, even in mixtures in which it was in excess, and this enabled it increasingly to dominate the soil and to extract much greater quantities of nitrogen. They were able to show that the nitrogen uptake rate of charlock in the early stages of competition was not reduced by small numbers of barley plants, though the growth rate was much lower (Table 8.2). Their explanation was that the primary factor competed for was light.

TABLE 8.2. Nitrogen uptake and growth rates of competing barley (*Hordeum vulgaris*) and charlock (*Sinapis arvensis*) (from Idris and Milthorpe, 1966).

	Nitrogen uptake rate[a] (mg mg^{-1} d^{-1})		Relative growth rate[b] (mg mg^{-1} wk^{-1})	
Mixture	Charlock	Barley	Charlock	Barley
Pure (95:0)	72·5	9·9	1·03	0·63
Excess (60:35)	80·5	16·0	0·82	0·68
Deficit (35:60)	48·9	13·8	0·68	0·81

[a] Uptake rate per unit root dry weight in the first two weeks of the experiment.
[b] Polynomials of the form $\ln W = \ln W_0 + bt + 2ct^2$ were fitted to data. The value quoted is of the first-order regression coefficient, b.

In contrast Aspinall (1960) grew white persicaria (*Polygonum lapathifolium*) with barley and found that, although suppressed plants of *P. lapathifolium* had typical shade adaptations (higher *LAR* and *SLA* for example), in shading experiments significant reductions in relative growth rate were not obtained until light intensities were reduced to 40–45% of full summer daylight. Since such reductions were not obtained in stands of barley until after the commencement of suppression of *P. lapathifolium* by barley, he inferred that nutrient competition resulting from the smaller root system of *P. lapathifolium* was the primary agent. This was confirmed by nutrient addition and by experiments in which the shoots and roots were separated.

The apparent contradiction between these two otherwise similar experiments may possibly be explained by the different growth forms of the competitors. *Sinapis arvensis* is a tall, single-stemmed plant, similar in general habitat to the barley it was grown with. *Polygonum lapathifolium* is a sprawling, weak-stemmed, much-branched plant that is unlikely ever to be able to compete effectively for light with the barley canopy. It may well be that selection has proceeded in different directions here; towards competitive ability for light in the case of *S. arvensis* and for nutrients with an approach to "shade" physiology for *P. lapathifolium*.

These examples underline the importance of considering the other interacting environmental factors under whose selective pressure the species has evolved. This is beautifully illustrated by the data of Snaydon (1971), who grew acid and calcareous-soil ecotypes of white clover, *Trifolium repens*, on both soils and in all combinations of root and shoot competition. His results (Table 8.3) show that the larger-leaved calcareous-soil plant outyielded the acid soil ecotype on both

TABLE 8.3. Yield of plants of an acid-soil ecotype of white clover *Trifolium repens* as a percentage of that of a calcareous-soil ecotype, when the two species were grown on both soils in all combinations of root and shoot competition (from Snaydon, 1971).

Competition	Acid soil	Calcareous soil
None	77_b	41_a
Shoots	53_a	38_{ab}
Roots	121_c	36_b
Shoots and roots	72_b	31_c

Within columns figures differently subscripted are significantly different by Duncan's test ($p = 0.05$).

soils whenever the shoots were in competition. The nearest approach to the acid-soil plants' native habitat is the full competition/acid soil combination, yet even here it is outyielded by the calcareous-soil plant: clearly this does not occur in the field. Only where the roots alone compete does the acid-soil plant gain its rightful advantage. The implication is that in the field the only form of effective competition is root competition, and that other factors, probably grazing pressure, prohibit the development of the intensity of shoot competition that occurs in a pot experiment.

The features that confer competitive superiority are relatively simple—leaf canopy architecture and height, rates of transpiration, and physiological characteristics of ion uptake—but their operation is complex. Selection may act to minimize these features and so confer competitive incompetence on a plant if their possession carries concomitant disadvantages in a particular field environment. In considering competitive relationships we may not ignore these factors, nor the many other environmental agents and behavioural adaptations that act to reduce the intensity of competition.

B. Avoidance of Competition in Space and Time

It is possible to demonstrate that under experimental conditions, of two plants grown together, one will usually exhibit competitive superiority over the other. Clearly, under field conditions, this frequently does not occur as co-existence is an apparently widespread phenomenon. It is often the case, however, that apparently cohabiting species, which would be listed by an ecologist together in a single species list for a community, are to only a small extent competing, through separation either in time or in space. Thus it is generally true that the species of diverse meadow communities have different, though overlapping phenologies (Fig. 8.4), at least for the above-ground organs. Little information is available on specific differences in the seasonality of root growth, and this would seem a fertile area for research.

Temporal separation can be achieved in respect of competition for any factor, though seasonal differences in its supply may make some growth times more favourable than others. However differences in the nature of competition for light, nutrients, and water (see above) mean that spatial separation of competing plants with respect to light can only occur either if there is no overlap between the two shoot systems (in which case ço-existence is apparent not real) or the lower-placed species in the canopy has a physiological adaptation to reduced light intensity. Thus, many woodland floor plants grow best at much higher light intensities than they actually experience—e.g. bluebell *Hyacinthoides non-scriptus* (Blackman and Rutter, 1946)—but survive under a leaf canopy because of a shade adaption in photosynthesis. Removal of the canopy would permit invasion by intolerant species, so that the bluebell and the trees in no sense compete for light, particularly as the bluebell is unable to influence the light supply to the tree leaves.

Spatial separation of root systems, however, is well known (Anderson, 1927; Coupland and Johnson, 1965; Whittaker and Woodwell, 1969; Kirikova, 1970) and may permit co-existence of species whose shoots intermingle. However, different soil layers will have distinct properties, in relation to water supply, nutrient content, microbial activity, and so on, so that such separation again involves physiological adaptation. This phenomenon has received surprisingly little experimental investigation, although it can be demonstrated that provision of distinct soil layers does promote co-existence (Table 8.4). O'Brien *et al.* (1967) were able to show that the massive yield depression of *Lolium perenne* by its hybrid with *Festuca pratensis*, x *Festulolium*, was associated with a reduction in P uptake from deep soil layers from 32% of the total to 7%. By contrast, the uptake pattern of x *Festulolium* was not altered by

Phenology

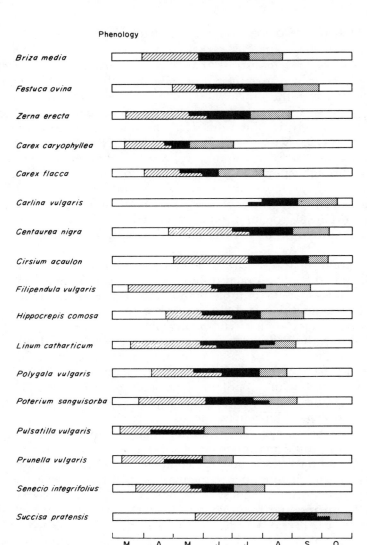

FIG. 8.4. Phenology and development of 17 chalk grassland species. (Reproduced, with permission, from Wells (1971). *Brit. Ecol. Soc. Symp.* **11**, 497–516. Blackwells, Oxford).

TABLE 8.4. Proportions of total yield of five species grown in a mixture on two soils arranged in different layers. Soil A is an acid sand (pH 3·8), soil B a fertile loam (pH 6·8). The first letter represents top 75 mm, second letter bottom 75 mm; A+B is a uniform mixture of the two soils (Fitter, unpublished).

Species	Soil arrangement				
	A/A	A/B	B/B	B/A	A+B
Holcus lanatus	0·97	0·89	0·17	0·43	0·48
Poa trivialis	0·00	0·00	0·04	0·07	0·09
Festuca rubra	0·02	0·08	0·10	0·09	0·07
Lolium perenne	0·01	0·02	0·60	0·44	0·34
Plantago lanceolata	0·00	0·01	0·09	0·06	0·02
Simpson Index	0·05	0·18	0·58	0·65	0·61
(±s.e.)	±0·02	±0·04	±0·03	±0·02	±0·02

H. lanatus, as the most calcifuge of the five species, dominates whenever the acid soil is the top layer, but *L. perenne* is favoured by the neutral soil. With the loam as top layer, altering the bottom layer radically alters the proportion of *H. lanatus* and raises the Simpson Index (1–S, a measure of dominance: 0=complete dominance of 1 species, maximum value here=0·80, if all species at equal proportions).

competition from either of its parents (Table 8.5). Such changes deserve to be more widely investigated.

C. Suppression of Competition

In many situations however, it cannot be argued that species are avoiding competition with one another in these ways, and here one must assume that other factors are acting to suppress the competitive advantage of one species to a greater or lesser extent, even possibly so far as to reduce growth sufficiently that no resources are in inadequate supply. Such factors can be divided into those that suppress both species and those that act only on the potential dominant.

1. Factors Acting to Suppress both Competitors

(i) There may be a balance of advantage between the two species, such that one has, say, superior nitrate gathering powers and the other pre-empts available light. Such interactions must be common and in appropriate situations could lead to co-existence; this has in

TABLE 8.5. Yield and phosphate uptake from 60 cm depth (as percentage of total) by *Lolium perenne*, *Festuca arundinacea*, and their triploid hybrid, *x Festulolium loliaceum*, when grown for hay (from O'Brien et al., 1967).

Competitor	Yield (g)			% P uptake from 60 cm		
	L. perenne	F. arundinacea	x Festulolium	L. perenne	F. arundinacea	x Festulolium
L. perenne	553	377	646	32	32	53
F. arundinacea	199	614	511	56	38	46
x Festulolium	71	164	789	7	16	47

fact been demonstrated for two unicellular algae, *Asterionella formosa* and *Cyclotella meneghiniana*. At all phosphate concentrations in pure culture *Asterionella* has the higher growth rate, whereas *Cyclotella* is superior at all silicate concentrations, if these are limiting. By adjusting the $SiO_2:PO_4$ ratio so that both are limiting it is possible to ensure co-existence in mixed cultures (Titman, 1976).

(ii) Physical or chemical features of the environment may be so extreme as to reduce the growth of both species to the point where either resources are no longer limiting or any possible competitive advantage of either species is nullified. This is possibly true of extremely cold or unstable environments, such as arctic scree, or of plants growing on toxic soils, such as lead mine spoils, but not of arid environments, such as deserts or shingle banks, where wide spacing of plants may occur, but the limiting factor is a resource—water.

2. *Factors Acting to Suppress the Potential Dominants*
These are of more general significance than those above and the following are among the most important:

(i) There may be a predator or parasite of the potentially dominant species whose population fluctuates in tandem, so that whilst that species is not eliminated from the community when rare, its population declines when it becomes very abundant. That this is likely to happen can be deduced from the effects of insect pests on crop plants in monoculture, but it has been demonstrated in mixed *Eucalyptus* forests in Australia and in competition between wheat and barley infected with powdery mildew (Burdon and Chilvers, 1974, 1977).

(ii) The potentially suppressed species may exhibit greater resistance to occasional catastrophes, either predictable or unpredictable. This may lead to clear-cut cycles in vegetational composition, if for example fire is a regular but infrequent habitat factor, but can also occur if of two species one is more winter- or drought-hardy, but the other is at an advantage during the growing season.

(iii) Different growth stages may vary in competitive ability. This can be observed on any scale, from the regeneration of species of one life-form to the basic difference between annuals and perennials. Typically an annual will outcompete a perennial during the first year of growth, but with time the perennial gains an increasing advantage. More significantly, perhaps, Watt (1947) showed that when a beech tree (*Fagus sylvatica*) falls in a pure beech canopy, the initial tree colonists are ash (*Fraxinus excelsior*). These are "tree weeds", fast-growing, and initially dominant, but eventually succumbing to the shade cast by the slower-growing but shade-tolerant beech seedlings. A full discussion of what he terms the "regeneration niche" is given by Grubb (1977).

(iv) A competitively subordinate plant may be able to produce chemicals which directly or indirectly impair the competitor's growth. This phenomenon is known as allelopathy and is fully discussed below (p. 291).

III. PREDATION AND PARASITISM

As Feeny (1976) has pointed out, the continued existence of plants is little short of miraculous. As stationary packages of food for several hundred thousand species of phytophagous insects and several thousand species of parasitic fungi, quite apart from herds of grazing mammals, it is at first sight hard to see how they avoid complete consumption. The devastation caused by locust swarms is of course well known, and occasionally one comes across totally defoliated plants in otherwise healthy vegetation. The winter moth *Operophtera brumata* is able almost to denude oak trees *Quercus robur* under certain conditions, and the chrysomelid beetle *Gastrophysa viridula* can similarly decimate docks *Rumex obtusifolius*. Typically, however, leaves of plants collected from field-grown plants show necrotic patches and nibbled margins, but not a bare skeleton of vascular tissue.

Clearly, plants discourage potential pathogens and herbivores from inflicting excessive damage. There appear to be three main mechanisms:

(i) Nutritional inadequacy. Most plants have relatively low protein contents. Southwood (1973) quotes figures suggesting that typical values for plant material are 10–30% of dry weight, compared with 50–60% in microbes, 40–60% in insects, and 25–40% in artificial diets for insects. It is an intriguing thought that plant breeders in attempting to improve the food quality of crop plants may be unwittingly removing this defence. Other nutritional factors may be important, such as low levels of sterols, of the amino-acids tryptophane and methionine in many plant proteins and even of sodium which is typically more abundant in animal than in plant tissues.

(ii) Physical barriers. Many plant organs have external coverings of scales, hairs, or glandular hairs. Beneath this there may be thick cuticles, thick epidermal cell walls, bands of collenchyma or sclerenchyma, or deposition of substances such as silica (in grasses) or resins (in conifers). All these provide problems for organisms attempting to penetrate plant tissues.

(iii) Toxins. Perhaps the most dramatic and widely discussed defences are chemical, recently reviewed by Levin (1976). These may be constitutive or induced by attack, and are chemically very diverse, including alkaloids, tannins, cyanogens, and a wide range of phenolic compounds. The reasons for the existence of this diversity are considered below.

These various types of defence have particular value in different situations, depending on the organisms involved and the nature of the attack. It is possible to distinguish two classes of plant-feeding organisms on the basis of the type of material removed. Some organisms obtain essential metabolites by removing whole cells including much structural material, principally cellulose, hemicellulose, and lignin: these are tissue feeders. Others, however, specifically remove cell contents and can be termed metabolite feeders, obtaining a diet containing less unutilizable material (cellulose, lignin, etc.) though not always well-balanced. It is also less damaging to the plant than tissue feeding; indeed small losses of metabolites may be quite inconsequential, and this is the basis of mutualistic symbiosis (cf. p. 288).

A. Nature of Attack

1. Metabolite Feeders

Three sources of metabolites are available to plant feeders—xylem contents, phloem contents, and parenchymatous or other cell contents; and two methods which they can use to obtain these metabolites—mechanical insertion of a probe to withdraw material, and systemic infection (Table 8.6).

As far as the insect is concerned, in the case of stylet-feeders the nutritional value declines in the order cell contents: phloem: xylem. Xylem is essentially a dilute solution of mineral salts and, depending on the nitrate reductase activity in the roots, which varies greatly with species, contains a small amount of amino-acids. Horsfield (1977) has shown that *Philaenus spumarius*, the well-known spittlebug, is a xylem feeder, and that it preferentially feeds on xylem vessels containing approximately 1 mM amino-acids. Indeed when required to utilize xylem containing less than 0·3 mM amino-acids, mortality of nymphs was around 90%. Xylem feeding clearly requires considerable specialization for an insect, though for higher plant hemiparasites such as *Euphrasia*, *Rhinanthus*, or *Melampyrum* it is more straightforward. All

TABLE 8.6.   Classification of metabolite feeders by type of food and mode
of attack.

Food source	Systemic infection	Mechanical probe
Xylem	many fungi: e.g. *Verticillium* often cause "wilt" diseases *Ceratostomella ulmi* (Dutch Elm disease)	insects; some Cercopidae: e.g. *Philaenus* plants; hemiparasites: e.g. *Rhinanthus*
Phloem	many fungi viruses: e.g. phloem necrosis in elms	insects; most Aphididae: e.g. *Myzus* plants; full parasites: e.g. *Orobanche*
Cytoplasm	many fungi: e.g. *Pythium, Botrytis* ("damping-off") Viruses	insects; some Mynidae: e.g. *Leptoterna* some Psyllidae

these are normally photosynthetic but have poorly developed root systems. By penetrating xylem vessels of adjacent plants they ensure a supply of minerals and water, and although organic compounds are transferred as well (Govier *et al.*, 1968) these are probably not of great significance. The best examples of such hemiparasites are provided by the annual members of the sub-family Rhinanthoideae of the Scrophulariaceae. It has been suggested (Karlsson, 1974) that the hemiparasitic habit enables these annuals to persist in the closed grassland communities of which they are characteristic and which are otherwise almost entirely composed of perennials, since they do not need to use resources in the production of an extensive root system. One further problem of xylem feeding is the very considerable negative pressures that may build up. For higher plant hemiparasites this is overcome by xylem to xylem continuity and by water secretion from leaf surface glands to increase the water potential gradient (Klaren, 1975; Govier *et al.*, 1968), but it is not known how insects cope.

Phloem, by contrast, contains a much more nutritious solution although its contents fluctuate greatly, both daily and seasonally. Its largest component is sucrose, which is typically 0·2–0·7 M, and it also contains normally up to 0·5% amino-acids and many other substances. For higher plant parasites phloem presumably contains an adequate diet; many such plants, such as *Orobanche* and *Lathraea*, derive all their nutrients from host phloem. For an insect, the main problem is the excessive C:N ratio. Aphids, the most successful phloem feeders, overcome this by sugar secretion, the well-known honeydew, and some indeed turn it to advantage by entering a symbiotic relationship with ants, who "farm" the aphids for the sugar. Phloem has the further advantage that it is under positive pressure and so the sucking insect has to control the inflow rather than expend energy on inducing it.

Cell contents are indubitably the best balanced diet for metabolite feeders, but are not renewable. Whereas an aphid stylet in a phloem vessel will receive a continuous flow of sap, once the contents of a cell have been used up, the organism must move on to a new one, explaining perhaps why this mode of feeding has proved most popular with the fungi, whose mode of infection requires them to grow through the host tissue, and to pass a series of cells anyway. An alternative is for the parasite to act more as a sink for metabolites without destroying the cell, much in the way that aphids do. Viruses, which to replicate must use cell contents, are renowned for their ability to incorporate themselves into the host genome, replicating in tandem, and most plants can be shown to contain virus particles without exhibiting disease symptoms.

2. Tissue Feeders

Metabolite feeders rarely cause dramatic damage to plants, and then often only incidentally. Tissue feeders, however, particularly leaf feeders, can destroy large proportions of a plant's assimilatory tissue, leading in some cases to total defoliation. Tissue feeders fall mainly into three groups—insects, molluscs and mammals, though birds and reptiles may be important in some situations. In marine habitats molluscs and fish are the most important. The basic qualification for a tissue feeder is the possession of biting or tearing mouthparts, but more subtly they must be able to cope with the problems of a cellulose-based diet. To obtain sufficient quantities of nitrogen and other, more minor dietary components, they must ingest very large quantities of cellulose, and to most animals this is unusable. The exceptions are a few molluscs, such as *Teredo*, which actually produce a cellulase, and those animals that have symbiotic bacteria or protozoa in the gut, notably termites (Isoptera) and ruminant mammals. Some insects—ants in South America and termites—cultivate fungi on leaves brought into the nest, and these break down the cellulose. The existence of non-microbial cellulases in molluscs is still disputed; certainly most herbivorous molluscs have cellulolytic bacteria in their guts, but Parnas (1961) by feeding the snail *Levantina hierosolyma* on antibiotics, claimed to show that the snails digestive gland also produced a cellulase, a conclusion disputed by Sumner (1968) on histochemical grounds. Similarly, *Scrobicularia plana* has been shown by Payne *et al.* (1972) to produce a complete cellulase system. Larvae of the goat moth, *Cossus cossus*, by contrast, feeding on wood but unable to use cellulose, take three years to reach maturity, and this appears to be due to poor nutritional quality, since on artificial diets they pupate within one year. Most tissue feeders are therefore faced with the problem of having to ingest an enormous quantity of material to obtain their requirements. Quantitatively this is measured as the ratio of the energy content of the ingested food to that of the biomass produced, the production–consumption efficiency. This is typically around 40–50 for phytophagous insects and 10–20 for carnovores.

B. Plant Defences

As briefly discussed above, plants can defend themselves by nutritional inadequacy, by physical barriers, and by chemical toxins. In addition, the activities of predators may be important, though the plant usually has little or no control over these. An exception is the relationship between some Central American *Acacia* species, which provide hollow thorns as nests and extra-floral nectaries and protein-rich appendages as food for colonies of ants, which deter potential herbivores. If the ants are removed, the plant is quickly defoliated (Janzen, 1975).

1. Nutritional Inadequacy
It appears to be generally true that plant tissue is only barely adequate as a diet for most insects (Southwood, 1973), although more useable for the herbivorous mammals and for fungi which benefit from symbiotic associations on the one hand and very versatile metabolic systems on the other. The failure of most animals to evolve a cellulase, even more striking in view of the fact that a handful of species have achieved it, is almost certainly explained by the very low protein contents of plant material, making cellulose unnecessary as an energy source since it is protein and not energy that is limiting. Many animal species have attempted to avoid this problem by feeding on sap, but as mentioned above, this too may have severe nutritional imbalances. The only species to avoid this problem to any great extent are the cytoplasm feeders, since cytoplasm has a much higher N content than whole plant tissue. There are, however, other problems associated with feeding on cytoplasm. Generally, increases in N content are likely to improve

growth and survival of the feeder, as has been shown for the aphid
Myzus persicae by van Emden *et al.* (1969) and for many other insects.
It is a striking consequence of this that nutrient deficiency for a plant
may actually be an important defence mechanism, and that there may
have been selection for low N contents. However, low N content may
not be a wholly adequate defence for a plant, since it could lead to a
grazing animal eating more tissue, so as to obtain sufficient, and this
would be more damaging to the plant. There is, therefore, a dilemma—
high N content increases palatability and so the likelihood of attack,
while low N content may make individual attacks more severe. However, low N content may also reduce both the individual and the
population growth rates of the herbivore and so reduce its equilibrium
population size, so that the total effect on the plant population is less
(Lawton and McNeill, 1979). Nevertheless, other defences may be
required.

2. *Physical Barriers*
Despite nutritional inadequacy, plants as primary producers are eaten.
All plants present, to a greater or lesser extent, physical problems to at
least some potential predators or pathogens. Tissue feeders can be
deterred by a variety of external morphological traits, whose scale
depends on the size of the animal. The ferocious spines of arid-zone
trees, such as *Acacia karoo*, have clearly evolved in relation to grazing by
large mammals, but less dramatic than these, there exists a wide range
of smaller structures. Spines are widespread, particularly on woody
plants, which can give them adequate strength, and give protection.
Some are detachable, as in *Rosa*, presumably to reduce the danger of
of stem breakage by passing animals catching them, others are out-
growths of the wood. Leaf-spines are also common in thistles (*Cirsium,
Carduus* etc.) and these grade into hairs. Most angiosperms are hairy in
some part, and Cronquist (quoted by Johnson, 1975) suggests that the
ability for shoot epidermal cells to produce hairs may be related to the
need for root epidermal cells to produce root hairs.

Hairs are found on higher plants in a bewildering variety of forms
(Fig. 8.5). Although once considered as a means of reducing transpiration by thickening the leaf boundary layer, numerous studies have
failed to show any such general relationship (but see Chapter 4 and
Chapter 5, p. 99). Undoubtedly in some cases they serve this function.
but more generally hairiness appears to be associated with defence
against insect attack. This was shown clearly for leaf-spines by Merz
(1959) who offered larvae of the moth (*Lasiocampa quercus*) which normally feed along the edges of leaves, leaves of holly (*Ilex aquifolium*),

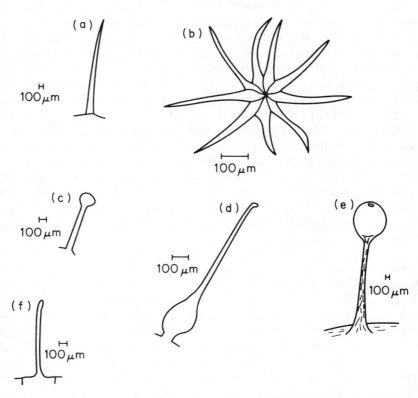

Fig. 8.5.   Types of hairs on plant surfaces. (a) simple hair from capsule of *Silene dioica*; (b) stellate hair from *Sida* (after Esau); (c) glandular hair from *Epilobium hirsutum*; (d) stinging hair from *Urtica dioica*; (e) glandular hair from *Drosera capensis*; (f) root hair from *Lolium perenne*.

which they refused to eat. The same leaves with the spines removed were avidly devoured. Leaf spines are therefore an effective deterrent and spiny or hooked hairs can also prevent insects feeding. Gilbert (1971) has shown that the hooked hairs of *Passiflora adenopoda* prohibit movement of and may even wound the caterpillars of Heliconid butterflies, damaging predators of other *Passiflora* species. Even soft hairs may be effective against smaller insects. Mutant lines of soybean varieties differing only in hairiness have been shown to have leafhopper (*Empoasca fabae*) infestations closely related to hair density (Singh *et al.*, 1971). In these experiments growth in height of the soybeans was closely related to the infestation of *E. fabae* suggesting that powerful selection pressures may be involved. The whole field of plant pubescence has been reviewed recently by Johnson (1975).

In addition to hairs, many other physical structures have been implicated in defence, including thick cuticles (important against fungal pathogens), silicious walls, oxalate raphides in cells, corky layers, resin and latex ducts and so on. Clearly the borderline between chemical and physical defences is hard to draw. Many hairs are glandular and can secrete either sticky substances, to immobilize insects, or toxins, and the full development of this line is seen in the stinging hairs of nettles (*Urtica*) and other families such as Loasaceae.

3. Chemical Defences

All plants contain compounds usually known as "secondary plant products", once considered to be waste products, but now generally accepted as largely defensive. There are at least 30,000 such compounds known from the relatively small sample of plants so far analysed (Harborne, 1977). The waste product theory seems in retrospect somewhat far-fetched, since organisms with a primarily anabolic biochemistry should be able to avoid producing wastes, but the clear toxicity of many of these compounds to fungi, insects, or other enemies is convincing evidence of their function.

One problem for a plant of adopting a chemical defence against predation of parasitism is that any chemical toxic enough to be effective is likely to be autotoxic—so where can it be stored? There are two compartments—the cell wall and the vacuole—which are remote from metabolism, and these are indeed found to contain many toxins. Alternatively two compounds (typically a glycoside and glycosidase enzyme), that are themselves innocuous but that if mixed produce a toxin, can be stored in separate compartments. Finally, special organs may occur, such as glandular hairs, which are wholly devoted to the storage and excretion of toxins. The extreme development of this can perhaps be seen on the leaf surface of sundews (*Drosera*), which is covered with stalked glands, and whose secretion of digestive enzymes turns a defensive into an offensive mechanism.

One class of compounds which may be of significance here has recently been found to be widespread—lectins or carbohydrate-binding proteins. Indeed the suggestion has been made that the mysterious "P-protein" found in the phloem, for which a generation of plant physiologists have vainly attempted to adduce a transport function, may be a defence mechanism against invasive pathogens for the otherwise vulnerable phloem (Gietl *et al.*, 1979). The P-proteins certainly possess lectin activity.

However, any diversion of resources away from what one might call primary plant activities—harvesting of resources, reproduction—into chemical defence incurs a metabolic cost, and one of the selective factors operating in this context will therefore be minimization of this cost. The most effective feeding deterrent must either (i) kill or otherwise rebuff all known feeders, or (ii) substantially reduce the food value of the plant. Flexibility of biochemical systems renders the first improbable, but the second is widely adopted. Many plants contain tannins which form complexes with plant proteins and so reduce still further the already low useable nitrogen content (see above, p. 282). Thus leaves of common oak, *Quercus robur*, contain up to 5% of tannins by weight in September, and these have been shown by Feeny (1968) significantly to reduce larval growth rate of winter moths, *Operophtera brumata*. Oak leaves also contain much less water in autumn, which may be a further deterrent. Such defence mechanisms have rather general effects in reducing the efficiency of predators, but are metabolically more expensive, and cannot provide complete immunity. They are, however, difficult for animals to circumvent.

Many plants have, therefore, apparently opted for compounds which have specifically toxic effects on predators and parasites. The range of such mechanisms is great, varying from the storage of organic acids to lower cell pH, which probably explains the immunity of *Oxalis* to attack by dodders, *Cuscuta* (Kuijt, 1969), through a variety of glycosides, non-protein amino-acids, terpenes, alkaloids, hormone mimics, and other compounds. The chemistry and mode of action of many of these is well described by Harborne (1977). Of significance here is the fact that all of these compounds, though toxic usually to a wide range of organisms, are capable of detoxification, and thus individual herbivore or pathogen species may become adapted to feed on one particular plant species or group of species, but be unable to cope with the toxins of others. This explains why most insect larvae have specific food plants, a point well known to lepidopterists. A neat illustration of this was provided by Erickson and Feeny (1974), who showed that the swallowtail butterfly, *Papilio polyxenes*, which normally feeds on leaves of various species of Umbelliferae, was unable to complete its reproduction successfully if fed on celery leaves (*Apium graveolens*, Umbelliferae) cultured in sinigrin, a mustard oil glucoside characteristic of crucifers. It is likely that this at least in part, explains the inability of *P. polyxenes* and other insects to eat crucifers. On the other hand, sinigrin is a specific attractant for other species adapted to feeding on crucifers and able to detoxify it.

Feeny (1976) has argued that the metabolic cost of producing large quantities of general feeding deterrents, such as tannins, is large and that they are characteristic of "apparent" species, that is those that are conspicuous either in time or space. Thus, long-lived, climax species, such as oak, would be expected to use this defence, whereas more fugitive species would go for the metabolically less expensive specific toxins. For such species the risk of an insect adapting by detoxification is not serious, as the plant populations are not sufficiently extensive or permanent to allow large predator populations to build up. Significantly most annual crops are descended from weeds of low "apparency" and are grown in monocultures: on this hypothesis one would therefore expect them to be particularly vulnerable to attacks by pests that can detoxify their specific defences.

If metabolic cost is an important consideration, then the optimum defence should be to possess inducible toxins, that are only produced when attack is likely. This, however, requires predictability of attack, which in the case of insects and other animals is not possible. The seasonal build-up of tannins in oak leaves, bracken fronds (Lawton, 1976), and other "apparent" species can be seen as a plastic response; closer to inducibility is the behaviour of chlorogenic acid (CGA), a widespread phenolic acid, in the sunflower, *Helianthus annuus*, in response to environmental stress (Del Moral, 1972b). Levels of CGA rise in response to a wide range of physical stresses, and it may be that, since under each stress, insect and other attacks would be more damaging, this can be seen as adaptive. Many plants, however, appear to produce proteinase inhibitors in unattacked parts after physical damage to one plant part (Green and Ryan, 1972) and these will confer protection to the rest of the plant and limit damage.

Where attack is systemic, however, the plant is able to predict the infection, since fungi, in particular, need actually to grow through tissue. Resistance to parasitic fungi often involves the phenomenon of hypersensitivity, where cells around the point of infection die. In such cases it is frequently found that chemicals capable of inhibiting fungal growth (phytoalexins) accumulate in the dying cells. Their role as agents limiting fungal growth in infected tissue is as yet not fully established, an alternative, though less probable explanation being that they accumulate as a consequence of fungal attack and necrosis (Deverall, 1977). However, the fact that their production declines after successful systemic infection, and that fungi capable of this often have enzymes capable of detoxifying them, strongly suggests that phytoalexins are indeed a form of inducible chemical defence in response to a predictable attack.

When the necrotrophic fungus *Botrytis fabae* attacks broad bean leaves it causes initially small brown lesions of necrotic tissue. This is the hypersensitive reaction. A phytoalexin wyerone acid, accumulates in these patches, but *B. fabae* reduces this to a less active form, grows through into living tissue, and starts the systemic infection (Mansfield and Deverall, 1974a, b). *B. cinerea*, by contrast, a much less specific necrotroph, is unable to reduce wyerone or to grow through the necrotic tissue.

It is possible, therefore, to recognize both general and specific forms of defence, the balance between the two being controlled by life-history and abundance, and also both constitutive and inducible defences. Because of the unpredictable nature of most insect and other animal predation on plants, inducible defence compounds are only found to any great extent in the plant : fungus relationship.

There is, however, a whole group of organisms feeding on plants for which chemical forms of defence would appear to be inadequate—the stylet feeders. Aphids and stylet-feeding nematodes only insert a relatively inert tube into the plant tissue and typically feed on phloem fluid which does not normally contain toxins. Nevertheless, some aphids at least show a high degree of host specificity, suggesting a chemical or possibly a physical relationship. It is known that the glandular hairs of some plants secrete toxins, and these may be important in controlling aphid infestations. Nevertheless, it seems possible that the primary defence of some plants against aphid attack is simply that in obtaining their food aphids make themselves very vulnerable to predators.

IV. MUTALISTIC ASSOCIATIONS

The distinction between mutualistic symbiotic associations and those that are parasitic is a fine one. It is most satisfactorily made on the basis of the flow of metabolites, this being one-way in parasitic but reciprocal in mutualistic associations. This is a quantitative distinction and the balance of flux is open to environmental influence. Very few mutualistic associations involving higher plants are obligate: in the two most important examples—root nodules and mycorrhiza—the plant can survive and reproduce in culture in sterile conditions, and it is to be expected, therefore, that the occurrence in the wild of such symbioses will be intimately linked to environmental conditions.

The significance of these associations to the plant ("host") is that they enable it to escape from environmental stress and so to extend the range of habitats they are capable of colonizing. It is no accident that these two associations have evolved to improve the supply to the host of the two most commonly deficient mineral nutrients—nitrogen by fixation from the atmosphere and phosphorus by long distance transport in the soil. There is, however, a price to be paid: the autotroph–heterotroph association depends on a supply of carbon to the heterotroph. Normally autotrophs have excess fixed carbon—or at least unused potential to produce it—but in conditions where photosynthesis is limited the plant may find it difficult to pay this biological tax.

Root nodules are a taxonomic mystery. For unknown but probably profound biochemical reasons only prokaryotic organisms have evolved the ability to fix nitrogen—which suggests that attempts to transfer *nif* genes for nitrogen fixation from bacteria to higher plants (Streicher *et al.*, 1972) are unlikely to be successful—and one bacterial genus, *Rhizobium*, has proliferated species capable of forming nodules with most members of the *Leguminosae*. Depending on the criteria used there are from two species upwards of *Rhizobia*, but infection of a legume host is highly specific to a particular variety. Nearly all species of the two sub-families Papilionoideae and Mimosoideae can form nodules, but only about a third of the more primitive and largely tropical Caesalpinoideae. Outside the *Leguminosae* nodule formation is known in 158 species of 14 genera—including *Alnus* (alder), *Myrica* (myrtle), *Casuarina*, *Hippophae* (sea buckthorn), and *Dryas* (avens)—but all bar one of these are infected by a different symbiont, probably an actinomycete, and form larger, clustered nodules (Bond, 1976). The one exception is *Trema cannabina* (Ulmaceae) from New Guinea which has recently been found to form nodules with *Rhizobium* (Trinick, 1973).

The almost universal response of natural vegetation to applied nitrogen renders it surprising that so valuable an association should be so taxonomically restricted. Certainly some tropical grasses can make use of fixed nitrogen by free-living bacteria in the rhizosphere, and this may be more widespread. In this latter case there is again a loss of carbon from the plant, since the rhizosphere bacteria rely on exudates and cell sloughing—indeed Martin (1977) found that up to 40% of the carbon translocated to wheat roots found its way into the soil. This can be compared with the figures of Minchin and Pate (1974) who found that over a 24 h period a pea plant (*Pisum sativum*) transported $11 \cdot 02$ mg of carbon to its roots, of which $6 \cdot 29$ mg (57%) were used as carbon skeletons for fixed nitrogen, and $4 \cdot 34$ (39%) for respiration.

The nodule acts as an important sink for fixed carbon and as long as the extra nitrogen supplied to the plant gives it an ecological advantage this will outweigh the loss. Legumes, therefore are typically pioneer species on N-deficient soils, as are many non-legumes capable of N-fixation, such as *Alnus*, *Casuarina*, and *Dryas*. Where soil nitrogen levels are higher, however, the advantage is lost and carbon used for growth lends more competitive ability than that used for fixing nitrogen.

Exactly the same applies to mycorrhizal infections. These are of various kinds, the most important being the sheathing (or ectotrophic), found mainly in trees; the vesicular–arbuscular (or V–A, often termed endotrophic), widespread amongst herbaceous plants; the ericaceous (Ericaceae) and the orchidaceous (Orchidaceae). The latter is odd, bearing some of the characteristics of a parasitic relationship, the parasite being the orchid, but the others operate on the basis of a carbon supply from host to fungus and a reciprocal phosphate supply.

In V–A mycorrhiza the fungus is one of a small group originally placed in the genus *Endogone* but now split into several genera such as *Glomus* and *Gigaspora*. They appear to be non-specific and infect a very wide range of hosts. Sheathing mycorrhiza by contrast are formed by Basidiomycetes and show more specificity, though by no means absolute. In each case the fungal mycelium ramifies through the soil, crossing the depletion zone around the roots (cf. Chapter 3) and obtains phosphate otherwise inaccessible to the plant. If plants are liberally supplied with phosphate, infection is reduced or eliminated just as nodule formation is inhibited by nitrate fertilizer. The evolutionary explanation of the mycorrhizal association probably lies in the fact that higher plants are unable to produce long strings of cells placed end to end in the manner of a fungal hypha, so that the fungus can explore soil for phosphate for a much lower input of structural carbon than a plant root, whose most appropriate structure, the root hair, rarely exceeds 5 mm. Indeed there is a good correlation between infection and root hair production, and plants which have very coarse root systems, such as the primitive Magnoliales, are in ecological, if not physiological terms obligately mycorrhizal (Baylis, 1975).

The ubiquity and lack of specificity of V–A mycorrhizal association poses a severe ecological problem: if all plants can form the association where is the selective advantage? It seems possible that under natural conditions mycorrhizal fungi may play an important role in competition between plants. Thus, Crush (1974) found that infection preferentially stimulated *Trifolium repens* in competition with *Lolium perenne*, while Fitter (1977) found that *Holcus lanatus*, which was only slightly suppressed by *L. perenne* in sterile culture, was almost completely eliminated when *Glomus fasciculatus* was introduced (Table 8.7).

TABLE 8.7.   Effect of inoculation with *Glomus fasciculatus* on growth and phosphate uptake of *Lolium perenne* in competition with *Holcus lanatus* (Fitter, 1977). Each pot contained 1 plant of each species.

	Dry weight as proportion of pot total		*Phosphate uptake in mg/plant*	
	non-mycorrhizal	mycorrhizal	non-mycorrhizal	mycorrhizal
Shoot competition only	0·48	0·42	3·0	2·4
Root and shoot competition	0·46	0·25	3·3	1·3

V. ALLELOPATHY

Allelopathy is the production of substances by one plant injurious to another plant (Muller, 1970) or to microbes as well (Rice, 1974). It is a most controversial topic, as can be judged from reading Harper's (1975) review of Rice's book. The problem is that plants contain an enormous range of more or less toxic substances and many experimenters have attempted to demonstrate allelopathic effects by applying extracts of a plant to the seeds or seedlings of another. Quite apart from the fact that the extracts are not appropriate experimental material, since they do not occur in nature, they are frequently not sterile so that bacterial transformations may have taken place, and usually the plants have no ecological relationship. Such experiments are hard to interpret. The critical question is whether some plants have a toxic influence on others growing in the field, and this must be separate from any competitive effects for light, water, and nutrients. Thus, one of the classic instances of allelopathy has always been held to be the effect of the crucifer *Camelina sativa* on flax, *Linum usitatissimum* (Grummer, 1958). Recently Kranz and Jacob (1977) have demonstrated that the interaction can be interpreted almost entirely in terms of competition for nutrients.

The clearest demonstration of such an effect is perhaps the work of Muller on the Californian chaparral (Muller, 1966). This vegetation comprises areas of annual grasses and extensive clumps of aromatic shrubs, particularly *Salvia leucophylla* and *Artemisia californica*. Around the shrubs there occurs characteristically a bare zone one to two metres wide and beyond that a zone of stunted growth three to eight metres wide. Such zones extend equally uphill or downhill. Muller and his co-workers systematically eliminated a range of possible explanations— competition for water or nutrients, grazing by animals sheltering in the shrubs, and the washing out of water-soluble toxins—and were left with the conclusion that volatile toxins were responsible. They demonstrated that a range of terpenes were given off by the shrubs, including α-pinene, β-pinene, camphene, cineole and camphor, and that these were capable of severely inhibiting seedling growth in the native grasses, *Festuca megalura*, *Bromus* spp. and *Stipa pulchra*, more so than in a standard test plant, cucumber. Finally, they showed that the terpenes were adsorbed by soil, remained toxic after at least two months' storage in soil, and could dissolve in cuticular waxes.

This is certainly the most complete demonstration of an allelopathic effect, and Muller has since described similar situations for a range of Californian arid-zone plants. The question that is unanswered is how important an influence is allelopathy in more mesic environments where no such dramatic patterning exists. Many workers have found inhibitory substances in plants, particularly in species such as *Mercurialis perennis* and *Allium ursinum*, which tend to form mono-specific stands.

Newman and Rovira (1975) found that when eight common British grassland plants were subjected to leachate of each of the other species, there were pronounced effects on yield. Leachates from all species caused yield reductions in at least some others, and the mean effect of each species as donor of leachate was a reduction of yield, averaged over all receiver species. Of the eight species tested, six had reduced yields from all donors, although of 48 combinations of these, only 10 were statistically significant. Strikingly *Trifolium repens* had its yield increased by leachate from all but one (*Holcus lanatus*) of the other species, though not from other clover plants; again however, only one effect was significant, when *Rumex acetosa* increased its yield by 25% (Table 8.8). These results are important as the species were not chosen because they showed many apparent allelopathic interactions. Indeed all commonly co-habit and all but one were collected from a single meadow. It is possible therefore that allelopathic influences are a normal phenomenon, but that their effect is generally small. Clearly a yield depression of a competitor of only a few percent could be highly beneficial.

TABLE 8.8.   Effect of leachate from various species (donors) on growth of those species in separate pots (receivers). Figures are percentage differences from the control donor with no plant leachates (from Newman and Rovira, 1975).

Receivers		Donors				
		Ao	Hl	Lp	Hr	Tr
Anthoxanthum odoratum	(Ao)	+4	−9	−1	−5	−26[a]
Holcus lanatus	(Hl)	−23[a]	−12	−22[a]	−18	−6
Lolium perenne	(Lp)	−22[a]	−24	−25[a]	−18	−10
Hypochaeris radicata	(Hr)	−22[a]	−30[a]	−16	−38[a]	−23[a]
Trifolium repens	(Tr)	+10	−8	+14	+9	0

[a] Effect significant at $p = 0.05$.
Plantago lanceolata showed no effects either as donor or receiver.
Cynosurus cristatus showed no effects as receiver, by a negative effect $(-20\%^a)$ as donor to Rumex acetosa.
Rumex acetosa also significantly increased yield $(+26\%^a)$ of Trifolium repens.

A. Mechanisms

The existence of the phenomenon is then well established, though its extent and significance are unclear. Still more obscure are the mechanisms of its action. It seems likely that many effects are indirect: perhaps the stimulation or depression of micro-organisms might be responsible, for this certainly occurs (Newman et al., 1977). Rice and Pancholy (1972) have established that a range of compounds produced by plants of a mature ecosystem (oak–pine forest) were capable of inhibiting the bacterial transformation of ammonium to nitrate. The likely explanation for this is that late-successional species tend to be more tolerant of acid conditions and hence ammonium as a nitrogen source than pioneers, because leaching and litter production typically lower soil pH during succession. Rice and Pancholy (1973, 1974) later identified a wide range of tannins, phenolic acids, flavonoids, and coumarins which completely inhibited the activity of Nitrosomonas at very low concentrations.

The role of phenolic acids is of great interest, since these are common breakdown products, for example of lignins, and have been identified as active agents in leaves of Adenostoma fasciculatum and Arctostaphylos glandulosa, two more Californian chaparral shrubs (McPherson and Muller, 1969). Phenolic acids are abundant in soils and have been identified in rhizosphere samples (Pareek and Gaur, 1973); they have been shown by Glass (1973, 1974) massively to inhibit uptake of phosphorus and potassium by barley (Fig. 6.1). The implications of this work are unexplored, but they might well help to explain the results of Newman and Miller (1977), who, following up the earlier work of Newman and Rovira (1975), found considerable effects of leachates on P uptake.

It seems possible, therefore, that phenolic acids may act by interfering with membrane function. W. H. Muller (1965) has suggested that volatile terpenes are inhibitors of cell division, and this may be true of many toxins, since inhibition of germination is one of the commonest effects. One would expect, however, to find that target plants had evolved resistance to allelopathic toxins, much as they have to heavy metals (Chapter 5) or as insects have to plant defence compounds. Unfortunately, our knowledge is far too piecemeal for it yet to be possible to investigate this, but it may be significant that the toxin, juglone, produced by the black walnut tree (*Juglans nigra*), which is lethal to many dicotyledonous herbs is ineffective against *Rubus fruticosus* and *Poa pratensis*, a shrub and a grass respectively.

B. Allelopathy in Perspective

The effects considered so far have involved toxic interactions between species mediated largely by terpenoids or phenolic compounds. Such effects are, however, both chemically and functionally only part of a wider spectrum. Plants exude from all parts a truly astonishing range of chemicals—sugars and scent compounds from flowers, terpenoids and soluble leachates from leaves, and an enormous range from roots. Rovira (1969) compiled reports of 10 sugars, 19 amino-acids, 10 organic acids, 2 flavonones, 3 enzymes, and a nucleotide in root exudates. A similar list now would be much longer. These various chemicals may have any number of functions:

(i) Simple excretion—it is widely assumed that plants do not require to excrete waste products but the salt produced by halophytes such as mangroves from salt glands (Chapter 5) is certainly excreted, as are protons from roots, and the anthocyanin which turns some nutrient-deficient plants purple is apparently a waste product. Some others may be too.

(ii) Discouragement of predators and pathogens—this function is well established and has already been discussed.

(iii) Encouragement of symbionts—for a symbiotic relationship to be established a recognition process has to be gone through. Roots spend much effort in repelling pathogens and these defences have to be circumnavigated for nodule or mycorrhizal symbiosis to occur. The legume—*Rhizobium* interaction is known to involve secretion of tryptophane by the legume, its conversion by the bacterium to IAA, which causes curling of the root, and enzyme degradation of root cell walls. Other such situations may involve exudates.

(iv) Direct effects on competitors—these are discussed above. Their existence can be taken as proven, but their significance is unclear. Potentially they could be highly potent in situations where the competitive balance is delicate.

(v) Autotoxicity—investigators may have found that some plants produce toxins with specific effects on their own seedlings. One of the classic investigations is that of Bonner and Galston (1944) who noticed that, in plantations of guayule (*Parthenium argentatum*—Compositae), edge plants were always larger than central ones. They eventually ascribed this to root-exuded *trans*-cinnamic acid, which they found to be toxic to *Parthenium* at 1 p.p.m., but to tomato only at 100 p.p.m. Such effects can presumably be explained on the grounds that, for a competitive dominant, the most severe form of competition is intra-specific. It was noticeable that in the experiments of Newman and Rovira (1975) species that were autotoxic were those that tended to grow naturally as isolated individuals, such as *Plantago lanceolata*, while species found naturally in pure stands, for example *Holcus lanatus*, were not autotoxic, and were more inhibited by other species.

Interactions between plants and other organisms, then, involve both the removal of resources from the environment (as in competition) and the addition of substances to it (as in defence and allelopathy). The range of compounds produced by plants is vast and we have as yet only scratched the surface in this field.

References

The numbers in square brackets in the margin are page references.

ABELES, F. B. (1973). "Ethylene in Plant Biology". Academic Press, New York and London. [247, 259]

ABEYAKOON, K. F. and PIGOTT, C. D. (1975). The inability of *Brachypodium sylvaticum* and other species to utilise apatite or organically bound phosphate in calcareous soil. *New Phytol.* **74,** 147–154. [216]

ACOCK, B., THORNLEY, J. H. M. and WARREN WILSON, J. (1970). Spatial variation of light in the canopy. *In* "Prediction and Measurement of Photosynthetic Productivity" (Ed. I. Setlik), pp. 91–102. Centre for Agricultural Publishing and Documentation, Wageningen. [37]

ADDICOTT, F. T. and LYON, J. L. (1973). Physiological ecology of abscission. *In* "Shedding of Plant Parts" (Ed. T. T. Kozlowski), pp. 85–124. Academic Press, New York and London. [176]

AHMAD, I. and WAINWRIGHT, S. J. (1976). Ecotype differences in leaf surface properties of *Agrostis stolonifera* from salt marsh, spray zone, and inland habitats. *New Phytol.* **76,** 361–366. [219]

ALBERDA, T. (1954). Growth and root development of lowland rice and its relation to oxygen supply. *Plant and Soil* **5,** 1–28. [236]

ALBERT, R. (1975). Salt regulation in halophytes. *Oecologia* **21,** 57–71. [213, 227]

ALLEN, S. E. (Ed.) (1974). "Chemical Analysis of Ecological Materials". Blackwell, Oxford. [88]

AMEN, R. D. (1966). The extent and role of seed dormancy in alpine plants. *Quart. Rev. Biol.* **41,** 271–281. [192, 193]

ANDERSON, J. M. (1975). The enigma of soil animal species diversity. *In* "Progress in Soil Zoology" (Ed. J. Vonek). *Proc. 5th Int. Coll. Soil Zool.* pp. 51–58. [107]

ANDERSON, M. C. (1964). Studies of the woodland light climate. I. The photographic computation of light conditions. *J. Ecol.* **52,** 27–42. [31]

ANDERSON, M. C. (1970). Radiation climate, crop architecture and photosynthesis. *In* "Prediction and Measurement of Photosynthetic Productivity" (Ed. I. Setlik), pp. 71–78. Centre for Agricultural Publishing and Documentation, Wageningen. [35]

ANDERSON, M. C. and MILLER, E. E. (1974). Forest cover as a solar camera: penumbra effect in plant canopies. *J. appl. Ecol.* **11,** 691–698. [35]

ANDERSON, V. L. (1927). Studies of the vegetation of the English chalk. V. The water economy of the chalk flora. *J. Ecol.* **15,** 72–129. [273]

ANDERSON, W. P. (1976). Transport through roots. *In* "Transport in Plants
[138]   IIB". *Encyclopaedia of Plant Physiology*, **2**, 129–156. Springer Verlag, Berlin.

ANDREW, C. S. and VANDEN BERG, P. J. (1973). The influence of aluminium
on phosphate sorption by whole plants and excised roots of some pasture
[208]   legumes. *Aust. J. agric. Res.* **24**, 341–351.

ANTONOVICS, J., BRADSHAW, A. D. and TURNER, R. G. (1971). Heavy metal
[218]   tolerance in plants. *Adv. Ecol. Res.* **7**, 2–85.

ARMSTRONG, W. (1964). Oxygen diffusion from the roots of some British bog
[235]   species. *Nature* **204**, 801–802.

ARMSTRONG, W. (1967). The oxidising activity of roots in waterlogged soils.
[236]   *Physiol. Plant.* **20**, 920–926.

ARMSTRONG, W. (1975). Waterlogged soils. *In* "Environment and Plant
[244]   Ecology" (Ed. J. R. Etherington), pp. 181–218. Wiley, London.

ARMSTRONG, W. (1978). Root aeration in the wetland condition. *In* "Plant
Life in Anaerobic Environments" (Eds. D. D. Hook and R. M. M. Craw-
[238]   ford), pp. 269–297. Ann Arbor Science Publishers Inc., Michigan.

[236, 243,   ARMSTRONG, W. and BOATMAN, D. J. (1967). Some field observations relating
244]   the growth of bog plants to conditions of soil aeration. *J. Ecol.* **55**, 101–110.

ARMSTRONG, W. and GAYNARD, T. J. (1976). The critical oxygen pressures for
[236, 245]   respiration in intact plants. *Physiol. Plant.* **37**, 200–206.

ARMSTRONG, W., BOOTH, T. C., PRIESTLY, P. and READ, D. J. (1976). The
relationship between soil aeration, stability and growth of Sitka spruce
(*Picea sitchensis* (Bong.) Carr.) on upland peaty gleys. *J. appl. Ecol.* **13**, 585–
[236]   591.

ASHENDEN, T. W. (1978). Growth reductions in cocksfoot (*Dactylis glomerata*
[256]   L.) as a result of SO_2 pollution. *Environ. Pollut.* **15**, 161–166.

ASHENDEN, T. W. (1979). The effects of long-term exposures to SO_2 and NO_2
pollution on the growth of *Dactylis glomerata* L. and *Poa pratensis* L. *Environ.*
[256]   *Pollut.* **18**, 249–258.

[252, 254,   ASHENDEN, T. W. and MANSFIELD, T. A. (1977). Influence of wind speed on
256]   the sensitivity of ryegrass to SO_2. *J. exp. Bot.* **28**, 729–735.

ASHENDEN, T. W. and MANSFIELD, T. A. (1978). Extreme pollution sensitivity
[252, 254,   of grasses when SO_2 and NO_2 are present in the atmosphere together.
256]   *Nature* **273**, 142–143.

ASHER, C. J. AND LONERAGAN, J. F. (1967). Response of plants to phosphate
concentration in solution culture. 1. Growth and phosphate content. *Soil*
[74]   *Sci.* **103**, 225–233.

ASPINALL, D. (1960). An analysis of competition between barley and white
persicaria. II. Factors determining the course of competition. *Ann. appl.*
[271]   *Biol.* **48**, 637–654.

ATKINSON, D. (1973). Some general effects of phosphorus deficiency on growth
[102]   and development. *New Phytol.* **72**, 101–111.

AUNG, L. H. (1974). Root-shoot relationships. *In* "The Plant Root and Its
[102]   Environment" (Ed. E. W. Carson), pp. 29–61. University Press, Virginia.

AUSTENFELD, F-A. (1974a). Der Einfluss des NaCl und anderer Alkalisalze
auf die Nitratreduktase aktivität von *Salicornia europaea* L. *Z Pflanzenphys.* **71**,

288–296. [201, 227]

AUSTENFELD, F-A. (1974b). Untersuchungen zum Ionenaushalt von *Salicornia europaea* L. unter besonderer Berücksichtigung des Oxalats in Abhängigkeit von der Substratsalinität. *Biochem. Physiol. Pflanzen.* **165**, 303–316. [201, 225, 227]

BAGSHAW, R., VAIDYANATHAN, L. V. and NYE, P. H. (1972). The supply of nutrient ions to plant roots in soil V. *Plant and Soil* **37**, 617–626. [83]

BALDWIN, J. P. (1975). A quantitative analysis of the factors affecting plant nutrient uptake from some soils. *J. Soil Sci.* **26**, 195–206. [79, 265, 267]

BALDWIN, J. P. and NYE, P. H. (1974). Uptake of solutes by multiple root systems from soil. IV. A model to calculate the uptake by a developing root system or root hair system of solutes with concentration variable diffusion coefficients. *Plant and Soil* **40**, 703–706. [265]

BALDWIN, J. P., NYE, P. H. and TINKER, P. B. (1973). Uptake of solutes by multiple root systems from soil. III. A model for calculating the solute uptake by a randomly dispersed root system developing in a finite volume of soil. *Plant and Soil* **38**, 621–635. [84]

BANGE, G. G. J. (1953). On the quantitative explanation of stomatal transpiration. *Acta Bot. Neerlandica* **2**, 255–296. [138]

BANNISTER, P. (1971). The water relations of heath plants from open and shaded habitats. *J. Ecol.* **59**, 51–64. [158]

BANNISTER, P. (1976). "Introduction to Physiological Plant Ecology". Blackwell, Oxford. [127, 158]

BARBER, D. A. (1972). "Dual isotherms" for the absorption of ions by plant tissue. *New Phytol.* **71**, 255–262. [73, 175]

BARBER, D. A., BOWEN, G. D. and ROVIRA, A. D. (1976). Effects of microorganisms on absorption and distribution of phosphate in barley. *Aust. J. Plant Physiol.* **3**, 801–808. [109]

BARBER, S. A. (1974). Influence of the plant root on ion movement in soil. *In* "The Plant Root and its Environment" (Ed. E. W. Carson), pp. 525–563. University Press, Virginia. [79, 81, 82, 83]

BARBER, S. A. (1979). Growth requirements for nutrients in relation to demand at the root surface. *In* "The Soil-Root Interface" (Eds. J. L. Harley and R. S. Russell), pp. 5–20. Academic Press, London and New York. [175]

BARLEY, K. (1970). The configuration of the root system in relation to nutrient uptake. *Adv. Agron.* **22**, 159–201. [103]

BARLEY, K. and ROVIRA, A. D. (1970). The influence of root hairs on the uptake of phosphate. *Comm. Soil. Sci. Pl. Anal.* **1**, 287–292. [103]

BAROSS, J. A. and MORITA, R. Y. (1978). Microbial life at low temperatures: Ecological aspects. *In* "Microbial Life in Extreme Environments" (Ed. D. J. Kushner), pp. 9–71. Academic Press, London and New York. [185]

BARROW, N. J. (1973). On the displacement of adsorbed anions from soil. I. Displacement of molybdate by phosphate and by hydroxide. *Soil Sci.* **116**, 423–431. [78]

BARROW, N. J. (1975). The response to phosphate of two annual pasture

[94] species. II. The specific rate of uptake of phosphate, its distribution, and use for growth. *Aust. J. Agric. Res.* **26,** 145–156.

[162] BARRS, H. D. (1968). Determination of water deficits in plant tissues. *In* "Water Deficits and Plant Growth" (Ed. T. T. Kozlowski), vol. 1, pp. 235–368. Academic Press, New York and London.

[228] BAUMEISTER, W. and KLOOS, G. (1974). Über die Salzsekretion bei *Halimione portulacoides* (L.) Aellen. *Flora* **163,** 310–326.

[114, 290] BAYLIS, G. T. S. (1975). The magnolioid mycorrhiza and mycotrophy in root systems derived from it. *In* "Endomycorrhizas" (Eds. F. E. Sanders, B. Mosse and P. B. Tinker), pp. 373–390. Academic Press, London and New York.

[77] BECKETT, P. H. T. (1964). Potassium–calcium exchange equilibria in soils: specific adsorption sites for potassium. *Soil Sci.* **97,** 376–383.

[257, 258] BELL, J. N. B. and CLOUGH, W. S. (1973). Depression of yield in ryegrass exposed to SO_2. *Nature Lond.* **241,** 47–94.

[250] BELL, J. N. B. and COX, R. A. (1975). Atmospheric ozone and plant damage in the United Kingdom. *Environ. Pollut.* **8,** 163–170.

[252, 260] BELL, J. N. B. and MUDD, C. H. (1976). Sulphur dioxide resistance in plants: a case study of *Lolium perenne. In* "Effects of Air Pollutants on Plants" (Ed. T. A. Mansfield), pp. 87–103. Cambridge University Press, Cambridge.

[223] BEN-AMOTZ, A. and AVRON, M. (1973). The role of glycerol in the osmotic regulation of the halophilic alga, *Dunaliella parva. Plant Physiol.* **51,** 875–887.

[256, 257, 259] BENNETT, J. H. and HILL, A. C. (1974). Acute inhibition of apparent photosynthesis by phytotoxic air pollutants. *In* "Air Pollution Effects on Plant Growth" (Ed. M. Dugger). *American Chemical Society Symposium Series* **3,** 115–127.

[176] BENSINK, J. (1971). On morphogenesis of lettuce leaves in relation to light and temperature. *Meded. Landbouw. Wageningen* **71** (15), 1–93.

[118, 119] BERNAL, J. D. (1965) The structure of water and its biological implications. *Symp. Soc. Exp. Biol.* **19,** 17–32.

[103] BHAT, K. K. S. and NYE, P. H. (1973). Diffusion of phosphate to plant roots in soil. I. Quantitative autoradiography of the depletion zone. *Plant and Soil* **38,** 161–175.

[5] BIDWELL, R. G. S. (1979). "Plant Physiology". Macmillan, London.

[187, 188, 189, 191] BILLINGS, W. D. (1974). Arctic and alpine vegetation: plant adaptations to cold summer climates. *In* "Arctic and Alpine Environments" (Eds. J. D. Ives and R. G. Barry), pp. 403–443. Methuen, London.

[186] BILLINGS, W. D. and BLISS, L. C. (1959). An alpine snowbank environment and its effect on vegetation, plant development and productivity. *Ecology* **40,** 388–397.

[182, 185, 187, 189] BILLINGS, W. D. and MOONEY, H. A. (1968). The ecology of arctic and alpine plants. *Biol. Rev.* **43,** 481–529.

[254] BISCOE, P. V., UNSWORTH, M. H. and PINCKNEY, H. R. (1973). The effects of low concentrations of sulphur dioxide on stomatal behaviour in *Vicia faba. New Phytol.* **72,** 1299–1306.

BJÖRKMAN, O. (1968). Further studies on differentiation of photosynthetic properties in sun and shade ecotypes of *Solidago virgaurea*. *Physiol. Plant.* **21,** 84–99.   [58]

BJÖRKMAN, O. and HOLMGREN, P. (1963). Adaptability of the photosynthetic apparatus to light intensity in ecotypes from exposed and shaded habitats. *Physiol. Plant.* **16,** 889–914.   [57, 59]

BJÖRKMAN, O., PEARCY, R. and NOBS, M. (1971). Hybrids between *Atriplex* species with and without β-carboxylation photosynthesis. *Carnegie Inst. Wash. Yearbook* **69,** 640–648.   [61, 62]

BLACK, C. C. (1971). Ecological implications of dividing plants into groups with distinct photosynthetic production capacities. *Adv. Ecol. Res.* **7,** 87–114.   [59, 60, 63]

BLACK, J. N. (1958). Competition between plants of different initial seed size in swards of subterranean clover (*Trifolium subterraneum*) with particular reference to leaf area and micro-climate. *Aust. J. Agric. Res.* **9,** 299–318.   [266]

BLACK, J. N. (1960). The significance of petiole length, leaf area, and light interception in competition between strains of subterranean clover (*Trifolium subterraneum* L.) grown in swards. *Aust. J. agric. Res.* **11,** 277–291.   [266]

BLACK, J. N. (1964). An analysis of the potential production of swards of subterranean clover (*Trifolium subterraneum* L.) at Adelaide, South Australia. *J. appl. Ecol.* **1,** 3–18.   [13, 14, 64, 65]

BLACK, M. (1969). Light controlled germination of seeds. *In* "Dormancy and Survival". *Symp. Soc. Exp. Biol.* **23,** 193–218.   [39]

BLACK, M. and WAREING, P. F. (1955). Growth studies in woody species. VII. Photoperiodic control of germination in *Betula pubescens* Ehrh. *Physiol. Plant.* **8,** 300–316.   [192]

BLACK, V. J. and UNSWORTH, M. H. (1979). A system for measuring effects of sulphur dioxide on gas exchange of plants. *J. exp. Bot.* **30,** 81–88.   [254]

BLACKMAN, G. E. and RUTTER, A. J. (1946). Physiological and ecological studies in the analysis of plant environment. I. The light factor and the distribution of the bluebell (*Scilla non-scripta*) in woodland communities. *Ann. Bot.* (N.S.) **10,** 361–390.   [38, 273]

BLACKMAN, G. E. and WILSON, G. L. (1951). Ibid. II. The constancy for different species of a logarithmic relationship between net assimilation rate and light intensity, and its ecological significance. *Ann. Bot.* (N.S.) **15,** 63–94.   [55]

BLACKMAN, V. H. (1919). The compound interest law and plant growth. *Ann. Bot.* **33,** 353–360.   [8]

BLAIR, G. J., MAMARIL, C. P. and MILLER, M. H. (1972). Effect of nitrogen status on short-term phosphate uptake. *Comm. Soil Sci. Pl. Anal.* **3,** 23–27.   [5, 100]

BLEASDALE, J. K. A. (1973). Effects of coal smoke pollution gases on the growth of ryegrass (*Lolium perenne* L.). *Environ. Pollut.* **5,** 275–285.   [252, 256]

BLISS, L. C. (1962). Adaptations of arctic and alpine plants to environmental conditions. *Arctic* **15,** 117–144.   [185, 186]

BLISS, L. C. (1975). Devon Island, Canada. *In* "Structure and Function of

Tundra Ecosystems" (Eds. T. Rosswall and O. W. Heal). *Ecol. Bull.* **20,**
[185, 187] 17–60. Swedish Natural Science Research Council, Stockholm.

BOGGIE, R. (1972). Effect of water-table height on root development of *Pinus*
[236] *contorta* on deep peat in Scotland. *Oikos* **23,** 304–312.

BÖHNING, R. H. and BURNSIDE, C. A. (1956). The effect of light intensity on
rate of apparent photosynthesis in leaves of sun and shade plants. *Amer.*
[55, 56] *J. Bot.* **43,** 557–561.

BOLE, J. B. (1973). Influence of root hairs in supplying soil phosphorus to
[104] wheat. *Can. J. Soil Sci.* **53,** 169–175.

BOND, G. (1951). The fixation of nitrogen associated with the root nodules of
Myrica gale L. with special reference to its pH relation and ecological
[209] significance. *Ann. Bot.* (N.S.) **15,** 447–459.

BOND, G. (1976). The results of the IBP survey of root nodule formation in
non-leguminous angiosperms. *In* "Symbiotic Nitrogen Fixation in Plants"
[289] (Ed. P. S. Nutman), **7,** 443–474. Cambridge University Press, Cambridge.

BONNER, J. and GALSTON, A. W. (1944). Toxic substances from the culture
[295] medium of Guayule which may inhibit growth. *Bot. Gaz.* **106,** 185–198.

BOORMAN, L. (1967). Biological flora of the British Isles: *Limonium vulgare* Mill.
[214] and *L. humile* Mill. *J. Ecol.* **55,** 221–232.

BOYSEN-JENSEN, P. and MÜLLER, D. (1929). Die maximale Ausbeute und der
tägliche Verlauf der Kohlensaureassimilation. *Jahrb. Wiss. Bot.* **70,** 493–
[56] 502.

BRADSHAW, A. D. (1965). Evolutionary significance of phenotypic plasticity
[15] in plants. *Adv. Genetics* **13,** 115–155.

BRADSHAW, A. D. (1972). Some of the evolutionary consequences of being a
[22] plant. *Evol. Biol.* **5,** 25147.

BRADSHAW, A. D. (1973). Environment and phenotypic plasticity. *Brook-*
[15] *haven Symp. Biol.* **25,** 75–94.

BRADSHAW, A. D., CHADWICK, M. J., JOWETT, D., LODGE, R. W. and SNAY-
DON, R. W. (1960a). Experimental investigations into the mineral nutrition
[90, 91] of several grass species III. Phosphate level. *J. Ecol.* **48,** 631–637.

BRADSHAW, A. D., LODGE, R. W., JOWETT, D. and CHADWICK, M. J. (1960b).
Experimental investigations into the mineral nutrition of several grass
[90, 91] species II. Calcium and pH. *J. Ecol.* **48,** 143–150.

BRADSHAW, A. D., CHADWICK, M. J., JOWETT, D. and SNAYDON, R. W. (1964).
[4, 90, Experimental investigations into the mineral nutrition of several grass
102] species IV. Nitrogen level. *J. Ecol.* **52,** 665–676.

BRADSHAW, A. D., MCNEILLY, T. S. and GREGORY, R. P. G. (1965). In-
dustrialisation, evolution, and the development of heavy metal tolerance
in plants. *In* "Ecology and the Industrial Society". *Brit. Ecol. Soc. Symp.* **5,**
[230] 327–343.

BRADY, N. C. (1974). "The Nature and Properties of Soils" 8th Edn. Mac-
[132] millan, New York.

BROCK, T. D. and DARLAND, G. K. (1970). Limits of microbial existence:
[3] temperature and pH. *Science* **169,** 1316–1318.

BROWN, A. D. H., MARSHALL, D. R. and MUNDAY, J. (1976). Adaptedness of variants at an alcohol dehydrogenase locus in *Bromus mollis* L. (Soft bromegrass). *Aust. J. biol. Sci.* **29**, 389–396. [239]

BROWN, J. C. (1972). Competition between phosphate and the plant for Fe from Fe^{++} ferrozine. *Agron. J.* **64**, 240–243. [90]

BROWN, M. E. (1975). Rhizosphere micro-organisms—opportunists, bandits, or benefactors. *In* "Soil Microbiology" (Ed. N. Walker), pp. 21–38. Butterworth, London. [87, 109]

BROWNELL, P. F. and CROSLAND, C. J. (1972). Requirement for sodium as a micro-nutrient for species having the C_4 dicarboxylic photosynthetic pathway. *Plant Physiol.* **49**, 794–797. [68]

BULL, J. N. and MANSFIELD, T. A. (1974). Photosynthesis in leaves exposed to SO_2 and NO_2. *Nature* **250**, 443–444. [256]

BURDON, J. J. and CHILVERS, G. A. (1974). Fungal and insect parasites contributing to niche differentiation in mixed species stands of eucalypt seedlings. *Aust. J. Bot.* **22**, 103–114. [277]

BURDON, J. J. and CHILVERS, G. A. (1977). The effect of barley mildew on barley and wheat competition in mixtures. *Aust. J. Bot.* **25**, 59–65. [277]

BURKE, M. J., GUSTA, L. V., QUAMME, H. A., WEISER, C. J. and LI, P. H. (1976). Freezing and injury in plants. *Ann. Rev. Pl. Physiol.* **27**, 507–528. [179, 194, 195]

BURSTRÖM, H. G. (1968). Calcium and plant growth. *Biol. Rev.* **43**, 298–316. [71, 208]

CALDWELL, M. M. (1968). Solar ultraviolet radiation as an ecological factor for alpine plants. *Ecol. Monogr.* **38**, 243–268. [39, 187]

CALLAGHAN, T. V. and LEWIS, M. C. (1971). The growth of *Phleum alpinum* L. in contrasting habitats at a sub-antarctic station. *New Phytol.* **70**, 1143–1154. [13, 46]

CANNON, W. A. (1911). The root habits of desert plants. *Carnegie Inst. Wash. Publ.* 131. [20]

CAPRON, T. M. and MANSFIELD, T. A. (1976). Inhibition of net photosynthesis in tomato in air polluted with NO and NO_2. *J. exp. Bot.* **27**, 1181–1186. [256]

CARTWRIGHT, B. (1972). The effect of phosphate deficiency on the kinetics of phosphate absorption by sterile excised barley roots, and some factors affecting the ion uptake efficiency of roots. *Comm. Soil. Sci. Pl. Anal.* **3**, 313–322. [96]

CASWELL, H., REED, F., STEPHENSON, F. N. and WERNER, P. A. (1973). Photosynthetic pathways and selective herbivory: a hypothesis. *Amer. Nat.* **107**, 465–480. [63]

CHAPIN, F. (1974). Morphological and physiological mechanisms of temperature compensation in phosphate absorption along a latitudinal gradient. *Ecology* **55**, 1180–1198. [97, 104]

CHAPMAN, V. J. (1977). "Wet Coastal Ecosystems". Ecosystems of the World, vol. 1. Elsevier, Amsterdam. [203]

CHENERY, E. A. and SPORNE, K. P. (1976). A note on the evolutionary status of aluminium accumulation among dicotyledons. *New Phytol.* **76**, 551–554. [227, 229]

[163]
CHEW, R. M. and CHEW, A. E. (1965). The primary productivity of a desert shrub (*Larrea divaricata*) community. *Ecology Monographs* **35,** 355–375.

[50, 268]
CHIPPINDALE, H. G. (1932). The operation of interspecific competition in causing delayed growth of grasses. *Ann. appl. Biol.* **19,** 221–242.

[240]
CHIRKOVA, T. V. (1978). Some regulatory mechanisms of plant adaptation to temporal anaerobiosis. *In* "Plant Life in Anaerobic Environments" (Eds. D. D. Hook and R. M. M. Crawford), pp. 137–154. Ann Arbor Science Publishers Inc., Michigan.

[100, 104]
CHRISTIE, E. K. and MOORBY, J. (1975). Physiological responses of arid grasses. I. The influence of phosphorus supply on growth and phosphorus absorption. *Aust. J. Agric. Res.* **26,** 423–436.

[110]
CHRISTIE, P., NEWMAN, E. I. and CAMPBELL, R. (1974). Grassland species can influence the abundance of microbes on each other's roots. *Nature* **250,** 570.

[116]
CLARKSON, D. T. (1965). Calcium uptake by calcicole and calcifuge species in the genus *Agrostis*. *J. Ecol.* **53,** 427–435.

[218]
CLARKSON, D. T. (1966). Aluminium tolerance within the genus *Agrostis*. *J. Ecol.* **54,** 167–178.

[90, 116, 218]
CLARKSON, D. T. (1967). Phosphorus supply and growth rates in species of *Agrostis* L. *J. Ecol.* **55,** 707–731.

[70]
CLARKSON, D. T. (1974). "Ion Transport and Cell Structure in Plants". McGraw-Hill, London.

[211]
CLARKSON, D. T. and SANDERSON, J. (1969). The uptake of a polyvalent cation and its distribution in the root apices of *Allium cepa*: tracer autoradiographic studies. *Planta* **89,** 136–154.

[208]
CLARKSON, D. T. and SANDERSON, J. (1971). Inhibition of the uptake and long-distance transport of calcium by aluminium and other polyvalent cations. *J. exp. Bot.* **23,** 837–851.

[103]
CLARKSON, D. T., SANDERSON, J. and RUSSELL, R. S. (1968). Ion uptake and root age. *Nature* **220,** 805–806.

[103]
CLARKSON, D. T., ROBARDS, A. W. and SANDERSON, J. (1971). The tertiary endodermis in barley roots: fine structure in relation to radial transport of ions and water. *Planta* **96,** 296–305.

[191]
CLEBSCH, E. E. C. (1960). "Comparative morphological and physiological variation in arctic and alpine populations of *Trisetum spicatum*". Ph.D. Thesis, Duke University (cited by Billings, 1974).

[203]
COE, M. D. (1964). The chinampas of Mexico. *Sci. Amer.* **211,** 90–98.

[164, 168]
CONNOR, D. J., LEGGE, N. J. and TURNER, N. C. (1977). Water relations of Mountain ash (*Eucalyptus regnans* F. Muell.) forests. *Aust. J. Plant Physiol.* **4,** 753–762.

[54]
COOK, C. D. K. (1972). Phenotypic plasticity with particular reference to three amphibious plant species. *In* "Taxonomy and Ecology" (Ed. V. H. Heywood), pp. 97–111. Systematics Association Special Volume No. 5. Academic Press, London and New York.

COOK, S. A. and JOHNSON, M. P. (1968). Adaptation to heterogeneous environments. I. Variation in heterophylly in *Ranunculus flammula* L. *Evolution* **22**, 496–516. [20]

COOMBE, D. E. (1966). The seasonal light climate and plant growth in a Cambridgeshire Wood. *In* "Light as an Ecological Factor". *Symp. Brit. Ecol. Soc.* **6**, 148–166. [38, 55]

COOMBE, D. E. and HADFIELD, W. (1962). An analysis of the growth of *Musanga cecropioides*. *J. Ecol.* **50**, 221–234. [64]

COOPER, A. J. (1973). "Root Temperature and Plant Growth". Res. Rev. 4, Commonwealth Bureau of Horticulture and Plantation Crops. [172, 176]

COOPER, J. P. and BREEZE, E. L. (1971). Plant breeding: forage grasses and legumes. *In* "Potential Crop Production" (Eds. P. F. Wareing and J. P. Cooper), pp. 295–318. Heinemann, London. [46]

COULT, D. A. and VALLANCE, K. B. (1958). Observations on the gaseous exchange which takes place between *Menyanthes trifoliata* and its environment. *J. exp. Bot.* **9**, 384–402. [238]

COUPLAND, R. T. and JOHNSON, R. E. (1965). Rooting characteristics of native grassland species in Saskatchewan. *J. Ecol.* **53**, 475–507. [150, 151, 273]

COWAN, I. R. and MILTHORPE, F. L. (1968). Plant factors influencing the water status of plant tissues. *In* "Water Deficits and Plant Growth" (Ed. T. T. Kozlowski), vol. 1, pp. 137–193. Academic Press, New York and London. [159]

COWLING, D. W., JONES, L. H. P. and LOCKYER, D. R. (1973). Increased yield through correction of sulphur deficiency in ryegrass exposed to sulphur dioxide. *Nature* **243**, 479–480. [252]

CRAFTS, A. S. (1968a). Water structure and water in the plant body. *In* "Water Deficits and Plant Growth" (Ed. T. T. Kozlowski), vol. 1, pp. 23–47, Academic Press, New York and London. [119]

CRAFTS, A. S. (1968b). Water deficits and physiological processes. In "Water Deficits and Plant Growth" (Ed. T. T. Kozlowski), vol. 2, pp. 85–133, Academic Press, New York and London. [122]

CRAWFORD, R. M. M. (1972). Some metabolic aspects of ecology. *Trans. Bot. Soc. Edin.* **41**, 309–322. [236, 240]

CRAWFORD, R. M. M. (1977). Tolerance of anoxia and ethanol metabolism in germinating seeds. *New Phytol.* **79**, 511–517. [242]

CRAWFORD, R. M. M. (1978). Metabolic adaptations to anoxia. *In* "Plant Life in Anaerobic Environments" (Eds. D. D. Hook and R. M. M. Crawford), pp. 119–136. Ann Arbor Science Publishers Inc., Michigan. [238, 239, 240, 241]

CRAWFORD, R. M. M. and McMANMON, R. M. (1968). Inductive responses of alcohol and malic dehydrogenases in relation to flooding tolerance in roots. *J. exp. Bot.* **19**, 435–441. [238]

CROCKER, R. L. and MAJOR, J. (1955). Soil development in relation to vegetation and surface age, Glacier Bay, Alaska. *J. Ecol.* **43**, 427–448. [86]

CROSS, J. R. (1975). Biological flora of the British Isles: *Rhododendron ponticum*. *J. Ecol.* **63**, 345–359. [50, 53]

CROSSLEY, G. K. and BRADSHAW, A. D. (1968). Differences in response to

[92]　　mineral nutrients of populations of ryegrass, *Lolium perenne* L. and orchard grass *Dactylis glomerata* L. *Crop Sci.* **8,** 383–387.

[111, 290]　CRUSH, J. R. (1974). Plant growth responses to vesicular–arbuscular mycorrhiza VII. Growth and nodulation of some herbage legumes. *New Phytol.* **73,** 743–749.

[39]　　CUMMING, B. G. (1963). Dependence of germination on photoperiod, light quality, and temperature in *Chenopodium. Can. J. Bot.* **41,** 1211–1233.

[146]　　DARWIN, F. (1876). On the hygroscopic mechanism by which certain seeds are enabled to bury themselves in the ground. *Trans. Linn. Soc. London. 2nd Series. Bot.* **1,** 149–167.

[20]　　DAUBENMIRE, R. F. (1947). "Plants and Environment". Wiley, New York.

[102]　　DAVIDSON, R. L. (1969). Effect of root-leaf temperature differentials on root–shoot ratios in some pasture grasses and clover. *Ann. Bot.* (N.S.) **33,** 561–569.

[241]　　DAVIES, D. D., GREGO, S. and KENWORTHY, P. (1974). The control of the production of lactate and ethanol by higher plants. *Planta* **118,** 297–310.

[22, 92, 231]　DAVIES, M. S. and SNAYDON, R. W. (1973a, b), (1974). Physiological differences among populations of *Anthoxanthum odoratum* L. collected from the Park Grass Experiment, Rothamsted. I. Response to calcium. *J. appl. Ecol.* **10,** 33–45; II. Response to aluminium. *J. appl. Ecol.* **10,** 47–55; III. Response to phosphorus. *J. appl. Ecol.* **11,** 699–670.

[118]　　DAVIS, K. S. and DAY, J. A. (1961). "Water". Heinemann, London.

[47]　　DAXER, H. (1934). Uber die Assimilations-ökologie der Waldbodenflora. *Jahrb. Wiss. Bot.* **80,** 363–420.

[259]　　DEAN, C. E. (1972). Stomate density and size as related to ozone-induced weather fleck in tobacco. *Crop Sci.* **12,** 547–548.

[4]　　DEL MORAL, R. (1972a). Diversity patterns in forest vegetation of the Wenatchee Mountains, Washington. *Bull. Torrey Bot. Club* **99,** 57–64.

[39, 287]　DEL MORAL, R. (1972b). On the variability of chlorogenic acid concentration. *Oecologia* **9,** 289–300.

[287]　　DEVERALL, B. J. (1977). "Defence mechanisms of plants". Cambridge University Press, Cambridge.

[95]　　DIRR, M. A., BARKER, A. V. and MAYNARD, D. M. (1973). Extraction of nitrate reductase from leaves of Ericaceae. *Phytochem.* **12,** 1261–1264.

[78]　　DITTMER, H. J. (1940). A quantitative study of the subterranean members of soybean. *Soil Conserv.* **6,** 33–34.

[94, 96]　DODDEMA, H., TELKAMP, G. P. and OTTEN, H. (1979). Uptake of nitrate by mutants of *Arabidopsis thaliana*, disturbed in uptake or reduction of nitrate. *Physiol. Plant.* **45,** 297–346.

[268, 270]　DONALD, C. M. (1958). The interaction of competition for light and nutrients. *Aust. J. agric. Res.* **9,** 421–435.

[247]　　DOWDELL, R. J., SMITH, K. A., CREES, R. and RESTALL, S. W. F. (1972). Field studies of ethylene in the soil atmosphere—equipment and preliminary results. *Soil Biol. Biochem.* **4,** 325–331.

[105]　　DREW, M. C. (1975). Comparison of the effects of a localized supply of phosphate, nitrate, ammonium and potassium on the growth of the seminal root system, and the shoot, in barley. *New Phytol.* **75,** 479–490.

DREW, M. C. (1979). Properties of roots which influence rates of absorption. *In* "The Soil-Root Interface" (Eds. J. L. Harley and R. S. Russell), pp. 21–38. Academic Press, London and New York. [237]

DREW, M. C. and NYE, P. H. (1969). The supply of nutrient ions by diffusion to plant roots in soil. II. *Plant and Soil* **31,** 407–424. [105]

DREW, M. C. and SAKER, L. R. (1975). Nutrient supply and the growth of the seminal root system in barley. II. *J. exp. Bot.* **26,** 79–90. [105]

DREW, M. C., SAKER, L. R. and ASHLEY, T. W. (1973). Nutrient supply and the growth of the seminal root system in barley. I. *J. exp. Bot.* **24,** 1189–1202. [105, 267]

DUBININA, I. M. (1961). Metabolism of roots under various levels of aeration. *Soviet Plant Physiology* **8,** 314–322. [240]

DUDNEY, P. J. (1973). An approach to the growth analysis of perennial plants. *Proc. Roy. Soc. London.* **B184,** 217–220. [12]

DUMBROFF, E. B. and COOPER, A. W. (1974). Effects of salt stress applied in balanced nutrient solutions at several stages during growth of tomato. *Bot. Gaz.* **135,** 219–224. [214]

DUNCAN, W. G. and OHLROGGE, A. J. (1958). Principles of nutrient uptake from fertiliser bands. II. *Agron. J.* **50,** 605–608. [105]

EATON, F. M., HARDING, R. B. and GANJE, T. J. (1960). Soil solution extraction at tenth-bar moisture percentages. *Soil Sci.* **90,** 253–258. [73]

EHLERINGER, J. R. (1978). Implications of quantum yield differences on the distributions of C_3 and C_4 grasses. *Oecologia* **31,** 255–267. [63]

EHLERINGER, J. R. and MOONEY, H. A. (1978). Leaf hairs: effects on physiological activity and adaptive value to a desert shrub. *Oecologia* **37,** 183–200. [159, 199]

ELGAWHARY, S. M. and BARBER, S. A. (1974). Root uptake coefficients for absorption of CaEDTA and Ca^{++} by tomato plants. *Plant and Soil* **40,** 183–191. [99]

ELKINGTON, T. T. and JONES, B. M. G. (1974). Biomass and primary productivity of birch (*Betula pubescens* S. Lat) in south-west Greenland. *J. Ecol.* **62,** 821–830. [184]

EMERSON, R. and ARNOLD, W. (1932). A separation of the reactions in photosynthesis by means of intermittent light. *J. Gen. Physiol.* **19,** 391–420. [35]

ENGLE, R. L. and GABELMAN, W. H. (1966). Inheritance and mechanism for resistance to ozone damage in onion, *Allium cepa* L. *Proc. Amer. Soc. Hort. Sci.* **89,** 423–430. [259]

EPSTEIN, E. (1961). The essential role of calcium in selective cation transport by plant cells. *Plant Physiol.* **37,** 682–685. [71, 72]

EPSTEIN, E. (1969). Mineral metabolism of halophytes. *In* "Ecological Aspects of the Mineral Nutrition of Plants". *Brit. Ecol. Soc. Symp.* **9,** 345–355. [216]

EPSTEIN, E. (1973). Mechanisms of ion transport through plant cell membranes. *Int. Rev. Cytol.* **34,** 123–168. [71, 72]

EPSTEIN, E. and HAGEN, C. E. (1952). A kinetic study of the absorption of alkali cations by barley roots. *Plant Physiol.* **27,** 457–474. [71, 72]

EREZ, A. and KADMAN-ZAHAVI, A. (1972). Growth of peaches under different filtered sunlight conditions. *Physiol. Plant.* **26,** 210–214. [41]

[286] ERICKSON, J. M. and FEENY, P. (1974). A chemical barrier to the black swallow-tail butterfly *Papilio polyxenes. Ecology* **55,** 103–111.

[165] ESAU, K. (1965). "Plant Anatomy", 2nd Edn. Wiley, New York.

[86] ETHERINGTON, J. R. (1967). Soil water and the growth of grasses. II. Effects of soil water potential on growth and photosynthesis of *Alopecurus pratensis. J. Ecol.* **55,** 373–380.

[51] EVANS, G. C. (1972). "The Quantitative Analysis of Plant Growth". Blackwells, Oxford.

[52] EVANS, G. C. and HUGHES, A. P. (1961). Plant growth and the aerial environment. I. Effect of artificial shading on *Impatiens parviflora. New Phytol.* **60,** 150–180.

[286] FEENY, P. (1968). Effect of oak leaf tannins on larval growth of the winter moth *Operophtera brumata. J. Insect Physiol.* **14,** 805–817.

[278, 286] FEENY, P. (1976). Plant apparency and chemical defence. In "Recent Advances in Phytochemistry. 10. Biochemical Interactions between Plants and Insects" (Eds. J. W. Wallace and R. L. Mansell), pp. 1–40. Plenum Press, New York.

[53] FEKETE, G., SZUJKÓ-LACZA, J. and HORVATH, G. (1973). Leaf anatomical and photosynthetical reactions of *Quercus pubescens* Willd. to environmental factors in various ecosystems. II. Photosynthetic activity. *Acta Bot. Acad. Sci. Hung.* **18,** 281–293.

[78] FERGUS, I. F., MARTIN, A. E., LITTLE, I. P. and HAYDOCK, K. P. (1972). Studies on soil potassium. II. The Q/I relation and other parameters compared with plant uptake of potassium. *Aust. J. Soil Res.* **10,** 95–111.

[92] FERRARI, G. and RENOSTO, F. (1972). Comparative studies on the active transport by excised roots of inbred and hybrid maize. *J. agric. Sci.* **79,** 105–108.

[45] FIRN, R. D. and DIGBY, J. (1980). The establishment of tropic curvatures in plants. *Ann. Rev. Plant Physiol.* **31,** 131–148.

[206] FIRTH, J. N. M. (1978). The origin and exploitation of non-ferrous metals. In "Environmental Management of Mineral Wastes" (Eds. G. S. Goodman and M. J. Chadwick), pp. 259–272. Sijthoff and Noordhoff, Alphen.

[85, 104, 107] FITTER, A. H. (1976). Effects of nutrient supply and competition from other species on root growth of *Lolium perenne* in soil. *Plant and Soil* **45,** 177–189.

[111, 290, 291] FITTER, A. H. (1977). Influence of mycorrhizal infection on competition for phosphorus and potassium by two grasses. *New Phytol.* **79,** 119–125.

[42, 45, 51, 52] FITTER, A. H. and ASHMORE, C. J. (1974). Response of two *Veronica* species to a simulated woodland light climate. *New Phytol.* **73,** 997–1001.

[77, 105] FITTER, A. H. and BRADSHAW, A. D. (1974). Root penetration of *Lolium perenne* on colliery shale in response to reclamation treatments. *J. appl. Ecol.* **11,** 609–616.

[215] FITTER, A. H., BROWNE, J., DIXON, T. and TUCKER, J. J. (1980). Ecological studies at Askham Bog Nature Reserve 1. Inter-relations of vegetation and environment. *Naturalist* **105,** 89–101.

FOOTE, B. D. and HOWELL, R. W. (1964). Phosphorus tolerance and sensiti-

vity of soybeans as related to uptake and translocation. *Plant Physiol.* **39,** 610–613.
[90]

FOWLER, D. and UNSWORTH, M. H. (1974). Dry deposition of sulphur dioxide on wheat. *Nature* **249,** 389–390.
[255]

FOX, R. L., HASAN, S. M. and JONES, R. C. (1971). Phosphate and sulphate sorption by latosols. *Proc. Int. Symp. Soil Fert. Evaln. New Delhi* **1,** 857–864.
[78]

FOY, C. D., CHANEY, K. L. and WHITE, M. C. (1978). The physiology of metal toxicity in plants. *Ann. Rev. Plant Physiol.* **29,** 511–566.
[206, 219]

FRANCK, J. and LOOMIS, W. E. (1949). "Photosynthesis in Plants". Iowa State College Press, Ames, Iowa.
[175]

FRIED, M. and BROESHART, H. (1967). "The Soil-Plant System". Academic Press, New York and London.
[83]

GALLAGHER, J. N. and BISCOE, P. V. (1979). Field studies of cereal leaf growth. III. *J. exp. Bot.* **117,** 645–655.
[176]

GARCIA-NOVO, F. and CRAWFORD, R. M. M. (1973). Soil aeration, nitrate reduction and flooding tolerance in higher plants. *New Phytol.* **72,** 1031–1039.
[238]

GARDNER, W. R. (1960). Dynamic aspects of water availability to plants. *Soil Sci.* **89,** 63–73.
[132]

GARNER, W. W. and ALLARD, H. A. (1920). Effect of length of day on plant growth. *J. Agr. Res.* **18,** 553–606.
[43]

GATES, C. T., HAYDOCK, K. P. and ROBINS, M. F. (1970). Response to salt in *Glycine*: 4. Salt concentration and the content of phosphorus, potassium, sodium and chloride in cultivars of *G. wightii* (*G. javanica*). *Aust. J. exp. Agric. Anim. Husb.* **10,** 99–110.
[219]

GATES, D. M. (1962). "Energy Exchange in the Biosphere". Harper and Row, New York.
[29]

GATES, D. M. (1968). Transpiration and leaf temperature. *Ann. Rev. Pl. Physiol.* **19,** 211–238.
[54]

GATES, D. M. (1976). Energy exchange and transpiration. *In* "Water and Plant Life" (Eds. O. L. Lange, L. Kappen and E.-D. Schulze). *Ecological Studies* **19,** 137–147. Springer Verlag, Berlin.
[118, 177, 197]

GATES, D. M. and PAPIAN, L. E. (1971). "Atlas of Energy Budgets of Plant Leaves". Academic Press, London and New York.
[177, 178]

GAUHL, E. (1969). Leaf factors affecting the rate of light-saturated photo-synthesis in ecotypes of *Solanum dulcamara*. *Carnegie Inst. Wash. Yrbk,* **68,** 633–636.
[59]

GAUHL, E. (1976). Photosynthetic response to varying light intensity in ecotypes of *Solanum dulcamara* L. from shaded and exposed habitats. *Oecologia* **22,** 275–286.
[58]

GAUHL, E. (1979). Sun and shade ecotypes in *Solanum dulcamara* L.: Photo-synthetic light dependence characteristics in relation to mild water stress. *Oecologia* **39,** 61–70.
[59]

GAUSE, G. F. (1934). "The Struggle for Existence" (Reprinted 1964). Hafner Publishing Company, New York.
[263]

[127] GEIGER, R. (1965). "Die Atmosphäre der Erde". Darmstadt, Perthes.

GEORGE, M. F., HONG, S. G. and BURKE, M. J. (1977). Cold hardiness and deep supercooling of hardwoods: its occurrence in provenance collections
[194] of red oak, yellow birch, black walnut and black cherry. *Ecology* **58,** 674–680.

GERDEMANN, J. W. and TRAPPE, J. M. (1975). Taxonomy of the Endogonaceae. *In* "Endomycorrhizas" (Ed. F. E. Sanders *et al.*), pp. 35–51. Academic
[113] Press, London and New York.

GERRETSEN, F. C. (1948). The influence of micro-organisms on the phosphate
[109] intake by the plant. *Plant and Soil* **1,** 51–81.

GIETL, C., KAUSS, H. and ZIEGLER, H. (1979). Affinity chromatography of a lectin from *Robinia pseudoacacia* L. and demonstration of lectins in sieve-
[285] tube sap from other species. *Planta* **144,** 367–371.

GIFFORD, R. M. (1974). A comparison of potential photosynthesis, productivity, and yield of plant species with differing photosynthetic metabolism.
[63] *Aust. J. Plant Physiol.* **1,** 107–117.

GIGON, A. and RORISON, I. H. (1972). The response of some ecologically distinct plant species to nitrate and ammonium nitrogen. *J. Ecol.* **60,**
[86, 215] 93–102.

GILBERT, L. E. (1971). Butterfly: plant co-evolution: has *Passiflora adenopoda*
[284] won the selectional race with Heliconid butterflies? *Science* **172,** 585–586.

GINZBURG, M. (1969). The unusual membrane permeability of two halo-
[229] philic unicellular organisms. *Biochem. Biophys. Acta.* **173,** 370–376.

[71, 110, GLASS, A. D. M. (1973). Influence of phenolic acids on ion uptake. I. Inhibi-
209, 294] tion of phosphate uptake. *Plant Physiol.* **51,** 1037–1041.

GLASS, A. D. M. (1974). Influence of phenolic acids on ion uptake. III.
[71, 210, 294] Inhibition of potassium absorption. *J. exp. Bot.* **25,** 1104–1113.

GLASS, A. D. M. (1978). Regulation of potassium influx into intact roots of
107] barley by internal potassium levels. *Can. J. Bot.* **56,** 1759–1764.

GLEAVES, T. J. (1973). Gene flow mediated by wind-borne pollen. *Heredity* **31,**
[23] 355–366.

GLOVER, J. and GWYNNE, M. D. (1962). Light rainfall and plant survival in
[152] East Africa. 1. Maize. *J. Ecol.* **50,** 111–118.

GODWIN, H., CLOWES, D. R. and HUNTLEY, B. (1974). Studies in the ecology
[86] of Wicken Fen. V. Development of fen carr. *J. Ecol.* **62,** 197–214.

[183] GOOD, R. (1964). "The Geography of Flowering Plants". Longman, London.

GOODLASS, G. and SMITH, K. A. (1978). Effect of pH, organic matter content and nitrate on the evolution of ethylene from soils. *Soil Biol. Biochem.* **10,**
[247] 193–199.

[13, 64, GOODMAN, P. J. (1968). Physiological analysis of the effects of different soils
65] on sugar beet crops in different years. *J. appl. Ecol.* **5,** 339–358.

GOODMAN, P. J., FOTHERGILL, M. and HUGHES, D. M. (1974). Variation in nitrate reductase, nitrite and nitrite reductase in some grasses and cereals.
[95] *Ann. Bot.* (N.S.) **38,** 31–37.

GORSKI, T. (1975). Germination of seeds in the shadow of plants. *Physiol.*
[39] *Plant* **34,** 342–346.

GOVIER, R. N., BROWN, J. G. and PATE, J. S. (1968). Hemiparasitic nutrition in Angiosperms. II. Root haustoria and leaf glands of *Odontites verna* (Bell) Dum. and their relevance to the abstraction of solutes from the host. *New Phytol.* **67**, 963–972. [280]

GRACE, J. (1977). "Plant Response to Wind". Academic Press, London and New York. [20]

GRACE, J. and MARKS, T. C. (1978). Physiological aspects of bog production at Moor House. *In* "Production Ecology of British Moors and Montane Grasslands" (Eds. O. W. Heal and D. F. Perkins). *Ecological Studies* **27**, 38–51. Springer Verlag, Berlin. [194]

GRACE, J. and WOOLHOUSE, H. W. (1974). A physiological and mathematical study of growth and productivity of a *Calluna-Sphagnum* community. IV. A model of growing *Calluna*. *J. appl. Ecol.* **11**, 281–296. [67]

GREACEN, E. L. and OH, J. S. (1972). Physics of root growth. *Nature New Biology* **235**, 24–25. [125]

GREAVES, M. P. and DARBYSHIRE, J. F. (1972). The ultrastructure of the mucilaginous layer on plant roots. *Soil Biol. Biochem.* **4**, 443–449. [108]

GREEN, D. G. and WARDER, F. G. (1973). Accumulation of damaging concentrations of phosphorus by leaves of Selkirk Wheat. *Plant and Soil* **38**, 567–572. [90, 201]

GREEN, M. S. and ETHERINGTON, J. R. (1977). Oxidation of ferrous iron by rice (*Oryza sativa* L.) roots: a mechanism for waterlogging tolerance? *J. exp. Bot.* **28**, 678–690. [243]

GREEN, T. R. and RYAN, C. A. (1972). Wound-induced proteinase inhibitor in plant leaves: a possible defence mechanism against insects. *Science* **175**, 776–777. [287]

GREENWAY, H. (1962). Plant response to saline substrates. I. Growth and ion uptake of several varieties of *Hordeum* during and after sodium chloride treatment. *Aust. J. Biol. Sci.* **15**, 16–38. [219]

GREENWAY, H. (1973). Salinity, plant growth, and metabolism. *J. Aust. Inst. Agr. Sci.* March 1973, 24–34. [219]

GREENWAY, H. and LEAHY, M. (1970). Effects of rapidly and slowly permeating osmotica on metabolism. *Plant Physiol.* **46**, 259–262. [207]

GREENWOOD, D. J. (1967). Studies on the transport of oxygen through the stems and roots of vegetable seedlings. *New Phytol.* **66**, 337–347. [236]

GRIME, J. P. (1966). Shade avoidance and shade tolerance in flowering plants. *In* "Light as an Ecological Factor". *Symp. Brit. Ecol. Soc.* **6**, 187–207. [45]

GRIME, J. P. (1979). "Plant Strategies and Vegetation Processes", Wiley, London. [39]

GRIME, J. P. and HODGSON, J. G. (1969). An investigation of the ecological significance of lime-chlorosis by means of large-scale comparative experiments. *In* "Ecological Aspects of the Mineral Nutrition of Plants". *Brit. Ecol. Soc. Symp.* **9**, 67–100. [218]

GRIME, J. P. and HUNT, R. (1975). Relative growth rate: its range and adaptive significance in a local flora. *J. Ecol.* **63**, 393–422. [8, 10, 12, 49, 91, 115]

[7] GRIME, J. P. and LLOYD, P. S. (1973). "An Ecological Atlas of Grassland Plants". Arnold, London.

[250] GROBBELAAR, N., CLARKE, B. and HOUGH, M. C. (1971). The nodulation and nitrogen fixation of isolated roots of *Phaseolus vulgaris* L. III. The effect of carbon dioxide and ethylene. *Plant and Soil* (Special Volume), 215–223.

[278] GRUBB, P. J. (1977). The maintenance of species-richness in plant communities: the importance of the regeneration niche. *Biol. Rev.* **52,** 107–145.

[86, 205] GRUBB, P. J. and SUTER, M. B. (1971). The mechanism of acidification of soil by *Calluna* and *Ulex* and the significance for conservation. *In* "The Scientific Management of Animal and Plant Communities for Conservation". *Brit. Ecol. Soc. Symp.* **11,** 115–135.

[291] GRÜMMER, G. (1958). Die Beeinflussung des Leinertrages durch *Camelina*-Arten. *Flora* **146,** 158–177.

[254, 255] GUDERIAN, R. (1977). "Air Pollution". *Ecological Studies* **22**. Springer Verlag, Berlin.

[78, 214] GUPTA, P. L. and RORISON, I. H. (1975). Seasonal differences in the availability of nutrients down a podzolic profile. *J. Ecol.* **63,** 521–534.

[180] HABESHAW, D. (1973). A reassessment of the part played by rapid intracellular ice formation in producing frost damage in the field. *J. agric. Sci.* **81,** 549–551.

[4] HACKETT, C. (1965). Ecological aspects of the nutrition of *Deschampsia flexuosa*. II. The effect of Al, Ca, Fe, K, Mn, N, P, and pH on the growth of seedlings and established plants. *J. Ecol.* **53,** 315–333.

[135] HALL, A. E., SCHULZE, E.-D. and LANGE, O. L. (1976). Currect perspectives of steady-state stomatal responses to environment. *In* "Water and Plant Life" (Eds. O. L. Lange, L. Kappen and E.-D. Schulze). *Ecological Studies* **19,** 169–188. Springer Verlag, Berlin.

[222] HALL, J. L., YEO, A. R. and FLOWERS, T. J. (1974). Uptake and localization of rubidium in the halophyte *Suaeda maritima. Z. Pflanzenphysiol.* **71,** 200–206.

[21, 22] HARBERD, D. J. (1961). Observations on population structure and longevity of *Festuca rubra* L. *New Phytol.* **60,** 184–206.

[285, 286] HARBORNE, J. (1977). "Introduction to Ecological Biochemistry". Academic Press, London and New York.

[112] HARLEY, J. L. (1971). Associations of microbes and roots. *Symp. Soc. Gen. Microbiol.* **23,** 309–332.

[111] HARLEY, J. L. and LEWIS, D. H. (1969). The physiology of ectotrophic mycorrhizas. *Adv. Microbiol. Physiol.* **3,** 53–58.

[262] HARPER, J. L. (1961). Approaches to the study of plant competition. *Symp. Soc. exp. Biol.* **15,** 1–39.

[63] HARPER, J. L. (1969). The role of predation in vegetational diversity. *In* "Diversity and Stability in Ecological Systems". *Brookhaven Symp. Biol.* **22,** 48–62.

[291] HARPER, J. L. (1975). Review of "Allelopathy" by E. L. Rice. *Quart. Rev. Biol.* **50,** 493–495.

HARPER, J. L. and BENTON, R. A. (1966). The behaviour of seeds in soil. II. The germination of seeds on the surface of a water supplying substrate. *J. Ecol.* **54,** 151–166. [147]

HARPER, J. L. and SAGAR, G. R. (1953). Some aspects of the ecology of buttercups in permanent grassland. *Proc. Br. Weed Control Conf.* **1,** 256–265. [245]

HARPER, J. L., WILLIAMS, J. T. and SAGAR, G. R. (1965). The behaviour of seeds in soil. 1. The heterogeneity of soil surfaces and its role in determining the establishment of plants from seed. *J. Ecol.* **53,** 273–286. [146]

HARRIS, G. A. and WILSON, A. M. (1970). Competition for moisture among seedlings of annual and perennial grasses as influenced by root elongation at low temperature. *Ecology* **51,** 530–534. [152]

HARRISON-MURRAY, R. S. and CLARKSON, D. T. (1973). Relationships between structural development and absorption of ions by the root system of *Cucurbita pepo. Planta* **114,** 1–16. [103]

HART, M. G. R. (1963). Observations on the source of acid in empoldered mangrove soils. II. Oxidation of soil polysulphides. *Plant and Soil* **19,** 106–114. [204]

HASSAN-PORATH, E. and POLJAKOFF-MAYBER, A. (1969). The effect of salinity on the malic dehydrogenase of pea roots. *Plant Physiol.* **44,** 103–104. [229]

HATRICK, A. A. and BOWLING, D. J. F. (1973). A study of the relationship between root and shoot metabolism. *J. exp. Bot.* **24,** 607–613. [101]

HAVILL, D. C., LEE, J. A. and STEWART, G. R. (1974). Nitrate utilisation by species from acidic and calcareous soils. *New Phytol.* **73,** 1221–1232. [95, 96]

HAY, R. K. M. (1977). Effects of tillage and direct drilling on soil temperature in winter. *J. Soil Sci.* **28,** 403–409. [183]

HAY, R. K. M. (1978). Seasonal changes in the position of the shoot apex of winter wheat and spring barley in relation to the soil surface. *J. agric. Sci.* **91,** 245–248. [161]

HAY, R. K. M. (1981). Timely planting of maize: a case history from the Lilongwe Plain. *Trop. Agr.* April 1981. [128]

HAY, R. K. M. and ALLEN, E. J. (1978). Tuber initiation and bulking in the potato (*Solanum tuberosum*) under tropical conditions: the importance of soil and air temperature. *Trop. Agric.* **55,** 289–295. [176]

HAYMAN, D. S. and MOSSE, B. (1972). Plant growth responses to vesicular-arbuscular mycorrhiza. III. Increased uptake of labile P from soil. *New Phytol.* **71,** 41–47. [112, 113]

HEATH, R. L. (1975). Ozone. *In* "Responses of Plants to Air Pollution" (Eds. J. B. Mudd and T. T. Kozlowski), pp. 23–55. Academic Press, New York and London. [225]

HEDBERG, O. (1964). "Features of Afroalpine Plant Ecology". Almqvist and Wiksells, Uppsala. [199]

HEICHEL, G. H. and MUSGRAVE, R. B. (1969). Varietal differences in net photosynthesis of *Zea mays.* L. *Crop Sci.* **9,** 483–486. [60]

HEIMER, Y. M. (1973). The effects of sodium chloride, potassium chloride

[222] and glycerol on the activity of nitrate reductase of a salt-tolerant and two non-tolerant plants. *Planta* **113,** 279–281.

[121] HELLKVIST, J., RICHARDS, G. P. and JARVIS, P. G. (1974). Vertical gradients of water potential and tissue water relations in Sitka Spruce trees measured with the pressure chamber. *J. appl. Ecol.* **11,** 637–667.

[118] HENDERSON, L. J. (1913). "The Fitness of the Environment". Macmillan, London.

[71] HEWITT, E. J. (1967). "Sand and Water Culture Methods Used in the Study of Plant Nutrition". C.A.B., London.

[53, 58, 59] HIESEY, W. M., NOBS, M. A. and BJÖRKMAN, O. (1971). Experimental studies on the nature of species. V. Biosystematics, genetics, and physiological ecology of the *Erythranthe* section of *Mimulus*. *Carnegie Inst. Wash. Publ.* **628.**

[102, 115] HIGGS, D. E. B. and JAMES, D. B. (1969). Comparative studies on the biology of upland grasses. I. Rate of dry matter production and its control in four grass species. *J. Ecol.* **57,** 553–564.

[70] HIGINBOTHAM, N. (1973). The mineral absorption process in plants. *Bot. Rev.* **39,** 16–70.

[228] HILL, B. S. and HILL, A. E. (1973). Enzymatic approaches to chloride transport in the *Limonium* salt gland. *In* "Ion Transport in Plants" (Ed. W. P. Anderson), pp. 379–384. Academic Press, London and New York.

[147] HILLEL, D. (1972). Soil moisture and seed germination. *In* "Water Deficits and Plant Growth" (Ed. T. T. Kozlowski), vol. 3, pp. 65–89. Academic Press, New York and London.

[135] HIRON, R. W. P. and WRIGHT, S. T. C. (1973). The role of endogenous abscisic acid in the response of plants to stress. *J. exp. Bot.* **24,** 769–781.

[187] HOCKING, B. and SHARPLIN, C. D. (1965). Flower basking by Arctic insects. *Nature* **206,** 215.

[70] HODGES, T. K. (1973). Ion absorption by plant roots. *Adv. Agron.* **25,** 163–207.

[201] HODGSON, D. R. and BUCKLEY, G. P. (1975). A practical approach towards the establishment of trees and shrubs on pulverised fuel ash. *In* "The Ecology of Resource Degradation and Renewal" (Eds. M. J. Chadwick and G. T. Goodman). *Brit. Ecol. Soc. Symp.* **15,** 305–330. Blackwell, Oxford.

[77] HOLFORD, I. C. R. (1976). Effects of phosphate buffer capacity of soil on the phosphate requirements of plants. *Plant and Soil* **45,** 433–444.

[42] HOLMES, M. G. and SMITH, H. (1975). The function of phytochrome in plants growing in the natural environment. *Nature* **254,** 512–514.

[36] HOLMES, M. G. and SMITH, H. (1977). The function of phytochrome in the natural environment. II. The influence of vegetation canopies on the spectral energy distribution of natural daylight. *Photochem. Photobiol.* **25,** 539–546.

[53, 57] HOLMGREN, P. (1968). Leaf factors affecting light-saturated photosynthesis in ecotypes of *Solidago virgaurea* from exposed and shaded habitats. *Physiol. Plant.* **21,** 676–698.

HOLMGREN, P., JARVIS, P. G. and JARVIS, M. S. (1965). Resistances to carbon

dioxide and water vapour transfer in leaves of different plant species.
Physiol. Plant. **18,** 557–573. [137]

HOLST, G. (1974). Über die Stickstoffdisposition in der Nährstoffaufnahme
der Pflanzen. *Angew. Botanik* **48,** 77–95. [88]

HOOK, D. D. and SCHOLTENS, J. R. (1978). Adaptations and flood tolerance
of tree species. *In* "Plant Life in Anaerobic Environments" (Eds. D. D.
Hook and R. M. M. Crawford), pp. 299–331. Ann Arbor Science Publishers Inc., Michigan. [236]

HOOK, D. D., BROWN, C. L. and KORMANIK, P. P. (1971). Inductive flood
tolerance in swamp tupelo (*Nyssa sylvatica* var *biflora* (Walt.) Sarg.). *J.
exp. Bot.* **22,** 78–89. [235]

HOPE-SIMPSON, J. F. (1938). A chalk flora of the Lower Greensand, and its use
in determining the calcicole habit. *J. Ecol.* **26,** 218–235. [89]

HORAK, O. and KINZEL, H. (1971). Typen des Mineralstoffwechsels bei den
höheren Pflanzen. *Oster. bot. Z.* **119,** 475–495. [225]

HORN, H. (1971). "The Adaptive Geometry of Trees". University, Princeton. [46, 53, 67]

HORSFIELD, D. (1977). Relationships between feeding of *Philaenus spumarius*
(L.) and the amino acid concentration in the xylem sap. *Ecol. Entomol.* **2,**
259–266. [279]

HORSMAN, D. C. and WELLBURN, A. R. (1976). Guide to the metabolic and
biochemical effects of air pollutants on higher plants. *In* "Effects of Air
Pollutants on Plants" (Ed. T. A. Mansfield), pp. 185–199. Cambridge
University Press, Cambridge. [255]

HSIAO, T. C. (1973). Plant responses to water stress. *Ann. Rev. Pl. Physiol.* **24,**
519–570. [125, 126, 157]

HSIAO, T. C., ACEVEDO, E., FERERES, E. and HENDERSON, D. W. (1976).
Water stress, growth and osmotic adjustment. *Phil. Trans. R. Soc. London*
B273, 479–500. [125, 126, 152, 157, 168]

HUBER, B. (1928). Weitere quantitative Untersuchungen über das Wasser-
leitungssystem der Pflanzen. *Jahrb. Wiss. Bot.* **67,** 877–959. [167]

HUBER, W. and SANKHLA, N. (1976). C_4 Pathway and regulation of the
balance between C_4 and C_3 metabolism. *In* "Water and Plant Life" (Eds.
O. L. Lange, L. Kappen and E.-D. Schulze). *Ecological Studies* **19,** 335–363. [160]

HUGHES, A. P. (1959). Effects of the environment on leaf development in
Impatiens parviflora D.C. *J. Linn. Soc. (Bot)* **56,** 161–165. [52]

HULTÉN, E. (1962). "The Circumpolar Plants, II, Dicotyledons". *K. svenska.
Vetensk. Akad. Handl. ser.* **5,** 13 (1). [188]

HUNT, R. (1970). "Relative growth rate: its range and adaptive significance
in a local flora". Ph.D. Thesis, University of Sheffield. [102]

HUNT, R. and PARSONS, J. F. (1974). A computer program for deriving growth-
functions in plant growth analysis. *J. appl. Ecol.* **11,** 297–308. [10]

HUNTER, J. R. and ERICKSON, A. E. (1952). Relation of seed germination to
soil moisture tension. *Agron. J.* **44,** 107–109. [147]

HUTCHINGS, M. J. (1976). Spectral transmission and the aerial profile in
stands of *Mercurialis perennis* L. *Ann. Bot.* **40,** 1207–1216. [64]

[50] HUTCHINSON, T. C. (1967). Comparative studies of the ability of species to withstand prolonged periods of darkness. *J. Ecol.* **55,** 291–299.

[35] HUXLEY, P. A. (1969). The effect of fluctuating light intensity on plant growth. *J. appl. Ecol.* **6,** 273–276.

[203] HYAMS, E. (1952). "Soil and Civilization". Thames and Hudson, London.

[263, 270, 271] IDRIS, H. and MILTHORPE, F. L. (1966). Light and nutrient supplies in the competition between barley and charlock. *Oecologia Plant.* **1,** 143–164.

[222] INGRAM, M. (1957). Micro-organisms resisting high concentrations of sugars or salts. *Symp. Soc. Gen. Microbiol.* **7,** 90–133.

[182] IVES, J. D. and BARRY, R. G. (Eds.) (1974). "Arctic and Alpine Environments". Methuen, London.

[53] JACKSON, L. W. R. (1967). Effect of shade on leaf structure of deciduous tree species. *Ecology* **48,** 498–499.

[249] JACKSON, M. B. and CAMPBELL, D. J. (1975). Movement of ethylene from roots to shoots, a factor in the responses of tomato plants to waterlogged soil conditions. *New Phytol.* **74,** 397–406.

[249] JACKSON, M. B. and CAMPBELL, D. J. (1976). Waterlogging and petiole epinasty in tomato: the role of ethylene and low oxygen. *New Phytol.* **76,** 21–29.

[116] JACKSON, W. A., FLESHER, D. and HAGEMAN, R. H. (1973). Nitrate uptake by dark-grown corn seedlings. *Plant Physiol.* **51,** 120–127.

[203] JACOBSEN, T. and ADAMS, R. M. (1958). Salt and silt in ancient Mesopotamian agriculture. *Science* **128,** 1251–1258.

[19, 95] JANIESCH, P. (1973). Beitrag zur Physiologie der Nitrophyten:Nitrat-Speicherung und Nitratassimilation bei *Anthriscus sylvestris* Hoffm. *Flora* **162,** 479–491.

[282] JANZEN, D. H. (1975). *Pseudomyrmex nigropilosa*: a parasite of a mutualism. *Science* **188,** 936–937.

[133] JARVIS, M. S. (1963). A comparison between the water relations of species with contrasting types of geographical distribution in the British Isles. *Symp. Brit. Ecol. Soc.* **3,** 289–312.

[59] JARVIS, P. G. (1964). The adaptability to light intensity of seedlings of *Quercus petraea* (Matt.) Liebl. *J. Ecol.* **52,** 545–571.

[88] JEFFERIES, R. L. and WILLIS, A. J. (1964). Studies on the calcicole-calcifuge habit. I. Methods of analysis of soil and plant tissues and some results of investigations on four species. *J. Ecol.* **52,** 121–138.

[96, 116] JEFFERIES, R. L., LAYCOCK, D., STEWART, G. R. and SIMS, A. P. (1969). The properties of mechanisms involved in the uptake and utilisation of calcium and potassium by plants in relation to an understanding of plant distribution. *In* "Ecological Aspects of the Mineral Nutrition of Plants". *Brit. Ecol. Soc. Symp.* **9,** 281–308.

[158] JEFFREE, C. E., JOHNSON, R. P. C. and JARVIS, P. G. (1971). Epicuticular wax in the stomatal antechamber of Sitka Spruce and its effects on the diffusion of water vapour and carbon dioxide. *Planta* **98,** 1–10.

[91] JEFFREY, D. W. (1964). The formation of polyphosphate in *Banksia ornata*, an Australian heath plant. *Aust. J. biol. Sci.* **17,** 845–854.

Jeffrey, D. W. and Pigott, C. D. (1973). The response of grasslands on sugar limestone in Teesdale to application of phosphorus and nitrogen. *J. Ecol.* **61,** 85–92. [90]

Jensen, R. D., Taylor, S. A. and Wiebe, H. H. (1961). Negative transport and resistance to water flow through plants. *Plant. Physiol.* **36,** 633–638. [139]

Jeschke, W. D. (1973). K^+-stimulated Na^+ efflux and selective transport in barley roots. *In* "Ion Transport in Plants" (Ed. W. P. Anderson), pp. 285–296. Academic Press, London and New York. [227]

John, C. D. (1977). The structure of rice roots grown in aerobic and anaerobic environments. *Plant and Soil* **47,** 269–274. [235]

John, C. D. and Greenway, H. (1976). Alcoholic fermentation and activity of some enzymes in rice roots under anaerobiosis. *Aust. J. Pl. Physiol.* **3,** 325–336. [239]

John, M. K. (1972). Cadmium adsorption maxima of soils as measured by the Langmuir isotherm. *Can. J. Soil Sci.* **52,** 343–350. [78]

Johnson, H. B. (1975). Plant pubescence: an ecological perspective. *Bot. Rev.* **41,** 233–258. [159, 283, 285]

Jones, H. E. (1971). Comparative studies of plant growth and distribution in relation to waterlogging. II. An experimental study of the relationship between transpiration and the uptake of iron in *Erica cinerea* L. and *E. tetralix* L. *J. Ecol.* **59,** 167–178. [243]

Jones, H. E. and Etherington, J. R. (1970). Comparative studies of plant growth and distribution in relation to waterlogging. I. The survival of *Erica cinerea* L. and *E. tetralix* L. and its apparent relationship to iron and manganese uptake in waterlogged soil. *J. Ecol.* **58,** 487–496. [243]

Jones, R. (1972). Comparative studies of plant growth and distribution in relation to waterlogging. V. The uptake of iron and manganese by dune and slack plants. *J. Ecol.* **60,** 131–140. [243]

Jordan, C. F. and Kline, J. R. (1977). Transpiration of trees in tropical rainforests. *J. app. Ecol.* **14,** 853–860. [165]

Jordan, W. R. and Ritchie, J. T. (1971). Influence of soil water stress on evaporation, root absorption and internal water status of cotton. *Plant Physiol.* **48,** 783–788. [157]

Juniper, B. E. and Roberts, R. M. (1966). Polysaccharide synthesis and the fine structure of root cap cells. *J. Roy. Micro. Soc.* **85,** 63–72. [108]

Karlsson, T. (1974). Recurrent ecotypic variation in Rhinantheae and Gentianaceae in relation to hemi-parasitism and mycotrophy. *Bot. Not.* **127,** 527–539. [280]

Kasperbauer, M. J. (1971). Spectral distribution of light in a tobacco canopy and effects of end-of-day light quality on growth and development. *Plant Physiol.* **47,** 775–778. [34, 41, 43]

Kasperbauer, M. J. and Peaslee, D. E. (1973). Morphology and photosynthetic efficiency of tobacco leaves that received end-of-day red or far-red light during development. *Plant Physiol.* **52,** 440–442. [41]

Katznelson, H. (1946). The 'rhizosphere effect' of mangels on certain

[107]　　　groups of soil micro-organisms. *Soil Sci.* **62**, 343–354.

KAUFMANN, M. R. (1972). Water deficits and reproductive growth. *In* "Water Deficits and Plant Growth" (Ed. T. T. Kozlowski), vol. 3, pp. 91–124.

[161]　　　Academic Press, New York and London.

KAY, Q. O. N. (1971). Biological Flora of the British Isles: *Anthemis cotula* L.

[22]　　　and *A. arvenis* L. *J. Ecol.* **59**, 623–648.

KEAY, J., BIDDISCOMBE, E. F. and OZANNE, P. G. (1970). The comparative rates of phosphate absorption by eight annual pasture species. *Aust. J. Agr.*

[94]　　　*Res.* **21**, 33–44.

KEELEY, J. E. (1978). Malic acid accumulation in roots in response to flooding: evidence contrary to its role as an alternative to ethanol. *J. exp. Bot.*

[243]　　　**29**, 1345–1349.

KEELEY, J. E. and FRANZ, E. H. (1979). Alcoholic fermentation in swamp and upland populations of *Nyssa sylvatica*: temporal changes in adaptive

[235, 243]　　strategy. *Amer. Nat.* **113**, 587–592.

[182]　　　KEVAN, P. G. (1972). Insect pollination of arctic flowers. *J. Ecol.* **60**, 831–847.

KEVAN, P. G. (1975). Sun-tracking solar furnaces in high-arctic flowers:

[29, 187]　　significance for pollination and insects. *Science* **189**, 723–726.

KIMBALL, S. L., BENNETT, B. D. and SALISBURY, F. B. (1973). The growth and development of montane species at near-freezing temperatures. *Ecology*

[186]　　　**54**, 168–173.

KING, T. J. (1975). Inhibition of seed germination under leaf canopies in *Arenaria serpyllifolia, Veronica arvensis,* and *Cerastium holosteoides. New Phytol.*

[39]　　　**75**, 87–90.

KINZEL, H. (1969). Ansätze zu einer vergleichenden Physiologie der Mineralstoffwechsel und ihre ökologischen Konsequenzen. *Ber. deutsch.*

[226]　　　*Bot. Ges.* **82**, 143–158.

KIRIKOVA, L. A. (1970). Razmeshchemie podzemaykh chaste; nekotoykh vidor traryanokustarnikorogo yarusa yelorogo yesa. (The distribution of underground parts of certain species of the herbaceous/dwarf-shrub layer

[273]　　　in a spruce forest.) *Bot. Zh.* **55**, 1290–1300.

KIYOSAWA, K. (1975). Studies on the effects of alcohols on membrane water

[235]　　　permeability of *Nitella. Protoplasma* **86**, 243–252.

KLAREN, C. H. (1975). "Physiological Aspects of the Hemiparasite *Rhinanthus*

[280]　　　*serotinus*". Groningen.

KLEIN, R. M. (1978). Plants and near-ultraviolet radiation. *Bot. Rev.* **44**,

[185, 187]　　1–127.

KLEINKOPF, G. E. and WALLACE, A. (1974). Physiological basis for salt

[228]　　　tolerance in *Tamarix ramosissima. Plant Sci. Lett.* **3**, 157–163.

KLIKOFF, L. G. (1969). Temperature dependence of mitochondrial oxidative rates in relation to plant distribution. *In* "Physiological Systems in Semi-Arid Environments" (Eds. C. C. Hoft and M. L. Riedesell), pp. 263–269.

[191]　　　University of New Mexico Press, Albequerque.

KLUGE, M. (1976). Crassulacean acid metabolism (CAM): CO_2 and water economy. *In* "Water and Plant Life" (Eds. O. L. Lange, L. Kappen and

E.-D. Schulze). *Ecological Studies* **19**, 313–322. Springer Verlag, Berlin.   [160]

KOCH, K. and MENGEL, K. (1974). The influence of the level of potassium supply to young tobacco plants on short-term uptake and utilisation of nitrate nitrogen. *J. Sci. Fd Agric.* **25**, 465–471.   [100]

KOCHENDERFER, J. N. (1973). Root distribution under some forest types native to West Virginia. *Ecology* **54**, 445–449.   [105]

KOLLER, D. (1972). Environmental control of seed germination. *In* "Seed Biology" (Ed. T. T. Kozlowski), vol. 2, pp. 1–101. Academic Press, New York and London.   [145, 146]

KOLLER, D. and NEGBI, M. (1966). Germination of seeds of desert plants. Final report to USDA, project no AlO–FS–6, Department of Botany, Hebrew University, Jerusalem, Israel.   [144, 145]

KONINGS, H. and JACKSON, M. B. (1975). Production of ethylene, and the promoting and inhibiting effects of ethylene on root elongation, in various species. *A.R.C. Letcombe Lab. Ann. Rep.* 1974, 23–24.   [248]

KOZLOWSKI, T. T. (1964). "Water Metabolism in Plants". Harper and Row, New York.   [150, 159]

KOZLOWSKI, T. T. (1972). Shrinking and swelling of plant tissues. *In* "Water Deficits and Plant Growth" (Ed. T. T. Kozlowski), vol. 3, pp. 1–64. Academic Press, New York and London.   [140]

KOZLOWSKI, T. T. (1976). Water relations and tree improvement. *In* "Tree Physiology and Yield Improvement" (Eds. M. G. R. Cannell and F. T. Last), pp. 307–327. Academic Press, London and New York.   [168]

KRAMER, P. J. (1969). "Plant and Soil Water Relationships". McGraw Hill, New York.   [149, 168]

KRANZ, E. and JACOB, F. (1977). Zur Mineralstoff-Konkurrenz zwischen *Linum* und *Camelina* II. Aufnahme von ^{32}P-Phosphat und ^{86}Rubidium. *Flora* **166**, 505–516.   [291]

KRAUS, H. (1969). Osmoregulation mit α-galactosyl-glyceriden bei *Ochromonas malhamensis*. *Ber. deutsch. bot. Ges.* **82**, 115–125.   [223]

KRIEDEMANN, P. E. and TÖRÖKFALVY, R. and SMART, R. E. (1973). Natural occurrence and photosynthetic utilisation of sunflecks by grapevine leaves. *Photosynthetica* **7**, 18–27.   [35]

KROG, J. (1955). Notes on temperature measurements indicative of special organisation in arctic and subarctic plants for utilisation of radiated heat from the sun. *Physiol. Plant.* **8**, 836–839.   [187]

KROH, G. C. and BEAVER, D. L. (1978). Insect response to mixture and monoculture patches of Michigan old-field annual herbs. *Oecologia* **31**, 269–275.   [63]

KU, H. S., SUGE, H., RAPPAPORT, L. and PRATT, H. K. (1970). Stimulation of rice coleoptile growth by ethylene. *Planta* **90**, 333–339.   [248]

KUIJT, J. (1969). "The Biology of Parasitic Flowering Plants". University of California Press, Berkeley.   [286]

KYLIN, A. and KÄHR, M. (1973). The effect of magnesium and calcium on adenosine triphosphatases from wheat and oat roots at different pH. *Physiol. Plant.* **28**, 452–457.   [229]

LAMM, C. G., TJELL, J. C., MØLLER, O. and CHRISTIANSEN, T. F. (1969). Plant nutrient availability in soils. II. Quantity-intensity relationships of phosphorus and manganese as influence by soil pH. *Acta agric. Scand.* **19,** [78]   135–140.

LANCE, J. C. and PEARSON, R. W. (1969). Effects of low concentrations of aluminium on growth and water and nutrient uptake by cotton roots. *Soil* [208]   *Sci. Soc. Amer. Proc.* **33,** 95–98.

LANE, S. D., MARTIN, E. S. and GARROD, J. F. (1978). Lead toxicity effects on [212, 221]   indole-3-ylacetic acid induced cell elongation. *Planta* **144,** 79–84.

LANGE, O. L. and ZUBER, M. (1977). *Frerea indica*, a stem succulent CAM [62]   plant with deciduous C_3 leaves. *Oecologia* **31,** 67–72.

LANGE, O. L., KAPPEN, L. and SCHULZE, E.-D. (1976). "Water and Plant [149, 159]   Life". *Ecological Studies* **19**. Springer Verlag, Berlin.

LANGRIDGE, J. and McWILLIAM, J. R. (1967). Heat responses of higher plants. *In* "Thermobiology" (Ed. A. H. Rose), pp. 231–292. Academic Press, [194]   London and New York.

[152–4,   LARCHER, W. (1975). "Physiological Plant Ecology". Springer-Verlag, 174, 196–8]   Berlin.

LARCHER, W., HEBER, U. and SANTARIUS, K. A. (1973). Limiting temperatures for life functions. *In* "Temperature and Life" (Eds. H. Precht, J. Christopherson, H. Hensel and W. Larcher), pp. 195–263. Springer-[179, 194]   Verlag, Berlin.

LARKUM, A. W. D. (1968). Ionic relations of chloroplasts *in vivo*. *Nature* [222]   **218,** 447–449.

LARSEN, S. (1964). On the relationship between labile and non-labile phos-[76]   phate in soils. *Acta agric. Scand.* **14,** 249–253.

[77]   LARSEN, S. (1967). Soil phosphorus. *Adv. Agron.* **19,** 151–210.

LATIES, G. G. (1969). Dual mechanisms of salt uptake in relation to compartmentation and long distance transport. *Ann. Rev. Pl. Physiol.* **20,** [73]   89–116.

LAW, R., BRADSHAW, A. D. and PUTWAIN, P. (1977). Life history variation [19]   in *Poa annua*. *Evolution* **31,** 233–246.

LAWTON, J. H. (1976). The structure of the arthropod community on bracken [287]   *Bot. J. Linn. Soc.* **73,** 187–216.

LAWTON, J. H. and McNEILL, S. (1979). Between the devil and the deep blue sea: on the problem of being a herbivore. *In* "Population Dynamics". [283]   *Brit. Ecol. Soc. Symp.* **20,** 223–244.

LAZENBY, A. (1955). Germination and establishment of *Juncus effusus* L. II. [242]   The interaction effects of moisture and competition. *J. Ecol.* **43,** 595–605.

LEACH, G. J. and WATSON, D. J. (1968). Photosynthesis in crop profiles, [64]   measured by phytometers. *J. appl. Ecol.* **5,** 381–408.

[233]   LEHNINGER, A. L. (1965). "Bioenergetics". Benjamin, New York.

LEIGH, R. A., WYN JONES, R. G. and WILLIAMSON, F. A. (1973). The possible role of vesicles and ATPases in ion uptake. *In* "Ion Transport in Plants" (Ed. [72]   W. P. Anderson), pp. 407–418. Academic Press, London and New York.

LEOPOLD, A. C. and KRIEDEMANN, P. E. (1975). "Plant Growth and Development", 2nd Edn. McGraw-Hill, New York. [172]

LEVIN, D. A. (1976). The chemical defences of plants to pathogens and herbivores. *Ann. Rev. Ecol. Syst.* **7**, 121–160. [279]

LEVITT, J. (1972). "Responses of Plants to Environmental Stresses". Academic Press, New York and London. [16, 163, 195, 197, 199]

LEVITT, J. (1978). An overview of freezing injury and survival, and its interrelationships to other stresses. *In* "Plant Cold Hardiness and Freezing Stress" (Eds. P. H. Li and A. Sakai), pp. 3–15. Academic Press, New York and London. [180]

LEWIS, M. C. (1972). The physiological significance of variation in leaf structure. *Sci. Prog., Oxf.* **60**, 25–51. [155, 156]

LIORET, C. (1974). L'analyse des courbes de croissance. *Physiol. Veg.* **12**, 413–434. [9]

LOCHHEAD, A. G. and ROUATT, J. W. (1955). The "rhizosphere effect" on the nutritional groups of soil bacteria. *Soil Sci. Soc. Amer. Proc.* **19**, 48–49. [108]

LOCK, J. M. and MILBURN, T. R. (1971). The seed biology of *Themeda triandra* Forsk. in relation to fire. *Symp. Brit. Ecol. Soc.* **11**, 337–349. [146]

LOMMEN, P., SMITH, S., YOCUM, C. and GATES, D. (1975). Photosynthetic model. *In* "Perspectives of Biophysical Ecology" (Eds. D. Gates and R. Schmerl), pp. 33–43. Springer-Verlag, Berlin. [53]

LONERAGAN, J. F. and ASHER, C. J. (1967). Response of plants to phosphorus concentration in solution culture. II. Rate of phosphorus absorption and its relation to growth. *Soil Sci.* **103**, 311–318. [99, 116]

LONG, R. C. and WOLTZ, W. G. (1972). Depletion of nitrate reductase activity in response to soil leaching. *Agron. J.* **64**, 789–792. [94]

LONGMAN, K. A. (1969). The dormancy and survival of plants in the humid tropics. *Symp. Soc. Exp. Biol.* **23**, 471–488. [144, 145]

LONGMAN, K. A. and JENIK, J. (1974). "Tropical Forest and its Environment". Longman, London. [199]

LOUGHMAN, B. C. (1969). The uptake of phosphate and its movement within the plant. *In* "Ecological Aspects of the Mineral Nutrition of Plants". *Brit. Ecol. Soc. Symp.* **9**, 309–322. [101]

LUDLOW, M. M. (1976). Ecophysiology of C_4 grasses. *In* "Water and Plant Life" (Eds. O. L. Lange, L. Kappen and E.-D. Schulze). *Ecological Studies* **19**, 364–386. Springer-Verlag, Berlin. [161, 199]

LYNCH, J. M. (1975a). The formation of ethylene by soil micro-organisms. *A.R.C. Letcombe Laboratory Ann. Rep.* 1974, 88–95. [246]

LYNCH, J. M. (1975b). Ethylene in soil. *Nature* **256**, 576–577. [250]

LYONS, J. M. (1973). Chilling injury in plants. *Ann. Rev. Pl. Physiol.* **24**, 445–466. [179]

MABRY, J. J., HUNZIKER, J. H. and DiFEO, D. R. (1977). "Creosote Bush. Biology and Chemistry of *Larrea* in New World Deserts". US/1BP synthesis series 6. Dowden, Hutchinson and Ross Inc., Stroudsburg, Pennsylvania. [163]

MacArthur, R. (1968). The theory of the niche. *In* "Population Biology and Evolution" (Ed. R. C. Lewontin), pp. 159–176. Syracuse University
[6]   Press.
MacRobbie, E. A. C. (1970). The active transport of ions in plant cells.
[98]   *Quart. Rev. Biophys.* **3**, 251–294.
McCormick, L. H. and Bowden, F. Y. (1972). Phosphate fixation by
[208]   aluminium in plant roots. *Soil Sci. Soc. Amer. Proc.* **36**, 799–802.
McCree, K. J. and Troughton, J. H. (1966). Prediction of growth rate at different light levels from measured photosynthesis and respiration rates.
[47, 49] *Plant Physiol.* **41**, 559–566.
McLaren, J. S. and Smith, H. (1978). Phytochrome control of the growth and development of *Rumex obtusifolius* under simulated canopy light
[266]   environments. *Plant Cell Env.* **1**, 61–68.
McManmon and Crawford, R. M. M. (1971). A metabolic theory of flooding tolerance: the significance of enzyme distribution and behaviour. *New
[238, 240] Phytol.* **70**, 299–306.
McNaughton, S. J., Folsom, T. C., Lee, T., Park, F., Price, C., Roeder, O., Schmitz, J. and Stockwell, C. (1974). Heavy metal tolerance in *Typha
[231]   latifolia* without the evolution of tolerant races. *Ecology* **55**, 1163–1165.
McNeilly, T. and Bradshaw, A. D. (1968). Evolutionary processes in
[22]   populations of copper-tolerant *Agrostis tenuis* Sibth. *Evolution* **22**, 108–118.
McPherson, J. K. and Muller, C. H. (1969). Allelopathic effects of *Adenostoma fasciculatum*, "chamise", in the California Chaparral. *Ecol. Monogr.*
[293]   **39**, 117–198.
[93, 216, Madhok, P. O. and Walker, R. B. (1969). Magnesium nutrition of two
217]   species of sunflower. *Plant Physiol.* **44**, 1016–1022.
Mahmoud, A. and Grime, J. P. (1974). A comparison of negative relative
[49, 268] growth rates in shaded seedlings. *New Phytol.* **73**, 1215–1220.
Mallott, P. G., Davy, A. J., Jefferies, R. L. and Hutton, M. J. (1975). Carbon dioxide exchange in leaves of *Spartina anglica* Hubbard. *Oecologia*
[61]   **20**, 351–358.
Malone, C., Koeppe, D. E. and Miller, R. J. (1974). Localisation of lead
[222]   accumulated by corn plants. *Plant Physiol.* **53**, 388–394.
Mancinelli, A. L. and Rabino, I. (1978). The "high irradiance responses" of
[44]   plant photomorphogenesis. *Bot. Rev.* **44**, 129–180.
[182]   Manley, G. (1952). "Climate and the British Scene". Collins, Glasgow.
Manohar, M. S. (1966). Effect of "osmotic" systems on germination in peas
[207]   (*Pisum sativum* L.). *Planta* **71**, 81–86.
Mansfield, J. W. and Deverall, B. J. (1974a). The rates of fungal development and lesion formation in leaves of *Vicia faba* during infection by
[288]   *Botrytis cinerea* and *B. fabae*. *Ann. appl. Biol.* **76**, 77–89.
Mansfield, J. W. and Deverall, B. J. (1974b). Changes in wyerone acid concentration in leaves of *Vicia faba* after infection by *Botrytis cinerea* or
[288]   *B. fabae*. *Ann. appl. Biol.* **77**, 227–235.
Mansfield, T. A. (1976). The role of stomata in determining the responses of

plants to air pollutants. *In* "Commentaries in Plant Science" (Ed. H. Smith), pp. 13–22. Pergamon Press, Oxford.   [253, 254, 255]

MANSFIELD, T. A. and DAVIES, W. J. (1981). Responses of stomata: the primary mechanisms of drought avoidance in mesophytes. (1981.)   [135, 137, 157]

MARKS, G. C. and KOZLOWSKI, T. T. (1973). "Ectomycorrhizae. Their Ecology and Physiology". Academic Press, New York and London.   [110]

MARSHALL, D. R., BROUÉ, P. and PRYOR, A. J. (1973). Adaptive significance of alcohol dehydrogenase isoenzymes in maize. *Nature New Biology* **244**, 16–17.   [239]

MARTIN, J. K. (1977). Factors influencing the loss of organic carbon from wheat roots. *Soil Biol. Biochem.* **9**, 1–7.   [108, 289]

MARTIN, J. T. and JUNIPER, B. E. (1970). "The Cuticles of Plants". Arnold, London.   [159]

MARTIN, M. H. (1968). Conditions affecting the distribution of *Mercurialis perennis* in certain Cambridgeshire woodlands. *J. Ecol.* **56**, 777–793.   [243]

MATHYS, W. (1973). Vergleichende Untersuchungen der Zinkaufnahme von resistenten und sensitiven Populationen von *Agrostis tenuis* Sibth. *Flora* **162**, 492–499.   [218]

MATHYS, W. (1975). Enzymes of heavy-metal-resistant and non-resistant populations of *Silene cucubalus* and their interaction with some heavy metals *in vitro* and *in vivo*. *Physiol. Plant* **33**, 161–165.   [211, 224]

MATHYS, W. (1977). The role of malate, oxalate, and mustard oil glucosides in the evolution of zinc resistance in herbage plants. *Physiol. Plant* **40**, 130–136.   [224]

MATSUMOTO, H., HIRASAWA, F., MORIMURA, S. and TAKAHASHI, E. (1976). Localisation of aluminium in tea leaves. *Plant Cell Physiol.* **17**, 890–885.   [227]

MAY, D. S. and VILLAREAL, H. M. (1974). Altitudinal differentiation of the Hill Reaction in populations of *Taraxacum officinale* in Colorado. *Photosynthetica* **8**, 73–77.   [191]

MAYER, A. M. and POLJAKOFF-MAYBER, A. (1975). "The Germination of Seeds", 2nd Edn. Pergamon, Oxford.   [241, 242, 250]

MEDINA, E. and TROUGHTON, J. H. (1974). Dark CO_2 fixation and the carbon isotope ratio in Bromeliaceae. *Plant Sci. Letters* **2**, 357–362.   [62]

MEIDNER, H. (1954). Measurements of water intake from the atmosphere by leaves. *New Phytol.* **53**, 423–426.   [152]

MEIDNER, H. and MANSFIELD, T. A. (1968). "The Physiology of Stomata". McGraw-Hill, London.   [133, 134, 135, 136, 137, 158]

MEIDNER, H. and SHERIFF, D. W. (1976). "Water and Plants". Blackie, Glasgow.   [119, 121, 123, 125, 133, 137, 141]

MERZ, E. (1959). Pflanzen und Raupen. Uber einigen Prinzipien der Futterwahl bei Grossschmetterlingsraupen. *Biol. Zentrbl.* **78**, 152–158.   [283]

MEWISSEN, D. J., DAMBLON, J. and BACQ, Z. M. (1959). Comparative sensitivity to radiation of seeds from a wild plant grown on uraniferous and non-uraniferous soil. *Nature* **183**, 1449.   [200]

MILLER, E. C. (1938). "Plant Physiology". McGraw-Hill, London.   [175]

[262] MILNE, A. (1961). Definition of competition among animals. *Symp. Soc. Exp. Biol.* **15,** 40–61.

[140] MILTHORPE, F. L. and MOORBY, J. (1974). "An Introduction to Crop Physiology". Cambridge University Press, Cambridge.

[176] MILTHORPE, F. L. and MOORBY, J. (1975). Potato. *In* "Crop Physiology" (Ed. L. T. Evans), pp. 225–57. Cambridge University Press, Cambridge.

[52] MILTHORPE, F. L. and NEWTON, P. (1963). Studies on the expansion of the leaf surface. III. The influence of radiation on cell division and expansion. *J. exp. Bot.* **14,** 483–495.

[289] MINCHIN, F. R. and PATE, J. S. (1974). Diurnal functioning of the legume root nodule. *J. exp. Bot.* **25,** 295–308.

[41] MOHR, H., DRUMM, H. and KASEMIR, H. (1974). Licht und Farbstoffe. *Ber. deutsch. Bot. Ges.* **87,** 49–70.

[29] MONTEITH, J. L. (1973). "Principles of Environmental Physics". Arnold, London.

[43, 58, 190, 191] MOONEY, H. A. and BILLINGS, W. D. (1961). Comparative physiological ecology of arctic and alpine populations of *Oxyria digyna. Ecol. Monog.* **31,** 1–29.

[58, 190] MOONEY, H. A. and JOHNSON, A. W. (1965). Comparative physiological ecology of an arctic and an alpine population of *Thalictrum alpinum. Ecology* **46,** 721–727.

[43] MORGAN, D. C. and SMITH, H. (1979). A systematic relationship between phytochrome-controlled development and species habitat for plants grown in simulated natural conditions. *Planta* **145,** 253–258.

[114] MOSSE, B. (1972). The influence of soil type and *Endogone* strain on the growth of mycorrhizal plants in phosphate deficient soils. *Rev. Ecol. Biol. Sol* **9,** 529–537.

[145] MOTT, J. J. (1972). Germination studies on some annual species from an arid region of Western Australia. *J. Ecol.* **60,** 293–304.

[147] MOTT, J. J. (1974). Factors affecting seed germination in three annual species from an arid region of Western Australia. *J. Ecol.* **62,** 699–709.

[256, 257] MUDD, J. B. and KOZLOWSKI, T. T. (Eds.) (1975). "Responses of Plants to Air Pollution". Academic Press, New York and London.

[105] MUKERJI, S. K. (1936). Contribution to the autecology of *Mercurialis perennis* L. *J. Ecol.* **24,** 38–81.

[291] MÜLLER, C. H. (1966). The role of chemical inhibition (allelopathy) in vegetational composition. *Bull. Torrey Bot. Club* **93,** 332–351.

[291] MÜLLER, C. H. (1970). Phytotoxins as plant habitat variables. *Recent Advances in Phytochemistry* **3,** 106–121.

[294] MÜLLER, W. H. (1965). Volatile materials produced by *Salvia leucophylla*: effect on seedling growth and soil bacteria. *Bot. Gaz.* **126,** 195–200.

[248] MUSGRAVE, A. and WALTERS, J. (1973). Ethylene-stimulated growth and auxin transport in *Ranunculus sceleratus* petioles. *New Phytol.* **72,** 783–789.

[248] MUSGRAVE, A., JACKSON, M. B. and LING, E. (1972). *Callitriche* stem elongation is controlled by ethylene and gibberellin. *Nature New Biology* **238,** 93–96.

NASSERY, H. (1971). Phosphate absorption by plants from habitats of different phosphate status. III. Phosphate fractions in the roots of intact plants. *New Phytol.* **70,** 949–951. [91]

NASYROV, Y. S. (1978). Genetic control of photosynthesis and improving productivity. *Ann. Rev. Pl. Physiol.* **29,** 215–237. [61]

NEILSON, R. E., LUDLOW, M. M. and JARVIS, P. G. (1972). Photosynthesis in Sitka spruce (*Picea sitchensis* (Bong.) Carr.). II Response to temperature. *J. appl. Ecol.* **9,** 721–745. [190]

NEWMAN, E. I. (1973). Competition and diversity in herbaceous vegetation. *Nature* **244,** 310. [270]

NEWMAN, E. I. (1974). Root and soil water relations. *In* "The Plant Root and its Environment" (Ed. E. W. Carson), pp. 363–431. University of Virginia Press, Charlottesville. [132]

NEWMAN, E. I. and ANDREWS, R. E. (1973). Uptake of P and K in relation to root growth and root density. *Plant and Soil* **38,** 49–69. [104]

NEWMAN, E. I. and MILLER, M. H. (1977). Allelopathy among some British grassland species. II. Influence of root exudates on phosphate uptake. *J. Ecol.* **65,** 399–412. [294]

NEWMAN, E. I. and ROVIRA, A. D. (1975). Allelopathy among some British grassland species. *J. Ecol.* **63,** 727–738. [292, 293, 294, 295]

NEWMAN, E. I., CAMPBELL, R. and ROVIRA, A. D. (1977). Experimental alteration of soil microbial populations for studying effects on higher plant interactions. *New Phytol.* **79,** 107–118. [293]

NEWTON, J. E. and BLACKMAN, G. E. (1970). The penetration of solar radiation through canopies of different structure. *Ann. Bot.* (N.S.) **34,** 329–348. [37]

NEWTON, P. (1963). Studies on the expansion of the leaf surface. II. The influence of light intensity and photoperiod. *J. exp. Bot.* **14,** 458–482. [52, 55]

NICHOLLS, A. O. and CALDER, D. M. (1973). Comments on the use of regression analysis for the study of plant growth. *New Phytol.* **72,** 571–581. [10]

NISSEN, P. (1974). Uptake mechanisms: organic and inorganic. *Ann. Rev. Pl. Physiol.* **25,** 38–80. [73]

NYE, P. H. (1966). The effect of nutrient intensity and buffering power of a soil, and the absorbing power, size and root-hairs of a root, on nutrient absorption by diffusion. *Plant and Soil* **25,** 81–105. [79, 82]

NYE, P. H. (1969). The soil model and its application to plant nutrition. *In* "Ecological Aspects of the Mineral Nutrition of Plants". *Brit. Ecol. Soc. Symp.* **9,** 105–114. [104]

NYE, P. H. (1973). The relation between the radius of a root and its nutrient absorbing power (α). *J. exp. Bot.* **24,** 783–786. [104]

NYE, P. H. and MARRIOTT, F. H. C. (1969). A theoretical study of the distribution of substances around roots resulting from simultaneous diffusion and mass flow. *Plant and Soil* **30,** 459–472. [79, 80]

NYE, P. H. and TINKER, P. B. H. (1969). The concept of a root demand coefficient. *J. appl. Ecol.* **6,** 293–300. [98, 102, 265, 267]

NYE, P. H. and TINKER, P. B. H. (1977). "Solute Movement in the Soil-Root System". Blackwell, Oxford. [74, 78, 79, 98]

O'BRIEN, T. A., MOORBY, J. and WHITTINGTON, W. J. (1967). The effect of management and competition on the uptake of ^{32}phosphorus by ryegrass, meadow fescue, and their natural hybrid. *J. appl. Ecol.* **4,** 513–520.   [273, 276]

OERTLI, J. J. (1971). The stability of water under tension in the xylem. *Z. Pflanzenphysiol.* **65,** 195–209.   [119]

OLMSTED, C. E. (1944). Growth and development in range grasses. IV. Photoperiodic responses in twelve geographic strains of side-oats grama. *Bot. Gaz.* **100,** 46–74.   [43]

OLSEN, C. (1971). Selective ion absorption in various plant species and its ecological significance. *C. R. Trav. Lab. Carlsberg* **38.** 399–422.   [93, 216]

OLSEN, S. R. and KEMPER, W. D. (1968). Movement of nutrients to plant roots. *Adv. Agron.* **20,** 91–151.   [79]

ORSHAN, G. (1963). Seasonal dimorphism of desert and Mediterranean chamaephytes and its significance as a factor in their water economy. *Symp. Brit. Ecol. Soc.* **3,** 206–222.   [157]

OSMOND, C. B., ZIEGLER, H., STICHLER, W. and TRIMBORN, P. (1975). Carbon isotope discrimination in alpine succulent plants supposed to be capable of crassulacean acid metabolism (CAM). *Oecologia* **18,** 209–218.   [61]

OSONUBI, O. and DAVIES, W. J. (1978). Solute accumulation in leaves and roots of woody plants subjected to water stress. *Oecologia* **32,** 323–332.   [126, 152, 168]

OWEN, P. C. (1952). The relation of germination of wheat to water potential. *J. exp. Bot.* **3,** 188–203.   [147]

OWUSU-BENNOAH, E. and WILD, A. (1979). Autoradiography of the depletion zone of phosphate around onion roots in the presence of vesicular–arbuscular mycorrhiza. *New Phytol.* **82,** 133–140.   [113]

OZANNE, P. G. and SHAW, T. C. (1967). Phosphate sorption by soils as a measure of the phosphate requirement for pasture growth. *Aust. J. agric. Sci.* **18,** 601–612.   [77]

PAREEK, R. P. and GAUR, A. C. (1973). Organic acids in the rhizosphere of *Zea mays* and *Phaseolus aureus* plants. *Plant and Soil* **39,** 441–444.   [110, 294]

PARKER, J. (1968). Drought-resistance mechanisms. *In* "Water Deficits and Plant Growth" (Ed. T. T. Kozlowski), vol. 1, pp. 195–234. Academic Press, New York and London.   [150, 152, 157, 159, 162, 163]

PARKER, J. (1972). Protoplasmic resistance to water deficits. *In* "Water Deficits and Plant Growth" (Ed. T. T. Kozlowski), vol. 3, pp. 125–176. Academic Press, New York and London.   [162, 163]

PARNAS, I. (1961). The cellulolytic activity in the snail *Levantina hierosolyma* Boiss. *J. cell. comp. Physiol.* **58,** 195–201.   [281]

PASSIOURA, J. B. (1963). A mathematical model for the uptake of ions from the soil solution. *Plant and Soil* **18,** 225–238.   [79]

PASSIOURA, J. B. (1972). The effect of root geometry on the yield of wheat growing on stored water. *Aust. J. agric. Res.* **23,** 745–752.   [150]

PASSIOURA, J. B. (1976). The control of water movement through plants. *In* "Transport and Transfer Processes in Plants", pp. 373–380. Academic Press, London and New York.   [161]

PAYNE, D. W., THORPE, N. A. and DONALDSON, E. M. (1972). Cellulolytic activity and a study of the bacterial population in the digestive tract of *Scrobicularia plana* (da Costa). *Proc. Malacl. Soc. London* **40**, 147–160. [282]

PEACOCK, J. M. (1975). Temperature and leaf growth in *Lolium perenne*. II. The site of temperature perception. *J. appl. Ecol.* **12**, 115–123. [172]

PEARSALL, W. H. (1938). The soil complex in relation to plant communities. *J. Ecol.* **26**, 180–193. [86]

PEARSALL, W. H. (1968). "Mountains and Moorlands", 2nd Edn. Collins, Glasgow. [178]

PENMAN, H. L. (1963). "Vegetation and Hydrology". Technical Bulletin no. 53, Commonwealth Bureau of Soils. [168]

PETERSON, H. B. and NIELSEN, R. F. (1978). Heavy metals in relation to plant growth on mine and mill wastes. *In* "Environmental Management of Mineral Wastes" (Ed. G. T. Goodman and M. J. Chadwick), pp. 297–310. Sijthoff and Noordhoff, Alphen. [206]

PETERSON, P. J. (1969). The distribution of zinc—65 in *Agrostis tenuis* Sibth. and *A. stolonifera* L. tissues. *J. exp. Bot.* **20**, 863–887. [221]

PHILIPSON, J. J. and COUTTS, M. P. (1978). The tolerance of tree roots to waterlogging. III. Oxygen transport in lodgepole pine and Sitka spruce of primary structure. *New Phytol.* **80**, 341–349. [236]

PIGOTT, C. D. (1975). Experimental studies on the influence of climate on the geographical distribution of plants. *Weather for 1975* 82–90. [172]

PISEK, A., LARCHER, W., MOSER, W. and PACK, I. (1969). Kardinale Temperaturbereiche der Photosynthese und Grenztemperaturen des Lebens der Blätter verschiedener Spermatophyten. III. Temperaturabhängigkeit und optimaler Temperaturbereich der Netto-Photosynthese. *Flora* **B158**, 608–630. [190]

PISEK, A., LARCHER, W., VEGIS, A. and NAPP-ZIN, K. (1973). The normal temperature range. *In* "Temperature and Life" (Eds. H. Precht, J. Christopherson, H. Hensel and W. Larcher), pp. 102–194. Springer-Verlag, Berlin. [172, 173, 189, 190, 192]

PITMAN, M. G. and CRAM, W. J. (1973). Regulation of inorganic ion transport in plants. *In* "Ion Transport in Plants" (Ed. W. P. Anderson), pp. 465–482. Academic Press, London and New York. [72, 101]

POLONENKO, D. R. and MAYFIELD, C. I. (1979). A direct observation technique for studies of rhizoplane and rhizosphere colonisation. *Plant and Soil* **51**, 405–420. [108]

PONNAMPERUMA, F. N. (1972). The chemistry of submerged soils. *Adv. Agron.* **24**, 29–96. [233, 244]

PORATH, E. and POLJAKOFF-MAYBER, A. (1964). Effect of salinity on metabolic pathways in pea root tips. *Israel J. Bot.* **13**,, 115–121. [210]

POWELL, C. L. (1975). Rushes and sedges are non-mycotrophic. *Plant and Soil* **42**, 481–484. [114]

POWELL, C. L. (1976). Mycorrhizal fungi stimulate clover growth in New Zealand hill country soils. *Nature* **264**, 436–438. [114]

[172] PRECHT, H., CHRISTOPHERSON, J., HENSEL, H. and LARCHER, W. (1973). "Temperature and Life". Springer-Verlag, Berlin.

[227] PRISCO, J. T. and O'LEARY, J. W. (1972). Enhancement of intact bean leaf senescence by NaCl salinity. *Physiol. Plant* **27**, 95–100.

[93, 201, 209, 216, 225] PROCTOR, J. (1971a). The plant ecology of serpentine. II. Plant response to serpentine soils. *J. Ecol.* **59**, 397–410.

[93, 201, 209, 216, 225] PROCTOR, J. (1971b). The plant ecology of serpentine. III. The influence of a high magnesium/calcium ratio and high nickel and chromium levels in some British and Swedish serpentine soils. *J. Ecol.* **59**, 827–842.

[63] QUEIROZ, O. (1977). CAM: rhythms of enzyme capacity and activity in adaptive control mechanisms. In "Encyclopaedia of Plant Physiology: Photosynthesis Vol. 2" (Ed. M. Gibbs and E. Latzko), pp. 126–137. Springer-Verlag, Berlin.

[9] RADFORD, P. J. (1967). Growth analysis formulae—their use and abuse. *Crop Sci.* **7**, 171–175.

[102] RAPER, D. R., OSMOND, D. L., WANN, M. and WEEKS, W. W. (1978). Interdependence of root and shoot activities in determining nitrogen uptake rate of roots. *Bot. Gaz.* **139**, 289–294.

[135] RASCHKE, K. (1975). Stomatal action. *Ann. Rev. Pl. Physiol.* **26**, 309–340.

[153, 158] RASCHKE, K. (1976). How stomata resolve the dilemma of opposing priorities. *Phil. Trans. R. Soc. Lond.* **B273**, 551–560.

[114] READ, D. J., KOUCHEKI, H. K. and HODGSON, J. (1976). Vesicular-arbuscular mycorrhiza in natural vegetation. I. The occurrence of infection. *New Phytol.* **77**, 641–653.

[235] REID, D. M. and CROZIER, A. (1971). Effects of waterlogging on the gibberellin content and growth of tomato plants. *J. exp. Bot.* **22**, 39–48.

[227] REILLY, A. and REILLY, C. (1973). Copper-induced chlorosis in *Becium homblei*. *Plant and Soil* **38**, 671–674.

[252] REINERT, R. A., HEAGLE, A. S. and HECK, W. W. (1975). Plant responses to pollutant combinations. In "Responses of Plants to Air Pollution" (Eds. J. B. Mudd and T. T. Kozlowski), pp. 159–175. Academic Press, London and New York.

[46] RHODES, I. (1969). Yield, canopy structure and light interception in two ryegrass varieties in mixed culture and monoculture. *J. Br. Grassld Soc.* **24**, 123–127.

[111, 113] RHODES, L. H. and GERDEMANN, J. W. (1975). Phosphate uptake zones of mycorrhizal and non-mycorrhizal onions. *New Phytol.* **75**, 555–562.

[291] RICE, E. L. (1974). "Allelopathy". Academic Press, New York and London.

[293] RICE, E. L. and PANCHOLY, S. K. (1972). Inhibition of nitrification by climax ecosystems. *Amer. J. Bot.* **59**, 1033–1040.

[293] RICE, E. L. and PANCHOLY, S. K. (1973). Inhibition of nitrification by climax ecosystems. II. Additional evidence and possible role of tannins. *Amer. J. Bot.* **60**, 691–702.

[293] RICE, E. L. and PANCHOLY, S. K. (1974). Inhibition of nitrification by climax ecosystems. III. Inhibitors other than tannins. *Amer. J. Bot.* **61**, 1095–1103.

RICHARDS, A. J. (1972). The *Taraxacum* Flora of the British Isles. *Watsonia.* **9,** Suppl.   [89]

RICHARDS, F. J. (1969). The quantitative analysis of growth. *In* "Plant Physiology" (Ed. F. C. Steward), vol. VA, pp. 1–76. Academic Press, London and New York.   [9]

RICHTER, H. (1976). The water status in the plant. Experimental evidence. *In* "Water and Plant Life" (Eds. O. L. Lange, L. Kappen and E.-D. Schulze). *Ecological Studies* **19,** 42–58. Springer-Verlag, Berlin.   [153, 163]

RILEY, D. and BARBER, S. A. (1971). Effect of ammonium and nitrate fertilisation on phosphorus uptake as related to root-induced pH changes at the root-soil interface. *Soil Sci. Soc. Amer. Proc.* **35,** 301–306.   [86, 215]

RITTER-STUDNIČKA, J. (1971). Zellensaft-Analysen zum Problem der Serpentinvegetation. *Österr. Bot. Z.* **119,** 410–431.   [225]

RORISON, I. H. (1958). The effect of aluminium on legume nutrition. *In* "Nutrition of the Legumes" (Ed. E. G. Hallsworth), pp. 43–61. Butterworth, London.   [211]

RORISON, I. H. (1965). The effect of aluminium on the uptake and incorporation of phosphate by excised sainfoin roots. *New Phytol.* **64,** 23–27.   [211]

RORISON, I. H. (1968). The response to phosphorus of some ecologically distinct plant species. I. Growth rates and phosphorus absorption. *New Phytol.* **67,** 913–923.   [91, 92]

RORISON, I. H. (1971). The use of nutrients in the control of the floristic composition of grassland. *In* "The Scientific Management of Plant and Animal Communities for Conservation". *Brit. Ecol. Soc. Symp.* **11,** 65–77.   [71, 88]

RORISON, I. H. (1975). Nitrogen source and metal toxicity. *J. Sci. Fd. Agric.* **26,** 1426.   [201, 215]

RORISON, I. H., SUTTON, C. D. and HALLSWORTH, E. G. (1958). The effects of climatic conditions on aluminium and manganese toxicities. *In* "Nutrition of the Legumes" (Ed. E. G. Hallsworth), pp. 62–68. Butterworth, London.   [215]

ROSS, J. (1970). Mathematical models of photosynthesis in a plant stand. *In* "Prediction and Measurement of Photosynthetic Productivity" (Ed. I. Setlik), pp. 29–45. Centre for Agricultural Publishing and Documentation, Wageningen.   [37]

ROSSWALL, T, and HEAL, O. W. (Eds.) (1975). "Structure and Function of Tundra Ecosystems". *Ecol. Bull.* **20**. Swedish Natural Science Research Council, Stockholm.   [182]

ROSSWALL, T., FLOWER-ELLIS, J. G. K., JOHANSSON, L. G., JONSSON, S., RYDEN, B. E. and SONESSON, M. (1975). Stordalen (Abisko). Sweden. *In* "Structure and Function of Tundra Ecosystems" (Eds. T. Rosswall and O. W. Heal). *Ecol. Bull.* **20,** 265–294. Swedish Natural Science Research Council, Stockholm.   [185]

ROVIRA, A. D. (1969). Plant root exudates. *Bot. Rev.* **39, 35–57.**   [108, 294]

ROVIRA, A. D. and BOWEN, G. D. (1973). The influence of root temperature on ^{14}C assimilates profiles in wheat roots. *Planta* **114,** 101–107.   [176]

ROVIRA, A. D. and DAVEY, C. B. (1974). Biology of the rhizosphere. *In* "The

Plant Root and its Environment" (Ed. E. W. Carson), pp. 153–240.
[108] University Press of Virginia.

ROVIRA, A. D., NEWMAN, E. I., BOWEN, H. J. and CAMPBELL, R. (1974).
Quantitative assessment of the rhizoplane microflora by direct microscopy.
[108, 110] *Soil Biol. Biochem.* **6,** 211–216.

ROZEMA, J. (1976). An ecophysiological study of the response to salt of four
[213, 216] halophytic and glycophytic *Juncus* species. *Flora* **165,** 197–209.

[120, 130, RUSSELL, E. W. (1973). "Soil Conditions and Plant Growth", 10th Edn.
131, 232, 246] Longman, London.

RUSSELL, R. S. (1940). Physiological and ecological studies on an arctic
vegetation. II. The development of vegetation in relation to nitrogen and
[191] soil micro-organisms on Jan Mayen Island. *J. Ecol.* **28,** 269–288.

[148, 233] RUSSELL, R. S. (1977). "Plant Root Systems". McGraw-Hill, London.

RUSSELL, R. S. and CLARKSON, D. T. (1976). Ion transport in root systems. *In*
"Perspectives in Experimental Biology" (Ed. N. Sunderland), vol. 2,
[104] pp. 401–411. Pergamon, Oxford.

RUTTER, A. J. (1968). Water consumption by forests. *In* "Water Deficits and
Plant Growth" (Ed. T. T. Kozlowski), vol. 2, pp. 23–84. Academic Press,
[164] New York and London.

SAKAI, A. (1970). Freezing resistance in willows from different climates.
[193, 194] *Ecology* **51,** 485–491.

SAKAI, A. and WEISER, C. J. (1973). Freezing resistance of trees in North
[193] America with reference to tree regions. *Ecology* **54,** 118–126.

SALISBURY, E. J. (1916). The oak-hornbeam woods of Hertfordshire. *J. Ecol.*
[38] **4,** 83–117.

SALISBURY, E. J. (1952). "Downs and Dunes: their Plant Life and its En-
[150] vironment". Bell, London.

[32] SALISBURY, F. B. (1963). "The Flowering Process". Pergamon, Oxford.

SALISBURY, F. B. and SPOMER, G. G. (1964). Leaf temperatures of alpine
[186] plants in the field. *Planta* **60,** 497–505.

SALSAC, L. (1973). Absorption du calcium par les racines de Féverole (cal-
[96] cicole) et de Lupin jaune (calcifuge). *Physiol. Veg.* **11,** 95–119.

SANDERS, F. E. and TINKER, P. B. (1973). Phosphate flow into mycorrhizal
[111, 112] roots. *Pestic. Sci.* **4,** 385–395.

[184, 185, SAVILE, D. B. O. (1972). "Arctic Adaptations in Plants". Monograph 6,
189, 193, 197] Canada Department of Agriculture, Ottawa.

SCHILLER, W. (1974). Versuche zur Kupferresistenz bei Schwermetallö-
[224] kotypen von *Silene cucubalus* Wib. *Flora* **163,** 327–341.

SCHOLANDER, P. F., VAN DAM, L. and SCHOLANDER, S. I. (1955). Gas ex-
[236] change in the roots of mangroves. *Am. J. Bot.* **42,** 92–98.

SCHULZE, E. D. (1972). Die Wirkung von kicht und Temperatur auf den CO$_2$-
Gaswechsel verschiedener Lebensformen aus der Krautschicht eines
[55] montanen Buchenwaldes. *Oecologia* **9,** 235–238.

SHEEHY, J. E. and COOPER, J. P. (1973). Light interception, photosynthetic activity and crop growth rate in canopies of six temperate forage grasses. *J. appl. Ecol.* **10,** 235–250.   [51, 64, 65]

SHEEHY, J. E. and PEACOCK, J. M. (1975). Canopy photosynthesis and crop growth rate of eight temperate forage grasses. *J. exp. Bot.* **26,** 679–691.   [46]

SHELDON, J. C. (1974). The behaviour of seeds in soil. III. The influence of seed morphology and the behaviour of seedlings on the establishment of plants from surface-lying seeds. *J. Ecol.* **62,** 47–66.   [146]

SHERIFF, D. W. (1977a). Evaporation sites and distillation in leaves. *Ann. Bot.* (N.S.) **41,** 1081–1082.   [120]

SHERIFF, D. W. (1977b). The effect of humidity on water uptake by, and viscous flow resistance of, excised leaves of a number of species: physiological and anatomical observations. *J. exp. Bot.* **28,** 1399–1407.   [157]

SHERWIN, T. and SIMON, E. W. (1969). The appearance of lactic acid in *Phaseolus* seeds germinating under wet conditions. *J. exp. Bot.* **20,** 776–785.   [241]

SHIRLEY, H. L. (1929). The influence of light intensity and light quality on growth of plants. *Am. J. Bot.* **16,** 354–390.   [57]

SHROPSHIRE, W. (1971). Photoinduced parental control of seed germination and the spectral quality of solar radiation. *Solar Energy* **15,** 99–105.   [30, 34, 40]

SINGH, B. B., HADLEY, H. H. and BERNARD, R. L. (1971). Morphology of pubescence in soybeans and its relation to plant vigour. *Crop Sci.* **11,** 13–16.   [284]

SKENE, MACGREGOR (1924). "The Biology of Flowering Plants". Sidgwick and Jackson, London.   [52]

SLAYTER, R. O. (1967). "Plant-Water Relationships". Academic Press, London and New York.   [121, 142, 152]

SLAVIK, B. (1974). Methods of studying plant water relations. *Ecological Studies* **9**. Chapman and Hall, London.   [122]

SMALL, E. (1972). Photosynthetic rates in relation to nitrogen recycling as an adaptation to nutrient deficiency. *Can. J. Bot.* **50,** 2227–2233.   [75, 86]

SMITH, A. M. (1976). Ethylene in soil biology. *Ann. Rev. Phytopathology* **14,** 53–73.   [249, 250]

SMITH, A. M. and AP REES, T. (1979). Pathways of carbohydrate fermentation in the roots of marsh plants. *Planta* **146,** 327–334.   [243]

SMITH, F. A. (1973). The internal control of nitrate uptake into excised barley roots with differing salt contents. *New Phytol.* **72,** 769–782.   [96]

SMITH, K. A. (1977). Soil aeration. *Soil Sci.* **123,** 284–291.   [246]

SMITH, K. A. (1978). Ineffectiveness of ethylene as a regulator of soil microbial activity. *Soil Biol. Biochem.* **10,** 269–272.   [250]

SMITH, K. A. and DOWDELL, R. J. (1974). Field studies of the soil atmosphere. I. Relationship between ethylene, oxygen, soil moisture content and temperature. *J. Soil Sci.* **25,** 219–230.   [245]

SMITH, K. A. and JACKSON, M. B. (1974). Ethylene, waterlogging and plant growth. *A.R.C. Letcombe Lab. Ann. Rep.* 1973, 60–75.   [248, 249]

SMITH, K. A. and ROBERTSON, P. D. (1971). Effect of ethylene on root extension of cereals. *Nature* **234,** 148–149.   [248]

SMITH, P. F. (1962). Mineral analysis of plant tissues. *Ann. Rev. Pl. Physiol.* **13,**
[93]   81–108.

SNAYDON, R. W. (1970). Rapid population differentiation in a mosaic environment. I. The response of *Anthoxanthum odoratum* populations to soils.
[22]   *Evolution* **24,** 257–269.

SNAYDON, R. W. (1971). An analysis of competition between plants of *Trifolium repens* populations collected from contrasting soils. *J. appl. Ecol.* **8,**
[219, 272]   687–698.

SNAYDON, R. W. and BRADSHAW, A. D. (1961). Differential responses to
[92]   calcium within the species *Festuca ovina* L. *New Phytol.* **60,** 219–234.

SNAYDON, R. W. and BRADSHAW, A. D. (1969). Differences between natural populations of *Trifolium repens* L. in response to mineral nutrients. II.
[92]   Calcium, magnesium and potassium. *J. appl. Ecol.* **6,** 185–202.

SOUTHWOOD, T. R. E. (1973). The insect–plant relationship—an evolutionary perspective. *In* "Insect–plant Relationships" (Ed. H. F. van Emden). *Roy.*
[278, 282]   *Ent. Soc. Symp.* **6,** 3–30.

SPANSWICK, R. M. (1976). Symplastic transport in tissues. *In* "Transport in Plants IIB". *Encyclopaedia of Plant Physiology* **2,** 35–53. Springer-Verlag,
[138]   Berlin.

SPARLING, G. P. and TINKER, P. B. (1975). Mycorrhizas in Pennine grassland. *In* "Endomycorrhizas" (Eds. F. E. Sanders, B. Mosse and P. B. Tinker),
[114]   pp. 545–560. Academic Press, London and New York.

SPEDDING, D. J. (1969). Uptake of sulphur dioxide by barley leaves at low
[254]   sulphur dioxide concentrations. *Nature* **224,** 1229–1231.

STÅLFELT, M. G. (1972). "Plant Ecology". Trs Jarvis, M. S. and P. G.
[86]   Longman, London.

STARKEY, R. L. (1929). Some influences of the development of higher plants
[107]   upon the micro-organisms in the soil. *Soil Sci.* **27,** 319–334.

STEWART, G. R. and LEE, J. A. (1974). The role of proline accumulation in
[223, 224]   halophytes. *Planta* **120,** 279–289.

STEWART, G. R., LEE, J. A. and OREBAMJO, T. (1972). Nitrogen metabolism of halophytes. I. Nitrate reductase activity in *Suaeda maritima. New Phytol.* **71,**
[95]   263–267.

STEWART, G. R., LEE, J. A. and OREBAMJO, T. (1973). Nitrogen metabolism of halophytes. 1. Nitrate reductase activity in *Suaeda maritima. New Phytol.*
[95]   539–546.

STOCKER, O. (1976). The water-photosynthesis syndrome and the geographical plant distribution in the Sahara deserts. *In* "Water and Plant Life" (Eds. O. L. Lange, L. Kappen and E.-D. Schulze). *Ecological Studies*
[154]   **19,** 506–521. Springer-Verlag, Berlin.

STONE, E. C. (1957a). Dew as an ecological factor. I. A review of the literature.
[152]   *Ecology* **38,** 407–413.

STONE, E. C. (1957b). Dew as an ecological factor. II. The effect of artificial dew on the survival of *Pinus ponderosa* and associated species. *Ecology* **38,**
[152]   414–422.

STOREY, R., AHMAD, N. and WYN JONES, R. G. (1977). Taxonomic and ecological aspects of the distribution of glycine-betaine and related compounds in plants. *Oecologia* **27**, 319–332.   [224]

STOUTJESDIJK, P. H. (1972). Spectral transmission curves of some types of leaf canopies with a note on seed germination. *Acta Bot. Neerl.* **21**, 185–191.   [36, 39]

STOUTJESDIJK, P. H. (1974). The open shade, an interesting micro-climate. *Acta Bot. Neerl.* **23**, 125–130.   [33, 42]

STREET, H. E. (1963). "Plant Metabolism". Pergamon, Oxford.   [175]

STREICHER, S. L., GURNEY, E. G. and VALENTINE, R. C. (1972). The nitrogen fixation genes. *Nature* **239**, 495–499.   [289]

SUMNER, A. T. (1968). A substrate-film method of the histochemical detection of cellulase. *Histochemie* **14**, 160–168.   [282]

SUTCLIFFE, J. (1977). "Plants and Temperature". Arnold, London.   [172, 174, 175, 195]

SZEICZ, G. (1974). Solar radiation in crop canopies. *J. appl. Ecol.* **11**, 1117–1156.   [33]

TADANO, T. (1975). Devices of rice roots to tolerate high iron concentrations in the growth media. *Jpn Agric. Res. Quart.* **9**, 34–39.   [215]

TAERUM, R. (1970). Comparative shoot and root growth studies of six grasses in Kenya. *East Afr. Agr. and For. J.* **36**, 94–113.   [150]

TAL, M. (1971). Salt tolerance in the wild relatives of the cultivated tomato: response of *Lycopersicon esculentum, L. peruvianum,* and *L. esculentum minor* to sodium chloride solutions. *Aust. J. agric. Res.* **22**, 631–638.   [219]

TAYLOR, G. E. and MURDY, W. H. (1975). Population differentiation of an annual plant species, *Geranium carolianum,* in response to sulphur dioxide. *Bot. Gaz.* **136**, 212–215.   [259]

TAYLOR, O. C., THOMPSON, C. R., TINGLEY, D. T. and REINERT, R. A. (1975). Oxides of nitrogen. *In* "Responses of Plants to Air Pollution" (Eds. J. B. Mudd and T. T. Kozlowski), pp. 121–139. Academic Press, New York and London.   [259]

TEAL, J. M. and KANWISHER, J. W. (1966). Gas transport in the marsh grass *Spartina alterniflora. J. exp. Bot.* **17**, 355–361.   [235]

TENHUNEN, J. D., YOCUM, C. S. and GATES, D. M. (1976). Development of a photosynthesis model with an emphasis on ecological applications. I. Theory. *Oecologia* **26**, 89–100.   [53]

TERBORGH, J. (1973). On the notion of favourableness in plant ecology. *Amer. Nat.* **107**, 481–501.   [4]

THELLIER, M. (1973). Electrokinetic formulation of ionic absorption by plant samples. *In* "Ion Transport in Plants" (Ed. W. P. Anderson), pp. 47–64. Academic Press, London and New York.   [98]

THOMAS, M. D. (1951). Gas damage to plants. *Ann. Rev. Pl. Physiol.* **2**, 293–322.   [252]

THOMPSON, K., GRIME, J. P. and MASON, G. (1977). Seed germination in response to diurnal fluctuations of temperature. *Nature* **267**, 147–149.   [172]

THOMSON, W. W., DUGGER, W. M. and PALMER, R. L. (1966). Effects of ozone on the fine structure of the palisade parenchyma cells of bean leaves. *Can. J. Bot.* **44**, 1677–1682.   [255]

[146]
THURSTON, J. M. (1960). Dormancy in weed seeds. *Symp. Brit. Ecol. Soc.* **1,** 69–82.

[4]
THURSTON, J. M. (1968). The effect of liming and fertilizers on the botanical composition of permanent grassland, and on the yield of hay. *Brit. Ecol. Soc. Symp.* **9,** 3–10.

[225]
TIFFIN, L. D. (1972). Translocation of micronutrients in plants. *In* "Micronutrients in Agriculture" (Eds. J. J. Mortrest, P. M. Giodano and W. L. Lindsay), pp. 199–229. Soil Science Soc. Amer., Madison.

[219]
TIKU, B. L. and SNAYDON, R. W. (1971). Salinity tolerance within the grass species *Agrostis stolonifera. Plant and Soil* **35,** 421–431.

[79, 80, 81]
TINKER, P. B. (1969). The transport of ions in the soil around plant roots. *In* "Ecological Aspects of the Mineral Nutrition of Plants". *Brit. Ecol. Soc. Symp.* **9,** 135–148.

[111]
TINKER, P. B. (1978). Effects of vesicular-arbuscular mycorrhizas on plant nutrition and growth. *Physiol. Veg.* **16,** 743–751.

[277]
TITMAN, D. (1976). Ecological competition between algae: experimental confirmation of resource-based competition theory. *Science* **192,** 463–465.

[182–5, 187, 195]
TRANQUILLINI, W. (1964). The physiology of plants at high altitudes. *Ann. Rev. Pl. Physiol.* **15,** 345–362.

[113]
TRAPPE, J. M. (1962). Fungus associates of ectotrophic mycorrhizae. *Bot. Rev.* **28,** 538–606.

[223]
TREICHEL, S. (1975). Der Einfluss von NaCl auf die Prolinkonzentration verschiedener Halophyten. *Z. Pflanzenphysiol.* **76,** 56–68.

[45]
TRENBATH, B. R. and HARPER, J. L. (1973). Neighbour effects in the genus *Avena*. I. Comparison of crop species. *J. appl. Ecol.* **10,** 379–400.

[289]
TRINICK, M. J. (1973). Symbiosis between *Rhizobium* and the non-legume *Trema aspera. Nature* **244,** 459–460.

[62]
TROUGHTON, J. H., MOONEY, H. A., BERRY, J. A. and VERITY, D. (1977). Variable carbon isotope ratios of *Dudleya* species growing in natural environments. *Oecologia* **30,** 307–311.

[41]
TUCKER, D. J. (1975). Far-red light as a suppressor of side-shoot growth in the tomato. *Plant Sci. Letters* **5,** 127–130.

[46]
TURESSON, G. (1922). The genotypical response of the plant species to the habitat. *Hereditas* **3,** 211–350.

[221]
TURNER, R. G. (1969). Heavy metal tolerance in plants. *In* "Ecological Aspects of the Mineral Nutrition of Plants". *Brit. Ecol. Soc. Symp.* **9,** 399–410.

[220, 221]
TYLER, G. (1976). Soil factors controlling metal ion absorption in the wood anemone *Anemone nemorosa. Oikos* **27,** 71–80.

[241, 242]
TYLER, P. D. and CRAWFORD, R. M. M. (1970). The role of shikimic acid in waterlogged roots and rhizomes of *Iris pseudacorus* L. *J. exp. Bot.* **21,** 677–682.

[254, 255]
UNSWORTH, M. H., BISCOE, P. V. and BLACK, V. (1976). Analysis of gas exchange between plants and polluted atmospheres. *In* "Effects of Air Pollutants on Plants" (Ed. T. A. Mansfield), pp. 5–16. Cambridge University Press, Cambridge.

VAARTAJA, O. (1954). Photoperiodic ecotypes of trees. *Can. J. Bot.* **32**, 392–399. [43]

VAN BEERS, W. F. J. (1962). Acid sulphate soils. *Int. Inst. Land Reclam. Imp. Bull.* **3**. [204]

VAN DEN BERGH, J. P. (1969). Distribution of pasture plants in relation to the chemical properties of the soil. *In* "Ecological Aspects of the Mineral Nutrition of Plants". *Brit. Ecol. Soc. Symp.* **9**, 11–23. [105]

VAN DEN HONERT, T. H. (1948). Water transport as a catenary process. *Disc. Faraday Soc.* **3**, 146–53. [138]

VAN DER PIJL, L. (1969). "Principles of Dispersion in Higher plants". Springer-Verlag, Berlin. [147]

VAN EMDEN, H. F., EASTOP, V. F., HUGHES, R. D. and WAY, M. J. (1969). The ecology of *Myzus persicae*. *Ann. Rev. Ent.* **14**, 197–270. [283]

VAN STEVENINCK, R. F. M. (1965). The significance of calcium in the apparent permeability of cell membranes and the effects of substitution with other divalent cations. *Physiol. Plant* **18**, 54–59. [208]

VARTAPETIAN, B. B. (1978). Life without oxygen. *In* "Plant Life in Anaerobic Environments" (Eds. D. D. Hook and R. M. M. Crawford), pp. 1–11. Ann Arbor Science Publishers Inc., Michigan. [235]

VEIHMEYER, F. J. and HENDRICKSON, A. H. (1948). Soil density and root penetration. *Soil Sci.* **65**, 487–493. [105]

VIETS, F. G. (1965). The plant's need for and use of nitrogen. *In* "Soil Nitrogen" (Eds. W. V. Bartholomew and F. E. Clark), pp. 543–554. Agronomy Series 10. Academic Press, London and New York. [105]

VILLIERS, T. A. (1972). Seed dormancy. *In* "Seed Biology" (Ed. T. T. Kozlowski), vol. 2, pp. 219–281. Academic Press, London and New York. [144]

VINCE-PRUE, D. and COCKSHULL, K. E. (1981). Photoperiodism and crop production. *In* "Physiological Processes Limiting Plant Production". *30th Easter School in Agricultural Science, University of Nottingham*. Butterworth, London. [34]

VOGEL, S. (1968). "Sun" leaves and "shade" leaves: differences in convective heat dissipation. *Ecology* **49**, 1203–1204. [54]

VON WILLERT, D. J. (1974). Der Einfluss von NaCl auf die Atmung and Aktivität der Malatdehydrogenase bei einigen Halophyten und Glykophyten. *Oecologia* **14**, 127–137. [223]

VON WILLERT, D. J., TREICHEL, J., KIRST, G. O. and CURDTS, E. (1976). Environmentally controlled changes of phosphoenolpyruvate carboxylases in *Mesembryanthemum*. *Phytochem.* **15**, 1435–1436. [63]

WAINWRIGHT, S. J. and WOOLHOUSE, H. W. (1975). Physiological mechanisms of heavy metal tolerance in plants. *In* "The Ecology of Resource Degradation and Renewal". *Brit. Ecol. Soc. Symp.* **15**, 231–258. [209, 216, 229]

WALKER, D. A. (1973). Photosynthetic induction phenomena and the light activation of ribulose diphosphate carboxylase. *New Phytol.* **72**, 209–231. [58]

WALLACE, W. (1973). A nitrate reductase inactivating enzyme from the maize root. *Plant Physiol.* **52**, 197–201. [94]

[230] WALLEY, K. A., KHAN, M. S. I. and BRADSHAW, A. D. (1974). The potential for evolution of heavy metal tolerance in plants. I. Copper and zinc tolerance in *Agrostis tenuis. Heredity* **32**, 309–319.

[149] WALTER, H. (1963). The water supply of desert plants. *Symp. Brit. Ecol. Soc.* **3**, 199–205.

[128] WALTER, H. and LIETH, H. (1960). "Klimadiagramm Weltatlas". Fischer Verlag, Jena.

[182] WARDLE, P. (1974). Alpine timberlines. *In* "Arctic and Alpine Environments" (Eds. J. D. Ives and R. G. Barry), pp. 371–402. Methuen, London.

[192] WAREING, P. F. (1969). The control of bud dormancy in seed plants. *Symp. Soc. Exp. Biol.* **23**, 241–262.

[172, 175] WASSINK, E. C. (1972). Some notes on temperature relations in plant physiological processes. *Meded. Landbouw. Wageningen* **72** (25), 1–15.

[64] WATSON, D. J. (1947). Comparative physiological studies on the growth of field crops. I. Variation in net assimilation rate and leaf area between species and varieties, and within and between years. *Ann. Bot.* (N.S.) **11**, 41–76.

[277] WATT, A. S. (1947). Pattern and process in the plant community. *J. Ecol.* **35**, 1–22.

[172] WATTS, W. R. (1973). Soil temperature and leaf expansion in *Zea mays. Expl. Agric.* **9**, 1–8.

[150] WEAVER, J. E. (1958). Classification of root systems of forbs of grassland and a consideration of their significance. *Ecology* **39**, 393–401.

[61] WEBSTER, G. L., BROWN, W. V. and SMITH, B. N. (1975). Systematics of photosynthetic carbon fixation pathways in Euphorbia. *Taxon* **24**, 27–34.

[130, 131] WEBSTER, R. and BECKETT, P. H. T. (1972). Matric suctions to which soils in South Central England drain. *J. agric. Sci.* **78**, 379–387.

[105] WELBANK, P. J. (1961). A study of the nitrogen and water factors in competition with *Agropyron repens* (L.) Beau. *Ann. Bot.* **25**, 116–137.

[255] WELLBURN, A. R., MAJERNIK, O. and WELLBURN, A. M. (1972). Effects of SO_2 and NO_2 polluted air upon the ultrastructure of chloroplasts. *Environ. Pollut.* **3**, 37–49.

[274] WELLS, T. C. E. (1971). A comparison of the effects of sheep grazing and mechanical cutting on the structure and botanical composition of chalk grassland. *In* "The Scientific Management of Animal and Plant Communities for Conservation" (Eds. E. Duffey and A. S. Watt). *Brit. Ecol. Soc. Symp.* **11**, 497–516. Blackwell, Oxford.

[172, 176] WENT, F. W. (1953). The effect of temperature on plant growth. *Ann. Rev. Pl. Physiol.* **4**, 347–362.

[24] WENT, F. W. (1974). Reflections and Speculations. *Ann. Rev. Pl. Physiol.* **25**, 1–26.

[100] WHITE, R. E. (1973). Studies on mineral ion absorption by plants. II. The interaction between metabolic activity and the rate of phosphorus uptake. *Plant and Soil* **38**, 509–523.

WHITEHEAD, F. H. (1971). Comparative autecology as a guide to plant distribution. *In* "The Scientific Management of Animal and Plant Communities for Conservation". *Symp. Brit. Ecol. Soc.* **11**, 167–176. [43]

WHITTAKER, R. H. (1975). "Communities and Ecosystems". MacMillan, London. [66]

WHITTAKER, R. H. and WOODWELL, C. M. (1969). Structure, production, and diversity of the oak-pine forest at Brookhaven, New York. *J. Ecol.* **57**, 155–174. [273]

WIGNARAJAH, K. and GREENWAY, H. (1976). Effect of anaerobiosis on activities of alcohol dehydrogenase and pyruvate decarboxylase in roots of *Zea mays. New Phytol.* **77**, 575–584. [239]

WILD, A., SKARLOU, V., CLEMENT, C. R. and SNAYDON, R. W. (1974). Comparison of potassium uptake by four plant species grown in sand and in flowing solution culture. *J. appl. Ecol.* **11**, 801–812. [99, 100, 104, 116]

WILLIAMS, D. E. (1961). The absorption of potassium as influenced by its concentration in the nutrient medium. *Plant and Soil* **15**, 387–399. [99]

WILLIAMS, D. E., VLAMIS, J., HALL, H. and GOVANO, K. D. (1971). Urbanisation, fertilisation, and manganese toxicity in Alameda mustard. *Calif. Agric.* **25**, 8–14. [227]

WILLIAMS, R. F. (1964). The growth of grasses. *In* "Grasses and Grasslands" (Ed. C. Barnard), pp. 89–101. MacMillan, London. [9]

WILLIAMSON, M. H. (1972). "The Analysis of Biological Populations". Arnold, London. [262]

WILLIS, A. J. (1963). Braunton Burrows: the effects on the vegetation of the addition of mineral nutrients to the dune soils. *J. Ecol.* **51**, 353–374. [90]

WILMOTT, A. and MOORE, P. D. (1973). Adaptation to light intensity in *Silene alba* and *S. dioica. Oikos* **24**, 458–464. [56]

WILSON, J. W. (1966). An analysis of plant growth and its control in arctic environments. *Ann. Bot.* **30**, 383–402. [191, 194]

WINTER, K. (1974). Einfluss von Wasserstress auf die Aktivität der Phosphoenolypyruvat—Carboxylase bei *Mesembryanthemum crystallinum. Planta* **121**, 147–153. [63]

WOLEDGE, J. (1971). The effect of light intensity during growth on the subsequent rate of photosynthesis of leaves of tall fescue. *Ann. Bot.* (N.S.) **35**, 311–322. [56]

WOODELL, S. R. J., MOONEY, H. A. and HILL, A. J. (1969). The behaviour of *Larrea divaricata* (creosote bush) in response to rainfall in California. *J. Ecol.* **57**, 37–44. [163]

WOODS, D. B. and TURNER, N. C. (1971). Stomatal responses to changing light by four tree species of varying shade tolerance. *New Phytol.* **70**, 77–84. [35]

WOOLHOUSE, H. W. (1966). The effect of bicarbonate on the uptake of iron in four different species. *New Phytol.* **65**, 372–375. [71]

WRIGHT, K. E. (1943). Internal precipitation of phosphorus in relation to aluminium toxicity. *Plant Physiol.* **18**, 708. [90]

WU, L. and ANTONOVICS, J. (1975). Zinc and copper uptake by *Agrostis stolonifera*, tolerant to both zinc and copper. *New Phytol.* **75**, 231–237. [218]

[230, 231] WU, L. and BRADSHAW, A. D. (1972). Aerial pollution and the rapid evolution of copper tolerance. *Nature* **238,** 167.

[163] YANG, T. W. (1967). Ecotypic variation in *Larrea divaricata*. *Am. J. Bot.* **54,** 1041–1044.

[227] YEO, A. R., LAUCHLI, A., KRAMER, D. and GULLASCH, J. (1977). Ion measurements by X-ray microanalysis in unfixed, frozen, hydrated plant cells of species differing in salt tolerance. *Planta* **134,** 35–38.

[175] YUDKIN, M. and OFFORD, R. (1973). "Comprehensible Biochemistry". Longman, London.

[53] ZELITCH, I. (1971). "Photosynthesis, Photorespiration, and Plant Productivity". Academic Press, London and New York.

[256] ZIEGLER, I. (1972). The effect of SO_2 on the activity of ribulose-1, 5-diphosphate carboxylase in isolated spinach chloroplasts. *Planta* **103,** 155–163.

[167] ZIMMERMANN, M. H. (1978). Hydraulic architecture of some diffuse-porous trees. *Can. J. Bot.* **56,** 2286–2295.

[165, 166, 167] ZIMMERMANN, M. H. and BROWN, C. L. (1971). "Trees: Structure and Function". Springer-Verlag, New York.

[167] ZIMMERMANN, M. H. and McDONOUGH, J. (1978). Dysfunction in the flow of food. *In* "Plant Disease" (Eds. J. G. Horsfall and E. B. Cowling), vol. 3, pp. 117–140. Academic Press, New York and London.

SYSTEMATIC INDEX

SUBJECT INDEX

A

Abscisic acid, 102
  stomatal opening, 135
Abscission, 168
Acetaldehyde, 233, 238
Acidification, 85–86
Adaptive responses, 16
  "pre-adaptation", 20
Adsorption of ions, 74
Aerenchyma, 235–236
After-ripening, 144
Algae, 12, 30
Alkaloids, 278, 286
Allelopathy, 262, 291–293
  and diversity, 292
  and succession, 293
  in chaparral, 291–292
  in grassland, 292
  microbial effects, 293
  occurrence, 291
Alpine environments, 43, 180
Aluminium, 201–205
  and iron deficiency, 218
  binding by roots, 218
  causes for toxicity, 206
  cell division, 211, 219
  effects on seedling growth, 215
  excretion, 225
  membrane damage, 209
  phosphate precipitation, 208
Amelioration, 24, 212
Amino-acids, 278, 286
Ammonium, 74–75, 86–87
  adsorption by soil, 75
  uptake, 215
Annuals, 10, 19, 24, 149, 266, 277, 280

B

Anthocyanin, 185, 187
Ants, 281
Aphids, 280–282, 288
Apoplast, 103, 119, 122, 138, 140, 179, 216
  water potential, 122
Arctic, 43, 180, 183
Arsenic, 204
Avoidance, 24
Awn, hygroscopic, 146

Bacteria, 3, 25, 75, 86, 107, 222, 229, 281, 289
Behavioural responses, 19, 47
  animals, 24
Boron, 201
Boundary layer, 155, 283
  resistance, 54, 137, 254
Breeding system, 18, 22
Bud scales, 193
Bulbs, 47, 187, 192

C

Cacti, 24
Cadmium, 78, 201, 205–206
Calcicoles and calcifuges, 86, 205, 215, 218–219, 224, 229
Calcium, 71–72, 81, 83, 85, 88, 93, 201, 205
  ATPases, 229
  cell wall elongation, 211
  contents of plants, 88
  form in plant, 103, 225